REVOLUTION AND WORLD ORDER

Revolution and World Order

THE REVOLUTIONARY STATE IN INTERNATIONAL SOCIETY

David Armstrong

CLARENDON PRESS · OXFORD

Oxford University Press, Walton Street, Oxford OX2 6DP
Oxford New York
Athens Auckland Bangkok Bombay
Calcutta Cape Town Dar es Salaam Delhi
Florence Hong Kong Istanbul Karachi
Kuala Lumpur Madras Madrid Melbourne
Mexico City Nairobi Paris Singapore
Taipei Tokyo Toronto
and associated companies in
Berlin Ibadan

Oxford is a trade mark of Oxford University Press

Published in the United States by
Oxford University Press Inc., New York

First published 1993

British Library Cataloguing in Publication Data
Data available

Library of Congress Cataloging in Publication Data
Armstrong, J. D. (James David), 1945–
Revolution and world order: the revolutionary state in
international society/David Armstrong.
p.   cm.
Includes bibliographical references (p.) and index.
1. International law.   2. International relations.   3. Revolutions.   I. Title.
JX3091.A77 1993 341.2—dc20 92-40619
ISBN 0-19-827528-5

3 5 7 9 10 8 6 4 2

Printed in Great Britain
on acid-free paper by
Ipswich Book Co., Suffolk

To
Maggie

PREFACE

This book, in its current form, has its origins in a conversation with Hedley Bull as long ago as 1975. I had just completed a Ph.D. in his Department at the Australian National University on the role of ideology in Chinese foreign policy. In this thesis, subsequently published by California University Press, I had developed the concept of China's 'socialization' within international society and I informed Professor Bull of my intention to elaborate upon this idea in a much more ambitious study of the impact of international society upon the international relations of revolutionary states. He suggested that a two-way interaction was involved in this context, since revolutions had also affected the evolution of international society, and I have attempted to incorporate this insight into this book. Bull's influence is to be found throughout this study, as in the work of so many of his former students and I share their regret that he did not live to witness the extent to which his ideas came virtually to dominate an entire school of thought within International Relations (a development he would have regarded with amused detachment). I also deeply regret that my friend and fellow graduate student at the ANU, John Vincent, never saw the publication of a book which he did so much to encourage me to complete.

After 1975 numerous professional and personal distractions cropped up to prevent me from doing more than the bare minimum of work on this book until 1987, when the generosity of the Nuffield Foundation enabled me to spend most of a year at Oxford, researching the French and American revolutions. While at St Antony's College, I met Mark Zacher of the University of British Columbia and Mark's subsequent invitation to spend two summers teaching at UBC gave me another opportunity to concentrate on the book in the extremely congenial setting of Vancouver. I am far from being the first academic to experience Mark's extraordinary generosity, collegiality, and hospitality, but I am glad to have this opportunity to thank him. I should also like to thank others at the UBC who made my stay there so enjoyable and contributed valuable suggestions for this book, especially Paul Marantz and Kal Holsti.

Past and present colleagues at Birmingham University have made many useful suggestions in the course of my writing this book and I should particularly like to acknowledge John Haslam, Erik Goldstein, Stuart Croft, Steve Greenwold, and Peter Lassman, who all read and commented upon various parts of the text. I have also benefited from discussions with Cornelia Navari, Ian Clark, Adam Roberts, Geoffrey Warner, and Fred Halliday. Fred Halliday also provided an invaluable set of reader's comments for OUP, of which I have attempted to take some account in the final draft of this book. A particular debt is owed to Royston Greenwood, whose cheerful disbelief in the possibility of this work ever appearing in print was a constant spur to action. Linda Wall worked her usual magic on the computer to produce an elegant final draft and endured my constant anxiety with equanimity. Rosamund Annetts copy-edited my first draft with meticulous care and intelligence and the Desk-Editing Department of OUP did an equally thorough job on the final draft. Needless to say, none of the above shares my responsibility for any errors of fact or interpretation that appear here.

Maggie has read every page of this book, sometimes in several drafts. It would not have been completed without her patience, support, and tolerance over several years.

CONTENTS

Introduction   1

1. The Westphalian Conception of International Society   12

2. State and People: The American Revolution   42

3. State and Nation: The French Revolution   79

4. State and Class: The Russian Revolution   112

5. The Revolt against the West and International Society   158

6. Norms, Rules, and Laws   199

7. Diplomacy   244

8. Statecraft and the Balance of Power   273

Conclusion   299

Bibliography   312

Index   325

Introduction

A common dilemma for a revolutionary state is to find itself in a relationship with international society that is profoundly ambiguous, if not entirely paradoxical. The belief system on which its revolution was founded and which legitimized the assumption of state power by the revolutionary élite is certain to run counter to the prevailing political doctrines of most other states, many of which may represent the 'old regime' values against which the revolution was aimed. The notion that, simply by virtue of being a state, the revolutionary state has joined an international society in which it is expected to share certain interests, rules, and norms and co-operate in the working of certain common institutions with 'old regime' states is likely to seem unacceptable to the revolutionary leaders.

The immediate response of the revolutionary state to this dilemma may be to reject, if not seek to overturn, what it is likely to perceive as an unequal, oppressive, and immoral structure of international authority, devised by the established powers in their own interests. Or it may react more ambivalently by seeking to avoid contamination by the outside world at the same time as attempting to restructure it in its own image. But whether its reaction to the international society is to seek world revolution, isolation, or international reform, from the moment a revolution assumes the form of statehood, it encounters strong pressures to conform to the conventions of the society of states: to become 'socialized'.

In essence, this study asks: to what extent do revolutionary states succeed in altering the international society of which they find themselves members, and to what extent does it succeed in 'socializing' them? On what basis can international order be built in a world where revolutionary states may even deny the very existence of a society of states with common interests, rules, and institutions? Do revolutionary states inevitably constitute a serious challenge to the prevailing norms of international society and, if so, why is this the case, how is the challenge manifested, and in what ways does the international society respond? In some cases the revolutionary state may be confronted by a fundamental conflict between the principles on which its revolution was based and the obligations imposed on it by the fact that it is now no longer a faction or a political party but a state trying to function in a world of states. How does it resolve this conflict? Is 'socialization' within the international community inevitable: does the 'system' tend to impose a uniform pattern on all of its components? If so, how does the socialization process take place, how long does it take, and what kinds of stresses and strains are involved for the state experiencing it? Or does the international system itself change with time in response to the advent of revolutionary states?

None of the key terms that are employed throughout this book—'revolutionary state', 'world order', 'international society', and 'socialization'—is uncontroversial, self-evident in its meaning, or unambiguous. It is appropriate, therefore, to begin with a discussion of how they will be used in this study and how they relate to each other.

There has been much dispute over the exact meaning of the term 'revolution'.[1] There may be some consensus that any definition must encompass the occurrence of some fundamental change and, more debatably, the use of violence. But a definition along these lines leaves open many important questions as well as embracing too wide a range of phenomena for it to be very useful for analytical purposes. For example, must the fundamental change occur in the social or only in the political field? If in the latter, is a change of government sufficient or must the revolution embrace the entire political structure? How essential to the definition is the use of violence? What differentiates a revolution from a *coup d'état*?

While these are undoubtedly significant questions, this study will not investigate them further because its focus is not upon the revolutionary process as such but upon the outcome of certain revolutions: the particular outcome that has been termed here a

---

[1] For some valuable contributions to this debate, see L. S. Stone, 'Theories of Revolution', *World Politics*, 18 (1966), 159–76; P. Amann, 'Revolution: A Redefinition', *Political Science Quarterly*, 86 (Mar. 1962), 36–53; A. Hatto, 'Revolution: An Inquiry into the Usefulness of an Historical Term', *Mind* (Oct. 1949), 459–517; J. C. Davies, 'Towards a Theory of Revolution', *American Sociological Review* (Feb. 1962), 5–18.

'revolutionary state'. The term 'revolutionary state' may be used to describe a state undergoing a revolution, in which case it refers purely to internal aspects of that state. However, the term as it is employed throughout this book, refers to the external consequences of the revolution. A revolutionary state is one whose relations with other states are revolutionary because it stands, in some sense, for fundamental change in the principles on the basis of which states conduct their relations with each other. Hence a 'revolutionary state' may be defined as one that deliberately adopts a posture of confrontation with the society of states, or is objectively involved in such a confrontation by virtue of the external implications of its revolution, or is perceived by significant numbers of other states to be in such a posture of confrontation. In any of these three cases the revolutionary state may be said to be alienated to some degree from the society within which it finds itself: the society of states.

Although a revolutionary state defined in these terms may emerge following any change of government, including one brought about by peaceful, democratic means, the circumstances most likely to give rise to a state that is revolutionary in its international behaviour are those attendant upon what Chalmers Johnson defined as a 'Jacobin Communist Revolution', that is, one involving 'a sweeping fundamental change in political organization, social structure, economic property control and the predominant myth of a social order'.[2] Such revolutions are inherently challenging to the prevailing international order because, as Richard Falk notes, they threaten 'all governments that resemble the first victim of the revolutionary cause'.[3] They are also, implicitly or explicitly, likely to find themselves in opposition not only to the 'predominant myth of a social order' internally but also to the ideas, rules, and practices which underpin the social order among states.

The crucial relationship, therefore, considered in this study is that between revolutionary states and the international society of which, as states, they are potential members but which, as revolutionary movements, they are liable to reject. What is meant here by the term 'international society' is outlined more fully in the following chapter, but a few preliminary points may be made at this

[2] Chalmers Johnson, *Revolution and the Social System* (Hoover Institution, ser. 3; Stanford, Calif., 1964), 6.
[3] R. A. Falk, 'World Revolution and International Order', in C. J. Friedrich (ed.), *Revolution* (New York, 1969), 155.

stage. A society may be defined as an association based upon certain common interests which accepts and maintains such rules and practices as its members deem necessary to achieve their common interests. There are several senses in which it is possible to talk about an 'international society' in these terms, depending largely upon the type of membership that is envisaged, but in this study a modified form of Hedley Bull's well-known usage in *The Anarchical Society* is employed. 'International society', therefore, is here synonymous with 'the society of states', and denotes the interests, rules, and practices that states in association hold in common. In the next chapter the phrase 'the Westphalian conception of international society' is used as a shorthand expression for the particular set of rules and practices that defined the society of states as it emerged in the seventeenth century and which revolved around the concept of sovereignty.

Order is yet another elusive concept in the study of international relations. To some it is interchangeable with the word 'peace', while others favour 'stability' or 'predictability' as synonyms. J. D. B. Miller finds Percy Cohen's explanation of social order helpful in clarifying the particular uses of the term in international relations. Cohen, Miller writes,

distinguishes five meanings for the term 'social order', all of which, in his view, are both logically and empirically related. They are a certain restraint, especially of violence; some mutuality or reciprocity in social life; some predictability, so that people know what to expect of one another; consistency; and persistence.[4]

Raymond Aron, by contrast, distinguishes five quite separate ways in which the term 'world order' has been employed: as any arrangement of reality; as the relation between the parts; as the maximum conditions for coexistence; as the minimum conditions for existence; as the conditions for the good life.[5] Alan James discusses two approaches to the idea of order, within which two distinct emphases may be found. In the first approach order is defined in an essentially formal way, with the emphasis on means

---

[4] P. S. Cohen, *Modern Social Theory* (London, 1968), ch. 2, summarized in J. D. B. Miller, 'World Society and International Economic Interdependence'. Unpublished paper in the Seminar on World Society given by the Department of International Relations, Australian National University, 7 July 1975.

[5] Cited in S. Hoffmann, 'Report of the Conference on the Conditions of World Order', *Daedalus* (Spring, 1966), 455–6.

rather than ends and on the manner of behaviour rather than its content. In this conception order has two aspects. The first is encapsulated in the word 'system' and denotes the existence of method and regularity and limits to areas of unpredictability in the affairs of a particular society. The second aspect recognizes that social life is essentially dynamic rather than static and emphasizes the need for clear procedures within which change may take place. James's second approach to order stresses substance rather than form and the need for what takes place within a society to merit the word 'orderly'. In this sense order may be defined in a limited way as equivalent to security or, far more ambitiously, as closely related to justice.[6] Stanley Hoffmann offers a more succinct suggestion, to the effect that order in international relations consists of 'formal or informal rules that allow for the moderation of disputes and for a measure of security and stability'.[7]

Hedley Bull concentrates upon one meaning of order: a particular disposition, sequence, or pattern of things for a given purpose. This results in a definition of international order that contrives to avoid undue specificity about the substantive content of order. International order, he suggests, is 'a pattern or disposition of international activity that sustains those goals of the society of states that are elementary, primary or universal'.[8] Hence the emphasis in Bull's approach to order is upon its consequences for the 'goals' of international society, which, he suggests, include such objectives as preserving the society of states itself, maintaining the independence of states, establishing peace as the normal condition of international relations, and achieving such common goals of all social life as limiting violence, keeping promises, and stabilizing possession. Order, he goes on to say, is maintained by a sense of common interest in these goals, by rules of conduct, and by common institutions, such as the balance of power, diplomacy, war, and the special role of the great powers.

Bull's outline of the goals of international society and the means by which they are sustained is followed in its essentials in this study. However, although he was one of the foremost thinkers on the question of international order, his definition of the term itself is curiously elusive. If the subordinate clause in his definition is

[6] A. James (ed.), *The Bases of International Order* (New York, 1973), 61–3.
[7] S. Hoffmann, *Primacy or World Order* (New York, 1978), 3.
[8] H. Bull, *The Anarchical Society* (London, 1977), 16.

omitted, we are left with the conception of order as 'a pattern or disposition of activity'. This is an accurate rendering of one dictionary definition, but it does not address the substantive senses in which the term is actually used in international affairs, as some of the other definitions do when they talk of stability, predictability, security, and restraints upon violence. These are all qualities that are commonly associated with the word when it is used to refer to civil or public order, which in turn are the broad categories to which discussion of international order belongs. The following definition of order in social life, which incorporates some of the important insights of the other writers who have been discussed in this section, is adopted in this study:

> Order denotes stability and regularity in the pattern of assumptions, rules, and practices that are accepted as legitimate among the members of a given society and that concern the mechanisms of and limits to the process of change within that society.

One further important point about international order needs to be made. Order in international affairs is as much a state of mind as a state of being. International order is not simply a condition that exists as a consequence of the effective working of various *objective* structures or institutions like the balance of power, diplomacy, or international law. It is dependent also on certain *subjective* or psychological requirements, of which the two most important are perception and communication. For example—to indulge in a rather large generalization but one that does make the point—the difference between the international situation in 1913 and 1914 was not simply the fact that the institutions that had upheld order in 1913 had broken down a year later, but that, for various reasons, the great powers had ceased to perceive international affairs as fundamentally orderly and had failed to communicate or signal adequately to each other the lengths to which they were prepared to go to defend what they regarded as vital interests. This is a significant point in connection with the impact of revolutionary states on international relations, since there have been many instances of a revolution having a profoundly disordering effect on international society in part because the revolutionary state and the established powers misperceived each other's intentions or because neither could understand the language being used by the other: revolutionary rhetoric on the one hand, stylized diplomatic jargon on the other. This psychological dimension to international order was well appreciated in eighteenth- and nineteenth-century European international society, whose diplomatic documents make frequent reference to measures designed to ensure the 'tranquillity' or 'repose' of Europe. Thomas Hobbes might have claimed for individuals that 'The Felicity of this life consisteth not in the repose of a mind satisfied', but the benefits of peace of mind and a sense of security were perceived differently by states.

If a revolutionary state finds itself at odds with international society, a threat to order is a probable consequence. The threat is likely to apply both to international order—the order that obtains among states—and to 'order within the wider world political system of which the states system is only a part', or to world order, to employ a distinction favoured by Hedley Bull.[9] This is because of the dual identity of revolutionary states as states and as the centres of would-be universal movements. Hence a revolutionary state may put in jeopardy not just 'stability and regularity in the pattern of assumptions, rules, and practices' that operates among states but the same qualities within individual states. As will be seen, international society has itself progressed, partly in response to the impact of revolutionary states, from a strict concern with order between states to the beginning of an involvement with the domestic order of states. Moreover, the conception within international society of what constitutes a legitimate state has been subtly amended over the last three hundred years. Hence, although the primary interest of this study is in the society of states and in international order, its main title is 'Revolution and World Order', which is intended to reflect, first, the fact that revolutions straddle both the society of states and the larger society of mankind as a whole, and, second, the way in which the distinctions between these two have become more blurred over the years.

Revolutions and international society affect and change each other. Although both aspects of this interaction are considered in this study, its main emphasis is upon the effect of international society on the revolutionary state. The term 'socialization' has been borrowed from anthropology to describe the mechanism through which international society influences the revolutionary state. Socialization denotes the process 'whereby men consciously or unconsciously conform to the conventions of the society in which

[9] Ibid. 20–3.

they live in order to function more effectively within it [and] whereby an increasing entanglement within an existing structure of relationships brings about an increasing degree of adaptation to the normal behaviour patterns of that structure'.[10] It may be objected that a term that is used to describe relationships such as that between the individual and his family or tribe is inapplicable in the context of what are essentially two inanimate juridical constructs: the state and the society of states. There is some force in this objection and I should not wish to press the analogy too far. However, the pressures experienced by revolutionary states to behave 'responsibly', to accept rules and norms that are acknowledged by other states, and in short to *be* states rather than revolutionary movements, are sufficiently like those experienced where the term 'socialization' is more conventionally employed for its use here to be warranted.

This book is not primarily intended to be a theoretical work. Although it undoubtedly has certain implications for the current discussion about the theory of international relations, I have not felt it necessary to spell these out or to 'take sides' in any of the debates over theoretical questions within the field. My aim has been to investigate the interaction between revolutionary states and international society over more than two hundred years and this is far too vast a canvas for more than a small part of this relationship to be considered, let alone for any rigorous, universally applicable theoretical conclusions to be drawn. I have allowed myself to be taken wherever there have seemed to be significant questions to ask or interesting phenomena to speculate about rather than to be strictly confined to a narrow and overly systematic 'research agenda'. There are indeed numerous suggestive analogies between the experiences of different revolutionary states and I have pointed some of these out, without trying to imply that I am devising some general theory about the international consequences of revolutions.

However, this book has one important and explicit theoretical objective. The concept of an 'international society' is not merely descriptive of certain contemporary or historical features of the relations among states but it is a term with very significant possibilities for International Relations theory. We may take as a starting-point Bull and Watson's definition of international society:

[10] J. D. Armstrong, *Revolutionary Diplomacy: Chinese Foreign Policy and the United Front Doctrine* (Berkeley and Los Angeles, 1977), 12.

By an international society we mean a group of states (or, more generally, a group of independent political communities) which not merely form a system, in the sense that the behaviour of each is a necessary factor in the calculations of the others, but also have established by dialogue and common consent rules and institutions for the conduct of their relations, and recognize their common interest in maintaining these arrangements.[11]

This offers, first of all, a set of basic observations about the political universe, namely that it contains states which may share common interests, rules, and institutions. More detailed observation might tell us more about the precise character of these various components of international society as well as something about the overall nature of international society at a certain point in time: whether it was hierarchical or hegemonial, for example. All this would be either essentially descriptive or theoretical only in the broadest sense of being part of the great tradition of speculation and interpretation that is sometimes termed 'political theory'.

The international society concept may also contribute to theory in the narrower sense of a hypothesis or set of hypotheses that purport to explain, and not just describe, some part of reality. As Waltz suggests:

By a theory the significance of the observed is made manifest. A theory arranges phenomena so that they are seen as mutually dependent; it connects otherwise disparate facts; it shows how changes in some of the phenomena necessarily entail changes in others.[12]

In this sense, the fact that states are members of a society has consequences for their internal as well as external behaviour, their relations with each other and the way in which the international system as a whole operates (where 'international system' means the general pattern of interaction among states and other international actors). In particular, the existence of an international society tends to condition states to behave in rule-governed ways. Moreover, it means that they are participants in a single discourse which takes place in accordance with shared assumptions and conventions and, to some extent, common cultural norms.

Revolutionary states, by definition, begin their international life outside this discourse. This has helped to marginalize their study

[11] H. Bull and A. Watson (eds.), *The Expansion of International Society* (Oxford, 1984), 1.
[12] K. Waltz, *Theory of International Politics* (Reading, Mass., 1979), 9–10.

within the academic discipline of International Relations since, as Halliday notes, they have been seen as 'breakdowns of otherwise regular processes in national and international society'.[13] Yet it is precisely their disruptive character that makes them especially worthy of much greater academic attention. The concept of an international society has numerous possibilities for further theoretical development. It has many legal, political, social, economic, cultural, and anthropological dimensions, only a few of which have been explored. But if it is to begin to realize its potential in International Relations theory, it needs to be employed in less static and descriptive ways than has often been the case. For example, if their membership of a society tends to condition the way states act, this suggests the possibility of discovering behavioural regularities that might in turn be used as the basis for theoretical generalizations. The concept of socialization implies that the pressure to conform operates upon any entity that aspires to statehood. This in turn suggests that the experience of revolutionary states should not be seen as something apart from mainstream International Relations but as providing important empirical evidence with which to confirm or refute theoretical observations about the functioning of the international system as a whole. The interaction between revolutionary states and the international society may also contribute to the development of theories about the causes of change in international relations. If the underlying rules and norms of international society have altered over time—as they have—this is a consequence both of factors operating at a system-wide level, such as technological or economic developments, and also of a more deliberate and self-conscious process of decision-making by the principal agents in the international system: states. Frequently this latter process has intensified following major shocks to the system, such as those delivered by world war or revolution. In this way revolutionary ideas have influenced the evolution of international society both directly, as some of these ideas have been brought into the mainstream of international norms, and indirectly, as the nature of the international society's response to a perceived threat from a revolution has introduced significant amendments to the original Westphalian structure.

[13] F. Halliday, 'Revolutions and International Relations: Some Theoretical Issues'. Paper presented to the British International Studies Association Conference, 1989, p. 3.

To reiterate, this study is not tightly organized around a systematic set of theoretical propositions. Its essential aim is to elucidate the interaction between revolutions and revolutionary ideas, on the one hand, and the established norms and processes of international society, on the other. To the extent that it has succeeded in this purpose, it may also have contributed to our understanding of the broader issue of the role of ideas in the history of international relations. However, the two-way interaction between individual agents and the social setting in which they are located is the basis of much theorizing in all of the social sciences, not just in International Relations.[14] Hence, where appropriate, attention is also drawn to the theoretical implications of this study for such questions as the causes of change in international society and the ways in which the existence of an international society affects the behaviour of states.

[14] A. E. Wendt, 'The Agent–Structure Problem in International Relations Theory', *International Organization*, 41/3 (Summer, 1987), 335–70.

The Westphalian Conception of International Society

The word 'society' is capable of sustaining a great many different meanings. It may, for example, refer in the broadest sense to the condition of living in association, company, or intercourse with others of the same species, as in 'human society'. It may refer to a particular group of individuals so associated, as in 'village society'. One *Oxford English Dictionary* definition—'the aggregate of persons living together in a more or less ordered community'—essentially derives from this meaning of the term, while also introducing the requirement of some degree of order. Here, the term 'society' will be employed to describe 'an association based upon certain common interests which accepts and maintains agreed rules and practices to further those common interests'. This in turn draws attention to one of the central questions about any rule-bound association: what is its principle of obligation? In other words, what is the source of the society's rules and why do people obey them? In the case of societies that have been formally constituted for some specific purpose, such as trade unions, the answer to this question is straightforward: the members themselves have designed the rules and agreed to be bound by them. In the case of the state—a form of association that claims much more far-reaching authority over its members—more complex and sophisticated explanations of obligation have been advanced. Many revolve around the idea of a social contract: the notion that the ultimate source of the state's exercise of legitimate authority is the consent of its citizens.

It is not immediately obvious that the term 'society', as defined here, has any significant application to international relations. Where is the evidence that the members of the 'international society' consider themselves to be obligated by any rules? What is the source of these rules? Who, indeed, are the members of the international society? Practices and institutions which make, administer, and enforce rules within states do not appear to have obvious parallels in the world as a whole, and therefore theories which seek to answer such questions with regard to states do not immediately seem applicable.

In the theory and practice of international relations, it is possible to distinguish three distinct usages of the word 'society' in the sense in which it has been defined here. Each of these postulates a different principle of obligation and a different basis for membership. While the third of these, the 'society of states', has enjoyed the highest degree of legitimacy over some four hundred years, the other two, in various forms, have never been entirely absent from international discourse and may be said to represent alternative visions of world order. As will be seen, they have also been particularly important in determining the nature and course of the dialogue between revolutionary states and the society of states.

The first of these three notions of international society has many variants, but what they all have in common is some conception of universal authority, so they may appropriately be defined as describing types of 'universal society'. A world government would be one kind of universal society, as would an *imperium* or hegemony exercised world-wide by a single state. What Martin Wight terms a 'suzerain states system' is a variant of this latter form of universal society.[1] The first essential characteristic of a universal society is that its members do not enjoy full legal independence. They may be organized into semi-autonomous political units or into merely administrative subdivisions, but all acknowledge a central source of authority. Secondly, the nature of political obligation in a universal society resembles that in a state: the central authority possesses the means of enforcing obedience to its edicts. The ultimate justifications for such a monopoly of legitimate violence may be as various as they are for the state. Divine guidance, the consent of the governed, a contract in which freedom is traded for order, the special enlightenment of the rulers, their civilizing mission, or simply the fact that the power at their disposal leaves little choice but obedience, may all form the basis of the principle of obligation in a universal society.

The second conception of international society has, like the first, many variants, but what they have in common is some sense that

---

[1] M. Wight, *Systems of States* (Leicester, 1977), 21–45.

there are bonds among people that cut across their separation into territorially based political units. The oldest tradition in European political thought that conceives of the world in these terms is natural law, whose notion of international society is that of a 'great community of mankind' (*magna communitas humani generis*) of which men and women are members simply by virtue of their membership of the human race. As human beings they are subject to the universally applicable and unchangeable moral norms that constitute natural law. According to Grotius's definition,

The law of nature is a dictate of right reason, which points out that an act, according as it is or is not in conformity with rational nature has in it a quality of moral baseness or moral necessity; and that, in consequence, such an act is either forbidden or enjoined by the author of nature, God.[2]

Although God is said to be the ultimate source of authority for natural law, the main emphasis of this definition is on the exercise of 'right reason', which, Grotius argues, would lead men to a comprehension of universally binding norms even without the assumption of the existence of God.

The 'great community' idea was intended to provide a principle of obligation that was valid even for sovereign states, since these were governed by men who were no less bound by natural law than any other human beings. It was also used by sixteenth- and seventeenth-century theorists to derive rules that states were supposedly bound to observe in their relations with each other. However, the essential characteristic of the 'great community' idea was that it postulated obligations which cut across or transcended those owed by individuals to their states. In this respect natural law is part of a tradition in political thought that also embraces Marxism and Islam. Each of these belief systems contains an idea of 'transnational' solidarity—among the working class and the community of believers respectively—and each, like natural law itself, has been employed by revolutionaries to challenge the bases of the third notion of international society: the society of states or the 'Westphalian conception of international society'.

The essential attribute of the members of the society of states is their sovereignty: their independence from any higher source of authority. They are, therefore, members of a unique society, an

---

[2] Hugo Grotius, *De Jure Belli et Pacis*, ed. William Whewell (3 vols.; Cambridge, 1853), Bk. 1. ch. 1, sec. x.

'anarchical society', in the term popularized by Hedley Bull, which possesses no governing authority capable of laying down and enforcing rules of conduct. It is empirically clear that international relations, although 'anarchical' in the sense of having no government, are not 'anarchic' in the sense of chaotic. On the contrary, they display a large measure of observance of rules and even cooperation across a broad spectrum of international activity, including trade, finance, communications, transport, diplomacy, and even that area which seems to symbolize a fundamental breakdown of international order: war. Yet if the actual conduct of states may be taken as prima-facie evidence that they see themselves as members of a rule-bound society, it gives little guidance as to the common interests and principle of obligation upon which this society is based.

One answer to these questions is to place states within natural law's system of universal moral norms. Another is to argue that their 'society' derives merely from the imperatives of coexistence and that they therefore observe such rules as enable them to avoid a constant state of war. A third approach is to point to the common Judaeo-Christian heritage and values of Europe and see in these the foundations of the European international society whose essential principles formed the basis of the modern global international society. However, the perspective adopted here differs to some extent from all three of these ways of conceptualizing the society of states by depicting it in origin as an association drawn together by a single common interest—sovereignty itself—and accepting, in the first instance, only such common rules and institutions as would protect and enhance sovereignty.

The principle of obligation in the society of sovereign states is also defined by the nature of sovereignty. States observe the rules that arise out of their association because they have in some sense consented to them. Their consent may take an explicit form, such as the ratification of a treaty or an affirmative vote in an international organization. It may be indirect, as when the prior agreement of states to be bound by the decisions of the UN Security Council overrides their disagreement with particular measures adopted by the Security Council. It may be implied, or tacit, as when a state says or does nothing explicitly to indicate that it does not accept some obligation. There are also certain kinds of obligation to which states are deemed to have consented simply by virtue of being accepted into international society; these are obligations that are inseparable from statehood, such as the obligation to respect the rights of foreign diplomats. Until relatively recently these last obligations formed the core of customary international law, although since 1945 there has been an increasing tendency for states to insist upon more formal means of expressing their assent to obligations.

It is important to be clear about what, precisely, states have given their agreement to. They have not created an international Leviathan which thereafter exercises absolute authority over them. They have, in essence, consented to such common rules and practices as enhance their independence and make it the basis of political legitimacy at the same time as promoting orderly international relations. This is not to say that states are incapable of adopting closer forms of association, of accepting rules that foster co-operation and not just independence or even of pursuing common values or sustaining common institutions that limit their freedom to some degree. This study will indicate some of the ways in which international society has evolved in such directions. It is simply to assert that the basis of the society of states as it emerged in the seventeenth century was not the same as the basis of the social contract that some political thinkers suggest underpins the relationship between citizens and their legitimate state authority. States, like citizens, may fruitfully be thought of as having entered into a social contract with each other in order collectively to pursue their common interests. There the resemblance ends. In contractarian terms the international social contract may be seen as a 'pact of association' rather than a 'contract of government'.

The remainder of this chapter considers the ways in which these three conceptions of international society have been employed in the theory and practice of international relations.

THE UNIVERSAL SOCIETY

No truly universal society has ever existed, although all aspirants to world empire and many schemes for world government have had this as their ultimate objective. However, at their zeniths the Chinese tribute system, the Roman Empire, and the medieval European idea of Christendom all approximated in certain respects to actual universal societies, and indeed that was how they conceived of themselves, since they either exercised hegemony over much of the world that was known to them or, in the case of Christendom, were based upon an ideology with claims to universal moral and spiritual authority.

The Chinese and Roman empires were founded by conquest but their durability was due not simply to force but also to the fact that they came to embody distinctive and widely accepted principles of social order. In the Chinese case, the political structure was merely one part of a complete cosmology that perceived the social, moral, physical, and spiritual universes as aspects of a single, unified whole. The highest goal—never attained in practice—was to achieve an overall harmony which, in the Confucian system, would come about when society as a whole observed the moral and ethical norms that supposedly governed relationships within an ideal family: filial piety, wifely obedience, paternal moral authority, respect for elders, and so on. The emperor held his office by virtue of the 'mandate of heaven' but he too was obliged to perform certain duties, and to do so in a virtuous fashion, otherwise, in one variant of Confucianism at least, he could be legitimately overthrown. This suggests a form of social contract between ruler and ruled under which all co-operate to produce harmony instead of chaos by accepting their ordained position in the social hierarchy and behaving morally. An even clearer contractarian notion is evident in imperial Chinese theory and practice concerning relations with people living outside the area of China proper. China saw itself as the 'Middle Kingdom', the centre of civilization, to which the whole world, in principle, owed allegiance, while it was the emperor's duty to lead less civilized peoples toward the benefits of Chinese civilization. In practice, a more specific variant of this implied contract operated in China's relations with some of its immediate neighbours, who paid tribute and offered regular obeisance to the Chinese emperor through the performance of rituals such as the kowtow, receiving in return his protection and guidance along the one true way which led to full assimilation into Chinese culture.[3]

Although attempts were sometimes made to base political relationships in China upon something approximating to the

---

[3] I. C. Y. Hsu, *China's Entrance into the Family of Nations* (Cambridge, Mass., 1960), 3.

Western principle of the rule of law, the legal aspects of the Chinese structure of authority and obligation remained secondary to the moral, ethical, and mystical framework of Confucianism. By contrast, law was at the heart of Roman ideas both of Republic and Empire and was an important unifying factor amongst the various nationalities within the Empire, alongside cultural and economic bonds and the security brought by the *Pax Romana*. Since the Roman emphasis on law had a significant influence on later versions of international society, it is worth briefly outlining a few of the basic Roman ideas about the place of law in the universal society which, at its peak, they saw their empire as embodying.

The most basic concept in Roman jurisprudence is that any society is founded upon law (*ubi societas ibi lex*). For the Stoic philosophers of the third century BC, law, in one sense, was prior to the state and was the essential governing principle of the universe:

Law is the ruler over all the acts both of gods and men. It must be the director, the governor and the guide in respect to what is honourable and base and hence the standard of what is just and unjust. For all beings that are social by nature the law directs what must be done and forbids what must not be done.[4]

'Law' in this fundamental sense meant natural law (*jus naturale*), the underlying eternal and immutable rules of moral conduct that were thought to be discoverable by the exercise of reason. Law in the narrower sense of civil law (*jus civile*)—specific rules imposing obligations upon the members of a particular society—was, in Cicero's view, derived from principles of justice which in turn were determined by natural law.[5] For Cicero 'A commonwealth is the weal of the people (*Res Publica Res Populi*); but a people is not any and every sort of human association brought together in any fashion whatever, but an association of many united in partnership by consent to law and by sharing of interests.'[6] The necessity for popular consent to authority was emphasized by several Republican writers, with the logical implication of this—that lawfully exercised authority derives from a social contract—clearly dis-

---

[4] Chrysippus, cited in G. H. Sabine, *A History of Political Theory* (London, 1963), 150.
[5] R. W. Carlyle and A. J. Carlyle, *A History of Mediaeval Political Theory in the West*, i (Edinburgh and London, 1903), 1–18.
[6] Cited in A. P. d'Entreves, *The Notion of the State* (Oxford, 1967), 75–6.

cerned by Cicero: 'But since one fears another and no one dares trust to himself, a sort of compact (*pactio*) is made between the people and the powerful men.'[7] Sovereignty (*summa potestas*—literally supreme power) was thus seen to have its ultimate source in the people, a doctrine that was later employed in a somewhat perverted form to justify the possession of *summa potestas* by the emperor, since it could be argued that his power had been conferred upon him by the people.[8] Conversely, securing the people from external dangers (*salus populi*) and maintaining order within the empire were regarded as the fundamental duties of the Emperor, by which he fulfilled his part in the social contract.

Hence, for the Romans, the purpose of human association was the attainment of order; the primary means to this end was law, which was also the governing principle of the state and the ultimate guarantee that the social contract between ruler and ruled would be upheld. The same principles were thought to apply, by a natural extension, to the Romans' universal society: the Empire. But since many provinces of the Empire had their own local codes of law, further elaboration of these ideas was required to justify the notion that law (and not just Roman power) was the fundamental unifying principle within the Empire, as distinct from a mere set of oppressive rules imposed by force. Here the Romans employed two separate conceptions of law to explain its unifying function within the Empire. The first was the idea of natural law which, since it was thought to derive from man's universal characteristic of being a creature capable of reason, was seen as forming an obvious basis for the common law of a universal Empire. The second was the idea that all legal systems had certain basic principles in common, such as the prohibition of murder, or the protection of property, and that, taken together, these principles could be seen as a common code of law possessed by all the nations or peoples which made up the Roman Empire: a 'law of nations' (*jus gentium*). Two observations may be made immediately about these ideas. The first is that natural law and the law of nations have much in common since both envisage law as deriving from fundamental principles of morality or social coexistence. This led some Roman writers to the conclusion that the two were in fact identical: that *jus gentium* was

---

[7] Cited in C. H. McIlwain, *The Growth of Political Thought in the West* (New York, 1932), 117.
[8] d'Entreves, *The Notion of the State*, 78.

nothing more or less than a concrete form of *jus naturale*.[9] A similar blurring of distinctions is to be found in some of the literature on the law of nations in the sixteenth and seventeenth centuries. A second point is that *jus gentium*, as conceived here, is not the same as *jus inter gentes* (law between nations, or international law). If *jus gentium* is the general principles of law accepted by civilized nations, *jus inter gentes* is something much more specific: the rules of conduct observed by nations in their dealings with each other. Of course, it is possible to imagine a situation where *jus gentium* and *jus inter gentes* were in practice the same, that is to say one in which the relations between independent nations were governed not merely by specific rules designed to facilitate their mutual intercourse, but by general adherence to a body of rules derived from fundamental moral principles which had won universal acceptance. However, it is hard to conceive of such a state of affairs outside an overall social context in which there was, if not a common political authority wielding effective sanctions, at least a common source of moral authority that was capable of definitively interpreting the rules. This would seem to imply the existence of a particular kind of universal society in which there was no single dominant state, but instead a multiplicity of states which were independent but none the less regarded themselves as in some sense subordinate to a higher authority. We shall return to this argument later when we consider the work of Christian von Wolff, who postulated just such an arrangement; for the moment it is sufficient to note that *jus naturale*, *jus gentium*, and *jus inter gentes*, although containing some points of similarity or overlap, encapsulate distinct ideas of law and are seen as separate by most Roman writers.

The idea of a universal society had taken such a strong hold in Europe during the Roman *imperium* that an attempt was made to retain it for several centuries after Rome's decline, albeit in the substantially amended form of Christendom. This extraordinarily complex amalgam of abstract theoretical notions and living institutions could, at its peak (under such emperors as Charlemagne or Otto the Great, and during the Crusades), sometimes exercise a major influence on events, but its real force was as an idea of world unity which persisted long after its decline.

[9] Carlyle, *Mediaeval Political Theory*, i. 36. See also the discussion in J. Goebel, *The Equality of States* (New York, 1923), 8–9.

At the heart of the notion of Christendom was the idea—with roots in Roman natural law theories as well as in Christianity—that mankind was inherently unified since all men were ultimately under the same divine ruler. In so far as man could achieve unity, therefore, he was working towards the earthly goal which he had been set by God.[10] As the Pope was God's representative on earth, he could claim universal dominion over lesser, temporal rulers. The crowning of Charlemagne as Roman Emperor by Pope Leo III in AD 800 was seen as creating a dual global overlordship, with the Church supreme in the spiritual domain while the new Roman Empire (first called 'Holy Roman Empire' in 1157) mirrored the Church's authority in secular matters.[11] In theory, the Church was the superior body, a position that was acknowledged in the performance of various ceremonial rituals,[12] but, in practice, the relationship between the two was never easy.

Neither Church nor Empire ever possessed sufficient power to realize their ambition of world government—or even undisputed dominion in the region of Western Christendom where their authority was recognized—and the Empire, though not formally abandoned until 1806, soon became, in effect, little more than another great power. But in an age when power was extremely widely diffused among many hundreds of feudal princelings the Church, despite its schisms and periods of corruption, retained its importance as a symbol of unity and source of moral authority. It also acted as the head of what amounted to a general system of law throughout Christendom, both in its roles as mediator, arbitrator, and court of final appeal and in its capacity as originator of new laws.[13] This law was both *jus gentium* and, in a rudimentary form, *jus inter gentes*, as the Church tried to regulate the relations amongst the many quarrelsome entities over which it claimed overlordship by subordinating them to rules of conduct. It is in this respect that Christendom may most clearly be seen as marking the transition between the universal society of Rome and the emerging society of sovereign states, as one writer suggests:

This papal world monarchy was also the bridge builder between Roman and modern times. All the characteristic Roman features had impressed

---

[10] O. Gierke, *Political Theories of the Middle Ages* (Cambridge, 1900), 9–19.
[11] J. Bryce, *The Holy Roman Empire* (London, 1907), 196.
[12] Goebel, *The Equality of States*, 39–40.
[13] G. Mattingly, *Renaissance Diplomacy* (London, 1955), 17–25.

themselves upon the physiognomy of the papacy, the Roman Church. Not only the law; also the conception of the universality of government. It was as universal monarchs that the popes partly applied Roman principles, partly developed them, and partly created new ones, which have since gained universal recognition in international law. The protection of legates; safe conduct of ambassadors; secrecy in diplomatic negotiations; insistence on the adherence to treaties made between secular rulers; condemnation of treaty violations; papal annulment and rescission of treaties and compacts; fixation of treaty conditions; excommunication and deposition of rulers; orders for the release of prisoners, for their humane treatment and that of hostages; protection of exiles, aliens and Jews; condemnation of 'unjust' wars and piracy; confirmation of peace treaties; orders for the free passage of troops engaged in a 'just' campaign; orders to rulers to enter into alliances; ascription of occupied territories to a victorious belligerent party, and so forth.[14]

Christendom was a universal society to the extent that it possessed a common religion, law, and culture, and, amongst the educated classes, a common language. The Church, as the major repository of learning, the principal provider of education, and the head of the legal system, was well placed to play a central role in such a society. It also possessed in the priesthood a cadre of individuals—a 'massive international bureaucracy', in Martin Wight's words[15]—who were clearly a cosmopolitan (or transnational) force, who were held in awe by much of the population, and who conceived their role to be upholding the authority of the Church. But what of its claim to universal authority; its claim to be able to command the obedience of kings and princes? Here it is immediately clear that the basis of the Church's claim to pre-eminence was very different from Rome's. At its peak Rome's power was far greater than that of any possible competitor, whereas the Church, even on the few occasions when it was able to work in harmony with the Empire, never enjoyed anything remotely approaching that degree of military ascendancy. But this is not to say that its perception of its own position *vis-à-vis* the temporal potentates was completely without foundation. Apart from those components of its dominance and prestige that have already been considered, it had another power which was both important in maintaining its standing in its own would-be universal

---

[14] W. Ullman, *The Growth of Papal Government in the Middle Ages* (London, 1962), 450.
[15] Wight, *Systems of States*, 28.

society and significant in its influence upon the later society of states. The Church was able to confer legitimacy upon temporal monarchs, and also to withdraw it from them, by the device of excommunication or by directly deposing them.[16] The theoretical basis of this capacity lay in the belief that the authority to rule derived from God, so that the Pope, as God's vicar on earth, was able to grant such authority to temporal rulers. As the feudal structure of authority came gradually to be supplanted by the new order of sovereign states, so that monarchs increasingly asserted their claims to absolute sovereignty over barons and other lesser lords, such monarchs needed to bolster their claims with as much external support as they could, and to surround themselves with as much pomp and circumstance as possible. The Church was uniquely able to assist in both respects.[17] Of course monarchs could choose to ignore the Church, and did so in increasing numbers as its prestige diminished and it came to have little real capacity to enforce its will. This lack of executive power, in principle at least, was not a problem for it, since it had, at a very early stage in its history, distinguished between the *auctoritas* (authority) that it possessed, which was sacred, and the mere *potestas* (power) of kings. *Auctoritas* was, in the words of one writer, the 'faculty of shaping things creatively and in a binding manner', while *potestas* was merely 'the power to execute what the *auctoritas* has laid down'.[18] While few monarchs would have interpreted their *potestas* in quite such a limited way, the belief in some kind of overall primacy possessed by the Pope was widely accepted in the Middle Ages. So also was the idea that the legitimacy of monarchs derived from the universal society of Christendom as personified by its head, the Pope.[19] The conception of international society as a whole acting as a source of legitimacy was one that was to have a lingering influence in later versions of international society.

[16] Ullman, *The Growth of Papal Government*, 281–301.
[17] J. H. Shennan, *The Origins of the Modern European State* (London, 1974), 19–23.
[18] Ullman, *The Growth of Papal Government*, 20–1.
[19] W. Ullman, 'Juristic Obstacles to the Emergence of the Concept of the State in the Middle Ages', in the same author's *The Church and Law in the Earlier Middle Ages* (London, 1975). For the fullest discussion of the theoretical underpinnings of these ideas, see W. Ullman, *Medieval Papalism* (London, 1949), esp. 76–137.

THE GREAT COMMUNITY

As the authority of the Church gradually diminished in the face of the venality of many of its rulers and, even more, the increasing self-confidence and assertiveness of national monarchs, so too did the fragile basis of unity that had existed through the Middle Ages come under threat. With sovereigns declaring themselves to be emperors in their own domains and hence unconstrained by any notion that their actions were subject to laws laid down by a higher authority, even the limited structure of international order that Christendom represented seemed likely to be replaced by unbridled anarchy. This was the context within which a number of thinkers from the sixteenth century onwards began to consider whether the international relations of the newly emerging sovereign states could still be said to be conducted within the framework of a larger international society and therefore to be subject to some kind of external constraint. They were particularly concerned to discover a sound foundation for the assertion that international law (variously defined and described) had a binding force even in a world of sovereign states. Given a fundamental belief in the inseparability of the concepts of law and society, they inevitably felt obliged first of all to find a new formulation of the idea of international society to replace that of the universal society of Christendom, with its hierarchical structure that had no place in the modern world. In the course of this exercise several of them advanced versions of the second major conception of international society that we wish to consider here. This is the idea that the whole world can be seen as constituting a 'great community of mankind' (*magna communitas humani generis*), that since the only qualification for membership of this community is to be a human being it cuts across national boundaries, and that it is governed by a set of fundamental moral and ethical norms which even sovereign states are obliged to observe.

This central thesis was backed by a wide range of supporting arguments of which the most common was an attempt to reassert the old Stoic idea of natural law, which the medieval Church had kept alive while adapting it to its own purposes. From a natural law perspective men were united by their possession of reason and by virtue of being all God's creatures, so to that extent they were all members of a single society. It was possible to ascertain what the rules governing this society were, either by consulting what were believed to be divine revelations or by the exercise of reason. In either case the various moral injunctions and prohibitions of natural law were deemed by some writers to be binding upon states as well as upon individuals.[20] Another Roman concept revived in the sixteenth century was that of *jus gentium*. In some works this retained its original meaning: the general principles of law held in common by civilized nations. In this sense it functioned as a second legal basis of the great community of mankind, since it denoted those specific legal norms which had developed amongst men by custom and practice over centuries but which were not necessarily parts of natural law. However, another school of thought emerged in which *jus gentium* took on rather more of the character of *jus inter gentes*: the actual rules governing the relations amongst states. In this case *jus gentium* was seen as a voluntary system of law, covering such matters as the rights of ambassadors or the treatment of aliens, that had evolved over time as nations sought to bring some degree of order and regulation to their dealings with each other. The voluntary law of nations existed alongside the necessary or compulsory law of nature.

A further analysis of the work of these writers is beyond the scope of this study. However, it is useful to describe in more detail the conceptions of international society that underpinned their ideas. We may begin with the two sixteenth-century Spanish theologians Francisco de Vitoria and Francisco Suarez, since they may be seen as occupying a transitional point between the idea of Christendom and that of the modern society of states. For Vitoria *jus gentium*, which he saw as deriving from and closely related to natural law, represented the outcome of a consensus amongst nations, and so functioned as a kind of binding social contract:

jus gentium has not only the force of a pact and agreement among men, but also the force of a law; for the world as a whole, being in a way one single State, has the power to create laws that are just and fitting for all persons, as are the rules of the *jus gentium* . . . moreover, in the gravest matters . . . it is not permissible for one country to refuse to be bound by the *jus gentium*, that latter having been established with the authority of the whole world.[21]

[20] For the most detailed study of the place of the concept of natural law in the evolution of international law, see E. B. F. Midgley, *The Natural Law Tradition and the Theory of International Relations* (London, 1975).

[21] Vitoria, *De Potestate Civili*, 21, cited in Midgley, *The Natural Law Tradition*, 84.

Hence, Vitoria's great community functions as if it were one state, with the authority to create binding obligation for all. Suarez was not prepared to go this far, and saw the real foundation of *jus gentium* as its utility rather than any sort of contract:

it is easily apparent that this system of law, simply as the result of usage and tradition, could have been gradually introduced throughout the whole world . . . without any special and simultaneous compact or consent on the part of all people. For the body of law in question has such a close relationship to nature and so befits all nations, individually and collectively, that it has grown, almost by a natural process, with the growth of the human race; and therefore it does not exist in written form, since it was not dictated by a legislator, but has, on the contrary, waxed strongly through usage.[22]

Similarly, Suarez envisaged international society, not as an authoritative lawmaker, but as a looser association deriving from the natural unity amongst human beings:

the human race, into howsoever many different peoples and kingdoms it may be divided, always preserves a certain unity, not only as a species, but also a moral and practical unity (as it were) enforced by the natural precept of mutual love and mercy; a precept which applies to all, even to strangers of every nation.

Therefore, although a given sovereign state, commonwealth or kingdom may constitute a perfect kingdom in itself, consisting of its own members, nevertheless, each one of these states is also, in a certain sense, and viewed in relation to the human race, a member of that universal society; for these states, when standing alone, are never so self sufficient that they do not require some mutual assistance, association, and intercourse, at times for their own greater welfare and advantage, but at other times because also of some moral necessity or need. This fact is made manifest by actual usage.[23]

Although Suarez also emphasizes the role of 'the habitual conduct of nations' (custom) in giving rise to law, his theory of society was still essentially a conception of a community of the human race rooted in the idea of natural law, rather than an early version of a society of states. The same emphasis was apparent in Alberico Gentili's *De Jure Belli*: 'All this universe which you see in which many things divine and human are included is one, and we

---

[22] Francisco Suarez, *Selections from Three Works*, ed. J. B. Scott (2 vols.; Classics of International Law; Oxford, 1944), ii. 351.
[23] Ibid. 348–9.

are members of a great body. Moreover nature had made us all kindred, since we have the same origin and the same abode.'[24]

Hugo Grotius, the most famous of these publicists, likewise based his version of the law of nations ultimately upon a conception of a society of men, although it is also possible to interpret his work as containing an implicit notion of a society of states. One translator, for example, has him saying: 'as the Laws of each Community regard the Utility of that Community, so also between different Communities, all or most forms might be established, and it appears that Laws have been established, which enjoined the Utility, not of special communities but of that great aggregate system of communities' (*magnae illius universitatis*).[25] A 'system of communities' would clearly be a society of social entities rather than of human beings, but this may be slightly to overstretch the definition of the rather vague term *magna universitas*. Elsewhere Grotius sees all society as stemming from man's essentially sociable nature: 'among these properties which are peculiar to man is a desire for society, that is a desire for a life spent in common with fellow man, and not merely spent somehow but spent tranquilly, and in a manner corresponding to the character of his intellect'.[26] A slightly different imperative is seen to operate for states: 'there is no State so strong that it may not, at some time, need the aid of others external to itself: either in the way of commerce, or in order to repel the force of many foreign nations combined against it'.[27] But even in this formulation society is still deemed to be an inescapable necessity for states, which remains essentially a proposition derived from the idea of natural law. However, elsewhere Grotius is careful to distinguish the law of nations from natural law: 'this Law of Nations is not like Natural Law, which flows in a sure way from certain reasons; but this takes its measure from the will of nations'.[28] Grotius also draws a number of specific distinctions which take him closer to a conception of international law as a system of law requiring the positive consent of states or deriving from well-established custom. For example, he distinguishes between acquisition of ownership

---

[24] Cited in F. S. Ruddy, *International Law in the Enlightenment* (New York, 1975), 17–18.
[25] Hugo Grotius, *De Jure Belli*, Prolegomena, p. 1.
[26] Ibid.   [27] Ibid.   [28] Ibid. ii. 206.

based on natural law and acquisition deriving its legitimacy from the law of nations, a law which, he says, pertains to 'the mutual society of nations amongst themselves'.[29] Finally, he defines *jus gentium* in a way that makes it virtually indistinguishable from *jus inter gentes*.[30]

If ultimately Grotius's conception of an international society remains somewhat unclear, this may be because he himself was torn between the *magna communitas* of natural law and the society of independent states to which his emphasis on voluntarism seemed to be pointing. No such uncertainty troubled the last two thinkers whom we shall briefly consider. Pufendorf, writing some years after Grotius, was quite emphatic in his view that 'the law of nature and the law of nations are one and the same thing, differing only in their external denomination . . . Nor do we feel that there is any other voluntary or positive law of nations which has the force of a law, properly so called, such as binds nations as if it proceeded from a superior.'[31] A rather different conclusion is reached by Christian von Wolff, writing in the middle of the eighteenth century. For him the 'great society', and its fundamental laws which existed in a state of nature, remain in being after the formation of states, with natural law having the same binding force upon states that it had upon individuals:

If we should consider that great society, which nature herself has established among men, to be done away with by the particular societies which men enter when they unite into a state, states would be established contrary to the law of nature, in as much as the universal obligation of all toward all would be terminated; which assuredly is absurd . . . individual men do not cease to be members of that great society which is made up of the whole human race, because several have formed together a certain particular society . . . After the human race was divided into nations, that society which before was between individuals continues between nations.[32]

Wolff believed that logically a necessary condition for a system of law with binding force upon states (which he thought existed) was a central authority, with the power to compel states to fulfil their

---

[29] Hugo Grotius, *De Jure Belli*, Prolegomena, i. 395–6.
[30] Ibid. i. 416.
[31] Cited in L. Krieger, *The Politics of Discretion and the Acceptance of Natural Law* (Chicago and London, 1965), 156.
[32] Christian von Wolff, *Jus Gentium Methodo Scientifica Pentractum*, trans. J. H. Drake (Oxford, 1934).

obligations to the international society of which they were a part, and to force them to comply with the law. This led him to the assertion that the states of the world as a whole could be deemed to constitute a *civitas maxima* (supreme state) with just such a capacity. The absence of any formal international organization which could act as his *civitas maxima* was not theoretically a problem for Wolff: he simply argued that since natural law bound all men and states automatically, and since the advantages of this were evident to all who were capable of experiencing 'right reason', states could be deemed to have given their tacit consent to it, 'if they know their own interests'.[33] However, even Wolff was troubled by the evident gap between his own logic and reality, so he introduced an additional component to his international society: the balance of power, which he defined as 'such a condition of several nations so related to each other in power that the combined power of the others is equal to the power of the strongest or to the joint power of certain ones'.[34] Equilibrium he believed to be conducive to the liberty of states, although he added, rather sadly:

If nations were to live by such a standard of ethics that they would perform for each other duties which by nature they owe, and if some would not injure others for their own advantage, equilibrium among nations would be of no use, as there would be no wars to be feared. Since the contrary is the case, equilibrium is especially useful to protect the common security.[35]

All of the ideas that have been discussed in this section have three features in common:

1. They are all attempts to find a new basis for order in the international relations of sovereign states, to replace the universal society of the Romans and its somewhat weaker reformulation as Christendom.

2. They all derive from the idea of natural law: the notion that man in a state of nature is governed by certain fundamental moral and ethical principles which remain in force despite the emergence of new social entities—states—claiming absolute authority in their own domains. In this view man is a human being before he is French or Spanish, and as such he has rights and obligations that stem from his membership of the great community of mankind,

---

[33] Ibid. 12.　　　　　[34] Ibid. 330.　　　　　[35] Ibid.

whose authority transcends that of the states to which it is morally as well as historically prior.

3. The idea of the great community is not dependent upon the existence of a formal structure of authority: it is essentially a transnational interpretation of international relations, and like all such approaches has potentially revolutionary or subversive implications for the claims of the sovereign state to undiluted internal authority.

THE SOCIETY OF STATES

The works discussed in the previous section may all be seen as attempts to discover an overall context for orderly social interaction amongst entities acknowledging no superior. Three crucial difficulties with their prescriptions are apparent. The first is that, against all evidence to the contrary, some of them try to cling to a belief in some kind of higher authority capable of limiting the freedom of states. Secondly, their emphasis on natural law is misplaced. This is not the place for a detailed critique of natural law theories, but there are some obvious problems with the concept: the use of the word 'law' is misleading since in this context the word has a meaning that is closer to the sense in which we speak of a scientific 'law' than to the juristic use of the word; the idea that 'right reason' will inevitably lead intelligent beings to the same conclusions about the application of natural law in specific cases is inherently dubious; the notion that human relations are naturally inclined towards co-operation and brotherly love is likewise not a self-evident truth. Finally, although when they deal with developments like the acceptance by states of rules relating to diplomacy and other matters these writers are accurately perceiving phenomena that are genuinely suggestive of some sort of society, they find it hard to come to grips with the precise nature of this society. Instead, they tend to resort to generalizations that are more appropriate to a universal society like Christendom than to the complexities of a society whose members recognize no authority higher than themselves.

Hence the question remains: if their perception of certain features indicative of the existence of a society is indeed valid, what kind of society is it? One approach to answering this question has been to suggest that in the eighteenth and nineteenth centuries the idea of an international society based upon a common European culture emerged. This was a period during which Europe faced no serious challenge from external powers such as it had faced in the past from Turkey and the Mongols, and this enabled the European powers to develop a sense of their own superiority and to begin to conceive of themselves as a kind of exclusive club, managing the world in their own interests, an idea which reached its peak in the second half of the nineteenth century. As Bull puts it:

As the sense grew of the specifically European character of the society of states, so also did the sense of its cultural differentiation from what lay outside: the sense that European powers in their dealings with one another were bound by a code of conduct that did not apply to them in their dealings with other and lesser societies.[36]

The members of this society were states, but states having in common values, culture, a system of law, and a standard of civilization.

There is considerable evidence that such a conception was clearly discernible by the beginning of the eighteenth century and commonplace after 1815. In 1716 François de Callières saw the interdependence of European states as the foundation-stone of their society:

we must think of the states of which Europe is composed as being joined together by all kinds of necessary commerce, in such a way that they may be regarded as members of one Republic and that no considerable change can take place in any one of them without affecting the condition, or disturbing the peace of all others.[37]

His reference to Europe as a kind of republic was echoed by Vattel, Voltaire, Burke, Gentz, and others, while, as we shall see later, one of Britain's stated reasons for going to war against revolutionary France was an objection to France's apparent intention of annulling the 'political system of Europe', and the British war aims included the restoration of 'a general System of Public Law in Europe'.

Although a conception of a European international society was clearly shared by many writers and statesmen by the end of the eighteenth century, it is important to distinguish between the

[36] H. Bull, *The Anarchical Society* (London, 1977), 33.
[37] A. F. Whyte, *The Practice of Diplomacy*, trans. of François de Callière's *De la manière de négocier avec les souverains* (London, 1919).

primary and secondary features of this society. The former are its defining characteristics: the essential common interests for whose protection and advancement it was formed. The latter are qualities which it acquired after the initial association—not necessarily superficial or unimportant qualities, but qualities subordinate to or derived from the central purpose of the society. The best analogy here is with the state itself, especially since it was the nature of the modern state that determined the fundamental character of the international society which developed in Europe after the collapse of Christendom. It is crucial to remember that the modern international society was not just a society of sovereign states but a society *for* sovereign states, with its most basic role that of legitimizing and protecting their sovereign status. The state itself was primarily a legal fiction in the sense that it was an attempt to provide a lawful basis and justification for the structure of power that emerged out of the collapse of medieval Christendom and feudalism. The concept of territorial sovereignty—the notion that all the inhabitants of a given territory, regardless of any other loyalties they might have, owed an overriding duty of obedience to the lawful sovereign of that territory—which defined the modern state was fundamentally a legal concept. Only secondarily might the state also function as a community of individuals sharing similar values or a common culture or religion, or as an association for promoting the welfare of its members. Similarly, the society of states was primarily a legal construct with the purpose of identifying the attributes of sovereign statehood which acted as membership qualifications, excluding entities that did not possess these attributes and legitimizing the supreme position of the state. Only secondarily might it acquire other features that would suggest a more fully developed community: the 'family of nations' of the late nineteenth century.

If one imagines an international social contract between states to establish a society of sovereign states, it would be reasonable to assume that its central principles of association would be similar to those outlined above, since these would be deemed most basic to the protection and advancement of its members' most vital interests. Of course no such social contract has ever been agreed, but one event has come to be seen as the symbolic origin of the modern system of international relations: the Peace of Westphalia, which brought to an end the Thirty Years War in 1648. Too much should not be claimed for this. The sovereign state, free in all but the legal theory of the Church, had emerged hundreds of years earlier, and Bodin's writings on sovereignty had been published in 1576. Diplomacy and the balance of power as tools of statecraft had both been apparent from the end of the fifteenth century. Moreover, the 'old' system of Christendom did not entirely disappear after 1648. Political entities that could not unambiguously be described as 'sovereign states' continued to exist up until the period of the French Revolution, and indeed were accepted by the Treaties of Munster and Osnabruck, which constituted the Westphalian settlement. Finally, the Peace was not, as is sometimes thought, a clearly formulated attempt to create a new international order, as were the League of Nations, the United Nations Organization, and, in a different way, the Concert of Europe. The principal aims of its most important signatories were to safeguard and advance their own immediate interests, and the great bulk of the clauses of the two treaties are concerned with setting out in minute detail precisely how they proposed to achieve these objectives.

None the less, the Peace of Westphalia may still be regarded as the symbolic origin of the society of states since it crystallized and gave legal weight to developments which had been taking place in a random and unfocused way for very many years. It also encapsulated in its terms seven of the most fundamental aspects of the emerging society of states in a way that no single event before or since 1648 has managed to do.

The first and most basic of these was the idea of sovereignty: the notion that the state and not the Church or Empire was the source of all legitimate authority. This acknowledgement of sovereignty came in the clauses permitting the various German states within the Empire the right to conduct their own diplomatic relations. Some of the larger states had been exercising this right for many years, but Westphalia gave it legal sanction for the first time and extended it to the other states within the Empire.[38] Secondly, the treaties marked a step towards the idea of equality amongst states: the principle of sovereign equality, or the notion that as all states are equally sovereign, however unequal they may be in other respects, they all merit equal respect by virtue of their statehood. This was

[38] G. Barraclough, *The Origins of Modern Germany* (Oxford, 1979), 381.

not so clearly and decisively accepted in Westphalia as the principle of sovereignty had been—many months of wrangling over precedence took place before the congress could begin and the idea of a hierarchy amongst states has persisted in different forms to the present day. However, the notion of sovereign equality is contained in two important decisions taken at Westphalia. First, Article 5 of the Treaty of Osnabruck declared that 'there be an exact and reciprocal Equality amongst all the Electors, Princes and States of both Religions, conformably to the State of the Commonweal, the Constitution of the Empire and the present Convention: so that what is just of one side shall be so of the other . . . '.[39] Second, decisions of the German Diet were not to be taken by majority vote but through a consensus or 'composition' between the Protestant and Catholic factions within the Diet.[40] This was primarily designed to ensure religious equality in the Empire, but it pointed the way to an important aspect of the principle of sovereign equality: the principle that since states were both sovereign and equal they could not be obligated without their consent, so that in international congresses decisions had to be unanimous.

The third key principle of the settlement was that of the balance of power. In this context the concept of balance of power implied that since states accepted no higher authority competent to uphold order amongst them, the chief ordering device in a society of states would be the maintenance of a balance of power so that no single state would be able to achieve preponderance over the rest. The balance of power principle was not specifically stated in a treaty until 1713, when the Treaty of Utrecht declared 'a just equilibrium of power' to be 'The best and most solid basis of mutual friendship and durable harmony'.[41] However, it was evident long before the end of the Thirty Years War that the war aims of many of the belligerents were increasingly limited to a territorial settlement that would establish a balance of power, rather than some form of total victory. In 1633 Sweden's chancellor, Oxenstierna, stated Sweden's primary objective in the war to be the preservation of a European equilibrium, although in 1646 Sweden's representative at the peace

[39] Treaty of Osnabruck, 24 Oct. 1648, in Clive Parry (ed.), *Consolidated Treaty Series*, i. (Dobbs Ferry, NY, 1969), 198–270.
[40] L. Gross, 'The Peace of Westphalia, 1648–1948', *American Journal of International Law*, 42 (1948), 22.
[41] Cited in E. V. Gulick, *Europe's Classical Balance of Power* (New York, 1967), 35.

congress, Count Salvius, lamented that the principle was being turned against Sweden: 'People are beginning to see the power of Sweden as dangerous to the "balance of power". Their first rule of politics is that the security of all depends on the equilibrium of the individuals. When one begins to become powerful . . . the others place themselves, through unions or alliances, into the opposite balance in order to maintain the equipoise.'[42] Even the papacy had come to see its interests in terms of the achievement of a balance of power rather than in terms of outright victory by a single state.[43] The territorial settlement clearly reflected this concern with the balance of power, and in particular the belief that a Germany united under the control of a single power represented a threat to the overall balance.

The fourth principle contained in the Peace was the idea of international society itself. Although this was not made explicit either, several aspects of the Treaties strongly suggest that the signatories conceived of themselves as acting, in certain respects, as members of a common society. The most obvious of these is that the settlement was agreed at a general congress of almost all of the states of Europe,[44] with the implication that all of them had the right to concern themselves with matters in which they might have no direct interest.[45] Furthermore, the signatories undertook a collective duty to 'protect all and every Article of this Peace against any one, without distinction of Religion'.[46] They also assumed the right to confer various entitlements upon individual rulers, as in the case of Alsace, to insist that states adhere to certain general practices of religious toleration in their internal policies, and, most important of all, formally to admit new members to the society of states (the United Provinces and the Swiss Confederation). A Marxist historian makes the additional point, concerning the Thirty Years War itself, that 'a precondition for the generalizing of the conflict was the presence in early seventeenth-century Europe, if

[42] G. Parker, *The Thirty Years War* (London, 1984), 184.
[43] Ibid.
[44] Article 17 of the Treaty of Osnabruck claimed several states which were not represented, including England, Denmark, and Poland, as allies of one side or another, thus associating them with the terms of the Treaty.
[45] On this point, see the discussion in T. Nardin, *Law, Morality and the Relations of States* (Princeton, NJ, 1983), 57–8.
[46] Article 123 of the Treaty of Munster, in Parry (ed.), *Consolidated Treaty Series*, i. 319–57.

not of an economic unity, at least of a framework for exchange and the first signs of a world market, whose centre of gravity was the whole area between the Baltic, Atlantic and Mediterranean'.[47]

Fifth, some of those characteristics of the Peace which seem to suggest a generally held conception of a society of states also imply that this international society had assumed Christendom's right to confer legitimacy upon individual states and to lay down a general principle of legitimacy. Martin Wight defines international legitimacy as 'the collective judgement of international society about rightful membership of the family of nations; how sovereignty may be transferred; and how state succession is to be regulated, when large states break up into smaller, or several states combine into one'. He adds that until the French Revolution 'the principle of international legitimacy was *dynastic*, being concerned with the status and claims of rulers'.[48] In practice, however, two separate facets of the principle of international legitimacy need to be distinguished. The first is that defined by Wight, which we may term the *specific* principle of legitimacy since it establishes the specific norm prevailing at any one time by which international society identifies the form of internal state authority (dynastic, national, popular, etc.) which it regards as acceptable. The second is a *general* principle, since it determines the general attributes looked for by states when they seek to identify a political unit as being worthy of admission to the society of states. At a basic level, they looked only for clear evidence of the existence of territorial sovereignty. As a more refined form of international society took shape in the nineteenth century, however, the general principle of legitimacy also came to require the achievement by would-be states of a certain 'standard of civilization', defined by Bull as demanding the ability 'to meet standards of performance (as in protection of basic rights of their citizens, standards of honesty and efficiency in administration, capacity to adhere to rules of international law and to enter into diplomatic relations, and avoidance of slavery and other odious practices)'.[49] The notions of religious equality and tolerance laid down at Westphalia had become firmly entrenched within the larger conception of a standard of civilization by the

---

[47] J. V. Polisensky, *The Thirty Years War* (London, 1974), 258.
[48] Wight, *Systems of States*, 153.
[49] H. Bull in the Foreword to Gerrit W. Gong, *The Standard of 'Civilization' in International Society* (Oxford, 1984).

time of the Congress of Berlin in 1878, as the following statement by M. Waddington, the French delegate, makes clear:

Mr. Waddington believes that it is important to take advantage of this solemn opportunity to cause the principles of religious liberty to be affirmed by the representatives of Europe. His Excellency adds that Serbia, who claims to enter the European family on the same basis as other states, must previously recognize the principles which are the basis of social organization in all states of Europe and accept them as a necessary condition of the favour which she asks for.[50]

The sixth underlying principle of the society of states to be implicitly acknowledged by the Peace of Westphalia was a conception of international law as neither the 'law of nations' in the sense of the general principles present in all legal systems, nor as natural law, but as a set of voluntarily accepted guidelines and rules of international conduct that were appropriate to a society of sovereign states. As such, its primary purpose was not to subordinate states to some higher authority, but the opposite: to establish the freedom of states as the supreme law, since it was only through the exercise of her freedom that each state was enabled 'properly to discharge the duties she owes to herself and to her citizens and to govern herself in the manner best suited to her circumstances'.[51] International law in this 'positivist' conception hence had the aim of regulating the relations between independent states in such a manner as to confirm their sovereignty, but since this was also the first objective of the society of states, international law had the additional purpose of protecting and preserving the society of states as a whole, and its system for the conduct of international relations. As the most influential eighteenth-century positivist put it, the 'voluntary law of nations' could be deduced 'from the natural liberty of nations, from the attention due to their common safety, from the nature of their mutual correspondence, their reciprocal duties, and the distinctions of their various rights, internal and external, perfect and imperfect'.[52] It was because the logic of sovereignty seemed to point to the impossibility of implementing a system for maintaining international order similar to those which operated within states that many statesmen and

[50] Gross, 'The Peace of Westphalia', 23.
[51] Emerich de Vattel, *The Law of Nations*, ed. J. Chitty (London, 1834), p. xiv.
[52] Ibid., pp. xiv–xv.

legal thinkers accepted that completely different ordering principles should apply, and they had no difficulty with the idea that devices like the balance of power could be seen as part of international law.[53]

Finally, the Peace may be seen as a triumph for the seventh major feature of the emerging society of states: diplomacy. In the basic sense of the word—negotiations between separate political entities—this is a practice as ancient as politics itself. But in the sense of a continuous attempt by states to manage their conflicting interests through a dialogue conducted by their official agents in accordance with certain widely accepted rules of procedure, norms of behaviour, and obligations concerning the treatment of foreign diplomats, diplomacy is of much more recent origin. The modern diplomatic system developed gradually from the later Middle Ages, especially in Italy, but Westphalia may be seen as the culmination of a long process of evolution and as the embodiment of the central idea of diplomacy: that, alongside and closely associated with the balance of power and international law, it provides the means by which sovereign states adjust their relations with each other, and the basis of order in international society.

THE STATE AND INTERNATIONAL SOCIETY

The seven elements of the Westphalian system outlined in the last section constitute the central or primary characteristics of the Westphalian conception of international society. They define an international society whose fundamental feature was an essentially juridical notion of statehood as conferring the sole legitimate entitlement to membership of a society of equals who acknowledged no higher authority than themselves and accepted only such mechanisms for international order as would preserve and enhance their sovereignty. As state practice evolved in the decades following Westphalia, certain additional features appeared which may be seen as a set of secondary characteristics of the Westphalian system, since they were either logical corollaries of it, or necessary principles of prudent statecraft within such a system in the context of the highly competitive European environment of the seventeenth and eighteenth centuries. The first of these was a doctrine of non-

[53] A. and D. F. Vagts, 'The Balance of Power in International Law: A History of an Idea', *American Journal of International Law*, 73 (1979), 555–80.

intervention: the principle that states had no right to interest themselves in the internal affairs of others. The Westphalian settlement had confirmed this principle in respect of religious matters and in the eighteenth century it came to acquire a more general applicability. The second was the closely related ideas of *raison d'état* and the primacy of foreign policy. As states were sovereign in their rights, so also were they in their duties: they could rely on no external authority for protection, hence self-preservation was the highest responsibility of any state. Moral considerations, such as those derived from natural law theories, could not constrain states in the same way as they did individuals. Necessity—reason of state—was the overriding imperative. As Richelieu put it:

In certain cases where the welfare of the State is concerned, it is necessary to employ a vigorous authority which sometimes oversteps the usual rules of prudence and which it is sometimes impossible to keep clear of certain evils.[54]

Since the threat to the security of the state came from outside, the attention of the state's rulers had to be focused first and foremost upon external affairs. Foreign policy took precedence over other goals such as internal reform. Moreover, since security was thought to depend ultimately upon power, developing a strong state was seen as the first purpose of national policy. One corollary of this was the belief that control over foreign policy should be firmly in the hands of the executive arm of the state, with little or no opportunity given to the judicial or legislative arms to hinder decisive action in the interest of the state. By the same token, diplomacy was not deemed to be a fitting subject of public debate. Open discussion of diplomatic negotiations would inevitably reduce the statesman's freedom to take measures in the name of expediency or urgency that might appear—or be—immoral if judged by the conventional standards of human beings in their private relations. It would also constrain foreign diplomats, whose freedom to discuss various matters depended upon an assumption that such discussions were confidential.

The seventeenth- and eighteenth-century concept of the state, which was at the root of doctrines like *raison d'état* and the primacy of foreign policy, perceived the state as primarily a provider of internal order and external security. While such views

[54] Cited in Shennan, *Origins of the Modern European State*, 104.

of the state remained unchallenged, the society of states did not develop much beyond the simple, even austere, form it had assumed after Westphalia. When other ideas about the role of the state—that it should embody the 'nation', that it should be responsive to the will of the 'people', that it was the standard-bearer of 'history', that it was responsible for the welfare of its citizens or of other states' citizens—began to take hold, there were inevitable consequences for the society of states. At the same time as this process, in which revolutionary states played a major part, was taking place, each great war raised fresh doubts about the mechanisms through which order was maintained within the Westphalian conception of international society. Once again, revolutionary states were critically involved, directly or indirectly, in this dialectic between old and new.

CONCLUSION

Since 1648 the dominant form of international society has been the 'Westphalian conception' of a loose association of sovereign states. The theoretical consequence of this which has received the greatest attention from scholars has concerned the freedom of states that is seen to derive from their sovereign status. Ideas like the competitive pursuit of separate national interests, the struggle for power among states and their security dilemma all relate to the perception that sovereignty is the key to explaining the behaviour of states. Some have suggested that the anarchical implications of sovereignty are tempered to some degree by the fact that, since no state has ever possessed sufficient power to achieve absolute dominance over the others, states are all parts of an interdependent international system that curbs their excesses through such means as the balance of power. Such constraints, however, are 'systemic' rather than 'societal': they derive from the system-wide consequences of the mutual antagonism of states, not from any shared sense of community among states.

If states are part of a society as well as a system, this suggests a very different set of theoretical implications. To take one obvious illustration, a balance of power that emerges out of the competitive pursuit of power is conceptually and theoretically distinct from one that is consciously sought by states as a means of promoting international order. In the one case a balance of power is a property of an international system, in the other of an international society. Similarly, when states seek to protect their sovereignty through military means, their behaviour is conceptually and theoretically distinct from attempts to defend their independence by supporting international efforts to affirm sovereignty as the central principle of a society of states. And when established states respond to doctrines of international revolution by restating their collective commitment to a common set of norms, rules, values, and practices, they are acting as members of an international society, not as units within an international system.

2

State and People
The American Revolution

The inclusion of the United States in a study of the interaction between revolutionary states and international society requires some preliminary explanation. Sober-minded and moderate individuals such as Washington, Adams, Jefferson, and Hamilton sit somewhat uneasily in the company of Robespierre, Trotsky, Castro, Khomeini, and Gaddafi. Their primary international goal was to win the right for their state to enter the society of states as a respectable member, not to overturn it. On achieving that aim they and their successors did not seek to export their revolution but at first tried to keep themselves free from political entanglements with the outside world. Later, as the United States rose to a pre-eminent position during the twentieth century, it often appeared to symbolize conservatism and counter-revolution rather than revolutionary change. Indeed, the United States—'imperialism' and 'the Great Satan' of Marxist and extremist Islamic demonology —came to be regarded as the principal enemy and leading target of many contemporary revolutionary movements.

Yet while there are clearly important differences between the United States and the other countries considered in this study, there are also some striking similarities. Throughout its history certain recurring features have appeared in America's approach to foreign relations, some of which are characteristic of revolutionary states generally. These include a belief in the universal significance of the American revolution and a sense of mission imparted by this belief, an underlying suspiciousness, occasionally verging on paranoia, about the intentions of foreigners, an idealistic optimism about America's potentialities which can sometimes lead to a readiness to exaggerate the capacity of limited means to achieve overly ambitious ends, a tendency to adopt a combative and self-righteous posture towards foreign rivals, a deep-seated distrust of traditional modes of conducting international relations, and a propensity towards doctrinal formulations of foreign policy, generally infused with ideological and moralistic rhetoric. A number of distinctively American traits, beliefs, and practices have also had implications for the US approach to foreign relations. These include a preference for legalistic solutions to international problems and ideally for the international application of the principle of the rule of law, the domestic separation of sovereign powers among several organs of state, a genuinely democratic influence in foreign policy-making, and a faith in the ability of commercial and economic means to achieve political ends. All of these facets of American foreign relations were discernible in the two decades following the Declaration of Independence and, although none is unique to the United States, taken together they amounted to a radical challenge to some of the established tenets and traditional modes of operation of international society.

FROM REVOLUTION TO CONSTITUTION: THE EMERGENCE OF AN AMERICAN FOREIGN POLICY

Many of the underlying assumptions and attitudes of American foreign relations were not products of the revolution as such. In most cases they had evolved over the previous 150 years as the colonists came to develop a view of themselves and their land as set apart from the tribulations and oppression of the old world, which indeed they had come to America to escape. To the image of America as a fortunate land was added an early sense of America's future importance in world affairs as its population came inevitably to outnumber the populations of the European mother countries and to take full advantage of the country's abundant resources. Hand in hand with this view of America as uniquely favoured by God and nature went a tendency to suspect powerful foreign nations of conspiratorial designs upon American happiness and liberty. After the defeat of France in 1763, Americans fed by radical opposition arguments in Britain itself, came to focus upon England as the chief source of this conspiracy.[1] One aspect of this notion was an image of Americans as virtuous and innocent, while

[1] See Bernard Bailyn, *The Ideological Origins of the American Revolution* (Cambridge, Mass., 1967) and *The Origins of American Politics* (New York, 1967).

foreigners—those who did not see the light and emigrate—were corrupt and cunning individuals with whom it was best to have as few dealings as possible. The success and impact of Thomas Paine's *Common Sense*, which articulated many of these ideas in 1776, is partly explicable by the degree to which the ground had already been prepared by countless earlier pamphlets on similar themes.

John Winthrop's 1630 characterization of America as a 'city upon a hill' was an early expression of the utopian vision of America as a land set apart, but more concrete manifestations of the same idea were also evident. During the seventeenth century, European states came to accept what Max Savelle terms the 'doctrine of the two spheres, resting upon the idea that Europe was one political and international sphere, with its own system of laws, institutions, and international connections, and that the "new world" was another', and treaties between European states would stipulate that a rift in their relationship in Europe should not be allowed to affect their relations in North America.[2] Another important influence was the extent to which American relations with the outside world were primarily commercial. This had two significant consequences. First, by the time of the revolution many Americans had come to believe that their commercial importance gave them a decisive form of leverage over European nations. Secondly, relations with Europe other than commercial ones were widely regarded as undesirable. As Thomas Paine put it, 'Our plan is commerce, and that, well attended to, will secure us the peace and friendship of all Europe; because it is the interest of all Europe to have America a free port. Her trade will always be a protection . . . As Europe is our market for trade, we ought to form no partial connection with any part of it. It is the true interest of America to steer clear of European contentions.'[3] Similarly, John Adams asserted that 'we should calculate all our measures and foreign negotiations in such a manner as to avoid a too great dependence upon any power of Europe—to avoid all obligations and temptations to take any part in future European wars: that the business of America with Europe was commerce, not politics or war.'[4] A

[2] Max Savelle, *The Origins of American Diplomacy* (New York, 1967), 106–7, 210–14.
[3] Cited in G. Stourzh, *Benjamin Franklin and American Foreign Policy* (Chicago, 1969), 117.
[4] Cited in F. Gilbert, 'The "New Diplomacy" of the Eighteenth Century', *World Politics*, 4/1 (Oct. 1951), 19.

further element in American thought concerning international relations at the time of the revolution may have been derived from the writings of the French *philosophes*, who rejected many aspects of the existing international system, such as traditional diplomacy and the balance of power, and saw free trade as the means of establishing a new international order based upon reason, morality, and openness.[5] The precise influence of the *philosophes* upon American foreign policy is a matter of controversy,[6] but the more general impact of Enlightenment thinking and natural law theories in particular is hardly to be doubted, being confirmed not least by the language of the Declaration of Independence.

Hence, as earlier remarked, the revolution did not create the political culture of the United States, but it did give a focus to the inchoate mixture of prejudice, philosophy, and reflection upon experience which had been taking shape during the eighteenth century as a characteristically American approach to foreign affairs. The first diplomatic acts of the thirteen colonies upon declaring themselves to have 'full Power to levy War, conclude Peace, contract Alliances, establish Commerce, and to do all other Acts and Things which Independent States may of right do' were marked by this distinctive style. However, the Declaration itself was far from being a clarion call to revolution elsewhere—indeed, it was the opposite, since its primary purpose, as Richard Henry Lee's resolution of 7 June 1776 proposing independence made clear, was to win acceptance as a legitimate state in order to make the search for foreign aid against Britain easier.[7] Thereafter the exigencies of the war as well as the quest for European recognition of America's legitimacy continued to dictate a policy of accommodation towards the international system within which the Americans would need to operate if they were to gain their objectives. But even during the period of the war there were signs of an unconventional approach to foreign affairs that was to reappear at intervals throughout the country's history, with important

[5] Gilbert, 'The "New Diplomacy" ', and *To the Farewell Address: Ideas of Early American Foreign Policy* (Princeton, NJ, 1961), 56–65.

[6] See J. H. Hutson, 'Early American Diplomacy: A Reappraisal', in L. S. Kaplan (ed.), *The American Revolution and 'A Candid World'* (Kent State, Ohio, 1977), 42–6, and the same author's *John Adams and the Diplomacy of the American Revolution* (Lexington, Ky., 1980), 143–55 for a critique of Gilbert's thesis.

[7] E. Dumbauld, 'Independence under International Law', *American Journal of International Law*, 70/3 (1976), 425.

consequences for the Westphalian conception of international society. In Felix Gilbert's words:

The utopian hopes which immigrants had connected with their settlement in America made it difficult for them to fit themselves meekly into the existing state system and to become a power like all other powers. Americans expected that the appearance of their country on the diplomatic scene would be instrumental in effecting a new departure in international relations and would usher in a new and better world. Americans would be inclined to listen to those voices which were critical of the existing methods of foreign policy and wanted to reform them rather than to accept them as appropriate and necessary.[8]

However, any thought in 1776 that America's arrival on the international scene might lead to a rapid transformation of the conduct of diplomacy soon disappeared. The initial hope of the more radical elements amongst the revolutionaries was that the prospect of commercial opportunities arising out of America's break with Britain would entice European powers, especially France and Spain, to help the United States without the need for a treaty of alliance, which might draw the United States into an undesirable entanglement with the amoral power politics of Europe. The principles laid down by John Adams as early as March 1776 regarding the correct approach to be taken towards France were:

1. No political connection. Submit to none of her authority, receive no governors or officers from her.
2. No military connection. Receive no troops from her.
3. Only a commercial connection; that is, make a treaty to receive our ships into her ports; furnish us with arms.[9]

These ideas influenced the draft treaty which Adams helped to write in 1776 and which was intended as a model for formal relations with Europe. This, although not as revolutionary a document as some have claimed, adopted the most liberal views then prevailing on such matters as free trade and the rights of neutral shipping.[10] It

---

[8] Gilbert, *To the Farewell Address*, 17.

[9] Ibid. 49.

[10] Ibid. 48–56 for the view that the Model Treaty represented 'the diplomacy of an entirely new era'. Hutson, 'Early American Diplomacy', 44–5, and W. C. Stinchcombe, 'John Adams and the Model Treaty', in Kaplan, *The American Revolution*, 69–70, both regard this as an exaggeration of the Treaty's significance.

was also, quite deliberately, opposed to the much more restrictive maritime principles which Britain had sought to impose since 1756, and the Americans confidently assumed that Britain's European rivals would be seduced by that feature of the Model Treaty, if its obvious commercial attractions did not suffice. Similarly, the instructions of the Continental Congress to the Commissioners it sent to Europe to seek assistance and recognition went to some lengths to rule out any possibility of a military alliance.[11] However, within three months the urgency of the American situation and the inability of the Commissioners to make much headway by offering commercial concessions alone had led the Congress to issue fresh instructions as follows:

Upon mature deliberation of all circumstances, Congress deem the speedy declaration of France and European assistance so indispensably necessary to secure the independence of these States, that they have authorised you to make such tenders to France and Spain as they hope will prevent any longer delay of an event that is judged so essential to the well-being of North America. Your wisdom, we know, will direct you to make such tenders to France and Spain as they hope will procure the thing desired on terms as much short of the concessions now offered as possible; but no advantages of this kind are proposed at the risk of a delay that may prove dangerous to the end in view.[12]

The Commissioners promptly offered France and Spain territorial gains in the West Indies and elsewhere if they aided the United States, albeit while continuing to point to 'advantages of that commerce, which in time will be immense'.[13] An alliance between the new republic and the Catholic monarchy of France followed in February 1778.

Although 'mature deliberation of all circumstances' had thus led Congress to retreat from its resistance to foreign entanglements, the underlying assumptions and attitudes that had produced its earlier stance remained and continued to influence the American approach to foreign relations throughout the War of Independence. Much recent American scholarship on the diplomacy of the revolution has

[11] S. F. Bemis, *The Diplomacy of the American Revolution* (New York and London, 1935), 48.

[12] B. Harrison *et al.*, Committee of Secret Correspondence to the Commissioners at Paris, 30 Dec. 1776, in F. Wharton (ed.), *The Revolutionary Diplomatic Correspondence of the United States* (4 vols.; Washington, 1889), ii. 240.

[13] Franklin, Deane, and Lee to Vergennes, ibid. 246.

emphasized the realism of the American leaders, their understanding and exploitation of such traditional devices of statecraft as the balance of power, and their disinclination to do or say anything that could be interpreted as indicating a desire to export their revolution.[14] This reappraisal of the revolutionary period can be supported by numerous contemporary American references to the balance of power (considered in Chapter 8) and by various statements urging a cautious, if not conservative, approach to the established states system, such as that by James Wilson in January 1777: 'In our Transactions with European States, it is certainly of Importance neither to transgress nor to fall short of those Maxims, by which they regulate their Conduct towards one another.'[15] However, while these studies decisively refute any notion that the first American diplomats were idealistic missionaries going forth with utopian plans to transform the world, they do not invalidate the interpretation offered here, one which seeks to portray American revolutionary diplomacy as possessing certain distinctive characteristics which had potentially radical implications for international society.

The first such characteristic was a continuing faith that America's commercial promise would ultimately enable her to achieve a commanding position and also, through the extension of her free trade principles, help bring about a more peaceful world. Referring to the American desire for a more liberal definition of wartime contraband than the dominant British doctrine, under which the British claimed extensive rights to confiscate goods transported by neutral ships, John Adams declared:

I think that the abolition of the whole doctrine of contraband would be for the peace and happiness of mankind; and I doubt not, as human reason advances, and men come to be more sensible of the benefits of peace, and less enthusiastic for the savage glories of war, all neutral nations will be allowed, by universal consent, to carry what goods they please in their own ships, provided they are not bound to places actually invested by an enemy.[16]

[14] For this 'revisionist' view of early American diplomacy, see the works by Hutson already cited and also J. R. Dull, *A Diplomatic History of the American Revolution* (New Haven, Conn., and London, 1985), J. H. Hutson, 'Intellectual Origins of Early American Diplomacy', *Diplomatic History*, 1/1 (Winter, 1977), 1–19, and L. S. Kaplan, *Colonies into Nations: American Diplomacy, 1763–1801* (New York, 1972).

[15] Hutson, *John Adams*, 153.

[16] Wharton, *The Revolutionary Diplomatic Correspondence*, iii. 612.

Adams believed that this commercial policy was an important part of America's revolutionary message to the world, since the economic interdependence which, in his view, would follow a shift from mercantilism to free trade would also lead to greater harmony among the nations.[17]

A second distinctive aspect of American foreign relations during the revolutionary period was the extent to which foreign policy was created by and debated in the Continental Congress. Although Congressional sessions were supposedly secret, Benjamin Franklin and Robert Morris were to remark, 'We find, by fatal experience, the Congress consists of too many members to keep secrets.'[18] During the revolution, the Continental Congress functioned in effect as the national government, largely because the individual states, who were jealously guarding their separate sovereignties, felt unable to entrust their affairs to a single executive body. Many also believed that such an arrangement approximated most closely to their republican ideals. However, in a world where other states exercised strong control over their foreign affairs, the American approach could be a source of weakness. Until 1781 the radical opponents of executive power had prevented the creation of a separate Department of Foreign Affairs, with its own Secretary, preferring to administer foreign policy through Congressional Committees whose membership was not constant and which were in any case unable to deal with the huge volume of business.[19] The Committees were subject to factional conflict which even led on occasion to disputing factions making open use of confidential diplomatic information to score points off each other.[20] It was in part the same factionalism that led Congress to send three Commissioners, supposedly of equal importance, to Paris so that different opinions and interests could be represented. Franklin offered a complete critique of this arrangement:

whatever advantage there might be in the joint counsels of three for framing and adjusting the articles of the treaty, there can be none in managing the common business of a resident here. On the contrary, all the advantages in negotiation that result from secrecy of sentiment and

---

[17] P. A. Varg, *The Foreign Policy of the Founding Fathers* (Baltimore, 1963), 3.
[18] Wharton, *The Revolutionary Diplomatic Correspondence*, i. 152.
[19] Ibid. i. 456–7.
[20] W. C. Stinchcombe, *The American Revolution and the French Alliance* (New York, 1969), 40–1.

uniformity in expressing it and in common business from dispatch are lost. In a court, too, where every word is watched and weighed, if a number of commissioners do not every one hold the same language in giving their opinion on any public transaction, this lessens their weight; and when it may be prudent to put on or avoid certain appearances of concern, for example, or indifference, satisfaction, or dislike, where the utmost sincerity and candour should be used, and would gain credit if no semblance of art showed itself in the inadvertent discourse perhaps of only one of them, the hazard is in proportion to the number. And where every one must be consulted on every particular of common business in answering every letter etc., and one of them is offended if the smallest thing is done without his consent, the interruptions by new applicants in the time of meeting etc., occasion so much postponing and delay, that correspondence languishes, occasions are lost, and the business is always behindhand.[21]

As the Commissioners possessed some of the New World's more sensitive egos, it was inevitable that their personal and political differences would lead to acrimony, with consequent damage to their ability to succeed in their appointed tasks. This damage was exacerbated by the self-righteous and pugnacious tone some of them occasionally adopted in their dealings with foreign powers. As the French foreign minister, Vergennes, commented after the Commissioners were recalled,

We think that Congress has acted wisely in recalling most of its agents in Europe; their character is too little conciliatory and their heads too much excited to admit of their being useful to their country. The calmness and prudence of Mr Franklin are certainly grave faults in their eyes; but it is by these qualities that this minister has inspired us with confidence.[22]

Although personality clashes undoubtedly contributed to the troubled atmosphere among the American diplomats, the root cause was Congressional reluctance to permit anything that resembled strong executive powers. As Alexander Hamilton remarked (employing the eighteenth-century usage of 'jealousy' to mean 'suspicion'): 'An extreme jealousy of power is the attendant on all popular revolutions, and has seldom been without its evils.'[23] 'Revolutionary suspiciousness' was also evident in the attitude of

---

[21] Franklin to Lovell, 22 July 1778, in Wharton, *The Revolutionary Diplomatic Correspondence*, ii. 659.

[22] Ibid. i. 489–90.

[23] 'The Continentalist', No. 1, 12 July 1781, in *The Papers of Alexander Hamilton*, ed. H. C. Syrett and J. E. Cooke (26 vols.; New York and London, 1961), ii. 650.

many Americans, including some Commissioners, towards foreigners.[24]

At the heart of American thinking on foreign as well as domestic affairs was a conviction that the highest priority, which even the exigencies of the war should not be allowed to displace, was to build and secure a republic in North America.[25] In the context of the time, this was taken to mean a form of society whose government would be answerable to the people and within which individuals would have the greatest possible freedom to pursue their own ends. Republics were conceived of as being particularly conducive to the promotion of virtue amongst their peoples, but two sources of corruption needed especially to be guarded against. The first was the emergence of too powerful a state, with strong central government and standing armies being the most obvious signs of this danger. The second was entanglement with the amoral monarchies and aristocracies of Europe. For some, such as the radical William Whipple, the alliance with France had already permitted the infiltration of this latter corruption: 'I fear we place too much dependence on foreign alliances, which will tend to introduce a servility destructive to true Republicanism.'[26] The threat of contamination by Europeans was considered great enough by Elbridge Gerry for him to urge, after the war, a cessation of diplomatic contacts with Europe:

I can see no necessity but great inconvenience in sending Ministers abroad and receiving them at home, inconveniences of being entangled with European politics, of being the puppets of European Statesmen, of being gradually divested of our virtuous republican principles, of being a divided, influenced and dissipated people; of being induced to prefer the splendor of a court to the happiness of our citizens; and finally of changing our form of government for a vile Aristocracy or an arbitrary Monarchy.[27]

It was in part this desire to protect the Republic against corrupting foreign influences that kept many Americans from any inclination to spread their revolutionary doctrines. They always

[24] See J. H. Hutson, 'The American Negotiations: The Diplomacy of Jealousy', in R. Hoffman and P. J. Albert (eds.), *Peace and the Peacemakers: The Treaty of 1783* (Charlottesville, Va., 1986), esp. 55–6, and also J. R. Dull, 'France and the American Revolution Seen as Tragedy', in R. Hoffman and P. J. Albert (eds.), *Diplomacy and Revolution: The Franco-American Alliance of 1778* (Charlottesville, Va., 1981), 73–106.

[25] For the definitive exposition of this thesis, see G. S. Wood, *Creation of the American Republic, 1776–87* (Chapel Hill, NC, 1969).

[26] Cited in Hutson 'Early American Diplomacy', 73.

[27] Ibid. 49.

saw their revolution as having a universal significance, however, and this belief, much later in their history, helped to ensure that the notion that the United States did indeed have an international mission fell on fertile ground. But during and for many years after the revolution the American leaders saw their country's world role as primarily one of leadership by example. Franklin did suggest one additional contribution to the cause of universal liberty: 'tyranny is so generally established in the rest of the world, that the prospect of any asylum in America for those who love liberty, gives general joy, and our cause is esteemed the cause of all mankind. We are fighting for the dignity and happiness of human nature.'[28] He also thought that in order to counter the threat of mass emigration, the European tyrannies 'must relax and allow more liberty to their people. Hence it is a common observation . . . that we are fighting for their liberty in defending our own.'[29] Some European leaders did look with concern upon the popularity of the American cause with their own peoples, while welcoming the blow to British power.[30] However, the definitive American view on this subject for more than fifty years after 1776 was stated by John Quincy Adams in 1821:

Wherever the standard of freedom and independence has been or shall be unfurled, there will her (America's) heart, her benedictions and her prayers be. But she goes not abroad in search of monsters to destroy. She is the well wisher to the freedom and independence of all. She is the champion and vindicator only of her own. She will commend the general cause by the countenance of her voice, and the benignant sympathy of her example. She well knows that by once enlisting under other banners than her own, were they even the banners of foreign independence, she would involve herself beyond the power of extrication, in all the wars of interest and intrigue, of individual avarice, envy and ambition, which assume the colors and usurp the standard of freedom: The fundamental maxims of her policy would insensibly change from *liberty* to *force* . . . She might become the dictatress of the world. She would be no longer the ruler of her own spirit.[31]

After the war, the interaction between America's foreign relations and its domestic policy continued to be a major theme of

[28] Wharton, *The Revolutionary Diplomatic Correspondence*, ii. 287–8.
[29] Ibid. 312.
[30] Bemis, *Diplomacy of the American Revolution*, 113.
[31] Cited in P. L. Geyelin, 'The Adams Doctrine and the Dream of Disengagement', in S. J. Ungar (ed.), *Estrangement: America and the World* (New York, 1985), 200.

political life, with an increasingly obvious tension between the republican ideal of a confederal form of government with limited central powers, and the weakness this led to in American dealings with foreign nations. For example, the British made it clear to John Adams during his mission to London that one obstacle to a commercial treaty between the two countries was the uncertain location of sovereign powers in the United States, leading to doubts about whether an American government could enforce the terms of a treaty, given that some states had ignored the terms of the peace treaty.[32] These matters came to a head in 1787 when the thirteen states debated whether to replace the loose association of their Articles of Confederation with a new federal Constitution. The 'antifederalist' argument, which repeated some of the familiar pro-republican assertions about the need for limited central powers, a diffusion of sovereignty, and only commercial relations (if any) with the outside world, is encapsulated in Charles Pinckney's speech, in which he declared the United States to be:

a new extensive Country containing within itself the materials for forming a Government capable of extending to its citizens all the blessings of civil and religious liberty—capable of making them happy at home. This is the great end of Republican Establishments. We mistake the object of our government, if we hope or wish that it is to make us respectable abroad.[33]

Alexander Hamilton, who was about to begin a period of ascendancy in the making of American foreign policy, put the ultimately successful opposing view:

It has been said that respectability in the eyes of foreign nations was not the object at which we aimed; that the proper object of republican Government was domestic tranquility and happiness. This was an ideal distinction. No Government could give us tranquility and happiness at home, which did not possess sufficient stability and strength to make us respectable abroad.[34]

At the very core of Hamilton's understanding of American foreign policy was a belief, which he was to reiterate many times over the next ten years, that in order to participate in international

[32] G. L. Lycan, *Alexander Hamilton and American Foreign Policy: A Design for Greatness* (Norman, Okla., 1970), 102.
[33] Cited in G. Stourzh, *Alexander Hamilton and the Idea of Republican Government* (Stanford, Calif., 1970), 126–7.
[34] Ibid.

relations on equal terms with other states it would be necessary to adapt American ways to theirs, both domestically, by altering the form of government, and internationally, by accepting the prevailing rules of conduct of the existing international society. He was opposed in these aims by a group headed by Thomas Jefferson, and their conflict may be seen in part as a contest between two distinct sets of ideas about the relationship between a revolutionary state and the Westphalian conception of international society.

JEFFERSON, HAMILTON, AND AMERICA'S PLACE IN INTERNATIONAL SOCIETY

Hamilton in the 1790s was first and foremost a politician, and hence concerned with the acquisition and exercise of power, both for himself and for his emergent party, the Federalists. Jefferson was much more unworldly in some respects than Hamilton, and yet he became involved in a personal struggle for power with Hamilton when both were members of Washington's administration, and did so again later during the factional conflict between Republicans and Federalists. Jefferson's thinking on foreign affairs was influenced by an abiding hatred of England and affection for France, a predisposition which was reversed in the case of Hamilton. Jefferson stood for the predominantly agrarian interests of the South, while Hamilton was identified with Northern commercial interests. Thus neither man's political thought was immune from the effects of prejudice, factionalism, and personal rivalry, and it would be a mistake to see either of them purely as the disinterested representative of a particular political doctrine. Yet although their power struggle brought their conflicting political philosophies into the open, it did not create the fundamental ideological difference that underlay all of their conflicts. This difference was rooted in intrinsically opposed perceptions of the relationship between state and citizen.

Jefferson's ideal state would have been populated by yeoman farmers who, he believed, possessed the qualities necessary for the preservation of a true republic more than any other group: 'Cultivators of the earth are the most valuable citizens. They are the most vigorous, the most independent, the most virtuous, and they are tied to their country and wedded to its liberty and interests by the most lasting bonds.'[35] Commerce brought with it that corrupting love of luxury and degrading economic dependence which had supposedly corroded Britain's liberal constitution and led to the imagined British conspiracy against American freedom before 1776—'a deliberate, systematical plan for reducing us to slavery', as Jefferson put it.[36] However, Jefferson was sadly aware that the American people had a 'decided taste' for commerce, so that any thoughts of creating a society entirely free of the need to trade would have to remain 'theory only'.[37] Hamilton enthusiastically embraced the prospect of foreign trade, his attitude contrasting sharply with Jefferson's reluctant endorsement of its inevitability. In his view, trade would be just such a route to American greatness as it had previously been to British and French power.[38] However, Hamilton had little time for the idealistic fancy of some Americans that 'the spirit of commerce has a tendency to soften the manners of men and to extinguish those inflammable humours which have so often kindled into wars'. Had commerce, he asked, 'done anything more than change the objects of war?'[39] Commerce was not a means towards some new utopia, but a necessary activity for a strong state, able to compete on equal terms with the European great powers.

If for Jefferson the ideal economic base for ensuring maximum individual liberty was thus unattainable, he felt that all the more effort needed to go into preventing the emergence of too strong a state, which was the other great threat to freedom. Societies without any government at all, like that of the American Indians, were far happier, he believed, than those living under the oppressive governments of Europe, so it was obvious where the balance between state and citizen should lie.[40] But as American Minister to Paris between 1784 and 1789 Jefferson had seen only too clearly the damage that was being done to American interests by the lack of co-ordination of external affairs under the Articles of Confederation. Characteristically he was ambivalent about whether the effects of this were entirely to be lamented:

[35] Letter to John Jay, 23 Aug. 1785, *Thomas Jefferson, Writings*, ed. M. D. Peterson (New York, 1984), 818. (Hereafter *Writings*.)
[36] Cited in Wood, *Creation*, 39.
[37] Cited in Hutson, 'Early American Diplomacy', 49.
[38] Clinton Rossiter (ed.), *The Federalist Papers* (New York, 1901), 53–60.
[39] Ibid.
[40] Letter to Edward Carrington, 16 Jan. 1787, in *Writings*, 880.

American reputation in Europe is not such as to be flattering to its citizens. Two circumstances are particularly objected to us, the nonpayment of our debts, and the want of energy in our government. These discourage a connection with us. I own it to be my opinion that good will arise from the destruction of our credit. I see nothing else which can restrain our disposition to luxury, and the loss of those manners which alone can preserve republican government.[41]

A wider gulf could hardly be imagined than that between this last opinion and the views of Hamilton, whose major achievement in the 1790s as Washington's Secretary of the Treasury was to establish America's creditworthiness with foreign financiers (his success later enabled Jefferson, as President, to purchase Louisiana from Napoleon). However, Jefferson was at one with Hamilton on the need for a unified approach to other nations as a means of obtaining 'respectability' abroad. Such unity could only be brought about by changing the Articles of Confederation, and Jefferson perceived clearly that the nature of the international system was responsible for imposing upon the United States the need for this change. As he commented to James Madison in 1786, on hearing that Virginia had handed over the regulation of its commerce to the federal government:

The politics of Europe render it indispensably necessary that with respect to everything external we be one nation only, firmly hooped together. If it would be seen in Europe that all our states could be brought to concur in what the Virginia Assembly has done, it would produce a total revolution in their opinion of us, and respect for us. And it should ever be held in mind that insult and war are the consequences of a want of respectability in the national character.[42]

Jefferson's eventual formula on the need to move from a confederal constitution was that 'we should be made one nation in every case concerning foreign affairs, and separate ones in whatever is merely domestic'.[43] Some authors have seen this and similar statements as evidence of an essential consensus regarding the Constitution amongst most leading Americans, including Jefferson and Hamilton.[44] There was, however, an important difference of

[41] Letter to Archibald Stuart, 25 Jan. 1786, in *The Papers of Thomas Jefferson*, ed. C. T. Cullen, 1st ser. ix (Princeton, NJ, 1954), 217–18. (Hereafter *The Papers*.)

[42] Letter to James Madison, 8 Feb. 1786, ibid. 264.

[43] Letter to John Blair, 13 Aug. 1787, ibid. xii. 28.

[44] See, in particular, L. S. Kaplan, *Entangling Alliances with None: American Foreign Policy in the Age of Jefferson* (Kent, Ohio, and London, 1987), 67–78.

emphasis between the two men in that Hamilton, in effect, called for *strong* government for the conduct of America's foreign relations, while Jefferson merely required unified government. Jefferson, indeed was concerned that the Constitution might fail to maintain what he thought of as the correct balance between state and citizen if it did not also contain a Bill of Rights and limitations on the right of individual presidents to perpetual re-election. Against frequent Hamiltonian demands for the central government to be vested with 'energy' (in the eighteenth-century sense of 'effectiveness'), Jefferson argued that if the proposed Constitution was amended in the liberal direction he desired, 'union may be produced under a happy constitution, and one which shall not be too energetic, as are the constitutions of Europe'.[45] In a statement of his political philosophy in 1799, he would similarly continue to endorse the investment of power in the states and in the legislature, rather than in any executive arm of government.[46] Hamilton, by contrast, adhered to the view of the state that had become prevalent in Europe following the Peace of Westphalia, in which the primacy of foreign policy required a strong and effective central government. He believed that there were laws of life, and of politics, which were eternal and immutable and which applied to republics as much as to monarchies; these would make conflict inevitable in America if the thirteen states retained their effective sovereignty:

To look for a continuation of harmony between a number of independent, unconnected sovereignties, situated in the same neighbourhood, would be to disregard the uniform cause of human events, and to set at defiance the accumulated experience of the ages.[47]

There were 'visionaries' who believed in the possibility of perpetual peace amongst the thirteen states merely because these constituted a republic, and 'commercial republics, like ours, will never be disposed to waste themselves in ruinous contentions with each other'. They would be governed instead by mutual interest and would 'cultivate a spirit of mutual amity and concord'. But, enquired Hamilton, was it not 'the true interest of all nations to cultivate the same benevolent and philosophic spirit? If this be their true interest have they in fact pursued it?' The reality was that

---

[45] Letter to William Carmichael, 15 Dec. 1787, in *The Papers*, xii. 426.
[46] Letter to Elbridge Gerry, 26 Jan. 1799, *Writings*, 1056.
[47] Cited in Stourzh, *Alexander Hamilton*, 149.

'momentary passions and immediate interests have a more active and imperious control over human conduct than general or remote considerations of policy, utility or justice'. Republics were no more immune from such truths than monarchies—indeed popular pressures could drag a nation into war even against the real interests of the state. In short, Americans needed 'to awake from the deceitful dream of a golden age, and to adopt as a practical maxim for the direction of our political conduct that we, as well as the other inhabitants of the globe, are yet remote from the happy empire of perfect wisdom and perfect virtue'.[48]

For Jefferson, who once confessed to John Adams, 'I like the dreams of the future better than the history of the past',[49] the notion that republics were constrained by the same laws that bound monarchies was anathema. But far more dangerous were the implications Hamilton drew from his central thesis, that foreign policy had primacy and that the republic should serve its interests, which was the exact reverse of what Jefferson believed. Even during the revolution Hamilton had privately decried what he saw as an excess of the spirit of liberty and a consequent lack of sufficient means to meet public needs.[50] In his arguments for a federal constitution he similarly urged that there should be no constraint on the powers of government to raise armies, since it was impossible to foresee or define the extent of national exigencies. For the same reason, America needed a standing army.[51] To Jefferson, standing armies were a threat to liberty. The United States, he felt, should rely solely on militia forces until an invasion was actually threatened, and should have only a limited navy. These measures would be less costly than the maintenance of standing forces, and could never endanger American liberties.[52]

The same division of opinion over the necessity for a strong state conditioned their attitudes towards internal rebellion. Hamilton, who had participated enthusiastically in the war of independence, could hardly argue that rebellion was never justified. However, even during the war he had attempted to establish clear criteria for

---

[48] Cited in Stourzh, *Alexander Hamilton*, 149–52.
[49] Cited in A. A. Ekirch, *Ideas, Ideals and American Diplomacy* (New York, 1966), 30.
[50] Letter to James Duane, 3 Sept. 1780, in *The Papers of Alexander Hamilton*, ii. 401.
[51] Rossiter (ed.), *The Federalist Papers*, 154–5.
[52] *Writings*, 1056. See also *The Papers*, x. 225.

legitimate rebellion and to distinguish these from mere arbitrary violence.[53] Hamilton argued that only when there was a complete breakdown of the social contract which formed the basis of the relationship between ruler and ruled could rebellion be justified. In that event alone individuals ceased to be bound by their municipal laws and returned, in effect, to a state of nature in which their actions were governed by natural law.[54]

Jefferson had also accepted in the Declaration of Independence that 'Prudence, indeed, will dictate that Governments long established should not be changed for light and transient causes.' In many of his later writings, however, he showed a marked sympathy for rebellion that went far beyond this more limited view. For example, he greeted an outbreak of insurrection in several states in 1786 with a remarkable equanimity and tolerance: 'I hold it that a little rebellion now and then is a good thing and as necessary in the political world as storms in the physical.'[55] And on the same subject, in one of his more famous utterances, he asked:

what country can preserve its liberties, if its rulers are not warned from time to time, that its people preserve the spirit of resistance? Let them take arms. The remedy is to set them right as to facts, pardon and pacify them. What signify a few lives lost in a century or two? The tree of liberty must be refreshed from time to time, with the blood of patriots and tyrants.[56]

It was inevitable that differences of this magnitude on the subject of rebellion as such, combined with Jefferson's unrelenting hostility towards England and admiration for France, should lead the two men to a decisive parting of the ways over the correct American response to the French Revolution. Jefferson as Minister to Paris had witnessed the beginnings of the Revolution, which he saw from the start as strongly influenced by the American example, writing to Washington as early as December 1788, 'The nation has been awakened by our revolution, they feed their strength, they are enlightened, their lights are spreading and they will not retrograde.'[57] Later he expressed the hope that 'so beautiful a revolution' would 'spread through the whole world',[58] and tended,

[53] Stourzh, *Alexander Hamilton*, 24.
[54] Ibid. 10–26.
[55] Letter to James Madison, 3 Jan. 1787, in *Writings*, 882.
[56] Letter to W. S. Smith, 13 Nov. 1787, in *The Papers*, xii. 356.
[57] Letter to Washington, 4 Dec. 1788, ibid. xiv. 330.
[58] To Sinclair, 1791, cited in S. K. Padover, *Thomas Jefferson on Democracy* (New York, 1939), 141.

at least in the first few years, to see the French revolutionary wars as
fought for the cause of liberty everywhere, including the United
States, whose freedom, he believed, would be endangered by a
British victory. Even when the revolution grew increasingly violent
he saw this as a small price to pay for something of such universal
significance, arguing in his most emphatic assertion on this subject:

The liberty of the whole earth was depending on the issue of the contest,
and was ever such a prize won with so little innocent blood? My own
affections have been deeply wounded by some of the martyrs to this cause,
but rather than it should have failed, I would have seen half the earth
desolated. Were there but an Adam and Eve left in every country and left
free, it would be better than as it now is.[59]

Jefferson's approval of the Revolution did not extend to support for
the activities of the French diplomat Genêt, who was not only
propagandizing the revolutionary cause in America but attempting
to raise money to equip frigates for action against England.
However, he was initially a strong advocate of Genêt's reception by
the United States, as he believed that this would further the French
revolutionary government's quest for international legitimacy.
Hamilton had reservations about Genêt's admission for precisely
the same reason.[60]

   Hamilton saw in the French Revolution nothing but danger for
the United States, and he regarded with alarm what he viewed as
the misguided enthusiasm of Jefferson and very large segments of
American opinion, which seemed to him likely to embroil America
in a war with England. What is interesting, in this context, about
Hamilton's view is that his opposition to the French Revolution
was presented in terms of the threat posed by the Revolution to the
established tenets of international society, with which he clearly
believed America should align herself. Jefferson, Madison, and
others of their persuasion saw France and America as the only true
republics in the world and believed that this fact should be a major
determinant of American policy. Hamilton attempted to argue that
America could be republican without being revolutionary and that
those who asserted that the United States could be in danger from a
general counter-revolution because America would be seen as
embodying the same principles as France were wrong. If the United
States refrained from intervening on the side of France, a clear

[59] Letter to William Short, 3 Jan. 1793, in *Writings*, 1004.
[60] *The Papers of Alexander Hamilton*, xiv. 393–4 n.

differentiation would be made by foreign governments between the two revolutions, with the War of Independence being seen as having *restored* rights previously enjoyed by a people who behaved with moderation during the revolution, whose government was able to 'rest the foundations of Liberty on the basis of Justice, Order and Law' and who

at all times have been content to govern themselves; unmeddling in the Governments or Affairs of other Nations; in fine, they will see in us sincere Republicans but decided enemies to licentiousness and anarchy—decided Republicans but decided friends to the freedom of opinion, to the order and tranquillity of all Mankind. They will not see in us a people whose best passions have been misled and whose best qualities have been prevented from their true aim by headlong fanatical or designing leaders to the perpetration of acts from which humanity shrinks . . . to substitute confusion to order, anarchy to government.[61]

Hamilton dismissed out of hand what was for many Americans the most appealing aspect of the French Revolution: its claim to be acting on behalf of universal liberty. The revolution itself, he perceived as early as 1794, would inevitably end in military dictatorship.[62] Its pretensions to leadership of a crusade for liberty were fraudulent and opposed to a fundamental principle of sovereignty—that every nation had the right to its own political system.[63] Assisting 'a reasonable and virtuous struggle for liberty, already begun' might be justifiable but 'to incite to revolution everywhere by indiscriminate offers of assistance before hand, is to invade and endanger the foundations of social tranquillity'.[64] A prominent feature of the Revolution from the start had been its 'spirit of proselytism, or the desire of new modelling the political institutions of the rest of the world according to her standard'.[65] Stripped of its idealistic pretexts, this amounted to nothing less than a quest for universal empire:

The conduct of France from the commencement of her successes has by gradual developments betrayed a spirit of universal domination; an

[61] 'Americanus', No. 2, 7 Feb. 1794, ibid. xvi. 18–19.
[62] Lycan, *Alexander Hamilton and American Foreign Policy*, 145.
[63] Daniel Lang, 'Alexander Hamilton and the Law of Nations', in N. A. Graebner (ed.), *Traditions and Values: American Diplomacy, 1790–1865* (Lanham, Md., New York, and London, 1985), 13.
[64] *The Papers of Alexander Hamilton*, xxi. 394.
[65] Ibid. 396.

opinion that she has a right to be the legatrix of Nations; that they are all bound to submit to her mandates, to take from her their moral, political and religious creeds; that her plastic and regenerating hand is to mould them into whatever shape she thinks fit and that her interest is to be the sole measure of the rights of the rest of the world. The specious pretence of enlightening mankind and reforming their civil institutions is the varnish to the real design of subjugating them.[66]

Given that this was the reality behind the Revolution, the other European powers were perfectly justified in uniting against it. Indeed it was a general principle of the law of nations that whenever a nation 'adopts maxims of conduct tending to the disturbance of the tranquillity and established order of its neighbours, or manifesting a spirit of self-aggrandizement—it is lawful for other Nations to combine against it, and, by force, to control the effects of those maxims and that spirit'.[67] The French opening of the Schelde to navigation in defiance of the express terms of the Westphalian settlement, an act which brought Britain into the war, was particularly reprehensible.[68] The French Propaganda Decree of November 1792 he saw as a general invitation to revolution of a kind certain to 'disturb the repose of mankind'.[69]

In the course of their debate over the French Revolution Hamilton and Jefferson elaborated what amounted to two opposing theories of international relations with two alternative sets of hypotheses to govern American foreign policy. For Jefferson, in common with many of the eighteenth-century revolutionary thinkers, the underlying principles that should govern the behaviour of states as well as individuals were to be derived from natural law. In the course of arguing that America remained bound by the wartime treaty with France, even though France had undergone a change of regime, he asserted:

The Law of Nations, by which this question is to be determined, is composed of three branches. 1. The Moral law of our nature. 2. The Usages of nations. 3. Their special Conventions. The first of these only, concerns this question, that is to say the Moral law in which Man has been subjected by his creator, and of which his feelings, or Conscience as it is

---

[66] 'The Warning', No. 1, 29 Jan. 1797, ibid. xx. 494.
[67] Letter to Washington, 2 May 1793, ibid. xiv. 406.
[68] Ibid.   [69] Ibid.

sometimes called, are the evidence with which his creator has furnished him. The Moral duties which exist between individual and individual in a state of nature, accompany them into a state of society and the aggregate of the duties of all the individuals composing the society constitutes the duties of that society towards any other; so that between society and society the same moral duties exist as did between the individuals composing them while in an unassociated state, their maker not having released them from their duties on their forming themselves into a nation. Compacts then between nation and nation are obligatory on them by the same moral law which obliged individuals to observe their compacts.[70]

In August 1789 he had written to Madison along similar lines, arguing against those who believed that America owed no debt of gratitude to France:

To say in excuse that gratitude is never to enter into the motives of national conduct, is to revive a principle which has been buried for centuries . . . I know but one code of morality for man, whether acting singly or collectively . . . Let us hope that our new government will take some other occasion to show that they mean to proscribe virtue from the canons of their conduct with other nations.[71]

Jefferson's insistence upon the necessity for morality in international affairs was nothing new for him, nor was it a mere rationalization of his sympathy for the French Revolution. For example, he had long argued the case for greater humanity in warfare, writing in 1779 in relation to the treatment of prisoners of war: 'But is an enemy so execrable, that though in captivity, his wishes and comforts are to be disregarded . . . ? I think not. It is for the benefit of mankind to mitigate the horrors of war as much as possible.'[72] He was, in addition, alert to any possibility of extending judicial procedures to international relations, seeing in the arrangements for the settlement of disputes between American states during the confederation period a future model for the rest of the world.[73] A draft by Jefferson of a model treaty of amity and commerce between America and Denmark and Norway managed to combine the three main strands in his thinking: the idea that states had overriding moral obligations deriving from natural law, the desire to establish humanitarian principles in war, and the

[70] Opinion on the French Treaties, 28 Apr. 1793, *Writings*, 423.
[71] Letter to James Madison, 28 Aug. 1789, *The Papers*, xv. 367.
[72] Letter to Patrick Henry, 27 Mar. 1779, *Writings*, 770.
[73] *The Papers*, vi. 505–6.

intention to strengthen the legal constraints upon states. Article 23
of this draft stipulated that, if war should arise between the
contracting parties, merchants should be given nine months to
settle their affairs and then be allowed to depart freely, while a large
group, including women, children, farmers, artisans, manufac-
turers, and fishermen, whose occupations were 'for the common
subsistence and benefit of mankind' should be allowed to continue
their occupations; neither they nor their property should be injured.
Article 24 stated that prisoners of war should neither be sent 'into
distant and inclement countries' nor crowded into 'close and
noxious places', but kept in Europe or America 'in wholesome
situations'. Moreover, the Article concluded,

neither the pretence that war dissolves all treaties, nor any other whatever
shall be considered as annulling or suspending this and the next preceding
article, but on the contrary that the state of war is precisely that for which
they are provided, and during which they are to be as sacredly observed as
the most acknowledged articles in the law of nature or nations.[74]

In his arguments in support of these Articles, Jefferson said that
they were 'for the interests of humanity in general', and suggested
that the United States should take a progressive view of international law, which could go on improving in a humanitarian
direction.[75] As Secretary of State, he was similarly to urge that the
United States should adopt the most modern or liberal interpretations of international law.[76]

The implications for American foreign policy that Jefferson
derived from such views were, first, that America should be a moral
and progressive force in world affairs. 'Our interests soundly
calculated will ever be found inseparable from our moral duties', he
asserted as President.[77] Second, came a clear though less explicitly
stated inference that America should take account of the internal
nature of foreign regimes in determining its policy towards them.[78]
Third, America should, where possible, turn to economic sanctions
rather than war when its commercial interests were threatened.

[74] *The Papers*, vii. 486–7.
[75] Ibid. 491–2.
[76] D. G. Lang, *Foreign Policy in the Early Republic* (London, 1985), 144–5.
[77] 2nd Inaugural Address, 4 Mar. 1805, *Writings*, 518.
[78] Lang, *Foreign Policy*, 154–6 and L. S. Kaplan, 'Jefferson and the Franco-
American Alliance of 1778: Reflections on Francophilia', in C. Fohlen and J.
Godechot (eds.) *La Révolution américaine et l'Europe* (Paris, 1981), 410–12.

This, he suggested to Madison in 1793, would give America 'a happy opportunity of setting another example to the world, by showing that nations may be brought to do justice by appeals to their interests as well as by appeals to arms'.[79] However, he was also very jealous of America's 'dignity' and 'honour', particularly where real or imagined insults from Britain were concerned, and his pacifism was not without limits. In 1786 he even went so far as to advocate war against the Barbary states, which were in the habit of extorting tribute from states wishing to have their shipping protected from the activities of pirates operating off their coast. This course of action he justified by appeals to justice and honour, and by the assertion that 'it will procure us respect in Europe and respect is a safeguard to interest'.[80] As President he was to initiate the military action he had urged as Minister to Paris.

Jefferson's most fundamental foreign policy principle was isolation. The idea that America should keep clear of foreign entanglements had been accepted by all American statesmen since 1776; this included Hamilton, who played an important part in drafting Washington's Farewell Address, containing the most comprehensive statement of the principle to that date. However, there was a significant difference of emphasis between the isolation of Hamilton and Washington, on the one hand, and that of Jefferson, on the other. For Jefferson the primary purpose of isolation was to prevent the American republic, and its virtuous citizens, from being contaminated by the world outside. This objective was of such paramount importance that it should even prohibit involvement in struggles for freedom outside America. As Jefferson wrote to a friend in 1799:

I sincerely join you in abjuring all political connection with every foreign power; and tho I cordially wish well to the progress of liberty in all nations . . . yet they are not to be touched without contamination from their other bad principles.[81]

Jefferson made it clear that he particularly objected to the Europeans' system of international relations. In a letter to Monroe towards the end of his life (which summarized his thinking on this subject), he wrote:

[79] Letter to James Madison, 24 Mar. 1793, *Writings*, 1006–7.
[80] Letter to John Adams, 11 July 1786, *The Papers*, x. 123.
[81] Letter to Thomas Lomax, 12 Mar. 1799, *Writings*, 1063.

I have ever deemed it fundamental for the United States never to take active part in the quarrels of Europe. Their political interests are entirely distinct from ours. Their mutual jealousies, their balance of power, their complicated alliances, their forms and principles of government, are all foreign to us. They are nations of eternal war. All their energies are expended in the destruction of the labour, property and lives of their people. On our part, never had a people so favorable a chance of trying to oppose systems of peace and fraternity with mankind and the direction of all our means and faculties to the purpose of improvement instead of destruction.[82]

Hamilton, too, supported the ideas of isolation and a separate American system of international relations, but he interpreted them in ways significantly different from Jefferson's. For Hamilton the United States was still a relatively small and weak nation, which needed to pursue a policy of non-involvement with the outside world and appeasement of the only state with the capacity seriously to harm America: Britain. He also admired the British constitution, but his policy was less influenced by this admiration than by his determination to buy sufficient time for America to enable it to build up its strength to a point where it need have no fear of external powers but could pursue its own path to greatness. He argued:

In addition to the general motives to peace which are common to other nations—it is of the utmost consequence to us that our progress to that degree of maturity which puts humanly speaking our fortunes absolutely in our hands shall not be retarded by a premature war.[83]

The 'very large party infatuated by a blind devotion to France' was endangering this strategy by its readiness to risk war with Britain. But the idea that the United States should avoid entanglements with foreign quarrels because its republican purity might be sullied by their immoral ways was entirely alien to Hamilton. As he argued when urging federation, the aim was to develop American power until the United States was itself able to determine the nature of its relationship with Europe:

our situation invites and our interests prompt us to aim at an ascendent in the system of American Affairs . . . Let the Thirteen States, bound together

---

[82] Cited in Lang, *Foreign Policy*, 160.
[83] Letter to W. C. Smith, 10 Apr. 1797, *The Papers of Alexander Hamilton*, xxi. 30.

in a strict and indissoluble Union, concur in erecting one great American system, superior to the control of all trans-Atlantic force or influence, and able to dictate the terms of the connection between the Old and the New World.[84]

Hamilton's assessment of America's foreign policy needs stemmed from an understanding of international relations that was anchored firmly in the conventional assumptions and power politics of eighteenth-century Europe. A strong, 'energetic' state was the most fundamental requirement, which overrode the counter-claims of greater individual liberty. This was because security from external danger was 'the most powerful director of national conduct' and freedom was only possible in conditions which guaranteed adequate security.[85] Given this, the predominant motive of states was their own national interest; they had no other choice if they were to maximize their primary goal of security. The fact that states were obliged to pursue their self-interest meant that moral judgements of the kind applied to individuals could not be used to appraise the actions of states.[86]

The argument that states were subject to different norms from the moral rules of natural law which bound individuals went to the heart of the division between Hamilton and Jefferson. Hamilton employed it first to refute the claim that gratitude for previous favours should play any part in international relations. During the Nootka Sound Crisis of 1790, which might have led to war between Britain and Spain, he rejected the suggestion that America owed a debt of gratitude to Spain because the latter had fought Britain during the War of Independence. Gratitude, he said, was a fine sounding word,

But where a word may become the basis of a political system, affecting the essential interests of the state, it is incumbent upon those who have any concern in the public administration, to appreciate its true import and application. It is necessary then to reflect . . . that gratitude is a duty or sentiment which between nations can rarely have any solid foundation.[87]

Spain had been motivated by self-interest in helping America, and so had France, argued Hamilton when similar suggestions about moral obligations to France were voiced during the revolutionary

---

[84] Rossiter (ed.), *The Federalist Papers*, 90–1.
[85] Ibid. 67.
[86] 'Pacificus' IV, *The Papers of Alexander Hamilton*, xv. 84–5.
[87] 'Reply to George Washington', 15 Sept. 1790, ibid. 43.

wars. Indeed, he wrote, 'it may be affirmed as a general principle, that the predominant motive of good offices from one nation to another is the interest or advantage of the Nation which performs them'.[88] Similarly, Hamilton had no patience with those who constantly invoked 'national honour' in urging what he saw as dangerous courses of action upon America. 'True honour is a rational thing', he wrote, which 'cannot be wounded by consulting moderation . . . The ravings of anger and pride' must not be mistaken for honour. He also lamented the manner in which 'imposture and fraud should be so often able to assume with success the garb of patriotism and that this sublime virtue should be so frequently discredited by the usurpation and abuse of its name'.[89]

Central to Hamilton's approach was the belief that the United States should not see itself as something unique in world politics, but simply as a state in a world of states which constituted a rudimentary international society, whose rules of conduct America should observe. He was particularly anxious to take issue with those who thought 'that the most natural and happy state of Society is a state of continual revolution and change'.[90] As early as 1784 he saw potential harm to America's external relations in the arguments of those who said that America's was an essentially novel case—one of revolution—to which conventional principles governing other societies could not be expected to apply. His reply to such assertions was that America was no longer a revolutionary state, but a member of an established international society:

The answer to this must be, that there are principles eternally true and which apply to all situations . . . that we are not now in the midst of a revolution but have happily brought it to a successful issue—that we have a constitution formed as a rule of conduct—that the frame of our government is determined and the general principle of it settled—that we have taken our station among nations, have claimed the benefit of the laws which regulate them, and must in our turn be bound by the same laws.[91]

The essential nature of that international society he depicted in Westphalian terms, when he defined the 'voluntary law of nations' as

---

[88] Cited in Lang, *Foreign Policy*, 105.
[89] Cited in Lycan, *Alexander Hamilton and American Foreign Policy*, 246–7.
[90] *The Papers of Alexander Hamilton*, xii. 502.
[91] 'Second Letter from Phocion', Apr. 1784, ibid. iii. 550.

a system of rules resulting from the equality and independence of nations, and which in the administration of their affairs and the pursuit of their pretentions, proceeding on the principle of their having no common judge upon earth, attributes equal validity, as to external effects, to the measures or conduct of one as of another without regard to the intrinsic justice of those measures or that conduct.[92]

He also took some pains to criticize those who tended to adopt a truculent or overly assertive tone in their approach to other nations, or who saw America as having some kind of mission to modify the existing law of nations. 'It is not for young or weak nations', he asserted, 'to attempt to enforce novelties or pretentions of equivocal validity. It is still less proper for them to contend at the hazard of their peace against the clear right of others.'[93] He specifically opposed Jefferson's attempts to establish a more liberal international legal principle governing wartime contraband carried in neutral ships: 'An established rule of the law of Nations can only be deemed to be altered by agreements between all the civilized powers or a new usage generally adopted and sanctioned by time.'[94] The United States, in this as in other cases, ought to observe 'the received maxims or usages of nations'.[95]

THE UNITED STATES AND THE WESTPHALIAN CONCEPTION OF INTERNATIONAL SOCIETY

In the context of the main themes being considered here, Hamilton's foreign policy represented an attempt to bring about the socialization of the United States within the prevailing international society. Jefferson stood for an alternative approach which maintained the combative, suspicious style that had been apparent during the revolution, emphasized the primacy of domestic politics over foreign policy, constantly sought the high moral ground, and allowed the internal character of foreign regimes to be an important criterion in forming American policy towards them. Jefferson's was not a policy of revolutionary internationalism, but it was not without revolutionary implications for the Westphalian conception of international society. In many

[92] 'The Defence', No. XX, Oct. 1795, ibid. xvii. 329–30.
[93] 'The Defence', No. XXXI, 12 Dec. 1795, ibid. xviii. 478.
[94] 'No Jacobin', No. III, 8 Aug. 1793, ibid. xv. 205.
[95] 'Reply to George Washington', ibid. 38.

respects Jefferson stood for an earlier tradition, that of the 'Great Community of Mankind'. His emphasis on moral principles and natural law, his progressive approach to international law, and his preference for ideologically acceptable regimes, all pointed to a world involving bonds between peoples that cut across purely national boundaries, and governed by norms which transcended the limited rules and institutions that states were prepared to accept as part of a sovereignty-based international society. Jefferson's belief in the value of economic sanctions similarly derived from an underlying hypothesis of interdependent world economy, which relates more closely to the Great Community concept than to the idea of a society of independent sovereign states.

The Jeffersonians triumphed over the Hamiltonians at the end of the eighteenth century and the Jeffersonian tendency in American foreign relations has remained an important force up to the present day. As American power increased, the United States seemed at times to be drifting towards its own version of a universal society: a reformulated world order under American leadership, backed by American military and economic power and working for the realization of American values world-wide, in terms both of restructuring traditional modes of conducting international affairs and of promoting acceptable standards of internal governance. Presidents Wilson, Truman, Kennedy, and Reagan all represented in their rhetoric and some of their policies different facets of this position, which is located in the overlapping margins between the Great Community and Universal Society ideas. 'Purist' Jeffersonians were also to be heard from time to time, arguing that Americans should have nothing to do with the outside world, even in order to change it. And Hamiltonian counter-arguments to both were always present, urging the pre-eminence of interests over values, and the need to match ends to means, to accept the reality of other nations' sovereignty and to refrain from viewing the rest of the world as a global conspiracy against American virtue.

The Monroe Doctrine was almost a paradigm of the Jefferson tendency—indeed, Monroe asked Jefferson, by then 80 years old, for his advice in 1823, and was informed that North and South America should have 'a system of her own, separate and apart from that of Europe'.[96] Monroe's own original intention was to link his central message—the exclusion of the Europeans and their 'politi-

[96] *Writings*, 1481.

cal system' from the American hemisphere—with a strong statement of support for the Greek revolt against Turkish rule. In the event he was persuaded by his Secretary of State, John Quincy Adams, that such support would not be in accordance with the American tradition of non-entanglement with Europe, even in a good cause.[97] So the doctrine was essentially a reformulation for all America of well-established American principles such as the two hemispheres and the non-applicability of the European system (specifically the Holy Alliance) to the Americas.

Prince Metternich, the leader of Europe's conservative forces, professed to see in the Doctrine and other American statements evidence of an American alliance with European revolution:

The United States of America . . . have cast blame and scorn on the institutions of Europe most worthy of respect . . . In permitting themselves these unprovoked attacks, in fostering revolutions wherever they show themselves, in regretting those which have failed, in extending a helping hand to those which seem to prosper, they lend new strength to the apostles of sedition and reanimate the courage of every conspirator.[98]

A more typical European response was that of the Prussian Minister in Washington, Baron von Tuyll:

The document in question enunciates views and pretensions so exaggerated, it establishes principles so contrary to the rights of the European powers that it merits only the most profound contempt.[99]

This was also the view of latter-day Hamiltonians in America, such as the member of Congress who described the Doctrine as 'an unauthorized, unmeaning, and empty menace, well calculated to excite the angry passions and embroil us with foreign nations'.[100]

From roughly 1840 to 1917 discussion of American foreign policy may be characterized as an attempt to reconcile America's growing power with the perceived ideals of the American Republic. Three broad positions are discernible in this debate. The first relates most closely to the orthodox Hamiltonian perspective, in that its central assertion was that America needed to adapt to new realities and not allow itself to be shackled by the dogmas of an earlier era.

---

[97] T. A. Bailey, *A Diplomatic History of the American People*, 2nd edn. (New York, 1942), 184–5.
[98] Cited in N. A. Graebner, *Ideas and Diplomacy* (New York, 1964), 214.
[99] Ibid.
[100] Bailey, *A Diplomatic History*, 187.

One of the fullest and most representative statements of this position appeared in President Taft's Message of 3 December 1912:

We have emerged full grown as a peer in the great concourse of nations. We have passed through various formative periods. We have been self-centered in the struggle to develop our domestic resources and deal with our domestic questions. The Nation is now too mature to continue in its foreign relations those temporary expedients natural to a people whose domestic affairs are the sole concern. In the past our diplomacy has often consisted, in normal times, in a mere assertion of the right to international existence. We are now in a larger relation with broader rights of our own and obligations to others than ourselves . . . The successful conduct of our foreign relations demands a broad and modern view. We cannot meet new questions nor build for the future if we confine ourselves to outworn dogmas of the past and to the perspective appropriate to the emergence from colonial times and conditions . . . Congress should fully realize the conditions which obtain in the world as we find ourselves at the threshold of our middle age as a Nation.[101]

The second view may be termed 'Jeffersonian universalism', since it combined a self-righteous, moralistic, and often bombastic tone with an argument that it was America's special mission, if not 'manifest destiny', to spread republican ideals throughout the hemisphere and beyond.[102] Representative illustrations of this theme include President Polk's statement of 1845: 'Foreign powers do not seem to appreciate the true character of our government . . . To enlarge its limits is to extend the dominions of peace over additional territories and increasing millions',[103] and, three years later, Congress's message of congratulations to France on having overthrown its monarchy. President Lincoln's assumption that democracy would 'perish from the earth' if it died in America was a mild variant of universalist reasoning. A more forthright assertion, which tried to deal with traditionalist objections to a policy of overseas imperialism, came from Senator Albert J. Beveridge in 1900:

The Declaration of Independence does not forbid us to do our part in the regeneration of the world . . . [the Founding Fathers] knew that the Republic they were planting must, in obedience to the laws of our

[101] Cited in C. A. Beard, *The Idea of National Interest* (Chicago, 1966), 106–7.

[102] For a discussion of these ideas, and the distinction between them, see F. Merk, *Manifest Destiny and Mission* (New York), 1966.

[103] Cited in W. A. Williams, *The Roots of the Modern American Empire* (London, 1970), 84.

expanding race, necessarily develop into the greater Republic which the world beholds today, and into the still mightier Republic which the world will finally acknowledge as the arbiter, under God, of the destinies of mankind.[104]

The third line of argument may be termed 'Jeffersonian purism', since it maintained the essential Jeffersonian position: America should spread its doctrines by example only, and keep its distance from the outside world. Like Jefferson, it advocated the use of economic instruments to achieve international political ends. The Open Door Notes of 1899–1900 and America's 'dollar diplomacy' of 1909–13 are illustrations of this theme, stemming from an intrinsically Jeffersonian belief that economic interdependence had reduced the possibility of war and that America was well placed to exploit this both for its own interests and in order to advance an American vision of an alternative world order.[105] The period of dollar diplomacy also witnessed American attempts to promote international arbitration as a means of resolving disputes—a continuation of Jefferson's progressive legalism (although, ironically, the first step in what was to be a continuing American endeavour to promote arbitration came in the Hamiltonian Jay Treaty, with Britain, of 1794).

If the diplomacy of that most complex of American presidents, Woodrow Wilson, may be reduced to a single formula, it is Jeffersonian universalism. His belief in the international rule of law, his faith in the power of world public opinion—'the organized opinion of mankind'—his emphasis on the use of economic sanctions by the League of Nations, his strong moralism, his belief that constitutional democracies would be a force against war, and his sense of an American mission to fight for the rights of man were all unmistakably Jeffersonian in origin. Where he parted company with Jefferson was in his preparedness to intervene, as in Mexico in 1913, against what he believed to be an unconstitutional regime, and his willingness to embark upon a crusade to spread—if not impose—his ideals world-wide. 'I am proposing, as it were, that the nations should with one accord adopt the doctrine of President Monroe as the doctrine of the world', he said in 1917. 'These are American principles, American policies. We could stand for no

---

[104] Graebner, *Ideas and Diplomacy*, 370–3.
[105] A. Iriye, *From Nationalism to Internationalism: US Foreign Policy to 1914* (London, 1977), 213–20.

others. And they are also the principles and policies of forward-looking men and women everywhere, of every modern nation, of every enlightened community. They are the principles of mankind and must prevail.'[106]

The Cold War has variously been seen as an American response to Soviet imperialism and, by revisionist historians, as the embodiment of American counter-revolutionary doctrines. But considered from another perspective, the Cold War, or at least the American strategy of containment, may be interpreted as the apotheosis of Jeffersonian universalism. This may be seen most clearly in one of the definitive American documents of the Cold War, NSC68, particularly in four of its aspects. First, the perception of the Soviet enemy that emerges from the document is not simply one of a powerful rival, but one of a moral foe, a 'slave state' representing the very antithesis of freedom, making the Cold War, in essence, a moral crusade.[107] Second, the document explicitly rejects isolationism as a possible US response to the Soviet threat by asserting the indivisibility of freedom and the impossibility in modern conditions of America's any longer insulating itself, in pure Jeffersonian style, from the rest of the world. For freedom to survive in the United States, international society as a whole must be refashioned:

Our overall policy at the present time may be described as one designed to foster a world environment in which the American system can survive and flourish. It therefore rejects the concept of isolation and affirms the necessity of our positive participation in the world community.

Third, economic policy was regarded as a 'major instrument in the conduct of United States foreign relations' and one that was 'peculiarly appropriate to the Cold War'. Fourth, the aim of the containment strategy was not simply to achieve 'victory' in any conventional sense but to bring about internal change in the nature of the Soviet regime:

The only sure victory lies in the frustration of the Kremlin design by the steady development of the moral and material strength of the free world and its projection into the Soviet world in such a way as to bring about an internal change in the Soviet system.

[106] Cited in W. A. Williams, *The Tragedy of American Diplomacy* (New York, 1962), 84.
[107] All citations from NSC68 are taken from the version published in United States, Department of State, *Foreign Relations of the United States, 1950* (Washington, 1977), i. 235–92.

NSC68 perceived the Cold War as a conflict between opposing visions of world order. Unlike Jefferson, with his predilection for a mild degree of anarchy, it saw the absence of international order as 'less and less tolerable' in a shrinking world. The Kremlin, it believed, 'seeks to impose order among nations by means which would destroy our free and democratic system'. Only American world leadership would permit an alternative design for world order to prevail. However, as the American strategy itself had revolutionary implications for the conduct of international relations, the consequence was that the Westphalian conception of international society found itself squeezed between two powerful alternative visions which had their origins in two very different revolutionary experiences.

CONCLUSION

The international society into which the United States entered was not to the taste of many of the Founding Fathers. It seemed to be part of the amoral, aristocratic, decadent, and oppressive European world of which their republic was conceived to be the antithesis. None the less, there were two important respects in which most leading Americans believed that the United States ought to accommodate itself to the eighteenth-century international society. First, their revolution was fought to win the right for their country to exist as a sovereign state. Such a status was inseparable from acceptance of the juridical structure that alone made sovereign statehood legitimate: the society of states. Second, once victory over the British had been achieved, the Federalist case for facing the rest of the world as a single sovereign entity prevailed over the antifederalist alternative.

It is significant that the second of these two facets of America's socialization into international society occasioned far more controversy than the first. At issue was a debate between those who saw the United States as a new form of republic in which the pursuit of happiness by the individual would be facilitated by the absence of oppressive state structures and those who feared that thirteen weak states would not be able to cope with the rigours of existence in a ruthlessly competitive world. Even among the Federalists were several who were also apprehensive about the consequences for

American revolutionary ideals of creating a strong state and who therefore supported the numerous checks and balances that were built into the Constitution. Only Hamilton enthusiastically endorsed the notion that the United States should wholeheartedly embrace the post-Westphalian conception of the state and seek greatness on the power-political terms of the eighteenth century, rather than on some new idealistic basis.

What this underlying ambivalence about the Westphalian international society meant was that the United States was only partially socialized into it. Its need for legitimacy and 'respectability' entailed an acceptance of the central Westphalian idea of a world of sovereign states with rights and duties that were defined by their common membership of a society of states. But from the outset the three different responses to the complete Westphalian conception that have been identified here—isolation, reform, and participation—competed with each other as divergent tendencies of American foreign policy. As American power grew, a stream of declarations, 'doctrines', and policy initiatives began to appear and with time to have an increasingly profound impact upon international society. Two basic principles shaped the reformist strand in the US approach to international relations. The first was the essential republican idea that a state was legitimate to the extent that it was responsive to the needs and interests of its people. The second was the need for greater morality and democracy in the actual conduct of international affairs. The former of these contributed to the dilution of the specific principle of international legitimacy of the eighteenth century, which accorded legitimacy to any established government. At the same time the external pressure on states to observe certain minimum standards of democracy and protection of human rights steadily increased, with the United States taking a leading role in this process. The second aspect of American reformism made itself felt in a number of ways in the actual functioning of international society. European colonialism came under increasing attack as an affront to the ideals of freedom and as a means of denying important markets to the growing American economy. The United States sponsored the two post-war attempts to replace the balance of power system with a new approach based upon a commitment to collective security in the League of Nations and the United Nations. It was also more open than the European powers to the idea that the 'executive' arms of these two organizations—the League Council and the UN Security Council—should be broadly representative bodies rather than consisting only of the great powers.

The United States may hardly be said to be typical either of revolutionary states or of other international actors. However, the very uniqueness of the American experience is valuable because it enables us to examine two of the central hypotheses with which this study is concerned: that the existence of the international society is a reality with which all states, however unique, have to come to terms through a socialization process that is common to all new entrants and that while international society may change over time, it has certain essential features that are less susceptible to change. It also enables some preliminary observations to be made about the nature of the socialization process.

In the American case, although it did not espouse the cause of international revolution, the United States did have an international outlook that was revolutionary in certain respects. Although it was more willing than many revolutionary states to accommodate the requirements of international society, it is clear that some of the adjustments that it made were not the preferred options of many Americans. Hence, even in the American case the process of socialization was not entirely voluntary. The socialization of the United States was a consequence, primarily, of its need for legitimacy and 'respectability': a need that was greater initially than that of many revolutionary states for the obvious reason that the first objective of the American revolution was to become a state. An additional impetus was given by the requirements of security. In the early years of the war the need for allies against Britain prompted a shift away from the initial high-mindedness of America's envoys to Europe. After the revolution the need to deal with the European powers on a more equal footing was an important factor in bringing about a major revision in the earlier conceptions of how the new republic should be constituted. The fact that socialization had a powerful advocate in Alexander Hamilton should not be ignored.

The revolutionary origins of the United States, its relative isolation and high level of security in the nineteenth century, and its margin of power over any competitor in the twentieth century have combined to make it an unusual member of international society. It has, sometimes at the same time, been a leading advocate of reform of international society as well as its chief defender against other revolutionary states. Both instances illustrate the important role that may be played by a state that is prepared and able to assume a hegemonial position within international society, whether to reform it or defend it. However, they also illustrate the durability of the central feature of international society: its basis in the sovereign equality of its members. International society has developed a greater sensitivity concerning human rights, racism, colonialism, self-determination, and undemocratic practices to a point where they may be said to have amended the general principle of international legitimacy: international society's collective judgement about what it expects from its members for them to qualify for full and undisputed membership. The United States has played a leading role in promoting these norms. But even the great power of the United States has been unable to achieve more than the most marginal changes in the fabric of international society. What is remarkable about contemporary international society is how little, not how much, it has deviated from the Westphalian conception.

3

State and Nation
The French Revolution

INTRODUCTION

Two hundred years after the French Revolution controversy still surrounds all of its important events, personalities, and features. Although perhaps less heated than the debates over the roles of some of the revolutionary leaders, or the various social and economic aspects of the Revolution, discussion of its international dimension has also given rise to widely varying interpretations. While the purpose of this chapter is the limited one of assessing the interaction between the Revolution and the established society of states within which it took place, it is impossible to address this issue without paying some attention to the larger debate over the foreign policy of the Revolution. Inevitably this discussion is dominated by the question of the origins and nature of the French revolutionary wars.

Three schools of thought concerning the origins of the wars may be discerned. The first, and oldest, sees the wars as primarily ideological: as a French crusade to spread revolution abroad that inevitably provoked the formation of a coalition of conservative powers against it. This view of the wars as fundamentally involving a clash of principles was widely accepted at the time and later became the corner-stone of interpretations of the wars by von Ranke and others.[1] In sharp contrast with this approach is the perspective, first and most emphatically set out by Sorel and adopted with variations by numerous twentieth-century historians, from which the wars are seen as merely a continuation of the power politics and traditional rivalries of eighteenth-century Europe. For

---

[1] For a discussion of this and other approaches to the wars, see T. C. W. Blanning, *The Origins of the French Revolutionary Wars* (London and New York, 1986), 69–73.

Sorel in particular the wars, far from being an attempt to spread abroad the principles of the Revolution, were a perversion of those very principles. Since Sorel also explicitly rejects the view that the revolutionary wars were an assault on international society, it is worth considering his interpretation in more detail.

Sorel begins by taking issue with the notion that an organized international community existed before 1789:

There is one prejudice which must be put aside in setting out on this history. It is the representation of Europe under the *ancien régime* as a regularly constituted community of states, in which each directed its conduct by principles recognized by all, where respect for established law governed international relations and treaties, and good faith marked their implementation, where the sense of monarchical solidarity assured both the maintenance of public order and the permanence of engagements contracted by princes. This 'Christian republic', as some have been pleased to call it, has during modern times been nothing more than an august abstraction . . . A Europe in which the rights of each derived from the duties of all was something so foreign to the thinking of the statesmen of the old régime that it took a quarter of a century of war, the most tremendous that had yet been seen, to force the idea upon them and to demonstrate the necessity of it.[2]

Instead of a well-regulated community, there was only international anarchy and the principle of 'might is right': 'there was no security but in a sound understanding of self-interest, no principle of order but in the conflict of interests. The rules of conduct could be summed up in these empirical maxims: what is worth taking is worth keeping—a prompting of greed to which all responded.'[3] Pascal's aphorism 'Being unable to fortify justice, we have justified force' was an apt summary of the international system of the old regime. In the light of this, Sorel's conclusions about the impact of the Revolution upon Europe are hardly surprising:

I have thought it necessary to set forth these customs and to define their meaning because the French Revolution found them in full vigour in the old Europe. This was the public law which would have been applied to France, and which, in default of her submission, was applied afresh to Poland. France did not introduce it into Europe in 1892; she was

[2] A. Sorel, *Europe and the French Revolution*, vol. i, trans. and ed. by A. Cobban and J. W. Hunt (London, 1969), 35.
[3] Ibid. 60.

threatened with subjection to it, and if later she practised it herself, this was not innovation but imitation. Far from having imposed this system on Europe to undermine the rights of others, she was led to adopt it in order to come to terms with the old established states. It was on these conditions that she treated with them and obtained citizen status in Europe. By so doing she betrayed, corrupted and destroyed her own principles and the new system of right which she wanted to make prevail, but she did not betray, corrupt or destroy the ancient law of Europe; its foundations had been destroyed by the old Europe itself.[4]

Sorel's interpretation of the origins of the war is echoed in its essentials by Cobban, who argues that the history of the wars 'can be told almost exclusively in terms of power politics and explained by the traditions of the countries involved and the personalities of their rulers and ministers'.[5] Ross also follows Sorel in seeing *raison d'état* as the supreme principle of all eighteenth-century diplomacy, and in discerning striking similarities between the wars of the Revolution and those of Louis XIV.[6] Similarly, Blanning notes that the French agitators for war in 1791–2 'had not sprung ready-armed from the head of revolutionary ideology. Both their long-term assumptions and short-term calculations were rooted in past experience and preconceptions. Equally, the response of their enemies was not just to the Revolution but to France as well.'[7]

Many French historians incline towards a third interpretation of the wars that sees them as stemming essentially from vicissitudes of the domestic politics of the Revolution, although they differ sharply when they come to attribute personal responsibility for the wars. In fact many individual motives for supporting war were apparent in 1791–2. Some of the influential foreign exiles in Paris who were amongst the strongest advocates of universal revolutions, such as the Prussian Anacharsis Cloots or the Swiss Clavière, saw in war a means of revolutionizing and winning power in their own countries.[8] The Girondins, under Brissot, who led the clamour for war, may have been influenced in part by the belief that the economic interests of the Gironde would be best served by war.[9]

[4] Ibid. 66.
[5] A. Cobban, *Aspects of the French Revolution* (London, 1971), 10.
[6] S. T. Ross, *European Diplomatic History, 1789–1815: France Against Europe* (New York, 1969), 1, 375.
[7] Blanning, *Origins*, 36–7.
[8] A. Mathiez, *The French Revolution* (London, 1951), 279.
[9] G. Lefebvre, *La Révolution française* (Paris, 1951), 225.

The court faction saw in war a means of restoring the monarchy to its former power through the armed intervention that would follow what they believed would be the inevitable defeat of France.[10] Ambitious generals, like Lafayette and Dumouriez, believed that war held out the promise of their own advancement.[11] Finally, as the war developed, and particularly after its enlargement in 1793, its progress became a major factor in the power struggles between different revolutionary factions.

The question of the origins of the revolutionary wars is only one aspect, albeit the most important one, of the larger issue under consideration here: the interaction between the French Revolutionary state and the international society within which it found itself. There were nearly three years of peaceful international relations between the beginning of the Revolution and the outbreak of war, and even after 1792 France was never at war with all other states. But war or the threat of war has followed revolutions too frequently for the major focus of this chapter not to be the most dramatic instance in history of this sequence of events. Moreover none of the three interpretations of the war that have been suggested here necessarily refutes the possibility of a link between the Revolution and war, or, in other words, between the Revolution and a fundamental disturbance to international society. If the Rankian thesis of an ideological war could be accepted such a link would clearly be of the most direct kind, but as the more complex explanations of the war that are contained in the two alternative interpretations advanced here suggest, the notion that the Revolution was simply 'exported' needs, at the very least, to be substantially modified. There were, however, some influential groups committed to the cause of international revolution. Moreover, revolution and domestic instability or disorder are closely linked terms, and the possibility of internal factionalism which spills over into the international arena is clearly one that can be accommodated within the parameters of this study. The only real difficulty arises from the Sorel thesis, since he explicitly rejects the idea that *ancien régime* Europe comprised any sort of international society. However, it is clear that what Sorel has in mind is a conception of a community of states far more ambitious

---

[10] A. Soboul, *The French Revolution, 1787–1799*, trans. A. Forrest (2 vols.; London, 1974), i. 236.

[11] A. Cobban, *A History of Modern France*, i (London, 1957), 189.

than the limited idea of an international society that has been advanced here: one organized around the principle of sovereign statehood, with a commonly held view of what constitutes legitimate entitlement to membership, the acceptance of certain rules of conduct, and some basis of order provided by the balance of power.

It is equally clear that Sorel himself goes a considerable way towards accepting this narrower conception of international society. He accepts, for example, that 'if there was in Europe no Christian republic, there were nations and states. So long as they existed, and there were relations between them, there was such a thing as public law.'[12] The basis of this law was what states actually did: 'What we can see are the actual policies of governments; and we must try to understand the habits they acquired, on which their relations are based. They did not envisage these habits in terms of juridical deductions from abstract principles, but simply as the statement of relationships which derived from the nature of things.'[13] Legitimate statehood was not an automatic entitlement, but something conferred by other states through diplomatic recognition.[14] And, although the state was 'an end in itself, it is sovereign; it recognizes no authority beyond its own',[15] which meant that state policy must be governed by the selfish principle of *raison d'état*, this did not imply the absence of any constraints upon states, but rather its opposite: 'The principle and the object of politics thus posited, rules of conduct can be deduced from them.'[16] The chief constraint upon states stemmed from the existence of other states:

States recognize no judges other than themselves and no laws other than their own interests; but the very force that tends to drive this doctrine to excess served also to temper it. The antidote to the paradoxes of *raison d'état* is common sense; the curb on the excesses of covetousness is self-interest properly understood. This, the only rule states understood, is the sole foundation of their justice. Ambition may dictate the plan but prudence should govern its execution.[17]

---

[12] Sorel, *Europe and the French Revolution*, 36. [13] Ibid.
[14] Ibid. 39. [15] Ibid. 42.
[16] Ibid. 46. [17] Ibid. 56.

Prudence was especially dictated by the operation of the balance of power, which also, in Sorel's view, provided the foundations of an elementary form of international society, although Sorel continues to resist the use of this term, preferring instead a commercial metaphor:

all the great powers were agreed in refusing to let any one of them raise itself above the others. Any of them that wished to play the lion would find the others leagued against it. Thus the great powers constituted a joint stock company, in which all kept what they possessed, made profits according to their holdings, and prevented any of the associated from laying down the law to the others. This was called the balance of power, or the European equilibrium.[18]

We will argue here that the Revolution did pose a threat to international society thus conceived, although it did not bear the sole responsibility for the wars. Moreover, the link between Revolution and war did not pull in only one direction. While the international relations of the Revolution acquired a violent momentum that was, in the end, unstoppable except by the final defeat of France, the existing structure and processes of international society always exerted a countervailing pressure upon the revolutionary leaders to act within the constraints imposed by the prevailing norms of international society.

THE REVOLUTIONARY CHALLENGE TO INTERNATIONAL SOCIETY

International affairs were not a significant issue at the outset of the Revolution. Indeed, only a tiny proportion of the thousands of *cahiers* presented to the States-General were concerned with such matters.[19] Even when the Revolution had entered a much more radical phase, its foreign policy continued to display signs of realism and common sense and an awareness of France's traditional interests. However, despite such evidence of restraint in France's international behaviour—taken by some as proof of an underlying continuity in French foreign policy—the Revolution did pose a

[18] Sorel, *Europe and the French Revolution*, 59.
[19] T. Ruyssen, *Les Sources doctrinales de l'internationalisme* (3 vols.; Paris, 1954), iii. 32.

fundamental challenge to international society, directly as well as implicitly, and by its conduct as well as its rhetoric.

Five important revolutionary ideas, principles, or developments may be identified which undermined in some significant respect the central assumptions of the Westphalian conception of international society. All involved beliefs widely held amongst the revolutionary leaders and had practical implications or consequences. The first of these is considered in more detail in the next section. It stemmed from the most basic principle of the Revolution: that sovereignty is vested in the people, not in the ruler. This, in essence, advanced a novel principle of international legitimacy based upon national self-determination rather than dynastic rights, which meant that a people not happy with its lot within one sovereignty could opt to join another. The principle was used to support the French annexations of the Alsace, Avignon, and Savoy, which were at the time under the auspices of the Empire, the Holy See, and Sardinia respectively. It was given a potentially universal application in the famous Propaganda Decree of 19 November 1792, which granted 'fraternity and aid to all peoples who wish to recover their liberty'.[20]

The Revolution had a universal dimension in other respects that appeared threatening to an international society founded upon the principle of state sovereignty. When Brissot asserted that the Revolution had 'turned all diplomacy upside down',[21] he had in mind its potential capacity to transcend state boundaries and act in effect as the birthplace of a wholly different conception of international society: one more closely related to the idea of a 'great community of mankind' discussed in Chapter 1. In its most idealistic phase, this aspect of French revolutionary ideology took the form of a benevolent cosmopolitanism under which French citizenship was offered to 'lovers of liberty' from other lands,[22] and vague schemes were mooted for the French Assembly to become some kind of international legislature.[23] When the Assembly

[20] For the full terms of the Decree, see J. H. Stewart, *A Documentary Survey of the French Revolution* (New York, 1951), 381.

[21] *Archives parlementaires*, 29 Dec. 1791 (Paris, 1891), xxxvi. 602. The word he used was 'bouleverser'.

[22] S. S. Biro, *The German Policy of Revolutionary France* (2 vols.; Cambridge, Mass., 1957, i. 478–9.

[23] See, for example, the letter from Cloots cited in H. Kohn, *Prelude to Nation State* (Princeton, NJ, 1967), 15.

renounced all wars of conquest in 1790, it did so in part out of a conviction, explicitly stated by Volney and others, that all peoples were part of one great society governed by natural law.[24] A more ominous aspect of this cosmopolitanism was the fact that the revolutionary armies contained Swiss, German, and Venezuelan generals who led Belgian, German, Bavarian, and other foreign legions.[25] In the most extreme phase of the Revolution, the universalist ideas of the revolutionaries became calls for permanent revolution to 'overthrow all thrones, crush all kings and render universal the triumphs of liberty and reason'.[26] Not just kings but 'their accomplices, the privileged castes' must be overthrown in all liberated countries, and no people could be permitted to choose only a 'demi-liberty'.[27] No boundaries could be recognized either for enemies or friends: it was necessary 'to wage a united struggle of *sans culottes* of the whole world against the international coalition of tyrants, aristocrats and priests'.[28]

One of the specific aspects of the idea of the Revolution as the centre of a 'great community' that disturbed statesmen in other European countries was the frequent assertion by the revolutionaries of a clear distinction between 'peoples' and their governments, and the related claim that 'peoples' owed a higher loyalty to the Revolution than to their own governments.[29] Although subversive activities against enemies in European wars were hardly a new development, the emergence of an 'internationalist' cadre who did owe primary allegiance to the Revolution was relatively novel. Moreover, the numerous French revolutionary agitators sent abroad were able to present themselves in a nobler light than had been available to other foreign agents attempting to foment trouble in previous conflicts. It was all too easy to discern a link between

[24] *L'Ancien Moniteur*, iv. 403.

[25] S. Schama, *Patriots and Liberators: Revolution in the Netherlands, 1780–1813* (London, 1977), 160, and Mathiez, *The French Revolution*, 217.

[26] Instruction of Committee of Public Safety to Minister of Foreign Affairs, cited in F. Masson, *Le Département des affaires étrangères pendant la révolution, 1787–1804* (Paris, 1877) 288.

[27] Cambon, on behalf of the Committees of Finance and War and the Diplomatic Committee, 15 Dec. 1792, *Archives parlementaires* (Paris, 1899), lv. 70–2.

[28] A. Soboul, 'Anacharsis Cloots, l'orateur du genre humain', *Annales historiques de la révolution française*, 239 (Jan.–Mar. 1980), 42.

[29] For examples of such rhetoric, see Condorcet's speech, 25 Jan. 1792, *Archives parlementaires* (Paris, 1891), xxxvii. 647–51, and Brissot, 1 Feb. 1793, ibid. (Paris, 1900), lviii. 113.

such subversive activities and the increase in revolutionary violence throughout Europe in the early 1790s—however little substance such a link had in practice.[30]

A third way in which the Revolution challenged the bases of the Westphalian international society stemmed from its tendency to disregard arguments based on existing international law and its preference for appeals to natural law. The Peace of Westphalia itself was frequently denounced by name: it had guaranteed liberty for princes alone, the Revolution would now guarantee liberty for peoples.[31] Moreover, it specifically allowed the hated Austrians to keep the people of Alsace under a 'feudal yoke'.[32] Indeed, all existing treaties were suspect to some degree, since they had not been given the consent of the people; this was an argument advanced as early as 1790.[33] As for international order, which treaties were supposed to underwrite, despotism 'only affects a concern for the tranquility of nations because it guarantees the tranquility of despots'.[34] Shunning the old international law, of which treaties were a part, France would henceforth conduct itself in accordance with natural law. Its early annexations were justified on this basis since they took France towards the natural boundaries of ancient Gaul (an argument that would have been familiar to Louis XIV).[35] An appeal to natural law that was more serious, since it threatened a vital British interest, was made when France decided to challenge the exclusive Dutch right of navigation on the Schelde, which had been agreed at Westphalia. The 'law of nature, the law of nations and all the principles of justice and liberty held sacred by the French nation' demanded an end to this state of affairs, while treaties 'extracted by cupidity, agreed by despotism' could not bind a liberated Belgian people, in whose interest the French were ostensibly acting.[36] Alliances were another form of treaty obligation that could not be expected to bind a free nation basing its

[30] See C. Brinton, *A Decade of Revolution, 1789–1799* (New York, 1934), 164–89 for a fuller elaboration of this point.

[31] Biro, *The German Policy*, i. 63.

[32] M. Dumas, 18 Jan. 1792, *Archives parlementaires* (Paris, 1891), xxxvii. 482–3.

[33] In the context of the Nootka Sound affair, see Ch. 6.

[34] Brissot, 12 Jan. 1793, *Archives parlementaires* (Paris, 1900), lvii. 20.

[35] Kyung-Won Kim, *Revolution and International System* (New York, 1970), 47–8.

[36] Lebrun, Foreign Minister, 19 Dec. 1792, *Archives parlementaires* (Paris, 1899), lv. 165.

foreign policy on principles of universal fraternity. Dumouriez, who became Foreign Minister for a period in 1792, had written a year earlier that 'a great, free and just people is the natural ally of all people and must not have particular alliances which tie it to the destiny and interest of such and such a people'.[37] This argument was repeated by Brissot in attacking the treaty of 1756 with Austria. The future treaties of liberty, he asserted, would be mere friendship treaties, while diplomacy would be limited to the conduct of commercial relations.[38]

The fourth important way in which the Revolution disturbed the foundations of the Westphalian international society lay in its transformation of warfare. Eighteenth-century war had hitherto been constrained to some degree by an implicit understanding that wars should be limited both in their means and in their ends. The survival of international society as a whole depended upon the maintenance of a balance of power and upon a self-denying ordinance by which its members refrained from seeking the total destruction of any of their number. Such restraint was much less in evidence in the French revolutionary wars.[39] No stronger statement of the French ideology of total war was made than the speech of Barère, member of the Committee of Public Safety, in January 1794:

In ordinary wars after such successes, one would have sought . . . peace . . . But in the war of liberty, they [successes] are only a means . . . of exterminating despots . . . Neither peace nor truce nor armistice nor any treaty can be made with despots except in the name of a consolidated, triumphant republic . . . dictating the peace . . . Monarchies need peace; the Republic needs martial energy. Slaves need peace; republicans need the ferment of liberty. Governments need peace; the French Republic needs revolutionary activity.[40]

More important than such rhetoric was the fact that the Revolution was also able to will the means for total war in the *levée en masse* of August 1793, which instituted military conscription:

Henceforth, until the enemies have been driven from the territory of the Republic, the French people are in permanent requisition for army service.

[37] Masson, *Le Département des Affaires Étrangères*, 151.
[38] Brissot, 17 Jan. 1792, *Archives parlementaires* (Paris, 1891), xxxvii. 469.
[39] T. C. W. Blanning, *The French Revolution in Germany: Occupation and Resistance in the Rhineland, 1792–1802* (Oxford, 1983), 129, and Kim, *Revolution and International System*, 17.
[40] Barère, 22 Jan. 1794, cited in Biro, *The German Policy*, i. 210.

The young men shall go to battle; the married men shall forge arms and transport provisions; the women shall make tents and clothes, and shall serve in the hospitals; the children shall turn old linen into lint; the old men shall repair to the public places, to stimulate the courage of the warriors and preach the unity of the Republic and the hatred of kings.[41]

Finally, the slow, deliberate—and confidential—processes of conventional diplomacy that were thought essential to the smooth functioning of a society of sovereign states were at times obliged to give way to the open debates and bellicose posturing of the revolutionary assemblies. This question is considered in more detail in Chapter 7.

INTERNATIONAL LEGITIMACY

The French Revolution did not challenge the idea of international legitimacy as such but rather the specific conception of international legitimacy that prevailed after Westphalia. Hence, the notion that authority could only be rightfully exercised if it was held in accordance with some generally agreed principle remained and indeed was strengthened; it was the precise content of that principle which was threatened and eventually transformed by the Revolution.

The dominant principle of international legitimacy in the eighteenth century was dynastic. Although there were exceptions, sovereignty in most states was vested in monarchs, whose power derived from notions of the divine right of kings. Territory under the sovereignty of a particular monarch passed to his heirs. He alone had the right to commit his state to war, or to enter into obligations to other states, which automatically bound everybody within his domain. Ironically, Louis XVI himself had issued a firm declaration of this doctrine in November 1787, when he asserted:

that the sovereign power in the kingdom belongs to the king alone; that he is accountable only to God for the exercise of his supreme power . . . that the king is sovereign head of the nation and is one with it; finally that the legislative power resides in the person of the sovereign, independent and indivisible.[42]

[41] Decree establishing *levée en masse*, 23 Aug. 1793, in Stewart, *A Documentary Survey*, 472–4.
[42] Sorel, *Europe and the French Revolution*, 221 n.

Such ideas were challenged at a very early stage of the Revolution. The Declaration of the Rights of Man and of the Citizen adopted in August 1789 advanced an alternative doctrine: 'the source of all sovereignty resides essentially in the nation; no group, no individual may exercise authority not emanating expressly therefrom', with the corollary that 'law is the expression of the general will'.[43] These were principles with many applications to foreign affairs. They were invoked in May 1790 when Spain requested French help in a conflict with England, as it was entitled to do under the terms of a dynastic agreement known as the Family Compact. But since this agreement had not received the consent of the French people it could not, under the new doctrine, be binding upon them. The same principles were used to justify the Revolution's action in August 1789 in abolishing the feudal rights possessed by various princelings and bishops in Alsace under the terms of the Peace of Westphalia. As Merlin of Douai informed the National Assembly when the issue was debated in October 1790:

There is, between you and your Alsatian brethren no other legitimate deed of union than the social compact formed last year between all Frenchmen, ancient and modern, in this very Assembly . . . Without doubt a treaty was obligatory for the monarchy . . . But today, when kings are generally recognized . . . only as the delegates . . . of nations . . . of what importance to the people of Alsace, of what importance to the French people, are the conventions which, in the age of despotism, united the first to the second. The Alsatian people is united to the French people because it wants it to be; it is its will alone, and not the treaty of Munster, which has legitimized the union.[44]

At the heart of the new doctrines was the idea that a clear distinction could be drawn between the nation and its ruler. This gave rise to a new principle of legitimacy based upon popular will (the consent of the people being necessary to legitimize any state) and also upon the even more dangerous idea of nationality, which was to become a dominating element in the international politics of the nineteenth and twentieth centuries. But there were immediate as well as long-term consequences. As Sorel suggests, the counter-revolution may be seen in part as an attempt to defend the old principle of legitimacy against the new: 'This was what made possible the armed emigré, organizing a state against the state,

[43] Stewart, *A Documentary Survey*, 114.
[44] Biro, *The German Policy*, i. 41.

concluding alliances with foreign powers and invading France side by side with foreign armies, and all in the belief that they were acting within their rights, for the emigrés claimed to have on their side both state and country and to be fighting only against usurpers.'[45] In the debates leading up to the first revolutionary war, the refusal of Leopold of Austria to recognize the legitimacy of French national sovereignty was cited as one ground for war against him.[46] It was also possible to use the principle against foreign governments. In a distinction that was to be employed in numerous subsequent revolutions, Brissot asserted the existence of 'a demarcation line between societies and their governments', with the governments of certain states hating the principles of the revolution while their peoples supposedly adored them.[47] Since such governments were clearly not legitimate, according to the new standard of popular support, their views could be disregarded and their peoples appealed to directly by the French. Nine months later the French Foreign Minister, Lebrun, was declaring this distinction between peoples and governments to be the base on which he was building his new diplomacy.[48]

THE REVOLUTIONARY MIND

Although clear-headed pragmatism was always in evidence among some revolutionary leaders, it is undeniable that the heightened emotional atmosphere during the first few years of the Revolution affected the way in which many Frenchmen viewed the relationship between the outside world and themselves. At its worst, their distorted perception of reality helped to create illusory expectations, to nurture a sense of moral superiority and martial invincibility, and to feed xenophobic and paranoid suspicions and fears. The precise influence upon events of such intangibles is impossible to quantify, but they undoubtedly contributed to the disruptive impact of the Revolution on international society.

During the six months before the outbreak of war in April 1792 and also before the declaration of war against England in February 1793, the dominant mood was one of optimism, combined with a

45 Sorel, *Europe and the French Revolution*, 84.
46 *Archives parlementaires*, 18 Jan. 1792 (Paris, 1891), xxxvii. 495.
47 Ibid. 29 Dec. 1791 (Paris, 1891), xxxvi. 606.
48 Masson, *Le Département des Affaires étrangères*, 261.

belief in the decadence of the forces arraigned against France. 'The French people will utter a great shout', declared Isnard at the Jacobin Club, 'and every other nation will answer to its call.'[49] Despite Robespierre, who mocked the idea that any foreign nation would welcome 'armed missionaries' from France, and warned against exporting the Revolution before it was consolidated at home, the majority was swept along by the enticing vision of the Girondins.[50] England, it was confidently asserted, would not join Prussia and Austria against France because the English supported the Revolution.[51] The moral force of the Revolution would sweep all before it; foreign soldiers and peoples would compare the fraternal attitude of the French army with the oppressiveness of their own nobility and refuse to fight for the old order.[52] The rest of Europe was decadent and ripe for revolution; in particular, when England seemed likely to enter the war in late 1792, there was a widespread belief that an imminent English revolution would pre-empt her intervention. Such sentiments were not merely a product of the overblown rhetoric of the National Convention. The dispatches of the French ambassador in London, Chauvelin, fed the French expectations of an English revolution, as did the numerous French secret agents in London, to such an extent that Lebrun was able to report to the National Convention's Diplomatic Committee as late as 20 November 1792 that British public opinion was firmly behind France and that the country itself was on the verge of a revolution.[53] Chauvelin, Lebrun, and the secret agents might have been exaggerating England's potential for revolution in part because of the requirements of self-preservation in an atmosphere in which it was becoming increasingly important to demonstrate revolutionary zeal in order to survive. Alternatively, a tendency to view events through the distorting prism of France's recent experiences might have genuinely misled them about the meaning of the increase in political unrest in Britain and elsewhere during 1792. In either case, the Revolution had clearly had an impact upon the normal functioning of the international system in terms of its

[49] M. J. Sydenham, *The French Revolution* (London, 1965), 94.

[50] F. L. Kidner, 'The Girondists and the "Propaganda War" of 1792: A Re-evaluation of French Revolutionary Foreign Policy from 1791 to 1793', Ph.D. thesis (Princeton University, 1971), 89–90.

[51] e.g. *Archives parlementaires* (Paris, 1891), xxxvi. 602.

[52] Ibid. (Paris, 1891), xxxvii. 645–51.

[53] Kidner, 'The Girondists', 450, and J. T. Murley, 'The Origins and Outbreak of the Anglo-French War of 1793', D.Phil. thesis (Oxford University, 1959), 152.

effect on French perceptions and behaviour and also on British statesmen, who inevitably saw French predictions of a British revolution as evidence of French intrigues to bring about just such an outcome.[54]

As France began to suffer some military reverses during 1793, a different atmosphere started to prevail: one of suspicion, xenophobia, and imagined conspiracies. As with the early idealism when foreigners had been welcomed into Paris with open arms, and also the optimism of the first months of the war, it is possible to see this as characteristic of revolutions during a particular phase, when they come to feel besieged by the forces they have helped to unleash. In the case of some revolutionaries in France, hostility towards foreigners was never far below the surface. As early as June 1791 the British diplomat Lord Auckland detected a 'malignant jealousy' towards England on the part of the Diplomatic Committee.[55] Robespierre in particular made no secret of his distrust of 'cosmopolitan charlatans' such as Cloots and Thomas Paine, who were respectively executed and imprisoned during the Terror.[56] As he declared in October 1793:

I distrust without distinction all those foreigners whose face is covered with a mask of patriotism and who endeavour to appear more republican and energetic than we are. They are the agents of alien powers; for I am well aware that our enemies cannot have failed to say: 'Our emissaries must affect the most ardent and exaggerated patriotism' in order that they may the more easily insinuate themselves into our committees and assemblies. It is they who are sowing discord.[57]

Any contact with foreigners could lead to contamination, which made French diplomats a particular target. Most of them were betraying the Revolution, argued Robespierre in July 1794, an attitude which, leading as it did to the execution of numerous foreign ministers and subordinate officials, did not make it easy for French diplomats to practise their craft.[58]

[54] *The Manuscripts of J. B. Fortescue esq. Preserved at Dropmore (The Dropmore Papers)* (Historical Manuscripts Commission, London, 1892), ii. 112, 332–43.

[55] Ibid. 112.

[56] D. A. Silverman, 'Informal Diplomacy: The Foreign Policy of the Robespierrist Committee of Public Safety', Ph.D. thesis (University of Washington, 1973).

[57] Mathiez, *The French Revolution*, 418–19.

[58] Silverman, 'Informal Diplomacy', 12, and Masson, *Le Département des affaires étrangères*, 298–9.

THE INTERPLAY BETWEEN THE DOMESTIC AND INTERNATIONAL
POLITICS OF THE FRENCH REVOLUTION

Heeren, in his discussion of the French Revolution, remarked, 'It was the peculiarity of the age that the external relations of the states proceeded from the internal'.[59] Indeed the domestic politics of the Revolution acquired a powerful dynamic which had important repercussions in international relations and conversely external affairs, including the war, were sometimes exploited for purely domestic purposes. This latter phenomenon is not unique to revolutions, but revolutions are especially likely to give rise to conditions conducive to international affairs becoming inseparable from domestic tensions and conflicts: factionalism, a precarious hold on power together with extreme penalties for losing it, and a blindness to everything except the imperatives of the internal struggle.

The most basic effect of the Revolution was to demolish the former structure of authority without, for some time, replacing it with an equally clear-cut decision-making process that could be perceived by foreign observers as effective, stable, and cohesive.[60] That there was some awareness of the problems this created in the sensitive foreign affairs area is evident from the fact that subsequent constitutions reveal a marked retreat from the principles laid down in the Constitution of 1791, which gave significant powers over foreign policy to the legislature rather than concentrating them all in the executive.[61] For foreign statesmen, however, such evidence of caution and pragmatism was clouded by the confusion created by the many strident voices which appeared able to speak with authority on foreign policy issues—a confusion demonstrated by the fact that several foreign capitals during the crucial 1791–3 period were hosts to two or more rival diplomatic agents, all claiming to represent France.[62]

A much more direct connection between external events and the

---

[59] A. H. L. Heeren, *A Manual of the History of the Political System of Europe and its Colonies* (2 vols.; Oxford, 1833), ii. 172.

[60] Kim, *Revolution and International System*, 50.

[61] J. E. Howard, *Parliament and Foreign Policy in France* (London, 1948). 13–24.

[62] Kidner, 'The Girondists'. 64.

Revolution emerged from the growing body of opinion asserting. that war was necessary for the consolidation and further development of the Revolution. Brissot, the strongest advocate of war, believed that it would force the king into open opposition to the Revolution,[63] and that 'our honour, our public credit, the necessity for consolidating our Revolution and giving it a moral basis—all make this course of action [war] obligatory'[64] (16 December 1791). To this list of considerations in favour of war he added, two weeks later, French external security, internal tranquillity, and the need to restore French finances.[65] Others, such as Desmoulins, advanced what in another context would come to be described as a theory of permanent revolution: 'What does it matter, after all, if the tyrants of Europe unite to make war on us? I would go further and say that perhaps something of the sort is necessary in order to mature and carry out more rapidly the other national revolutions that are being prepared.'[66] Nor was this perceived linkage between revolution and war merely a matter of rhetoric. Just as the Revolution had nurtured the war, so did the development of the war lead to an intensification of the Revolution throughout 1793, although not perhaps in the manner desired by Brissot, who was to lose his head in the second revolution.

The symbiotic relationship between revolution and war acquired a dynamic that was substantially independent of the wishes of the leading revolutionaries and of their ability to control it. One of the most important aspects of this concerned the role of the army. Having had low status before 1789, the soldier achieved a new prestige during the war. The Revolution 'redefined the man in the ranks. He became a citizen-in-arms, a defender of his people and a paragon of revolutionary morality.'[67] But this prestige made the soldier more politically dangerous. As Clavière wrote to the French general, Custine, in December 1792, 'We must maintain a state of war; the return of our soldiers would increase the disorder everywhere and ruin us.'[68] Or, in the even blunter assessment of

[63] M. J. Sydenham, *The Girondins* (London, 1961), 104.
[64] Mathiez, *The French Revolution*, 144.
[65] *Archives parlementaires*, 29 Dec. 1791 (Paris, 1891), xxxvi. 607.
[66] P. Gaxotte, *The French Revolution*, (London and New York, 1932), 188.
[67] J. A. Lynn, *The Bayonets of the Republic: Motivation and Tactics in the Army of Revolutionary France, 1791–4* (Chicago, 1984), 63–5.
[68] Mathiez, *The French Revolution*, 286.

Roland: 'It is necessary to march the thousands of men whom we have under arms as far away as their legs will carry them, or else they will come back and cut our throats.'[69]

EXPORTING THE REVOLUTION OR EXPANDING FRANCE

Sorel's verdict on the wars is that the French:

commenced the war to defend their independence; they continued it to propagate their principles; then, by the force of things, by the pressure of tradition and of the national interest, the spirit of classical magistracy, inbred in the race and exalted by the revolutionary spirit, identified national defence, propaganda, supremacy, the grandeur of France and the happiness of humanity in a single design, that of conquest. Conquest, once commenced, followed the inevitable path of conquest. The war absorbed the state. The Revolution realized . . . this great, confused dream of Rome which smouldered in the French imagination.[70]

This interpretation of French policy in the war as progressing from initially defensive objectives through a programme of international revolution to a design for world conquest raises two questions that go beyond the narrow issue of French war aims. First, are revolutionary states inherently expansionist? Second, when a revolutionary state exhibits expansionist tendencies should these be regarded as no different in kind from expansionism on the part of any other state, and dealt with by international society in the same manner, or be seen as an essentially new phenomenon, posing a quite different challenge to international society and requiring equally novel solutions? In other words, should French territorial acquisitions be seen as expanding France or exporting the Revolution?

These questions admit of no easy answers. All long wars are capable of sustaining profound changes in their nature and in the purposes of those fighting them. Success on the battlefield creates its own military and political dynamic. Wars themselves create needs: soldiers must be fed, conquered territories must be governed, popular enthusiasm must be maintained. The Revolution unleashed huge reserves of previously latent power in France, but it did so by means of various measures of political and military modernization

---

[69] Mathiez, *The French Revolution*.
[70] A. Sorel, *L'Europe et la révolution française*, 21st ed., iv. (Paris, 1892), 462.

which others could emulate rather than by firing the masses with a proselytizing zeal. Moreover, these powers were not in the end harnessed and directed towards universal empire by some abstract revolutionary force, but by the unique genius of a single individual.

In practice, a complex mix of factors operated in all of the crucial developments in French policy during the wars. The war was begun for what seemed to many in France to be sound defensive reasons: it was a pre-emptive measure against what was perceived to be a concert of foreign powers that was being formed against France. But the concert was seen as being organized against the French constitution—and hence the Revolution—and not simply against the French state, so right at the outset France's dual identity as revolutionary state and great power complicates any analysis of the war. Moreover while its fundamentally defensive nature was asserted by all, many simultaneously believed that the war would be a war of liberation. At first it was believed that France would be a liberating influence mainly through the example it set. As the statement of French foreign policy on 14 April 1792 put it, France at war would 'present to the world the new spectacle of a nation truly free, subject to the rules of justice in the midst of the turmoils of war, and respecting everywhere at all times with regard to all men the rights which are the same for all'.[71] Later, French victories presented the country with foreign territory that had to be governed somehow and ideological considerations did influence at least the theory of how such government should be carried out. For example, the two decrees of November and December 1792, and the speeches accompanying them, which instructed French generals on the administration of the occupied territories told them to proclaim the sovereignty of the people and organize 'a form of free and popular government'. However, they also made it clear that the 'freedom' of the conquered peoples only extended as far as their willingness to select a form of government that was compatible with French principles. If they opted for only a 'semi-liberty' or for retaining their 'privileged orders' this would be unacceptable and French 'revolutionary power' would need to be employed to carry through a revolution that would be in the best interests of the conquered peoples—if only their consciousness were sufficiently awakened to enable them to see matters in the true light.[72]

[71] Stewart, *A Documentary Survey*, 285.
[72] See Cambon's revealing speech introducing the December Decree, *Archives parlementaires*, 15 Dec. 1792 (Paris, 1899), lv. 70–2.

A dualism in French perceptions and motivations, stemming from France's split personality as both revolutionary state and great power, is apparent throughout the first few years of the war—even after strategic and financial considerations had clearly come to dominate the conduct of the war. The truth was that French security, the interests of successive revolutionary factions holding power, and the survival of the Revolution had all come to be inextricably linked with each other and with the course of the war. When Brissot called for war against Spain and for revolution to be fomented in Spain's American colonies because 'our liberty will never be undisturbed so long as there is a Bourbon left on his throne',[73] he was advocating a policy that could be justified on ideological, national interest, and personal grounds. Similarly, the Committee of Public Safety, which had initially rejected a policy of international revolution, soon came to see practical advantages for France in supporting revolution in the territories of France's enemies. For instance in 1794 a statement of French policy on Catalonia argued that while annexation was against revolutionary principles, encouraging the establishment of an independent republic was not, although 'necessity, principles and interest' dictated the need to bind the new Catalan republic to France.[74] A similar mixture of practical calculation and principle appears in a letter sent by the Committee to a French diplomat in 1795, on the question of absorbing the Rhineland into France:

by what right could France, which ought to be giving lessons in philosophy to the world, and which has proclaimed herself the enemy of all oppression, by what right could she despoil of their lands five or six petty sovereigns who never had the will to make war against her, who were engaged only in self-defence, and from whom she has nothing to fear?[75]

A far better policy would be to make peace with the German princelings in order more effectively to prosecute the war against Austria. 'By this means, the odium of an unjust spoliation and the reproach of inconsistency with respect to principles professed would be avoided.'[76]

---

[73] Mathiez, *The French Revolution*, 280–6.
[74] Silverman, 'Informal Diplomacy', 217.
[75] Biro, *The German Policy*, i. 437.
[76] Ibid.

THE EUROPEAN RESPONSE

It has already been suggested that order in international affairs is a state of mind as much as a state of being: that it is dependent upon perceptions as well as upon objective circumstances. In the context of the French Revolution, this points to the importance of the response of the other European powers to the Revolution—particularly their appraisal of its significance for the European international system as a whole. French protestations of amicable intentions towards the rest of Europe may or may not have been sincere: as we have seen, the question of French foreign policy motivation is an exceptionally complex one. But an assessment of the Revolution's impact upon international order cannot be confined to a consideration of the intentions of French policy-makers in isolation. French actions sometimes had implications that went far beyond what was intended, as had the November 1792 Propaganda Decree. Such implications could also be perceived by foreign statesmen. In either case, the Revolution's impact upon international order was not simply dependent upon French action but also upon international reaction.

The initial response of some of France's traditional enemies to the Revolution was one of scarcely concealed glee. 'The French have done infinitely better for us than we could possibly have done', wrote Britain's Foreign Secretary, the Duke of Leeds, in July 1789.[77] In a similar vein, Lord Auckland gave his opinion of the troubles in France to the Duke of Leeds' successor, Lord Grenville, in 1791, 'I am not sure that the continued course of their struggles to maintain a disjointed and inefficient Government would not be beneficial to our political interests, and the best security to the permanence of our prosperity'.[78] Britain's ambassador to France warned that foreign intervention to help the king might bring an end to this happy state of affairs: 'Foreign forces would, in my mind, serve only to unite the country still stronger against him [Louis XVI], and would compel the French to form a good government; who, if left to themselves, would have frittered it away into a nondescript metaphysical permanent anarchy'.[79]

[77] H. Mitchell, *The Underground War against Revolutionary France: The Missions of William Wickham, 1794–1800* (Oxford, 1965), 14.
[78] 13 June 1791, *The Dropmore Papers* ii. 96–7.
[79] Earl Gower to Lord Grenville, 1 July 1791, ibid. 117.

Not everybody shared these sanguine views. In England, Burke was soon arguing that the European political system, which in his view had been underpinned by an aristocratic code of honour and by principles of chivalry and courtesy, was under serious threat from 'this new conquering empire of light and reason'.[80] Rumours of a French 'Propaganda Club' bent on fomenting revolution, and disquiet about the particular dangers of this with regard to Ireland, were widespread, both in the popular press and in the reports of British secret agents in France. In countries with closer links to the Bourbons or with more reason to feel threatened by the implications of what was happening in France, there was greater concern, although even here this took many months to crystallize into outright hostility to the Revolution. In general this was because of other preoccupations—Belgium in the case of Marie Antoinette's brother, Emperor Leopold of Austria, Poland and Turkey in the case of Russia, and expansionism in the case of Prussia. If the king of Sweden and the Bourbon king of Spain did express more immediate alarm, and if French *émigrés* were vociferously agitating for a counter-revolutionary crusade, their views were of relatively minor consequence during 1789–90.

When Austria and Prussia began seriously to consider the possibility of armed intervention against France from Spring 1791 onwards, they did so from several diverse motives. The desire to achieve a favourable balance of power was part of Leopold's calculations, insofar as this goal would be served by restoring a grateful Louis XVI to his former status in France.[81] Even more traditional considerations relating to possible territorial gains from a war against what was believed to be a severely weakened France were never far from the surface.[82] But alongside these *realpolitik* concerns went a genuine fear of the danger posed by a radical Revolution to the European political system as a whole—a fear exacerbated by the mutual incomprehension and misperception increasingly characterizing much of the communication between the Revolution and the established powers. In the words of the Austrian Chancellor, Kaunitz, in a note to Austrian diplomats in

[80] F. G. Selby (ed.), *Burke's Reflections on the Revolution in France* (London, 1906), 85–6.

[81] Ross, *European Diplomatic History*, 34.

[82] K. A. Roider, Jr., *Baron Thugut and Austria's Response to the French Revolution* (Princeton, NJ, 1987), 95–6.

July 1791, the spread of the 'spirit of insubordination and revolt' was so menacing that all governments needed to 'make common cause in order to preserve the public peace, the tranquillity of states, the inviolability of possessions and the good faith of treaties'. The prosperity and hegemony of Europe were 'intimately linked to a community of interests of all kinds, of internal administration, of gentle and calm manners, of well informed opinions and of a beneficent and pure religion, which groups them all in a single family of nations', and this could be threatened not only by the Revolution, but also by the necessary counter-measures that would have to be taken against it.[83]

Kaunitz was instrumental in drawing up in August 1791 the Declaration of Pillnitz, in which Leopold and Frederick William II of Prussia declared the fate of Louis XVI to be 'a matter of common concern to all the sovereigns of Europe' and asserted that they would use force on behalf of Louis and to impose a moderate constitution on France, albeit only if they were aided by the other states of Europe. Leopold's privately stated intention was to use the Declaration to 'curb the leaders of the violent party and forestall desperate decisions. This will still leave them an opportunity for honest repentance and the peaceful establishment in France of a regime which will preserve at least the dignity of the crown and the essentials of general tranquillity.'[84] In fact the Declaration was perceived in France as evidence of the formation of a concert of powers with the aim of overthrowing the Constitution and reversing the principle of equal rights, so it had the opposite effect to what was intended, since it gave Brissot's war faction some very useful ammunition.

Prospects for improvement in the steadily worsening relations between France and Austria and Prussia were thus made much more difficult by the fundamental ideological differences between the two sides. These affected their relationship in two important ways. First, each side came to see the other, not simply as a traditional great power rival with which a negotiated compromise might be possible, but as embodying a threat to its very existence. Second, this perception affected the way in which each viewed the other's motives, so that what were intended to be little more than

[83] Sorel, *L'Europe et la révolution française*, ii. 233.
[84] Stewart, *A Documentary Survey*, 220–4.

symbolic gestures were magnified out of all proportion to their true significance.

A similar process occurred during the deterioration of relations between Britain and France at the end of 1792. Certainly in this case the principal *casus belli* had nothing to do with ideology. The increasing French domination of the Low Countries, symbolized by the French decision to open the Schelde river, which had been closed to international shipping by the Peace of Westphalia, threatened a vital and long-standing British interest. The French, however, embellished this decision with various doctrinal layers about natural law and adopted a dogmatic and bellicose tone in their negotiations with the British that obscured the fact that they were anxious to reach a settlement. Similarly, the Propaganda Decree of 19 November, which was not thought of as particularly consequential by the French, was promulgated at the same time as an increase in radical upheavals in England, which meant that it could easily be seen as proof of a French design to foment revolution throughout Europe. Like the Austrians, the British came to believe that what was at stake was not simply the security of specific interests, however important, but that of the international system as a whole.

Nothing illustrates these points more clearly than the Anglo-French exchanges in December 1792. The French Foreign Minister, Lebrun, had attempted to appease England by playing down the significance of the opening of the Schelde and the Propaganda Decree.[85] But he accompanied this with a threat to appeal to the British people over the heads of its government, if necessary, by presenting the people with a situation in which 'a great nation is seen upholding the rights of nature, justice, liberty and equality against a Ministry which undertakes a rift only for reasons of simple personal convenience'.[86] Britain's response was to insist that the Decree of 19 November was 'the formal declaration of a design to extend universally the new principles of government adopted in France, and to encourage disorder and revolt in all countries, even in those which are neutral'. The French explanation of the Decree was unsatisfactory since it

still declares to the promoters of sedition in every country what are the cases in which they may count beforehand on the support and succour of

---

[85] Ross, *European Diplomatic History*, 65.
[86] Kidner, 'The Girondists', 288.

France; and . . . reserves to that country the right of mixing herself in our internal affairs whenever she shall judge it proper and on principles incompatible with the political institutions of all the countries of Europe.

France's claim to a unilateral right to set aside existing treaties on the Schelde in the name of natural law was similarly unacceptable, since it would jeopardize the very basis of the existing international system.

France can have no right to annul the stipulations relative to the Scheldt, unless she have also the right to set aside equally all the other treaties between all the powers of Europe, and all the other rights of England, or of her allies . . . England will never consent that France shall arrogate the power of annulling at her pleasure, and under the pretence of a pretended natural right of which she makes herself the only judge, the political system of Europe, established by solemn treaties, and guaranteed by the consent of all the powers.

The proposed French appeal to the British people was also dismissed as an attempted violation of the British constitution.[87] Lebrun attempted to reply to this in what he doubtless considered to be a conciliatory fashion, but still managed to repeat the rationale for French actions derived from the new revolutionary doctrines, which was a major cause of British concern. The Decree of 19 November, he maintained, was not seditious, it merely said that France would aid a nation 'in which the general will, clearly and unequivocally expressed, should call the French nation to its assistance and fraternity'. As for the opening of the Schelde, its closure had been concluded 'by treaty without consent of the Belgians' who 'now reenter into the rights which the house of Austria have taken away from them'.[88]

The ideas that some nebulous 'general will' could permit interference in their internal affairs and that some equally dubious 'natural rights' could override treaty obligations were both anathema to the British, who were rapidly losing patience with what they perceived as a dogmatic French insistence upon replacing the basic tenets of the Westphalian conception of international society with their own doctrines. As Pitt put it at the outset of the war on 12 February, the French

[87] H. Temperley and L. M. Penson (eds.), *Foundations of British Foreign Policy* (London, 1966), 3–8.
[88] Ibid.

will not accept, under the name of liberty, any model of government but that which is conformable to their own opinions and ideas and, unless they are stopped in their career, all Europe must soon learn its ideas of justice, the law of nations, models of government and principles of liberty from the mouth of the French cannon.[89]

Years later, in a lengthy review of the war, Pitt was to reiterate his conviction that the 'system' of the French Revolution—'the alliance of the most horrid principles with the most horrid means'—involved a fundamental attack on the existing principles of international society and an attempt to mould, 'at its discretion, a new and general code of the law of nations'. He supported this contention with four arguments. The French system 'was in itself a declaration of war against all nations'; it had disturbed the European balance of power; the instability of its Government 'has been of itself sufficient to destroy all reliance, if any such reliance could, at any time, have been placed on the good faith of any of its rulers'; finally, in the case of the Schelde and on many other occasions the French 'assumed the power which they have affected to exercise through the whole of the revolution, of superseding, by a new code of their own, all the recognized principles of the law of nations'.[90]

THE SOCIALIZATION OF REVOLUTIONARY FRANCE

It is perhaps ironic that, even during the most radical phase of the Revolution, there were many who were well aware of the impact of French actions and rhetoric upon opinion elsewhere in Europe, and who saw the need for the Revolution to reach an accommodation with the established society of states, to adopt some of its rules, to behave in accordance with its existing norms, and, in short, to become socialized within the prevailing order. In some respects they were successful in their efforts to persuade the revolutionaries of the need to adapt in order to survive; in other respects the pressure of circumstances forced France to adopt (or resume) patterns of

[89] Pitt's speech of 12 Feb. 1793 on the outbreak of the war, cited in Murley, 'The Origins and Outbreak of the Anglo-French War of 1793', 507–8.
[90] Pitt's speech on Overtures of Peace with France in the House of Commons, 3 Feb. 1800, in E. R. Jones (ed.), *Selected Speeches on British Foreign Policy* (London, 1914), 38–111.

behaviour little different from those of its more orthodox rivals. But the communications barrier imposed by the gulf between the revolutionary ideology and rhetoric of France and the conventional language and practices of traditional diplomacy proved too great to overcome. It was France's misfortune not to be believed when it tried to signal its willingness to play the diplomatic game by the old rules, in part because the Revolution seldom spoke with one voice; foreign statesmen found it safest to interpret such signals as evidence, not of France's socialization, but of French deceitfulness.

'Socialization' is not a phenomenon that is capable of precise measurement. Evidence for its occurrence here must be sought in diverse French acts suggestive of a desire to accommodate the imperatives of the international society within which Revolutionary France found itself to be unavoidably located. Such indications began to appear at an early stage of the Revolution. For instance, when Merlin of Douai introduced his report on the annexation of Alsace by France he justified the annexation first of all by reference to the new revolutionary principles: no treaty could override the social compact formed between all Frenchmen in 1789; the will of the people of Alsace was all that mattered. But he went on to offer a lengthy argument in support of French sovereignty over Alsace that was based entirely on the established practices of existing international law and long-standing treaties. Indeed, he felt obliged to apologize to the Assembly for having to speak to it in the unbearable language of the old diplomacy.[91] France also offered compensation to the dispossessed German princes of Alsace.

A retreat from rigid adherence to high principle was also evident in other areas. Despite the undeniable justice of abolishing slavery in French colonies, French commercial interests, and also the danger of losing the colonies if the slaves were emancipated, dictated a policy of maintaining slavery.[92] Appeals for French assistance from revolutionary factions in The Netherlands during 1790–1 were rejected. As the president of the Jacobin Club put it in May 1791, 'despite the absolutely sincere interest that we take in their cause, we will under no circumstances embark on a crusade against Holland and Prussia and so we must be content with expressing our wishes for universal liberty and the true happiness of the entire human race . . . After all, have we not got sufficient

[91] *L'Ancien Moniteur*, vi. 239–41.
[92] E. D. Bradley, *The Life of Barnave* (2 vols.; Oxford, 1915), i. 315–25.

enemies already at this time?'[93] Such realism was also reflected in the moderate Decree of French Foreign Policy of 21 June 1791, which called for a continuation of 'relations of friendship and good understanding' with those states which were officially represented at Paris.[94]

The Propaganda Decrees of November and December 1792 were widely interpreted as evidence of France's intention to foment revolution throughout Europe and elsewhere. In fact, the more controversial first Decree was never seen in France as having the significance that it was to acquire outside, while the second Decree clearly marked a shift away from the universalist pretensions of the first, towards a realistic set of guidelines to be observed by French generals in conquered territory. In April 1793 military setbacks, culminating in the defection of the leading French general, Dumouriez, produced a virtual stampede away from the idealism of November. In proposing that France adopt a decree of non-intervention in the internal affairs of other states, Danton referred to the November Decree in the following way:

It is time, citizens, that the National Convention makes known to Europe that it knows how to ally policy to republican virtues. We are reaching a point where it is necessary to disengage liberty in order to preserve it better for all these enthusiasms. Let me explain: in a moment of enthusiasm you produced a decree whose motive was doubtless lofty, since you gave yourself the obligation of giving protection to peoples who wished to resist the oppression of their tyrants. This decree would seem to commit you to come to the aid of a few patriots who wished to make a revolution in China. It is necessary, before all else to look to the conservation of our body politic and to lay the foundations of French greatness. (Applause)[95]

Danton was able to secure the rescindment of the November Decree. The December Decree remained in force, but its real purpose was not to proclaim France's devotion to universal liberty but to find a way of paying for the war by imposing the cost upon the conquered territories. As Cambon sadly noted on 10 December 1792, 'The farther we advance into enemy territory, the more ruinous the war becomes, especially with our principles of philosophy and generosity.'[96] Hence, although the Decree instructed French generals to proclaim the sovereignty of the people

---

[93] Schama, *Patriots and Liberators*, 150.
[94] Stewart, *A Documentary Survey*, 210–11.
[95] *Archives parlementaires*, 13 Apr. 1793 (Paris, 1902), lxii. 3.
[96] Mathiez, *The French Revolution*, 286.

in occupied territories, and to announce that they brought 'peace, aid, fraternity, liberty and equality', it also ordered the public treasury and the property of priests and nobles to be placed 'under the safeguard and protection' of France.[97]

A similar realism, coupled with a desire not to see France's approach to international relations diverge too far from that of the rest of Europe, was in evidence on other occasions during 1793. For example, Abbé Grégoire tried to secure the National Convention's agreement to a 'Declaration of the Rights of Peoples', which attempted to derive a set of principles of international law from the basic doctrines of the Revolution. Its articles, which are considered more fully in Chapter 6 on international law, contained numerous assertions drawn from natural law, and also the statement that only governments based on liberty and equality could conform to the rights of the people, and hence possess true legitimacy.[98] But the Convention was in no mood to agree to yet more rhetorical self-indulgence which would achieve few if any concrete results but might add to France's difficulties in dealing with other powers. It rejected the decree, accepting the argument of Barère: 'I invite the Convention not to forget the situation of France in the middle of Europe. You are not only a philosophical and legislative assembly, you are a political assembly.'[99]

The mood of the Convention in the three months before the fall of the Girondins in June 1793 was succinctly expressed by Danton's friend Pierre-François Robert, on 26 April:

We are not the representatives of the human race. I wish therefore that the legislator of France would forget the universe for a moment to concern himself with his country alone. I desire that kind of national egoism without which we shall prove false to our duties.[100]

From June onwards the increasing internal xenophobia was matched by an even more emphatic shift away from universalist notions. French representatives abroad were told that they were no longer to participate in local politics, and French generals were instructed to renounce every 'philanthropic idea' adopted earlier in the vain hope of making foreign nations understand the benefits of

---

[97] Stewart, *A Documentary Survey*, 382.
[98] Ruyssen, *Les Sources doctrinales*, iii. 57–63.
[99] Ibid. 59.
[100] Kohn, *Prelude*, 73.

liberty, and to observe the normal laws of war in the conquered territories.[101] All French agents abroad were instructed to respect neutral territory.[102] 'We must nationalize the Revolution,' urged French diplomat Soulavie, 'consider nothing but France—and return to the traditional policy of the nation.'[103] In like mood, Merlin of Thionville, while informing his colleagues that the people in some conquered territories actually preferred servitude to liberty, instructed them, 'Be happy at home. That is the means of revolutionizing other peoples—by causing them to envy our lot.'[104]

The problem for the French was that many of their other actions during the same period seemed to indicate an intensification of the Revolution and, as in the case of the *levée en masse*, an even greater mobilization of the resources of the state behind the Revolution's external objectives. In the event, their move in 1793 towards a less internationalist mood, accompanied by overtures towards Prussia with the aim of splitting the alliance, did not finally pay dividends until a separate peace was signed with Prussia in April 1795. Moreover, France's 'socialization' during 1793 was in large part a product of apprehensions caused by military reverses. Military success, combined with the leftist 'Fructidor' coup of 4 September 1797, produced a more vigorous and ambitious foreign policy. Now, though, the driving force was not universal liberty but universal empire.

During his sojourn at St Helena, Napoleon wrote that he had attempted to bring Europe into a 'unity of codes, principles, opinions, feelings and interest'. He added that the new forces unleashed by the French Revolution would eventually lead to this end under some new leader:

The impulse has been given, and I do not think that, after my fall and the disappearance of my system, there will be any other great equilibrium possible in Europe than the concentration and confederation of the great peoples. The first sovereign who, in the midst of the first great struggle, shall embrace in good faith the cause of the peoples, will find himself at the head of all Europe, and will be able to accomplish whatever he wishes.[105]

[101] *Archives parlementaires*, 15 Sept. 1793 (Paris, 1885), lxxiv. 231.
[102] Declaration of French Foreign Policy, 17 Nov. 1793, in Stewart, *A Documentary Survey*, 475–6.
[103] Biro, *The Germany Policy*, i. 190.
[104] Ibid. 208.
[105] Cited in P. Dukes, *A History of Europe, 1648–1948* (Basingstoke, 1985), 213.

There is, of course, more than an element of self-justification in this, and his prediction of a future 'universal society' of Europe has yet to be fulfilled. However, in his remarks on the impact of popular nationalism upon the balance of power system there is also a profound insight. The flexibility of the eighteenth-century balance of power depended upon the capacity of the great powers to move freely in and out of alliances and to dispose of their own and others' territory at will in order to serve the interest of an overall equilibrium. The wishes of their own and other populaces and the principle of nationality could safely be ignored. If an alliance, such as that between Austria and France, was unpopular, or a people was divided by some territorial redistribution, that mattered less than whether a balance of power was obtained to the satisfaction of the principal rulers of Europe. But the French Revolution had freed a genie from the bottle, and the best efforts of Metternich and the conservative powers after 1815 were not going to suffice to persuade it to return.

CONCLUSION

At the risk of over-simplifying complex events which do not quite fit any single interpretation, it may be argued that the Revolution began with a vaguely formulated conception of international affairs resembling in many respects the 'great community of mankind' outlined in the first chapter. It then graduated to a much clearer notion of a 'universal society' under French hegemony. In both cases the French Revolution posed a fundamental challenge to that general consensus about the ends, means, and essential structure of international relations that is termed here 'the Westphalian conception of international society'. But there were important differences between the challenges posed by these two alternative models of international society. In its first phase, the Revolution threatened the legitimacy of dynastic governments, the principle that states had no right to intervene in each other's internal affairs, and some of the basic tenets of international law. It made it difficult for diplomacy to function because of the mutual incomprehension between the Revolution and Europe. Most fundamentally, it opposed the idea of state sovereignty with the conception of national self-determination. However, the Revolutionary and

Napoleonic drive towards predominance threatened the European balance of power and ultimately the survival of independent states.

Just as there were two distinct challenges to the Westphalian order, so did international society offer a dual response. Those powers which were most threatened by the ideas associated with the 'great community' reacted by trying to make the Westphalian framework fit the end of strengthening, legitimizing, and preserving the political order of the *ancien régime*. In so doing they too diverged in significant ways from the Westphalian international society, in particular in their efforts to establish a general right of international intervention against revolutions, which culminated in the Protocol of Troppau in 1820.

England, which was much less threatened by the implications of France's would-be 'great community', concentrated instead upon the necessity of restoring the balance of power and preventing any future bid for universal hegemony. Hence, English diplomacy both during and after the war tended to resist proposals for a general right of intervention by the great powers against revolutionary developments in another country. The British aim was to develop some collective means to make the balance of power system function more effectively and, in Pitt's words, to re-establish 'a general system of Public Law in Europe'.

The two different preoccupations of the European powers led them to very different conclusions about the nature of the post-war order. Both accepted the necessity for a great power concert, which would institutionalize in some sense the wartime co-operation amongst the powers, but while the English saw the Concert as a means of protecting Europe against any future prospect of a universal society, their allies saw the re-emergence of the pernicious doctrines of the great community as the main danger, and pressed for the Concert to be organized accordingly. In the end the divisions amongst them were too great for the most ambitious aspirations for the Concert of Europe to be fully realized.

The Westphalian international society survived after 1815 but it did not survive unaltered. Just as Revolutionary France had been obliged to adjust to some of the conventions and patterns of the society of states, so too did a process of 'reverse socialization' operate, in which subtle changes began to appear in the underlying assumptions and *modus operandi* of the international society as a result of the influence of the revolutionary state. The revolutionary ideas of nationality and popular support gradually displaced dynastic convenience as principles of legitimacy. Dynastic wars similarly became a thing of the past. The notion that the international community could expect states to observe generally accepted standards in their conduct of their internal affairs slowly took hold. Indeed the very idea of an international community as something more than a loose association of completely independent sovereign states—of a family of nations—came to play an increasingly significant part in the international relations of the nineteenth century. The Concert of Europe was a clear reflection of this, with its acceptance of a great power role in the management of the international system, its use of conference diplomacy, and its attempt to give international law a more central position.

4

State and Class
The Russian Revolution

THE DEVELOPMENT OF INTERNATIONAL SOCIETY IN THE NINETEENTH CENTURY

One of the implications of the Westphalian system, and its sanctification of the state, was that an individual's membership of his state overrode competing aspects of his social identity: his duties as a citizen were greater than his obligations as a human being (or worker, artist, intellectual, etc.).[1] The continuing fascination of natural law doctrines for philosophers tended to obscure this central fact in much discussion of international relations until the early nineteenth century. Some contractarian theorists, for instance, represented state sovereignty as primarily an internal matter, involving a state authority's relationship with its citizens, with natural law providing some constraint upon the powers of sovereigns within their own domain and, by extension, in the state's foreign relations. The idea of a society of sovereign states, constrained mainly by such rules and obligations as could be derived from its own inner logic, as an association of independent entities which acknowledged no moral, political, or legal superior, was slow to take hold, even in the writings of Vattel, who had the clearest insight into the nature of the 'anarchical international society' of the eighteenth century.

The American Revolution, to some degree, and the French Revolution, to a considerable extent, were influenced by the conception of a 'great community of mankind', which derives from natural law. However, the most serious challenge posed by the French Revolution to the international system came not from the idealistic advocacy of the breaking down of national frontiers that

---

[1] A. Linklater, *Men and Citizens in the Theory of International Relations* (London, 1982), develops this distinction.

characterized its early years but from the threat that it might establish a universal French hegemony. The ideology of the French Revolution, as distinct from its practice, especially under Napoleon, did not attempt to refute the essential idea of the state, but tried rather to suggest a new basis of legitimacy in the doctrine of the 'will of the nation' to replace the old notion of dynastic right. The aim of the American Revolution, likewise, was not to do away with the state, but to create a more perfect state, founded on republican ideals. Indeed, the ideas of nationalism and liberalism promoted by these revolutions actually strengthened the notion of the overriding rights of the state, since one fostered a sense of emotional identification with the state that was far stronger than the previous, essentially legal, bond between state and citizen, while the other, by promising a state that was more responsive to the needs and wishes of its members, added material interest to the legal and emotional ties of sovereignty and nationalism. It would take a doctrine that attempted to reject nationalism and liberalism as well as the state to be thoroughly subversive of the Westphalian conception of international society.

This is not to say that the Westphalian international society survived entirely unchanged in the nineteenth century. The revolutionary ideas of nationalism and liberalism implied and eventually achieved a new basis of international legitimacy, while the endeavour made in 1815 to reimpose and enforce the old international order actually brought about various subtle amendments to it.

The most obvious of these was apparent as early as 1814, in the decision of the four leading opponents of France to reserve to themselves the working out of 'a system of real and permanent balance of power in Europe'.[2] This in effect created a special category of 'great powers', and, by implication, organized international society along hierarchical lines, contrary to a strict interpretation of the principle of the equality of states.

Potentially more far-reaching than this decision, which essentially ratified an already existing reality, was the intention of the great powers not merely to lay down the terms of the peace settlement but to play a subsequent role in the management of

---

[2] Secret article in the first Treaty of Paris, cited in C. K. Webster, *The Congress of Vienna* (London, 1934), 45.

international relations. The ordering instruments of eighteenth-century international society—the balance of power, diplomacy, and international law—had functioned in a decentralized fashion, as befitted a society organized around the principle of sovereign equality. The idea that the great powers should assume a special managerial role in the international system, and in particular that they should exercise a form of tutelage over smaller powers, might imply a centralized directorate or joint hegemony with extensive powers of intervention in the internal affairs of states as well as control over their external relations. Indeed, just such an arrangement was greatly desired by Austria and Russia, the two states with most to lose from the revolutionary ideas of nationalism and liberalism. However, the powers were divided amongst themselves as to the precise responsibilities of their proposed European Concert, and this, together with continuing rivalries and competition among them, meant that the Concert system was much less extensive and effective than had been envisaged by Metternich and Tsar Alexander.

The legal basis for the Concert was the suitably vague sixth article of the Quadruple Alliance of 1814, by which the powers agreed to continue meeting 'for the purpose of consulting upon their common interests and for the consideration of the measures which . . . shall be considered the most salutary for the repose and prosperity of Nations and for the maintenance of the Peace of Europe'. Metternich was in no doubt that the chief threat to Europe's 'repose' emanated from revolutionary doctrines, and that the powers should assert a general right of intervention to forestall revolutionary upheavals. He continued to uphold this position, with varying degrees of success, at the post-war Congresses of Aix-la-Chapelle (1818), Troppau (1820), and Laibach (1821).[3] The Holy Alliance sponsored by the Tsar had the similar aim of uniting the powers around the twin principles of Christianity and defence of the legitimacy of all established governments.

However, Castlereagh, Britain's foreign minister, resisted such unlimited commitments with equal consistency. The purpose of the Alliance in his view was specifically to contain France and, more generally, to uphold the balance of power that had been created at the Congress of Vienna. It should not concern itself with

---

[3] H. Kissinger, *A World Restored* (Boston 1957), although controversial as a work of history, still has the best general discussion of the conflicting principles of Metternich and Castlereagh.

'subordinate, remote and speculative cases of danger'.[4] Castlereagh was not opposed to a right of intervention under certain circumstances but, he argued:

The only safe principle is that of the law of nations: that no State has a right to endanger its neighbours by its internal proceedings, and that if it does, provided they exercise a sound discretion, their right of interference is clear.[5]

A 'universal alliance for the peace and happiness of the world' was, he believed, impractical, but the Quadruple Alliance had gone further than any previous agreement in accepting great power obligations to settle differences, watch over the peace of Europe, and secure the observance of treaties. All of these, however, essentially strengthened international society without altering its Westphalian principles. The idea of an 'Alliance Solidaire' to 'support the state of succession, government and possession within all other states from violence and attack' logically implied in his view the previous establishment of a system of international government capable of securing and enforcing 'upon all kings and nations an internal system of peace and justice'. As he saw it, without such an international government 'all notions of general and unqualified guarantee must be abandoned' and states must rely upon their own resources with only such assistance as other states were prepared to lend them according to circumstances, provided it was in line with international law.[6] This interpretation of the Concert of Europe, with its emphasis upon only a limited right of intervention, comes closest to describing the way in which the system actually operated during the nineteenth century.

Although no international government appeared, the nineteenth century did witness some strengthening of the principal devices by which order had been maintained in the Westphalian system: the balance of power, diplomacy, and international law. In the case of the balance of power this was achieved mainly through a more formal and self-conscious approach to maintaining that balance, particularly by Britain, and by a more complex and sophisticated understanding of the concept of balance than that which had

[4] Castlereagh's State Paper of 5 May 1820, H. Temperley and L. M. Penson (eds.), *Foundations of British Foreign Policy* (London, 1966), 48–63.
[5] 'Memorandum on the Treaties of 1814 and 1815', in Webster, *The Congress of Vienna*, 166–71.
[6] Ibid.

prevailed in the eighteenth century. Paul Schroeder has traced the development of the concept during the nineteenth century, from the classic 'balance of power' notion, which stressed 'balance through compensations and indemnities, the calculation of forces on the basis of territory, population and revenues and the management of threats and crises through hostile alliances and coalitions', to a much broader 'political equilibrium' involving a 'balance of satisfaction, a balance of rights and obligations and a balance of performance and payoffs, rather than a balance of power'.[7]

The principal development in the area of diplomacy was the greatly increased use of conferences to consider and sometimes settle matters of general interest. This strengthened the belief that European international society was moving beyond the loose and very limited association of the eighteenth century towards the idea of an international community with at least an informal decision-making structure in which all had the right to be involved. The most ambitious period of conference diplomacy, that of the congress system of 1815–22, foundered upon the irreconcilable differences between the British and Austrian approaches to the Concert of Europe, and later proposals by Metternich and others for permanent or standing conferences on specific questions also came to nothing.[8] However, permanent organizations, called public international unions, were created to deal with various technical issues, such as postal services, and conferences continued to be held up to the ambassadors' conference on the Albanian question in 1913. The two Hague Conferences of 1899 and 1907 were attended by many non-European states, marking a transition between a primarily European and a world-wide international society.

There were parallel developments in the field of international law. These occurred at several different levels. Fundamentally, the powers sought, with varying degrees of success, to adopt what Clark calls 'a procedure of international legitimation of change'.[9] In particular, there were repeated attempts throughout the century to affirm the principle that territorial settlements agreed to in treaties could only be revised with the consent of all signatories—if at all.

---

[7] P. W. Schroeder, 'The Nineteenth-Century System: Balance of Power or Political Equilibrium', *Review of International Studies*, 15/2 (Apr. 1989), 135–53.

[8] F. H. Hinsley, *Power and the Pursuit of Peace* (Cambridge, 1963), 213–16.

[9] I. Clark, *Reform and Resistance in the International Order* (Cambridge, 1980), 91.

This principle was ignored during the extensive territorial redistributions of the 1850s and 1860s, but it was striking that the leading revisionist powers immediately sought to have their gains confirmed by treaty, and the principle was formally reaffirmed in the London Protocol of 1871.[10] There were also several attempts by the powers collectively to guarantee certain treaties (such as those defining the status of Switzerland, Belgium, Luxembourg, and the Congo), and to underwrite treaties in another way, by accepting self-denying ordinances with respect to particular areas. Finally, there were a great many treaties establishing rules and regulations in various technical and economic areas and also in humanitarian matters of common concern, such as slavery. This development went alongside an increased use of arbitration procedures to deal with issues where, in the parlance of the time, 'neither honour nor vital interest' was involved.

All of these developments contributed to an increased awareness of the social context within which the European states conducted their international relations as well as to some refinement of the *modus operandi* of international society. Unsurprisingly, Metternich was one of the strongest advocates of the need for states to base their policies upon an acceptance of the reality of international society although, equally predictably, he saw the defence of legitimate rights rather than simply political equilibrium as the foundation-stone of international society:

Politics is the science of the vital interests of states in its widest meaning. Since, however, an isolated state no longer exists . . . we must always view the *society* of states as the essential condition of the modern world . . . The great axioms of political science proceed from the knowledge of the true political interests of *all states*; it is upon these general interests that rests the guarantee of their existence . . . Modern society . . . exhibits the application of the principle of solidarity and of the balance of power between states . . . The establishing of international relations on the basis of reciprocity under the guarantee of respect for acquired rights . . . constitutes in our time the essence of politics.[11]

Even some of the revolutionary governments formed during the 1848 revolutions showed that they had learned one lesson from the experience of the French Revolution when they sought to assure the

---

[10] F. R. Bridge and R. Bullen, *The Great Powers and the European States System, 1815–1914* (London, 1980), 11–13.
[11] Cited in E. V. Gulick, *Europe's Classical Balance of Power* (New York, 1967), 32.

great powers of their attachment to the basic principles of the European international society. The French Foreign Minister, Lamartine, for instance, while asserting in his 'Manifesto to Europe' that the new French republic did not require international recognition in order to exist, emphasized France's desire to enter into 'the family of established governments, as a regular power, and not as a phenomenon destructive of European order'. He also advocated an early version of the doctrine of peaceful coexistence:

Monarchy and republicanism are not, in the eyes of wise statesmen, absolute principles, arrayed in deadly conflict against each other; they are facts which contrast one with another and which may exist face to face by mutually understanding and respecting each other.[12]

Similar sentiments were expressed by Heinrich von Gagern, President of the Frankfurt Parliament, when he resisted demands for a pan-German union on the grounds that this would violate German obligations to the 'European family of peoples'.[13]

The fact that the European powers clearly perceived themselves as constituting a society of states is further evidenced by the manner in which they set out criteria for the admission of other states to full membership of the 'family of nations', or to the right to be accepted as equal sovereign states. These criteria were encapsulated in the concept of a 'standard of civilization' which had to be met by any aspirants to full statehood. This did not so much imply that the would-be state had to behave internally in a manner deemed 'civilized' as that it needed to show itself capable of performing, to a minimum standard, certain governmental functions including protecting foreign nationals, entering into diplomatic relations, and meeting obligations under international law.[14] When the governments of countries like China, and initially Japan, seemed unable to carry out these duties, they were forced to accept an 'unequal' relationship with the European powers, under which the latter demanded various extraterritorial rights on the grounds that the former could not perform the obligations expected of a sovereign state.[15]

[12] Cited in F. Eyck (ed.), *The Revolutions of 1848–49* (Edinburgh, 1972), 39.
[13] Ibid. 114–15.
[14] G. W. Gong, *The Standard of 'Civilization' in International Society* (Oxford, 1984), pp. vii-viii and *passim*.
[15] See the chapters on China and Japan by G. W. Gong and H. Suganami in H. Bull and A. Watson (eds.), *The Expansion of International Society* (Oxford, 1984), 171–200.

Although the nineteenth century witnessed developments of this kind which strengthened and refined the Westphalian international society, these proved incapable of preventing the general collapse of the international system in 1914–18. The root cause of this was the impact of nationalism upon the nineteenth-century structure of international relations. Although, as already suggested, nationalism did not pose a threat to the founding principle of the Westphalian international society—the pre-eminent position of the state—since it elevated the state, or at least the nation state, yet further, it did weaken four of the pillars of the system as it actually operated in the nineteenth century. The first of these was the balance of power. The creation of a powerful German state on the basis of nationality made it much more difficult for a general European balance to be created or sustained. At the same time, the threat of the total eclipse of the great multinational empires of Austria and Turkey left those two states permanently apprehensive and insecure. Moreover, the claims of nationality were inherently antagonistic to some of the mechanisms through which the balance of power had traditionally operated: for example, the notion that states should receive territorial 'compensation' for a rival's gains in the interests of preserving harmony within the system as a whole ran counter to the national rights of the residents of the compensatory territory. Secondly, national self-determination offered a powerful alternative to the specific principle of international legitimacy that had functioned during the eighteenth century and which Metternich had tried to restore in the nineteenth: the rights of existing rulers. The triumph of the new principle over the old was formally confirmed at the Paris Peace Conference of 1919. Thirdly, the great powers became less willing to exercise self-restraint in the general interest, partly because nationalism projected an even more exalted idea of the 'self' to be restrained than had some of the fantasies of the eighteenth-century despots, and one with a much stronger emotional appeal. Finally, the idea of the sanctity of treaties—and the territorial arrangements underwritten in them—was hard to reconcile with claims that territorial boundaries should be drawn along national lines.

The Paris Peace Conference of 1919 was an attempt to rebuild international society in accordance with the new principle of national self-determination, with a new concept of collective security to replace the old balance of power approach to international order, and a formalization of the Concert system in the shape of the League of Nations. This is considered in more detail in Chapter 5 but it may be briefly noted here that the new international system was intended, as the Concert system had been, to modify and improve upon the Westphalian conception of international society, not to overthrow it or even fundamentally to transform it. Piecemeal reform was not, however, among the aims of the Russian Revolution, which presented the international system with an even greater challenge than had Napoleon.

THE BOLSHEVIK THEORY OF INTERNATIONAL RELATIONS

The victorious faction in the Russian Revolution owed its legitimacy and even *raison d'être* to a doctrine which represented the most systematic and comprehensive denial of the validity of all the basis tenets of the Westphalian structure—including those of the 'reformed Westphalia' of 1919—yet to have appeared. The most pragmatic of the Bolsheviks soon appreciated that, whatever long-term aspirations they might cherish concerning the overthrow of the existing international order, for the present they needed to face certain harsh realities. These included the fact that to protect their own power, their revolution, and, as they saw it, the future of socialism, they had also to protect a doctrinal paradox: a revolution based upon an ideology that represented itself as the antithesis of the state had taken the concrete form of a state. This central paradox led to others, including the dilemma arising because in order to function as a state in a society of states, Soviet Russia needed to assume many of the attributes of other states, and accept some of the rules—if not outright membership—of what it believed to be a world system fundamentally antagonistic to itself. The Bolsheviks' ideology, despite the herculean contortions of Soviet theorists, was, in truth, wholly inadequate to the task of reconciling these contradictions, but since it alone legitimized their monopoly of power, it could not be discarded. Yet while it remained the official creed of the state and part of the belief system of the Soviet leadership, the Soviet Union would inevitably both perceive and encounter hostility from the established powers. The phase of paranoia that appears to be a normal accompaniment of radical revolutions was, in the Bolsheviks' case, virtually guaranteed by the inherent character of their ideology.

Four central aspects of Marxism are of particular importance in the context of this discussion: Marx's belief in an objectively determinable historical process, his view that the relations between economic classes constitute the motive force of history, his argument concerning the inevitability of struggle, and his assumption of the necessity of international revolution. Marx's thought, and its interpretation and development by Engels and Lenin, is not free from its own internal contradictions and ambiguities, including several in the four areas to be considered here, and Soviet theorists have found it convenient to stress different aspects of these theories as changing political circumstances have required. However, each cluster of ideas has a core sufficiently consistent and authoritative to be regarded as identifying the central Marxist position in that case, and thus to allow the implications of that position for the Westphalian international society to be assessed.

For Marx and his followers, history was not a series of random, unpredictable and unconnected events which could be given sense and meaning only subjectively, by the historian's attempt to impose his own intellectual framework of cause and effect upon them. Rather, history was a single process, governed by its own inner laws, through which society, which was conceived of as an organic whole, developed towards ends that were inherent in the nature of the historical process and therefore comprehensible to those who could discern the forces impelling the process.[16] The key to such insight into the laws of historical development was to be discovered by shifting the attention away from the traditional concerns of history with the doings of kings and queens and the interactions between their states towards deeper and far less limited forces: economics, changes in technology, and the social consequences of

[16] For this brief discussion of Marxism, I have relied primarily on the following: K. Marx, *Capital*, 1887 ed. (3 vols.; London 1954), F. Engels, *Anti-Dühring*, 1878 (Moscow, 1954), F. Engels, *Ludwig Feuerbach and the End of Classical German Philosophy*, 1888 ed. (Moscow, 1946) (including K. Marx, *Theses on Feuerbach*), K. Marx and F. Engels, *The Communist Manifesto*, ed. H. J. Laski (London, 1948). G. A. Cohen, *Karl Marx's Theory of History: A Defence* (Oxford, 1978), I. Berlin, *Karl Marx*, 2nd edn. (London, 1948), J. Plamenatz, *German Marxism and Russian Communism* (London, 1954) Z. A. Jordan, *The Evolution of Dialectical Materialism* (Harmondsworth, 1967), V. I. Lenin, *Karl Marx*, 1918 ed. (Peking, 1967), *The State and Revolution*, 1917 (Peking, 1976).

these. In his attempt to 'lay bare the economic law of motion of modern society',[17] Marx argued that technological changes gave rise to particular social orders, with all men and women belonging to one or another economic class according to their role in economic production. Their class membership gave them their primary social identity, with other claims to their allegiance being secondary, or, in the case of the state, essentially false, since the state was, in Lenin's words, 'an organ of class rule, an organ for the oppression of one class by another'.[18] It followed from 'historical materialism' that the true motive force of history was the struggle between classes, not conflict among nations or some other possible determinant. In the particular historical epoch during which Marx was writing, one class, the capitalist bourgeoisie, was dominant, while a new class, the industrial proletariat, was oppressed, exploited, and alienated from society. The chief difference between the current and previous epochs was to be that the inevitable victory of the proletariat over the bourgeoisie would bring about an end to class struggle—and to such instruments of class struggle, employed by previously dominant classes, as the state. The proletariat was more alienated from state and society than any class before it—'the working men have no country'—and was therefore more likely to be a truly international (or transnational) force. In Engels' words:

Because the condition of the workers of all countries is the same, because their interests are the same, they must also fight together, they must oppose the brotherhood of the bourgeoisie of all nations with a brotherhood of the workers of all nations.[19]

The proletariat was the instrument through which a new classless and stateless world order would be brought into being. 'National differences and antagonism between peoples', Marx believed, somewhat optimistically, 'are daily more and more vanishing, owing to the development of the bourgeoisie, to freedom of commerce, to the world market, to uniformity in the mode of production and in the conditions of life corresponding thereto.'[20] The historic role of the proletariat was to accelerate this process

[17] Marx, *Capital*, i. 20.
[18] Lenin, *The State and Revolution*, 10.
[19] Cited in F. Petrenko and V. Popov, *Soviet Foreign Policy: Objectives and Principles* (Moscow, 1981), 53.
[20] *The Communist Manifesto*, 142.

with the inevitable consequence spelled out in the most famous passage in Engels' *Anti-Dühring*:

The first act in which the state really comes forward as the representative of the whole of society—the taking possession of the means of production in the name of society—is at the same time its last independent act as a state . . . The government of persons is replaced by the administration of things. The state is not 'abolished', it withers away.[21]

This was inevitably going to be a process that was both dynamic and revolutionary. Nothing in history ever stood still; in fact, dialectical logic dictated that any existing state of things included its own negation—the seeds of its inevitable downfall. The outcome of a dialectical process was necessarily revolutionary since the dialectical method:

regards every historically developed social form as in fluid movement, and therefore takes into account its transient nature not less than its momentary existence; because it lets nothing impose upon it, and is in its essence critical and revolutionary.[22]

Revolutionary conditions were not just a theoretical imperative but were also created inevitably by the deepening hardship of the proletariat.

Finally, revolution, when it came, would be world-wide. This, too, was both a theoretical and a practical necessity. If states were artificial entities, without any genuinely independent existence, a revolution which was essentially a confrontation between two international classes could not be confined within the meaningless boundaries of one state. In Engels' words, revolution:

will take place simultaneously in all civilized countries . . . It will also exercise a considerable influence upon the other countries of the world and will completely change and much accelerate their former course of development. It is a world revolution and will therefore have the whole world as its arena.[23]

Moreover, if a revolution in a single country did not very quickly become international, it would be destroyed by the international bourgeoisie that encircled it. Marx declared that the proletariat 'must make the revolution permanent . . . until the Proletariat has

---

[21] Cited in Lenin, *The State and Revolution*, 20–1.

[22] Marx, *Capital*, i. 29.

[23] Cited in E. R. Goodman, *The Soviet Design for a World State* (New York, 1960), 2.

conquered State power . . . not only in one country but in all the dominant countries of the world'.[24]

What new social and political forms were to follow the withering away of the state—and the state system—was far from clear, mainly because of Marx's and Engels' assumption of the primacy of economic factors. The world-wide victory of the proletariat would complete the development of a single world economy, rendering any remaining national divisions unnecessary. A new type of society would emerge, based on fraternal solidarity among peoples, as depicted in Engels' idealized Paris Commune: 'the flag of the Commune is the flag of the World Republic'.[25] This did not provide much guidance for Marx's followers. When Lenin and Trotsky urged the working class to resist the call of patriotism during the First World War, they did so in the name of internationalism but found it difficult to go much further than Engels in defining their future world order with any clarity. Trotsky argued:

In the present historical conditions the proletariat is not interested in defending an anachronistic national 'Fatherland', which has become the main impediment to economic advance, but in the creation of a new, more powerful and stable fatherland, the republican United States of Europe, as the foundation for the United States of the World.[26]

Lenin similarly argued that Marxism 'puts forward in the place of any kind of nationalism an internationalism which is the fusion of all nations in a higher unity'.[27] He was, however, already envisaging the possibility of socialism existing, even if only for a short time, in a single country, and was therefore less happy with the implication of Trotsky's emphasis on a 'United States of Europe', that revolution had to occur simultaneously throughout Europe. But in the course of countering Trotsky's arguments he failed to furnish any real clarification of the nature of the future socialist world community:

The United States of the World . . . is that state form for the unification and freedom of nations, which we identify with socialism . . . As a separate slogan, however, the United States of the World would hardly be correct,

[24] Cited in E. R. Goodman, *The Soviet Design for a World State* (New York, 1960), 5.

[25] Ibid. 7.

[26] Cited in I. Deutscher, *The Prophet Armed: Trotsky, 1879–1921* (London, 1954), 215.

[27] Cited in E. H. Carr, *The Bolshevik Revolution, 1917–1923* (3 vols.; Harmondsworth, 1971), i. 432.

first because it means the same thing as socialism and second, because it might foster an incorrect interpretation about the possibility of a victory of socialism in one country, and about the relations of such a country to others. Unequal economic and political development is an unconditional law of capitalism. From this it follows that in the beginning the victory of socialism is possible in a few, or even in one capitalist country, taken separately.[28]

Although the precise form of the Marxists' new world order was extremely vague, the comprehensive nature of the challenge posed by Marxist doctrines to the Westphalian conception of international society was unmistakable. At the heart of the Westphalian system was a tacit assumption that the lawful authority of the state could be established within the context of an international society that would both legitimize state sovereignty and provide some degree of order for the system as a whole. The political philosophy underlying these ideas, with its stress on such concepts as 'the state', 'law', 'order', 'legitimacy', and 'international society', was deemed by Marxists to be not merely untenable but part of a structure of oppression of one class by another. The Marxian alternative was, in effect, a very distinctive version of the 'great community', in which the most important social relationships were economic rather than politico-legal, and which cut across state boundaries to create a focus for allegiance amongst people higher than that required by their state. The state was, in reality, an instrument of oppression, and its claim to provide order was a means of legalizing and perpetuating this oppression.[29] This meant, amongst other things, that there was no genuine basis for a principle of non-intervention amongst states. The concept of sovereign equality, corner-stone of the Westphalian system, implied that states had the right to conduct their internal affairs as they chose. The attempt by the conservative powers in the Concert of Europe to discard this principle had failed to make much headway, but the Marxian challenge to it had a far more profound intellectual content. If classes were international, it was quite natural for workers in one state to offer fraternal aid to the proletariat of another state. Moreover, given the need for revolution to be international for it to survive anywhere, the export of revolution was a practical as well as a philosophical necessity.

[28] Cited in Goodman, *The Soviet Design*, 129.
[29] Lenin, *The State and Revolution*, 10.

An additional divergence from the Westphalian structure derived from the Marxist view of history. The Westphalian system was essentially static in conception, having the aim of legitimizing an existing structure of authority and an international order based on the supremacy of the state. The shape of particular international orders might change as powers waxed and waned, but the essential principles of the international society within which states conducted their affairs would remain the same. The French and American revolutions had, it is true, introduced the new ideas of nationalism and liberalism, but it had eventually been possible to incorporate these into the Westphalian system, with only marginal amendments to its core principles. Marxist doctrines on the primacy of economics and of classes had contradicted the central tenet of the Westphalian system: sovereign equality. The Marxist view of history undermined other aspects of it. If all things were in a state of flux, not only was any particular social order doomed to collapse, but, since history always moved in a progressive direction, 'legitimacy' belonged not to authorities deemed lawful by the false criteria of bourgeois thought but to the forces working to overthrow them. For practical purposes, this implied a principle of international legitimacy based, not on dynastic right nor on national self-determination, nor even on the liberal democracy desired by Woodrow Wilson, but on the interests of the international proletariat and the cause of world revolution. Later chapters will show the fundamental conflict between Marxism and the principal corner-stones of the post-Westphalian approach to international order: diplomacy, the balance of power, and international law.

RECONCILIATION AND ADAPTATION: THE BOLSHEVIKS IN POWER

Experience can work to reinforce or to weaken previously held views.[30] This is not, however, a simple matter of incorrect ideas being modified or correct ideas being strengthened as evidence emerges to refute or confirm them. To use Kenneth Boulding's

---

[30] The following argument has also appeared in J. D. Armstrong, *Revolutionary Diplomacy: Chinese Foreign Policy and the United Front Doctrine* (Berkeley and Los Angeles, 1977), 11–12.

analogy, the Aztecs who offered human sacrifices to obtain good harvests would not necessarily have ceased to do this if one year's harvest were bad.[31] They might have increased the numbers being sacrificed in the belief that the bad harvest 'proved' that the gods were not satisfied with the existing offering. Similarly, if ideological tenets do not appear adequately to account for some event or to describe some situation, the adherents to the ideology may *adapt* their doctrines to make them fit reality more closely, or they may attempt to reconcile an apparent contradiction by depicting reality in such a way that it appears to fit the doctrine. Where a doctrine has near sacred qualities in the eyes of its adherents, or where a ruling élite owes its legitimacy to the doctrine, major difficulties are likely to be encountered in any serious attempt to adapt it, which means in practice that 'reconciliation' is the safer and more frequently adopted course. Where significant 'adaptation' does occur, it is likely to be part of a process of socialization, whereby the norms of the larger society are internalized and made a part of the belief system of those accepting the ideology—as when a revolutionary state finds itself conforming to the conventions of international society.

The case of Lenin in this context is a complex one. Even before 1917 he had made substantial amendments to Marxism, for example in his ideas about the nature and role of a revolutionary party. But he undoubtedly saw these as attempts to find more effective ways of putting into practice the core doctrines of Marx and Engels. Where he did attempt important theoretical revisions, as in his pamphlet on imperialism, he was motivated both by the desire for 'reconciliation'—the need to show that the world, despite certain appearances to the contrary, still conformed to Marxian explanations of its functioning—and by the requirements of 'adaptation', to take account of developments in capitalism since Marx's time. After the October Revolution his primary objective was to ensure the survival of Soviet Russia, at first against a majority of his colleagues who could not bring themselves to accept what they perceived to be an ideological absurdity. However, even here Lenin's approach had elements of both 'reconciliation' and 'adaptation'. The aim was not to become integrated into a capitalist world order but to secure a breathing space to enable the inevitable,

[31] J. C. Farrell and A. P. Smith (eds.), *Image and Reality in World Politics* (New York, 1967).

but seemingly delayed, international revolution to take place. Where policies appeared to lead the 'socialist fatherland' to act in ways that were indistinguishable from the behaviour of capitalist states, these were to be viewed as mere tactical expedients, not as denoting a fundamental change in long-term strategy. This provided a convenient means by which Lenin's successors—up to Mikhail Gorbachev—might rationalize their own actions and so preserve the sole basis of their legitimacy. But it meant that the Soviet Union was unable to discard its claim to be the vanguard of world revolution, or even, at times, the need to act as though it was. This meant that the Soviet state was always in a somewhat uneasy relationship to international society: both inside and outside, half accepted and half rejected.

As early as 1902, Lenin argued that 'the revolution itself must not be regarded as a single act . . . but as a series of more or less powerful outbreaks rapidly alternating with periods of more or less complete calm'.[32] This assertion, made in the context of his plans for a new type of revolutionary party, foreshadowed his later attempts to explain the non-appearance of international revolution by his theory of the uneven development of capitalism. His advice to ultra-revolutionaries not to insist on summoning 'all available forces for the attack right now',[33] his argument in 1901 that 'a political alignment is determined not only by ultimate aims, but also by immediate aims, not only by general views but by the pressure of direct practical necessity',[34] and his insistence on building up strength before confrontations with enemies, on forming temporary alliances, even with unreliable elements, and on utilizing 'contradictions' amongst enemies were all tactical arguments, derived from his Party's domestic political experiences, which he was to utilize in the international arena.[35]

Despite Lenin's consistent emphasis on cautious tactics, and the few indications that before 1917 he was already contemplating the possibility and working out the implications of 'socialism in one

[32] Lenin, 'What is to be Done', *Collected Works*, v. (Moscow, 1961), 514.
[33] 'Where to begin', ibid. 20.
[34] 'Review of Home Affairs', ibid. 301.
[35] In addition to the works of Lenin already cited, advice of this kind is to be found in 'The Agrarian Programme of Russian Social Democracy', *Collected Works*, vi. 125, 'One Step forward Two Steps Back', ibid. vii. 330–4, 'Two Tactics of Social Democracy in the Democratic Revolution', ibid. ix. 85 and 91–2, and 'The Attitude of Bourgeois Parties', ibid. xii.

country' if only for a short period, there is no evidence that he did not anticipate international revolution following quite soon after the success of a revolution in a single country, or that he expected a revolutionary state to pursue anything but an essentially revolutionary policy internationally. There is no hint in his pre-1917 writings of the possibility that a revolutionary state might need to assume some of the attitudes of 'bourgeois' states or accept some of the conventions of the existing society of states. 'Legitimacy', for example, belonged to the working class and to whatever actions it took in the interests of the class struggle, not to the nation state:

The socialist movement cannot triumph within the old framework of the fatherland. It creates new and superior forms of human society, in which the legitimate needs and progressive aspirations of the working masses of *each* nationality will, for the first time, be met through international unity, provided existing national partitions are removed.[36]

This new doctrine of legitimacy applied before the revolution as well as after it:

we regard civil wars, i.e. wars waged by an oppressed class against the oppressor class . . . as fully legitimate and necessary.[37]

Furthermore, the chief task of successful revolutionaries was to aid the revolutionary cause elsewhere:

After expropriating the capitalists and organizing their own socialist production, the victorious proletariat of that country will arise against the rest of the world—the capitalist world—attracting to its cause the oppressed classes of other countries, stirring uprisings in those countries against the capitalists, and in case of need using even armed force against the exploiting classes and their states. The political form of a society wherein the proletariat is victorious in overthrowing the bourgeoisie will be a democratic republic, which will more and more concentrate the forces of the proletariat of a given nation or nations in the struggle against states that have not yet gone over to socialism.[38]

The ultimate objective was not to ensure the survival of any sort of sovereign state system but to form a world socialist union:

[36] 'The Position and Tasks of the Socialist International', in J. Riddell (ed.), *Lenin's Struggle for a Revolutionary International: Documents, 1907–1916* (New York, 1986), 162.

[37] Lenin and Zinoviev, 'Socialism and War', ibid. 120–4.

[38] 'On the Slogan for a United States of Europe', ibid. 260.

The aim of socialism is not only to end the division of mankind into tiny states and the isolation of nations in any form, it is not only to bring the nations closer together but to integrate them.[39]

Shortly before the October Revolution Lenin was still expounding the position he had adopted in the first months of the First World War. The war was a conflict brought about by imperialism and since the latter was the final stage of capitalism it presaged imminent proletarian revolution. The correct international line for socialists was to work for the defeat of their own governments since this would hasten the revolution. If 'the proletariat' won power in Russia, its foreign policy should be to call for an immediate and unconditional peace, not in the expectation that this would be accepted by any imperialist government, but on the assumption that it would be rejected and that such rejection would form the catalyst for a global revolutionary uprising. The correct 'proletarian' foreign policy should be one of alliance with 'the revolutionaries of the advanced countries' and also with another anti-imperialist force perceived to be of growing importance, 'the peoples oppressed by imperialism, primarily our neighbours in Asia'.[40] It may be noted in passing that in his increased emphasis on 'oppressed nations'—that is upon social groups distinguished by their national rather than class characteristics—Lenin was by implication accepting a world structured to some degree along national lines, as well as along class lines. It is true that the distinctions between these two characterizations of international society were blurred by his refusal to acknowledge what might appear to be the logical corollary of 'oppressed nations': the existence of complementary 'oppressor nations'. While the victims of oppression could apparently be classified without reference to any economic divisions within their ranks as members of a single category—the nation—their oppressors remained the familiar representatives of 'international capital'. Lenin's attitude towards nationalism derived from his sense of tactical expediency, insofar as he perceived support for nationalism to be a useful weapon in the international revolutionary struggle, but it opened a veritable Pandora's box of dispute and confusion. Many Asian communists were dismayed to discover that Lenin expected them to subordinate

---

[39] 'The Socialist Revolution and the Right of Nations to Self Determination', ibid. 356.

[40] Lenin, 'The Foreign Policy of the Russian Revolution', *Collected Works*, xxv. 86–7.

their internal class struggle to the cause of national unity against the common imperialist enemy.[41] A few of them, however, went much further than Lenin towards a conceptualization of international society that departed from conventional class categories. One of the founders of the Chinese Communist Party, Li Ta-chao, went so far as to suggest that racial conflict occupied essentially the same position as class struggle in the determination of world events:

The white peoples [see themselves] as the pioneers of culture in the world; they place themselves in a superior position and look down on other races as inferior. Because of this the race question has become a class question and the races on a world scale have come to confront each other as classes . . . The struggle between the white and coloured races will occur simultaneously with the class struggle . . . Thus it can be seen that the class struggle between the lower class coloured races and the upper class white race is already in embryonic form and its forward movement has not yet stopped.[42]

Li also held the related opinion that because of its inferior status *vis-à-vis* the rich, white countries, China could be considered a 'proletarian nation'. Given the pre-eminent place of 'the proletariat' within Marxist ideology, this could be taken to imply the superiority of such 'proletarian nations' over other states, even including the Soviet Union. This was a point of view that had been specifically criticized by the Comintern when it was advanced in the 1920s by Sultan Galiev, with reference to Muslim countries. Galiev had in fact gone one step further than Li by arguing that the Western proletariat would retain a colonialist attitude even after it had won victory in the revolution, in which case the only solution would be to reverse Marxism and impose a dictatorship of the 'proletarian nations' of the East over the former colonial powers of the West.[43]

To return to the Bolsheviks, nothing in their analysis of world affairs or their actions in the first weeks after the October Revolution suggests any intention to deviate from their alternative world-view. The mood of the times is captured by Trotsky's famous (though possibly apocryphal) statement of his intention to 'issue a

[41] See, for example, the Comintern debate on the 'national and colonial question' in 1920: *The Second Congress of the Communist International* (Washington, DC, 1920).

[42] M. Meisner, *Li Ta-chao and the Origins of Chinese Marxism* (Cambridge, Mass., 1967), 190–1. See also Armstrong, *Revolutionary Diplomacy*, 31–2.

[43] H. C. d'Encausse and S. R. Schram, *Marxism and Asia* (London, 1969), 35–6.

few revolutionary proclamations and shut up shop' on his assumption of the office of People's Commissar for Foreign Affairs.[44] Why should a revolutionary state, which denied the validity of the existing state system, surround itself with the trappings of traditional diplomacy when the whole edifice was about to collapse? Amongst the first of these 'revolutionary proclamations' was the decree on peace of 8 November 1917 in which the Bolsheviks called for a 'just and democratic peace' without annexations or indemnities.[45] The decree contains several points that are of particular interest in the present context. First, it appealed to 'peoples and their governments', and later addressed itself directly to the 'class conscious workers of the three most advanced countries', referring to the service rendered by these workers to the cause of socialism and progress over many years and expressing confidence that they would understand 'the mission now lying before them of liberating humanity from the horrors of war'.[46] Second, it explicitly based the decree on a new doctrine of legitimacy, which superseded any previous standard employed to establish lawful title to territory containing one nationality that had been incorporated by another:

By annexation or seizure of foreign territory the Government, in conformity with the legal consciousness of democracy in general and of the working class in particular, understands any incorporation of a small and weak nationality by a large and powerful state without a clear, definite, and voluntary statement of acceptance and willingness by the weak nationality, regardless of when this forcible incorporation took place, regardless also of how developed or how backward is the nation forcibly attached or forcibly detained . . . and finally regardless whether or not this large nation is located in Europe or in far off countries beyond the seas.[47]

Finally, the decree stated the new government's intention to abolish secret diplomacy, to conduct its negotiations openly and to publish all secret treaties concluded by its predecessors. Hence the decree managed to undermine in several different ways not only most of the central tenets of the Westphalian international society but the particular international order then prevailing, including the

---

[44] Trotsky approved of the spirit of this quotation but denied actually making it. Leon Trotsky, *My Life* (New York, 1930), 341.

[45] *Dokumenty vneshnei politiky (DVP)*, i. (Moscow, 1957), 11–14.

[46] Ibid. 13.   [47] Ibid. 12.

colonial system and the claim of the great powers to special rights and privileges.

In accordance with its promise in this decree, the Foreign Affairs Commissariat duly published a number of secret diplomatic documents. In its accompanying statement it declared:

Secret diplomacy is an essential tool in the hands of the propertied minority, which is compelled to deceive the majority in order to subordinate it to its interests. Imperialism, with its world-wide plans of aggression and predatory alliances and deals has brought the system of secret diplomacy to its highest development. The struggle against imperialism, which has bled white and ruined the people of Europe, means at the same time a struggle against capitalist diplomacy, which has cause enough to dread exposure.[48]

The 'world's peoples' had the right to learn about 'those plans which the financiers and industrialists have secretly forged with their parliamentary and diplomatic agents'. Once again a new criterion of legitimacy was invoked to justify such a dramatic departure from established practice:

The abolition of secret diplomacy is the foremost condition of honesty, for a popular, really democratic foreign policy. Soviet power sets as its aim the putting into practice of such a policy. That is precisely the reason why, while openly proposing to all belligerent peoples and their governments a speedy armistice, we are at the same time publishing the treaties and agreements, which have lost all their obligatory force for the Russian workforce, soldiers and peasants, who have taken power into their own hands.[49]

The Bolsheviks also gave notice in many lesser ways of their determination to approach international relations in a radically different manner from that of the states they believed to be intent on destroying them, with their underlying objective remaining the furtherance of the cause of international revolution. In Trotsky's words 'If the peoples of Europe do not arise and crush imperialism, we shall be crushed—that is beyond doubt.'[50] Two million roubles were set aside to be used by Bolshevik representatives abroad 'for the needs of the revolutionary movement' and specifically to assist 'the left internationalist wing of the workers' movement of all

---

[48] Ibid. 21.   [49] Ibid.
[50] Cited in A. E. Senn, *Diplomacy and Revolution* (Notre Dame, Ind., and London, 1974), 12.

countries, whether these countries are at war with Russia or are allied with her or whether they are remaining neutral'.[51]

The clear implication of most of the Bolsheviks' international activity up to this point was that they were speaking as representatives of a world-wide class to other members of that class, rather than as a government to other governments: the social context within which they saw themselves as operating was a transnational great community rather than a society of states. This was explicitly stated in the declaration accompanying the two million rouble grant:

Taking into consideration that the Soviet Government is based on the principles of the international solidarity of the proletariat and on the brotherhood of the toilers of all countries; that the struggle against war and imperialism can be brought to a completely successful conclusion only if waged on an international scale.[52]

In the same spirit, the Bolsheviks followed the French, in the idealistic, cosmopolitan phase of their revolution, by offering citizenship on a very liberal basis to foreigners and employing a number of foreign sympathizers both as agents abroad and in departments of the People's Commissariat of Foreign Affairs (Narkomindel).[53] Later on, Soviet appeals to allied forces landing in Russia urged them instead to return home and lead revolutions in their own countries so that 'together we shall form a world-wide co-operative commonwealth'.[54] By the same token state to state relations were downgraded and any international obligations which depended logically upon a conception of a society of states capable of conferring rights and duties upon its members were ignored. For Trotsky, there existed 'only one unwritten but sacred treaty, the treaty of the international solidarity of the proletariat'.[55] Even as late as March 1918, when American President Woodrow Wilson sent a conciliatory telegram to the Congress of Soviets, the reply of the Congress was couched in the implacable language of proletarian revolutionary solidarity rather than in the polite

[51] Cited in A. E. Senn, *Diplomacy and Revolution* (Notre Dame, Ind., and London, 1974), 15.

[52] Cited in J. Degras, *Soviet Documents on Foreign Policy*, i. (London, 1951), 22.

[53] Senn, *Diplomacy and Revolution*, 208, No. 10, and T. J. Uldricks, *Diplomacy and Ideology: The Origins of Soviet Foreign Relations, 1917–30* (London, 1979), 20. The liberal citizenship entitlement of the 1918 Constitution was dropped in the 1936 version.

[54] Carr, *The Bolshevik Revolution*, iii. 99.

[55] Ibid. 26.

formulas of government to government diplomacy. Addressed to 'the labouring and exploited classes' of the United States, it expressed the belief of the Congress that

the happy time is not far distant when the toiling masses of all bourgeois countries will throw off the yoke of capitalism and establish a socialist order of society, which alone is capable of assuring a firm and just peace as well as the cultural and material welfare of all toilers.[56]

By this point Soviet policy-making was dominated by the internal and external politics surrounding the Brest-Litovsk negotiations with the Germans, which, more than any other single event, forced the Bolsheviks to cast aside any illusions about the nature of the international realities that confronted them. However, even in this case it is worth noting that Lenin, the first to see the inevitable necessity of accepting German terms, was never able to secure an absolute majority of his colleagues in favour of the treaty. It was only accepted because Trotsky and three other members of the Central Committee were eventually, and reluctantly, persuaded to abstain from voting rather than support their preferred option of revolutionary war, which would have brought about Lenin's resignation.[57]

For Lenin the initiation of negotiations with Germany may well have been wholly dictated by the entirely pragmatic consideration of the survival of Bolshevik power in Russia.[58] Certainly by January 1918 he was beginning to argue that the existence of a socialist government in a single country had created a situation that had not been anticipated by Marxist theory and in which the primary consideration had to be the survival of the revolutionary state:

The correct conclusion from this is that the moment a socialist government triumphed in any one country, questions must be decided . . . exclusively from the point of view of the conditions which best make for the development and consolidation of the socialist revolution which has already begun.

[56] R. K. Debo, *Revolution and Survival: The Foreign Policy of Soviet Russia, 1917–18* (Liverpool, 1979), 243. Text of Soviet reply in *DVP* i. 211.

[57] Debo, *Revolution and Survival*, 113–69 and J. W. Wheeler-Bennett, *Brest-Litovsk: The Forgotten Peace* (London and New York, 1966).

[58] For the thesis that Lenin was committed to the idea of 'socialism in one country' and everything that it entailed from the beginning, see Piero Melograni, *Lenin and the Myth of World Revolution* (Atlantic Highlands, NJ, 1989).

In other words, the underlying principle of our tactics must not be, which of the two imperialisms it is more profitable to aid at this juncture, but rather, how the socialist revolution can be most firmly and reliably ensured the possibility of consolidating itself, or, at least, of maintaining itself in one country until it is joined by other countries.[59]

In this he was strongly opposed by Bukharin and others who adhered to what they believed to be the correct 'internationalist' position, namely that the interests of world revolution overrode the interests of preserving Soviet power in Russia. Indeed, without world revolution Soviet power could not be maintained for much longer, so that a policy aimed at securing the survival of Soviet Russia at the expense of world revolution would inevitably be self-defeating. As Bukharin put it:

We said and we say that in the end everything depends on whether the international revolution conquers or does not conquer. In the end international revolution—and that alone—is our salvation . . . Renouncing international propaganda, we renounce the keenest edged weapons that we had.[60]

Trotsky's position was a little more ambiguous, since he was prepared to participate in the Brest-Litovsk negotiations, but only as a tactic to buy time while the proletariat in Germany and elsewhere readied itself for revolution. But both Trotsky and Bukharin shared a concern that Lenin's approach smacked of traditional nationalism and defence of the Russian state and accorded ill with the internationalism and anti-statism of Marxism.

These were charges that Lenin took some pains to deny. In the process of doing so, he developed what amounted to a fundamental adaptation of the Marxist approach to international relations. His aim was to demonstrate that the goal of world revolution was compatible with working for the survival of Soviet Russia; this inevitably meant that he had to confront the reality that, without world revolution, Soviet Russia could not be seen primarily as one part of a global class, but must be acknowledged to be a state in a world of other states with which it was obliged to coexist.

Four interrelated arguments were at the heart of this new perspective, which, although possibly apparent in embryonic form before the October Revolution, received its most comprehensive

[59] See Piero Melograni, *Lenin and the Myth of World Revolution* (Atlantic Highlands, NJ, 1989), 5.
[60] Cited in Carr, *The Bolshevik Revolution*, iii. 61.

formulation during and just after the period of the Brest-Litovsk negotiations (3 December 1917–3 March 1918). Lenin's first assertion was that defending the Soviet state was not the same as defending any other sort of state:

We do not stand for the state, we do not defend the status of a great Power: of Russia nothing is left save Great Russia. These are not national interests; we affirm that the interests of socialism, the interests of world socialism, are higher than national interests, higher than the interests of the state. We are 'defencists' of the socialist fatherland.[61]

He advanced the notion of a 'socialist fatherland' in an attempt to show that consolidating Bolshevik power and defending the Soviet state were not just compatible with advancing the interests of socialism world-wide—the two were virtually synonymous. The concept of a 'socialist fatherland' had both an internal and an external aspect. Internally the socialist revolution was far from complete, and the Bolshevik hold on power was still somewhat tenuous. On the other hand, the precise date of the outbreak of world revolution could not be predicted. Therefore in the conflict between a concrete reality and a mere hope the former had to win: internal affairs took precedence over external. As Lenin put it in the Twenty-One Theses for Peace with which he defended his approach to the Brest-Litovsk negotiations:

The situation in which the Socialist Revolution in Russia finds itself is to be taken as the point of departure for every definition of the international task confronting the new Soviet Government.[62]

Externally, the Soviet state faced numerous enemies bent upon destroying it. This meant that it needed to be militarily strong if it was to be able to defend itself:

We are living not merely in a state but in a system of states; and it is inconceivable that the Soviet republic should continue to exist for a long period side by side with imperialist states. Ultimately one or other must conquer. Until this end occurs a number of terrible clashes between the Soviet republic and bourgeois states is inevitable.[63]

Lenin's reference to 'a system of states' suggests that he was well aware that, in urging acceptance of the fact of Soviet statehood

---

[61] Ibid. 67.
[62] Cited in Wheeler-Bennett, *Brest-Litovsk*, 386.
[63] Cited in Carr, *The Bolshevik Revolution*, iii. 122–3.

upon his more reluctant colleagues, he was also accepting one
inevitable implication of this: that Soviet Russia would have to
assume some of the attributes of other states, in particular a
capacity to defend itself.

Revolutionary purists perceived risks in such developments.
Lenin's response was based on two further, closely connected
assertions. The first was essentially a tactical point: because the rest
of the world had clearly not moved to a revolutionary stage as
quickly as had the Soviet Union, a 'breathing space' was required
during which Soviet power could be consolidated in Russia while
proletarians elsewhere caught up with their Bolshevik comrades. As
Lenin put it in his report on foreign policy in May 1918:

We possess great revolutionary experience, which has taught us that it is
essential to employ the tactics of merciless attack when objective
conditions permit, when the experience of compromising has shown that
the people's indignation has been aroused and that attack will express this
change. But we have to resort to temporizing tactics, to a slow gathering of
forces when objective circumstances do not favour a call for a general
merciless repulse.

If we see that as a result of objective conditions the international
proletariat moves too slowly, we must nevertheless stick to our tactics of
temporizing and utilising the conflicts and contradictions between the
imperialists, of slowly accumulating strength; the tactics of preserving this
island of Soviet power in the strong imperialist seas, maintaining this island
which now already attracts the gaze of the working people of all
countries.[64]

He also argued that the current epoch should be seen as a
'transitional period' between capitalism and socialism.[65] This was a
thesis of greater theoretical significance, since it attempted to retain
the essential Marxian claim to be able to base policy upon a deep
insight into the workings of history. However, the implication was
clearly that 'transitional' compromises would have to be made in all
sorts of areas pending the socialist millennium.

Finally, Lenin tried to apply to international relations a
formulation that he had employed much earlier in planning
Bolshevik manœuvres during the 1905 revolution: the proposal
that all decisions should take the form of 'dual policies', which

[64] Full text in Lenin, *O vneshnei politike sovetskogo gosudarstva* (Moscow,
1960), 128–42.
[65] M. Light, *The Soviet Theory of International Relations* (Brighton, 1988),
148–57.

attempted to integrate short-term tactical expediency with the longer-term strategic goal of world revolution. While this was clearly a doctrine capable of rationalizing almost anything (as it did under Stalin), Lenin saw it as a means of retaining a revolutionary sense of purpose even while making unwelcome compromises with the 'international bourgeoisie':

To carry on a war for the overthrow of the international bourgeoisie, a war which is a hundred times more difficult, protracted and complex than the most stubborn of ordinary wars between states, and to renounce in advance any changes of tack, or any utilization of a conflict of interests (even temporary) among one's enemies, or any conciliation or compromise with possible allies (even if they are temporary, unstable, vacillating or conditional allies)—is that not ridiculous in the extreme?[66]

The combined effect of the four concepts of the 'socialist fatherland', the 'breathing space', the 'transitional period', and the 'dual policy' was, on the one hand, to impel Soviet Russia towards increasingly state-like behaviour, which inevitably implied some degree of 'socialization'—acceptance of the norms of international society—since these were designed to uphold and support the state. On the other hand, the Soviet state retained a parallel identity as a revolutionary force intent upon undermining international society. The ambiguity was resolved by Stalin (to his satisfaction at least) by his insistence that the international revolutionary movement should serve the interests of the Soviet state, as his most famous utterance on this point unequivocally asserts:

An internationalist is one who is ready to defend the USSR without reservation, without wavering, unconditionally; for the USSR is the base of the world revolutionary movement, and this revolutionary movement cannot be defended and promoted unless the USSR is defended.[67]

Soviet diplomacy continued to reflect the divided personality of the Soviet state throughout the 1920s and early 1930s. Whether out of conviction, or because they could not undermine their main claim to legitimacy, or because the allegiance of sections of the international labour movement was valuable when few other allies were available, the Bolsheviks could not renounce their commitment to international revolution. Nor, however, could they avoid the necessity of relations with other states. Russia was economically

---

[66] 'Left Wing Communism—an Infantile Disorder', *Collected Works*, xxxi. 70.
[67] Cited in Light, *The Soviet Theory of International Relations*, 157.

devastated and, as hopes of world revolution faded, it was soon evident that trade relations with at least the major powers would be a vital element in the reconstruction of the Russian economy. Moreover, a period of international peace would help to provide Soviet Russia with the 'breathing space' it required for internal reconstruction. Finally, there was the simple fact that important—indeed crucial—decisions were being taken in international fora without reference to the Soviets.

Two distinct principles and two organizational forms were devised to reflect this underlying duality. 'Proletarian internationalism' was meant to embody the Soviet commitment to working-class solidarity that derived from its social identity as head of an international class. 'Peaceful coexistence' was the corresponding principle for the Soviet Union's inter-state relations. The Communist International was established in 1919 as the institutional form of proletarian internationalism, while the Narkomindel was allocated the task of conducting Soviet relations with other states. This division of duties enabled Moscow to claim that it was not responsible for the utterances and actions of the Comintern—a claim that few other governments took seriously.

The distinction between governmental and party functions was always blurred, and it was never very clear whether peaceful coexistence was to be regarded merely as a tactic to buy time while the real work of the Soviet Union—preparing for world revolution—went on behind the scenes, or whether it implied a long-term commitment to a policy of integrating the Soviet Union within the state system through acceptance of the prevailing norms of the Westphalian international society. Both interpretations were advanced (sometimes by the same individual) at different times, in different circumstances, and to different audiences throughout the 1920s and 1930s. Stalin and the Comintern tended to take the view that peaceful coexistence was simply another form of struggle against capitalism.[68] However, Narkomindel spokesmen such as Chicherin and especially Litvinov argued that peaceful coexistence implied a much more fundamental reorientation of Soviet foreign policy in line with the Soviet Union's primary identity as a state in a world of states. For Chicherin, this was simply a matter of pragmatic politics:

[68] Cited in Light, *The Soviet Theory of International Relations*, 28–57, and X. J. Eudin and R. M. Slusser, *Soviet Foreign Policy, 1928–1934: Documents and Materials* (2 vols.; London, 1966), i. 138–9.

There may be differences of opinion as to the duration of the capitalist system but at present the capitalist system exists, so that a *modus vivendi* must be found in order that our socialist state and the capitalist states may coexist peacefully and in normal relations with one another.[69]

In the context of the extremely threatening international climate of the 1930s, Litvinov saw peaceful coexistence as requiring not simply an accommodation between the two systems but the adoption by the Soviets of many of the essential Westphalian values. Membership of an international society based upon principles of sovereignty and non-intervention seemed to offer greater security than maintaining a posture of revolutionary isolationism, whatever Marxist ideology might appear to dictate to the contrary.

It was in this spirit that the Soviets joined the League of Nations in 1934. Previously their attitude towards this organization had rested upon a basic rejection of the underlying premiss of the League Covenant, namely that all states did indeed constitute an international society with certain common values and interests. This was spelled out by Chicherin to Britain's ambassador to Germany in 1925:

As regards the League of Nations, it was and would remain impossible for Russia to join the League because this would involve an obligation to execute decisions taken by a body composed of States organized on a fundamentally different basis from that of the Soviet Republic. This objection was not transitory, it was fundamental.[70]

In the world as viewed through Marxist-Leninist spectacles, an international organization with authority to curtail the freedom of action of states would simply serve the aggressive designs of the imperialist states:

The Soviet Government feels that in an epoch such as ours, when the policy of all States is wholly dominated by their separate interests, any attempt to establish a system of international equity and of protection for the weak nations against the strong by means of an international organization is bound to fail . . . . [It] therefore rejects any plan for an international organization which implies the possibility of measures of constraint being

---

[69] Cited in Carr, *The Bolshevik Revolution*, iii. 166.

[70] Lord D'Abernon to Mr Austen Chamberlain, 8 Nov. 1925 (reporting a conversation with Chicherin). *Documents on British Foreign Policy, 1918–39*, ed. E. L. Woodward and R. Butler, ser. 1a, i. (London, 1952), 114.

exercised by any international authority whatsoever against a particular State. In the present state of international relations, a system of that kind would inevitably become, in the hands of a dominant group of Powers, an instrument of aggression against other Powers.[71]

By 1936 the Soviet position had undergone a complete reversal, with Litvinov calling for a greatly strengthened League and arguing that 'An end must be put to the situation wherein pleas of sovereignty and constitutional formalities are an obstacle to the performance of international obligations.'[72]

The ambiguous Soviet approach to peaceful coexistence continued after the war, and for much the same reasons. On the one hand, Soviet state interests were served by insisting that peaceful coexistence implied a policy of scrupulous respect for international law and the principle of non-intervention.[73] On the other hand, when the more radical Chinese challenged Soviet credentials as the leading revolutionary power by deriding Moscow's peaceful coexistence policies as un-Marxist, the Soviets were obliged to revert to their earlier contention that peaceful coexistence was a form of class struggle.

Similar ambiguities were apparent in many other areas of Soviet foreign relations. Trotsky, for example, was quite capable of invoking the norm of non-interference in domestic affairs to protest against other countries' policies towards the Soviet Union, while simultaneously threatening to appeal to their peoples over the heads of their governments.[74] Moscow could also see no contradiction between its refusal to pay various international debts contracted by previous Russian regimes, on the grounds that 'Governments and systems that spring from revolution are not bound to respect the obligations of fallen Governments', and its objections to great power attempts to settle certain international issues on the grounds that the Soviet Union possessed treaty rights deriving from earlier Tsarist agreements.[75]

As the Soviet Union's economic plight deepened in the early 1920s, Moscow's readiness to play the part of a responsible

[71] Chicherin's reply to the League of Nations' request for Soviet comments on the proposed Draft Treaty of Mutual Assistance, 12 Mar. 1924, in Degras, *Soviet Documents*, i. 430–4.
[72] Goodman, *The Soviet Design*, 384.
[73] Light, *The Soviet Theory of International Relations*, 41.
[74] Debo, *Revolution and Survival*, 26–7.
[75] Degras, *Soviet Documents*, i. 308–18.

member of the international community became more pronounced. Trade agreements were signed with Britain and other countries which included stipulations that the Soviets would not seek to spread their revolutionary creed in colonial territories. Turkey's persecution of its Communist Party was ignored in the interests of good state to state relations with the Kemalist regime. The Soviets began to participate in various technical and humanitarian aspects of the League of Nations' work. Partly as a reward for these signs of international good behaviour, the Soviet Union was invited to attend the 1923 Genoa Conference. There, in a remarkable *tour de force*, Chicherin attempted in his opening statement to reconcile ideological principles with Soviet state practice:

While maintaining the standpoint of their communist principles, the Russian delegation recognize that in the present period of history, which permits the parallel existence of the old social order and of the new order being born, economic collaboration between the States representing these two systems of property is imperatively necessary for the general economic reconstruction.

In our view the establishment of universal peace should be undertaken by a world congress, convened on the basis of the complete equality of all peoples and the recognition of the right of all of them to determine their own destiny. We think that the method of representation at these conferences should be changed. We consider the official participation of workers' organizations at these congresses absolutely essential.

The Russian Government is even willing to adopt as its point of departure the previous agreements of the Powers regulating international relations, with some necessary modifications, and to take part in the revision of the Covenant of the League of Nations so as to transform it into a real League of Peoples without any domination of some nations by others and without the existing division into victors and vanquished.[76]

Chicherin managed to suggest that, although the 'old social order' was destined to disappear, its system of international relations could be accepted by Moscow pending its demise, so long as it was modified to take account of the appearance of a new type of society. He made it clear that he was under no illusion that such a 'transitional' arrangement would do anything to remove the real causes of war and economic crisis, which were to be found in the nature of capitalism, but declared Moscow's readiness 'to support every effort calculated to bring an improvement, if only of a

[76] Ibid. 298–301.

palliative nature, into the world economy, and to remove the threat of new wars'.[77]

Chicherin's equivocal assurance that he would play by the capitalists' rules until the capitalists were overthrown attracted less interest at Genoa than his conclusion of the Rapallo Treaty with another outlaw state, Germany. Even without this dramatic event there would have been little likelihood of the leading Western powers changing their view of Soviet Russia as a deeply subversive force whose behaviour, whether conciliatory or belligerent, proceeded from the same revolutionary purpose. The opinion of the American Secretary of State in 1920 was that

the existing régime in Russia is based upon the negation of every principle of honor and good faith, and every usage and convention underlying the whole structure of international law; the negation, in short, of every principle upon which it is possible to base harmonious and trustful relations, whether of nations or individuals. In the view of this Government, there cannot be any common ground upon which it can stand with a Power whose conceptions of international relations are so entirely alien to its own, so utterly repugnant to its moral sense.[78]

Fifteen years later, Soviet attempts to project a more responsible image in the face of the threat from Nazi Germany did not signify any fundamental shift, in the view of the American ambassador to Moscow:

there has been no decrease in the determination of the Soviet Government to produce world revolution. Diplomatic relations with friendly states are not regarded by the Soviet Government as normal friendly relations but 'armistice relations' and it is the conviction of the Soviet Union that this 'armistice' can not possibly be ended by a definite peace but only by a renewal of battle.[79]

A year later, another American diplomat based in Washington was expressing his view that his country and the Soviet Union represented 'not only quite dissimilar systems but also conflicting policies with respect to the duties and obligations of members of the family of nations'.[80] In 1938 Soviet non-acceptance of the basic

[77] Degras, *Soviet Documents*.
[78] Cited in T. J. Uldricks, *Diplomacy and Ideology*, 51.
[79] United States, Department of State, *Foreign Relations of the United States: The Soviet Union, 1933–39* (Washington, 1952), 224–5.
[80] Ibid. 308.

norms of international society was still seen by American diplomats as constituting a major barrier to normal relations with Moscow:

The normal process of cooperation between countries in conformity with the established principles which govern the relations of the United States with friendly governments does not appear to constitute a basic factor in Soviet policy.[81]

Essentially the same perception of the Soviets governed American policy after the Second World War.

It is clear that almost from the beginning Soviet leaders were prepared to ignore those aspects of their ideology which seemed to require them to place pursuit of international revolution before all other goals including defence of the Soviet state. This inevitably led them in the direction of 'socialization'—of becoming more 'state-like'—both in their internal attributes and their external behaviour. Yet they were unable to relinquish their self-proclaimed identity as vanguard of the international proletarian revolution, for reasons ranging from genuine belief through fear of losing their legitimacy to the simple utility value of possessing credentials which gave them access to the Western labour movement, to intellectuals, to the likes of Kim Philby, and later to the radical regimes of a number of Third World countries. The consequent duality of purpose and identity coloured their public rhetoric and diplomacy even during periods of *détente* with the West such as occurred under Khrushchev and Brezhnev. This in turn meant that the West was unlikely to take at face value the evident Soviet wish to be accepted as a full and equal member of the international community. Western hostility in its turn confirmed the Soviets in two other ideologically induced perceptions contained in their world-view: the convictions that the 'imperialists' were continually conspiring against the Soviet Union and that the nature of 'imperialism' would lead inevitably to war.

Hence, the Soviets found themselves in an impasse: the established powers were unable to accept them as full members of an international society which, in any case, they themselves regarded with deep suspicion. In 1928 Litvinov went some way towards acknowledging criticisms of Soviet paranoia about external threats, but stopped well short of accepting that a sufficient basis of common interests and values existed for Moscow to be able to

[81] Ibid. 592–4.

place any trust in such institutions of the Versailles system as the League of Nations' disputes procedures:

We are often criticized for making bogeys of non-existent anti-Soviet blocs, for exaggerating and inflating the dangers threatening our Union, for placing too much confidence in reports of anti-Soviet plans and preparations. Of course, not all such reports deserve equal confidence and attention, not all the rumours reaching us can be precisely verified and documented. [But] The fight against our Union has never ceased; it has only assumed different forms according to changing circumstances . . . With such an attitude to the Soviet Union, the proposal that we should submit our disputes with other countries for settlement to organizations or persons whom we know to be hostile to us is ridiculous.[82]

During the 1930s the prevailing international order, the Versailles system, and even some of the foundation-stones of the Westphalian international society itself encountered their most serious challenge since Napoleon. Germany pursued a new European order, structured along racial lines, that paid little heed to the principle of sovereign equality or national self-determination, let alone to such ideas as non-intervention, legitimacy, a stable balance of power, or traditional diplomacy. Japan proposed to replace a European-dominated order in Asia with one controlled by a single power: itself. The doctrines of isolationism that had been formulated by the USA during its post-revolutionary phase were one factor that kept it from intervening to uphold a system that its ideology told it was decadent and corrupt. Within Europe, Soviet ideology initially led it completely to misjudge developments in Germany. The increasing threat from Japan and the non-appearance in Germany of any revolution against a regime which had made only too clear what the Slav races could expect at its hands, led the Soviets from 1933 onwards into an urgent quest for allies. In the process they sought to present themselves not only as respectable members of the Versailles system but as its most fervent upholders. Many factors conditioned the response of their prospective allies, Britain and France, but two are particularly salient in this context. First, the Soviet/Comintern (no other state accepted Soviet attempts to distinguish the two) line for fifteen years had been to depict any collaboration with capitalist powers as a tactical manœuvre. Second, Britain and France perceived Germany as less

[82] Degras, *Soviet Documents*, ii. 351.

revolutionary and hence ultimately less subversive of the existing order than the Soviet Union. So where Soviet overtures were greeted with suspicion if not hostility, Germany was dealt with as if it could be accommodated by the old ways that had kept the Westphalian structure intact for so long: secret diplomacy, territorial adjustments, compromises and concessions, with all business conducted within a framework of common assumptions, values, and rules. Not for the first or last time, revolution had disrupted the orderly functioning of the Westphalian system, on this occasion by helping to distort the perspectives of all those who shared the same basic interest in containing Germany and Japan.

'INTERNATIONAL RELATIONS OF A NEW TYPE'

While there was only one state owing its inspiration to Marxism-Leninism, the task of formulating the essential Soviet approach to international relations was relatively straightforward. The Soviet Union was an embattled island of socialism in a world dominated by capitalist powers. While, therefore, a relationship of peaceful coexistence with the capitalists was possible, the underlying character of Soviet–capitalist relations remained one of confrontation between a powerful but historically doomed force and one which, although currently weak, was destined to supplant capitalism. Because the capitalist powers would inevitably contend amongst themselves it was possible for the Soviet Union to seek tactical advantages by aligning with one side or the other—or with both successively between 1939–45—but this could never be taken to imply any fundamental acceptance of the capitalist international system. It was merely that during the 'transitional period' between capitalism and socialism an appropriate form of international relations was required: in essence this would involve going along with many aspects of the existing international system, if not actually exploiting it. But communists should never lose sight of the inherent antagonism and irreconcilability between the old world and the putative new one.

Several post-war developments posed serious problems for this relatively uncomplicated image of international relations. Nuclear weapons made accommodation with the capitalist powers an urgent long-term necessity rather than a short-term dialectical tactic. Decolonization was producing many new sovereign states which did not quite fit into orthodox Marxist-Leninist categories. This became evident when initial assessments of the nationalist regimes of most ex-colonies as puppets of their former colonial masters did not square with their evident independence in foreign policy, as demonstrated during the Korean War. Moscow shifted fairly rapidly from its early appraisal of the former colonies, which ranked them according to the degree of 'working class' involvement in government, to one that, in effect, judged them by their international orientation. The 1947 Zhdanov line, which put everybody into 'anti-fascist' or 'imperialist' camps, with neutrality impossible, was replaced under Khrushchev by a cluster of new concepts which depicted a 'zone of peace' between the two camps consisting of 'national democracies' which were capable of making a 'peaceful transition' to socialism.[83] This formulation went considerably beyond an attempt to reconcile ideology with certain awkward facts towards an adaptation of doctrine to take account of the possibility of close state to state relations with non-socialist countries—a development that did not go unremarked by the Chinese when they began their campaign against 'revisionism' in the late 1950s.

Far more complex theoretical and practical issues were raised by the post-war creation of socialist regimes in Eastern Europe. In the immediate aftermath of the October Revolution the Bolsheviks had rejected 'bourgeois' concepts such as sovereign equality, international law, and diplomacy, only to discover that the rest of the world was not prepared to deal with the Soviets on any other basis, and later to find the Westphalian/Versailles order of real value to Soviet interests.[84] But the underlying theoretical premiss of Soviet preparedness to enter into normal relations with other states on the terms expected within the Westphalian system was that such an arrangement was 'transitional', pending the transformation of the world into something more closely resembling the Marxian vision. Relations with 'bourgeois' states retained their dialectical duality: accommodation, coexistence, or alliance with them was always temporary and conditional; struggle between the two systems never

[83] M. Rush (ed.), *The International Situation and Soviet Foreign Policy* (Columbus, Ohio, 1970), 130, 159, 171–2.

[84] A process described by one author as a transition from 'the attitude of rejection, to cynical acceptance and then to one of obsessive reverence for the sovereignty principle'. R. A. Jones, *The Soviet Concept of 'Limited Sovereignty' from Lenin to Gorbachev* (London, 1990), 27.

ceased. Clearly this was wholly inappropriate for relations among socialist states but what principles were valid?

One interpretation of Marxism would seem to require the abolition of political boundaries within the socialist camp, but to the undiscerning gaze of the outside world that might have appeared to be mere annexation. In practice, Moscow employed two somewhat contradictory principles to explain relationships within the socialist camp. First, it was asserted that the Eastern European states were genuinely sovereign: indeed, they were more so than 'bourgeois' states, since it was only in the socialist camp that sovereignty was truly vested in the people rather than controlled by a ruling class that was under the yoke of 'American imperialism'.[85] However, sovereignty did not prevent harmonious and fraternal 'international relations of a new type' from developing in the socialist camp, since it was free from the principal source of international tension, which was deemed to be capitalist exploitation. Relations amongst the constituent republics of the Soviet Union were declared to be the model for international relations within the socialist camp.[86] The second principle was that of unity within what was sometimes referred to as 'the socialist commonwealth'—a conception of a universal society with obligations to the whole that sat somewhat uneasily alongside the equally strongly affirmed principle of sovereignty.

The reality of Soviet hegemony was at first something that it was not felt to be particularly important to disguise. Stalin personally retained great prestige among communists at the end of the war, Soviet experience and aid were thought to be invaluable in guiding the Eastern European countries along the path to full socialism, and Soviet power was believed to be necessary to guard the socialist camp against the designs that, as ever, the imperialists were assumed to be harbouring against it. The Soviets even felt able to repeat Stalin's famous definition of an internationalist as someone who was prepared unreservedly to defend the Soviet Union.[87] Tito's critique of Soviet domination of the bloc necessitated a shift towards more discreet formulations, but there was no real departure from the essential universalist principle that the socialist

[85] Ibid. 10–11, 21–2.
[86] Ibid. 73–5 and K. Grzybowski, *The Socialist Commonwealth of Nations* (New Haven, Conn., and London, 1964), 247.
[87] Jones, *The Soviet Concept of 'Limited Sovereignty'* 67.

countries owed obligations to the bloc and to socialism. For example, Vyshinsky's definition in a 1949 speech at the United Nations—'states of the period of transition charged with the task of developing the countries of Eastern Europe along the socialist path'—clearly implied an 'internationalist' duty that significantly constrained such states' freedom to conduct their internal affairs as they chose.[88]

By 1957 de-Stalinization, abortive anti-Soviet rebellions in Eastern Europe, and the emergence of polycentrist tendencies in the bloc had forced some re-evaluation of the basis of intra-bloc relations. Peaceful coexistence, now defined in terms of 'the principles of complete equality of respect for territorial sovereignty, of state independence and sovereignty and of non-interference in one another's internal affairs', was now declared to be applicable to relations within the bloc as well as with other countries.[89] The Soviet Union, as 'the first and mightiest socialist power', retained a special status and an entitlement to support from other bloc members.[90] Increasingly, though, the 'internationalist obligation' of socialist states was deemed to be primarily to the socialist camp as a whole and to what was now defined as a transnational 'socialist world system'. This duty embraced support for workers everywhere as well as the obligation to work with the iron laws of history, which had made the world socialist system the 'decisive factor in the development of society'.[91] In particular, socialism, in Khrushchev's words, had acquired the capacity to 'determine, in a growing measure, the character, methods and trends of international relations'.[92] The end product, Khrushchev speculated, was:

the amalgamation of all nations in a single Communist family. The question of borders as it is presently conceived will gradually cease to exist. No sovereign socialist country can shut itself up within its own borders and rely solely upon its own forces and its own wealth.[93]

The basis of unity within the 'socialist world system' was therefore defined in 'great community' terms as class solidarity,

---

[88] Jones, *The Soviet Concept of 'Limited Sovereignty'* 3.

[89] K. Grzybowski, *The Socialist Commonwealth*, 252. (Declaration of 30 Oct. 1956.)

[90] Light, *The Soviet Theory of International Relations*, 177. (1957 Declaration.)

[91] W. Zimmerman, *Soviet Perspectives on International Relations, 1956–67* (Princeton, NJ, 1969), 82–3.

[92] Ibid. 181–2.

[93] Goodman, *The Soviet Design*, 49.

together with the correct understanding of world affairs that was imparted by the shared ideology of Marxism-Leninism. The reality was closer to a universal society under the hegemony of Moscow, a fact that became very evident in 1968 with the Soviet invasion of Czechoslovakia. This was accompanied by a rationalization of the invasion which became known as the Brezhnev Doctrine, and which was seen by many as laying down formally a principle that had been clearly implied by many earlier statements, namely, that the sovereignty of socialist countries was limited by the obligations they owed to socialism. The charge that the invasion was a simple act of aggression was met by a restatement of earlier arguments to the effect that sovereignty was not to be measured by some 'bourgeois' yardstick, but by the only genuine standard of 'socialist self-determination', and that by straying from the correct socialist path the Czech leadership was placing this true sovereignty in jeopardy.[94] According to Brezhnev,

imperialist and reactionary forces are trying to rob the people of various socialist countries of the sovereign right earned by them to guarantee their national prosperity and the security and happiness of the masses of working people by constructing a society free from all oppression and exploitation.[95]

If a state deviated from the 'common natural laws of socialist construction' it might deviate from socialism as such.[96] This could endanger the socialist system as a whole, and this fact gave other socialist states the right (indeed, made it their duty) to intervene to protect the interests of the 'world revolutionary movement', which overrode those of any single country.[97] If socialist unity of purpose was maintained, the socialist camp would continue to make steady progress towards its ultimate goal of a socialist commonwealth, a process which Brezhnev claimed was to be well under way in 1976:

The ties between socialist states are becoming ever closer with the flowering of each socialist nation and the strengthening of their sovereignty, and elements of community are increasing in their policy,

---

[94] *Pravda*, 26 Sept. 1968 (article by S. Kovalev).
[95] Speech of 12 Nov. 1968, cited in R. J. Mitchell, *Ideology of a Superpower: Contemporary Soviet Doctrines on International Relations* (Stanford, Calif., 1982), 30.
[96] Ibid.
[97] Kovalev, *Pravda*, 26 Sept. 1968.

economy and social life. There is a gradual levelling up of their development. This process of a gradual drawing together of socialist countries is now operating quite definitely as an objective law.[98]

GORBACHEV AND THE PURSUIT OF SOCIALIZATION OF THE SOVIET UNION

It is possible to see the Brezhnev Doctrine as nothing more than a cynical attempt to justify a display of imperial might by the Soviet Union. That, however, would be to miss an important point about the Doctrine, namely that it followed inescapably from Soviet ideology. It was, in essence, an attempt to force—quite literally—the facts into line with the theory: to reconcile the two rather than adapt the theory. The alternative would have been to accept a series of propositions casting doubt not simply upon the reliability of the Soviet Union's security structure in Eastern Europe but upon the very basis of the Soviet system. Marxism-Leninism was supposed to lay down the foundations for a different kind of national society existing within a framework of like-minded fraternal nations, all progressing in unity towards a common goal which represented the future for mankind as a whole. The Czech experiment in effect implied a shift to something much closer to the Westphalian model of international relations, in which states had the right to pursue whatever internal policies they chose, even if these involved a move towards 'bourgeois' Western practices. Each state's obligation to itself, in other words, overrode its duties to its partners.

When Mikhail Gorbachev began his herculean task of restructuring Soviet society, he saw clearly enough the necessity for new political thinking to replace the strait-jacket of Marxist-Leninist orthodoxy that was stifling initiative and preventing genuine progress within the Soviet Union. What he may not have appreciated—as perhaps Brezhnev did—was the considerable dependence of the entire Soviet edifice upon the legitimation conferred by Marxism-Leninism. To call the latter into question was to remove the foundation-stone of unity, not only in the 'socialist camp', but among the nations that constituted the Soviet Union itself.

[98] Mitchell, *Ideology of a Superpower*, 96.

Gorbachev's revolution embraced almost all facets of Soviet theory and practice, but for our purposes three aspects of 'new thinking' in the field of international relations are particularly important. The first was the adoption of an open and questioning attitude to the shibboleths of the past. As Gorbachev observed in a major address to the United Nations in December 1988: 'Life is making us abandon established stereotypes and outdated views. It is making us discard illusions.'[99] Even more pointedly, the Soviet Foreign Minister, Eduard Shevardnadze, declared, 'In all frankness, we ought to admit that several of our foreign-policy doctrines, concepts and ideas of the past, and of current times, for that matter, were inspired by purely time-serving considerations.'[100] Singled out for particular criticism amongst such ideologically rooted thought patterns was the image of the West as an implacably hostile enemy, an image that was 'hampering the revamping of international relations on the principles of morality and civility, the development of productive dialogue, and clear-cut consideration of interests'.[101] Also criticized were the notion that the Soviet Union represented the one true model to be followed by all socialist states[102] and the effect of teleological or deterministic thinking on Soviet foreign policy, whereby the twin assumptions of socialism's inevitable triumph and capitalism's inevitable collapse constantly led the Soviet Union into overly optimistic assessments of the global 'correlation of forces'.[103]

Secondly, the Soviet leadership sought to adopt the basic norms of international society in a much more wholehearted and uncynical manner than previously. As Shevardnadze explained, 'We should not pretend, Comrades, that norms and notions of what is proper, of what is called civilized conduct in the world community do not concern us. If you want to be accepted in it you must observe them.'[104] Amongst these norms was international law as a whole. In the words of an *Izvestiya* attack on the Brezhnev Doctrine in October 1989:

[99] Gorbachev address to the UN, 7 Dec. 1988, UN Document A/43/PV.72, p. 7.
[100] *International Affairs* (Moscow), Oct. 1988, p. 25.
[101] Ibid.
[102] P. Marantz, 'The Gorbachev Revolution: Emerging Trends in Soviet Foreign Policy'. Paper delivered to the International Society of Political Psychology, Tel Aviv, 20 June 1989.
[103] Ibid. 21–5.
[104] *International Affairs*, Oct. 1988, p. 23.

It is impossible to expect complete trust in our new political thinking . . . until it is clearly said: There were not, and there could not have been any circumstances which could have justified a breach of the elementary norms of international law . . . The time has come to admit, publicly, and accept our responsibility for the Brezhnev Doctrine. It is dead to all intents and purposes.[105]

Another shift was away from the confrontational use of diplomacy as a tool for propaganda and point-scoring and towards an appreciation of its traditional value as a means for achieving peaceful resolution of disputes.

Gorbachev's acceptance of the idea of an international society with rules and norms of behaviour was founded essentially on the Westphalian conception of a society of sovereign states: 'In a nuclear age the effectiveness of international law should be based not on enforcing compliance but rather on norms reflecting a balance of State interests.'[106] However, just as a number of American leaders, while accepting the essential Westphalian principles, have also been animated by a reformist zeal, so too was Gorbachev. One of his most frequently reiterated themes was that the world today must be seen as a single organism in which 'the scientific and technological revolution has turned many economic, food, energy, environmental, information and population problems, which only recently we treated as national or regional into global problems'.[107] This interdependence had created 'universal human interests', solutions to which needed to be 'guided by the primacy of universal human values'.[108] This meant that 'the international community must learn how it can shape and guide developments in such a way as to preserve our civilization and to make it safe for all and more conducive to normal life'.[109] However, since sovereign equality remained the central principle of international relations, this had to be achieved through a process of consensus formation. Essentially, that implied a democratization of diplomacy and the need 'to internationalize dialogue and the negotiating process'.[110] In concrete terms, this meant a much enhanced role for the United Nations.

[105] *Izvestiya*, 14 Oct. 1989.
[106] Gorbachev address (above, n. 99), 23.
[107] Ibid. 6.   [108] Ibid. 8.
[109] Ibid. 9.   [110] Ibid. 16.

CONCLUSION

As suggested earlier, its ideology, combined perhaps with a traditional Russian suspiciousness towards the outside world, meant at one time that the Soviet Union could never see itself as a full member of the Westphalian international society, nor could it be viewed as such by the leading states within the Westphalian system. The adoption by Moscow of some of the Westphalian norms was always interpreted by itself and by other states as a temporary, tactical expedient. This contributed to the slide to war in 1938–9, to the Cold War, and to numerous other problems in Soviet foreign policy, particularly in its relations with the Third World.

A genuine effort to achieve socialization awaited the arrival of Mikhail Gorbachev. Yet it is perhaps significant that he did not simply adopt as his own the prevailing norms of international society but attempted to go beyond them. Gorbachev's impact, intentional or not, upon international relations at the end of the twentieth century has been so formidable that many sizeable volumes are likely to be written about the mainsprings of his revolution. Some of his ideas bear a striking resemblance to those of Woodrow Wilson. However, there is a humanistic strain in Marxist thought, together with a vision of a future, more interdependent world, and it is equally possible that this was an influence upon Gorbachev's intellectual development. The existence of the Soviet state, with its claims to represent the international proletariat and its support for 'national liberation', was one of many factors contributing to new international norms, such as improved labour conditions and anti-colonialism. If Gorbachev had been able to succeed in promoting a reformed version of international society, and if at least part of the inspiration for his ideas had been shown to be attributable to Marxist doctrines, this might have been interpreted as another instance of the two-way interaction between revolutionary state and international society.

In the event, Gorbachev's revolution brought to crisis point the central paradox of the Soviet state. Both its own legitimacy as a multinational empire and its right to exercise hegemony over Eastern Europe rested upon its claim to be the 'socialist fatherland': to be something other than a mere state whose conduct might be appraised by the same criteria as applied to other states. On the other hand, Moscow implied, by insisting upon all the entitlements due to a major state, that it was legitimate to regard it as such. While both claims remained in force, the Soviet Union was never likely to become fully integrated within the society of states. The decision to opt for respectability as a state at the expense of its revolutionary identity fatally weakened the basis of unity within the Soviet Union and the socialist camp.

Just as the challenge of Revolutionary and Napoleonic France had caused the established powers first to act together to defend the Westphalian international society, then to seek to improve its organizational forms and operational procedures in the Concert of Europe, so did the long international counter-revolution that was provoked by the events of 1917 help to cause a re-examination and reformulation of international society. Whatever may have been the motives behind Moscow's championing of the anti-colonial cause, its material support and constant propaganda about the evils of imperialism were instrumental in establishing the principle of self-determination as an accepted norm of international society. The International Labour Organization was set up in part because of fears that the Soviet Union might be able to manipulate the international labour movement. This helped to place social issues on the international agenda, as also did the Soviet Union's vocal opposition to racism and its declaratory posture in favour of various feminist issues.

But the most significant, indirect—and certainly unintended—Soviet contribution to the development of international society was in the nature of the US reaction to what it perceived to be a Soviet threat after 1945. Governance and management in international society had hitherto been either decentralized to the point of being virtually non-existent, as in the eighteenth century, or based on a loose concert of major powers, as in the nineteenth century. Britain is sometimes represented as enjoying a hegemonial position during this latter period because its geographical isolation and naval and industrial power enabled it to manipulate the European balance while remaining secure against external threat. However, even at the peak of its power it was at most first among equals and never able to determine the course of international affairs to the extent that the United States has done in the second half of the twentieth century. American hegemony was to a certain degree the inevitable outcome of long-maturing historical processes. But in several important respects, each of which has significance for the evolution of international society, the rise of American hegemony derived from its response to the Soviet Union.

The most important of these relates to the actual decision by the United States to assume a hegemonial role. In 1945 this was by no means inevitable. Roosevelt's vision of a post-war order assumed a continuation of the wartime alliance in another form. Congress and public opinion supported the demobilization of American forces and opposed further American involvement overseas. The United States had already possessed in 1919 the economic power and military potential to seek global hegemony but had chosen not to. The main reason why the same choice was not made after 1945 was the growing American apprehension about Soviet ambitions and the perceived threat from Soviet revolutionary doctrines. The chief consequences of this so far as our discussion of international society is concerned were twofold. First, there was a partial shift from the Westphalian basis of international society, the competitive coexistence of several roughly equal powers, all of whom accepted the essential rights of the others, to an effective declaration by the United States that its zone of influence—the 'free world'—alone possessed full international legitimacy. Second, the United States acted as a socializing agent on behalf of its own conception of international legitimacy, offering economic, diplomatic, and military support to opponents of communism. With the collapse of communism in Europe, the United States continued to act as 'socializer' by encouraging the former communist states to assume the characteristics that, in Washington's view, defined the fully legitimate state: free political institutions, guarantees of human rights, and an open market economy. International social engineering of this kind, to promote internal 'good governance', was also applied to numerous Third World states, now no longer able to balance the conflicting Soviet and American conceptions of the legitimate state against each other.

5

The Revolt against the West and International Society

The Bolshevik Revolution and the new approach promised by Woodrow Wilson had both appeared to portend radical changes to the international society of 1914. In the event, the essential Westphalian edifice survived intact, inasmuch as its constituents remained sovereign states and its institutions, rules, and norms were still those that could be accommodated within the confines of an anarchic, decentralized society, with authority distributed horizontally, on the basis of legal equality, rather than vertically, according to some hierarchical principle. However, just as the deliberations after the French revolutionary wars had given rise to a subtly amended international society, with a new category of great powers deemed to have special responsibility for the maintenance of international order, an increasing emphasis on nationality as the basis for statehood, and later a certain reformulation of the criteria for membership of the international society in the shape of a 'standard of civilization', so too did the aftermath of the First World War leave its mark. As with the post-Napoleonic order, this affected the primary attributes of the Westphalian system less than its secondary features: the cluster of ideas and assumptions that underpinned the array of legal instruments and informal mechanisms through which the members of international society went about their increasingly complex business. The most concrete expression of these secondary features was the League of Nations. It was inevitable that a deliberate endeavour by international society to reconstitute itself should be accompanied by a greater self-consciousness about its underlying principles as well as an awareness of the need to formulate them in ways that would be acceptable to a public opinion whose expectations had been aroused by the representative of an old revolutionary state, Woodrow Wilson, and that of a new one, Lenin.

Wilson's first public endorsement of the League of Nations idea in 1916 contained in embryo most of the central concepts that he was later to try to incorporate in the League Covenant. He advocated

a universal association of the nations to maintain the inviolate security of the high seas for the common good and unhindered use of all the nations of the world, and to prevent any war begun either contrary to treaty covenants or without warning and full submission of the causes to the opinion of the world—a virtual guarantee of territorial integrity and political independence.[1]

There was no questioning here of the basic Westphalian concept of sovereign equality; indeed, Wilson's speech in effect reaffirmed this, as did the League Covenant. However, Wilson placed great stress on the idea of international society itself, and on strengthening the foundations of order in a society of states, and it is here that it is possible to discern some important changes of emphasis from the original Westphalian structure.

International relations in Europe after 1648 constituted an international society only in so far as states perceived in their common interest of maintaining their sovereign status, the basis for some collaboration over rules and procedures to enshrine sovereignty as their cardinal principle. The primary purpose of the international society that emerged was not, however, to preserve the sovereignty of any particular state, but, through a balance of power and other devices, to uphold an international system in which it would be difficult for one state to achieve preponderance, or for some non-state entity, like the Church, to claim transcendent authority over states. In practice, the system served the interests of the great powers best, sometimes at the cost of the existence of a smaller state like Poland, and the special position of the great powers was formalized after 1815. Wilson, in effect, called for all states to guarantee each other's sovereignty, a commitment incorporated in a somewhat weaker form in Article 10 of the

[1] R. S. Baker and W. E. Dodd (eds.), *The Public Papers of Woodrow Wilson*, ii. (New York, 1927), 184–8. Some of the following discussion is drawn from D. Armstrong, *The Rise of the International Organisation* (London, 1982), 1–23.

Covenant. A further change foreshadowed in this and other Wilsonian statements was a move towards a more open diplomacy, which Wilson saw as one of the chief pillars of his new world order:

My conception of the League of Nations is just this, that it shall operate as the organized moral force of men throughout the world and that whenever and wherever wrong and aggression are planned or contemplated, this searching light of conscience will be turned upon them and men everywhere will ask, 'What are the purposes that you hold in your heart against the fortunes of the world?' Just a little exposure will settle most questions. If the Central Powers had dared to discuss the purposes of this war for a single fortnight, it never would have happened.[2]

Wilson was clearly contemplating a 'new diplomacy', which was to be substantially different in form from the traditional diplomacy of the post-Westphalian era in the sense that it would involve open, almost parliamentary debate, although its function would remain the peaceful resolution of differences.

Another foundation-stone of the Westphalian system, the balance of power, was to undergo an even more dramatic transformation into, in Wilson's words, a 'community of power'.[3] While the balance of power had the limited objective of preventing a single state from achieving preponderance, what would today be termed the 'collective security' provisions of the League involved the automatic application of sanctions against any state which went to war in violation of its Covenant obligations. The aim was to deter not just bids for universal hegemony but any act of aggression. The greatly expanded role for international law that was envisaged in 1919 also implied a change in its function, suggesting that the states endorsing it had progressed from a minimalist and static concern with rules whose primary aim was to legitimize and safeguard sovereignty to a more evolutionary and teleological interpretation of law as a means of bringing states to accept more civilized standards of conduct in their internal as well as their international affairs. This was apparent in the suggestion, taken up by Wilson, that the League should be involved in the development of international standards to apply to labour conditions—the proposal that led to the establishment of the Interna-

---

[2] *The Public Papers of Woodrow Wilson*, i. 330.
[3] Cited in D. F. Flemming, *The United States and the League of Nations, 1918–1920* (New York, 1932), 12.

tional Labour Organization.[4] It was also implied by Wilson's attempt to make the colonial powers responsible to the League for their management of their colonies. The fifth of Wilson's famous Fourteen Points had been concerned with this issue, and when Wilson's adviser, Colonel House, elaborated upon the point in 1918, he advanced a potentially far-reaching interpretation of the President's thinking: 'It would seem as if the principle involved in this proposition is that a colonial power acts not as owner of its colonies but as a trustee for the natives and for the society of nations.'[5] In the event, however, the League's mandates system only covered former enemy colonies.

The net effect of these proposals was to point the way towards a much more integrated, comprehensive, and highly developed international society than states had hitherto been prepared to contemplate. The society of states was to remain as such but the limited *association* of the Westphalian conception was to evolve towards a much closer *community*, sharing values, standards, practices, and institutions as well as interests. The League was to be the central instrument through which this evolution was to be achieved. In the words of the South African Jan Smuts, who had an important influence on the drafting of the Covenant, the League should be viewed

not only as a possible means for preventing future wars, but much more as a great organ of the ordinary peaceful life of civilization, as the foundation of the new international system which will be erected on the ruins of this war and as the starting-point from which the peace arrangements of the forthcoming conference should be made. Such an orientation of the idea seems to me necessary if the League is to become a permanent part of our international machinery. It is not sufficient for the League merely to be a sort of *deus ex machina*, called in in very grave emergencies when the spectre of war appears; if it is to last, it must be much more. It must become part and parcel of the common international life of states, it must be an ever visible, living working organ of the polity of civilization.[6]

In the event, the world between the wars bore little resemblance to the more integrated and multifaceted international community

---

[4] C. Seymour (ed.), *The Intimate Papers of Colonel House* (4 vols.; London, 1928), iv. 296.

[5] Ibid. 161.

[6] J. C. Smuts, 'A Practical Suggestion', in D. H. Miller, *The Drafting of the Covenant* (2 vols.; New York, 1928), ii. 24–5.

envisaged by Wilson and others. The League's membership was never universal, since the US Senate refused to ratify the Treaty of Versailles, Germany was not admitted until 1926 and left in 1933, the Soviet Union did not join until 1934, Japan withdrew in 1933, Italy in 1937, and several Latin American states on various occasions through the 1920s and 1930s. Of equal importance was the fact that European statesmen found it difficult to conduct their affairs in accordance with the 'new thinking' which required them to acknowledge a responsibility to international society as a whole. For example, in 1921 Lord Curzon reproved the Persian Foreign Minister for writing to reassure the League's Secretary-General that a recent Anglo-Persian agreement was not incompatible with the Covenant. The only effect of such a letter, he maintained, would be to afford the League a pretext to sit in judgement on Persia's sovereign right to interpret its treaty obligations in any way it chose.[7] Again, the League's Mandates Commission was given only marginal and indirect powers of supervision over former enemy colonies, which effectively became part of the colonial empires of the recipient powers. In one case, Japan's invasion of Manchuria, British diplomats argued that the League's principles were inapplicable because, given Japan's special rights in Manchuria, 'the ordinary canons of international intercourse have no application'.[8] On the only occasion when the League attempted to respond to an act of aggression through the new mechanisms of collective security, following Italy's invasion of Ethiopia, the endeavour failed in part because Britain and France reacted to this situation in accordance with 'Westphalian' balance of power thinking, which dictated that it was more important to retain Italy as a possible ally against the greater danger, Germany, than to risk Italy's alienation by adhering to the new 'Versailles' principle of collective response to an international lawbreaker.

If there ever had been any prospects of a more closely knit international community developing after 1918, they conclusively vanished with the advent in the 1930s of two major powers who were bent upon the wholesale restructuring of the existing order. Of the seven great powers, one, the United States, had resumed its traditional isolationism, two, Britain and France, were at best only

[7] *Documents on British Foreign Policy, 1918–39*, ed. E. L. Woodward and R. Butler, 1st ser. xiii. (London, 1963), 489.

[8] Ibid., ser. 2, vol. viii. pp. 826–9.

half-heartedly committed to the Versailles settlement and to sustaining the international order associated with it, while four, the Soviet Union, Germany, Italy, and Japan, were fundamentally opposed to it. Moreover, while Italy's requirements amounted to little more than a larger slice of the cake, the demands of the other three 'revisionist' powers had more revolutionary implications for the Westphalian system. The Soviet case has already been fully considered. Where Marxism-Leninism placed class rather than state at the heart of its rebuttal of Westphalia, Adolf Hitler dreamt of a world order reshaped along racial lines. Race would claim the central importance currently accorded to the outmoded concept of the sovereign state, with its fixed and inviolate territorial boundaries based on the equally erroneous Versailles notion of national self-determination:

The new order cannot be conceived in terms of the national boundaries of peoples with a historical past but in terms of race that transcends those boundaries . . . I have to liberate the world from dependence on its historical past . . . Just as the conception of the nation was a revolutionary change from the purely dynastic feudal states . . . as our own revolution is a further step or rather, the final step, in the rejection of the historical order and the recognition of purely biological values.[9]

Some races were to be physically eliminated, others enslaved, as part of a design for the domination of Europe by the German master race. Hitler's was a new formulation of the 'universal society' conception, and one unlikely to have universal appeal, but it was one which came as close to realization as the previous, Napoleonic bid for *imperium*.

Japan had not undergone any internal political revolution similar to Germany's, and its foreign policy in the 1930s, although highly disruptive of the existing order, derived from more conventional ambitions than those that animated Germany. In essence, Japan desired to be the single hegemonic power in a region that had always been contested by several would-be hegemons. The particular hierarchical principles that Japan intended to apply may have been drawn more from Asian than from European experience, but the outcome for the international relations of the region would

[9] Cited in K. J. Holsti, *Peace and War: Armed Conflicts and International Order, 1648–1989* (Cambridge, 1991), 222. I am grateful to Professor Holsti for giving me an early draft of his manuscript.

still have been the replacement of a pluralistic order by a universal *imperium*. In one respect, however, Japan's bid for predominance in Asia may be related analytically to the international outlook of certain revolutionary states: it sprang in part from a rejection of Western values and of the politico-economic order that the Western powers had tried to establish after 1918. One Japanese school of thought believed that the Western states had prevented Japan from obtaining the just fruits of war after the Sino-Japanese War (1894–5), the Russo-Japanese War (1904–5), and the First World War, as well as ganging up against Japan at the Washington Conference of 1921–2. To add insult to injury, Japanese immigrants in the USA were discriminated against and Japanese attempts to enshrine racial equality as one of the principles of the new Versailles world order had been rudely rebuffed at the Paris Peace Conference. Western society was seen by right-wing elements as decadent and potentially subversive of traditional Japanese values. The Great Depression, which hit Japan particularly badly, added an economic dimension to the general thesis: the international economic system was clearly structured so as to maintain Western dominance and Japanese subservience.[10] Hence politically, culturally, and economically the West was seen as something to be comprehensively rejected. Those sharing this outlook were in no mood to make fine distinctions between different facets of what they perceived to be a uniform system of oppression. The Westphalian system of international relations, and its latter-day Wilsonian refinements, were part and parcel of a single hate-object: the West. This was a theme that was to re-emerge in a different context after the Second World War.

Just as the Thirty Years War and the Napoleonic and First World Wars had been followed by attempts to lay down new ground rules for international society, the Second World War produced its own attempt to redefine the bases of international society, taking account of the development of thought since 1919. However, in 1945 there was far less international consensus about common values and rules to uphold them than there had been after previous wars, and this is evident in the principal 'constitutional' document of the post-war order: the Charter of the United Nations Organization. This brings together a wide-ranging set of principles,

[10] Cited in K. J. Holsti, *Peace and War: Armed Conflicts and International Order, 1648–1989*, 225–8.

rules, and institutions that supposedly define a new and much reformed version of the Westphalian international society. The chief problem with the Charter, conceived in this sense, is that frequently one principle is not entirely compatible with another. This has not prevented it from being regarded as a general statement of the norms, values, and rules that ought to operate in states' conduct of their international relations. As such, it forms part of the context within which the behaviour of post-1945 revolutionary states needs to be assessed.

One of the principal pillars of the Charter is the determination 'to establish conditions under which justice and respect for the obligations arising from treaties and other sources of international law can be maintained', as appears in the preamble. Except for the reference to 'justice', this could appear unamended in any of the defining documents of the Westphalian system. The same is true of the statement of UN principles in Article 2, which emphasizes sovereign equality and respect for the territorial integrity and political independence of states, and limits the United Nations' capacity to intervene in 'matters which are essentially within the domestic jurisdiction of any state'. However, this stress on the traditional rights of states is qualified by the opening words of the Charter, in which, on American insistence, 'we the peoples of the United Nations' express our various determinations, and by the 'Purposes' of the UN, expressed in Article 1, in which reference is made to the need to promote respect for human rights and fundamental freedoms without distinction as to race, sex, language, or religion (and, on Soviet insistence, to the 'self-determination of peoples').[11] These references go some distance towards a new and more tightly defined standard of international legitimacy, whose ideal would be a popular government which respected human rights and possessed no colonies. A similar shift in the balance between the obligations and the freedom of states occurs in relation to a state's right to go to war. International conventions before 1919 had generally accepted that this right existed where a state's 'honour or vital interest' was involved. The League Covenant, while it attempted to place various limitations and constrictions upon the right, did not prohibit it in all circumstances. By contrast, the Charter recognizes only an 'inherent right of individual or collective self defence' under certain circumstances defined in Article 51. Similarly, diplomacy under Article 33 becomes not simply a possible way for states to resolve their differences, but a requirement for states in dispute. The Charter's stress upon the equality of states is somewhat qualified by the extensive powers it places in the hands of the Security Council, headed by its five permanent members, all of whom possess a veto. In this instance the Charter combines the traditional Westphalian principle that a state may not be legally bound without its consent (although restricting its full application to five states) with the idea of a great power concert, introduced in 1815 and formalized in 1919. Finally, the Charter invokes a new and potentially far-reaching set of norms when, in Article 55, it declares part of the purpose of international society to be the promotion of higher standards of living, full employment, and conditions of economic and social progress and development.

This extensive set of rules, values, aspirations, and institutions may be said to constitute an amalgam of the various views in 1945 of what international society did and should comprise. Its ambiguities and contradictions left it open for later generations to emphasize different parts of it in accordance with their differing national interests. After 1960, with a clear Third World majority in the General Assembly and the Security Council emasculated by the Cold War, the dominant themes in UN debates came to be opposition to racism and colonialism and the right of poorer countries to development. This led at times to a confrontational atmosphere between many former colonies and the leading Western powers, who were often depicted as the last bastions of colonialism and supporters of the racist state of South Africa. To the more radical within the Third World, the divisions between themselves and the West went much further than a difference of opinion over values. The West was seen not simply as resisting progress in the shape of the drive against colonialism and racism, but as the dominant element in a political, social, and economic order that systematically exploited the Third World through unfair economic practices, cultural imperialism, and support for the more reactionary forces in the Third World. Such thinking inevitably coloured their view of international society. Although the idea of sovereignty—the corner-stone of the Westphalian system—was enthusiastically adopted by all of the new states, the notion of an underlying solidarity among sovereign states was rejected by some of them. 'What has international law done for the people of Iran?', the Ayatollah Khomeini once reportedly asked,[12] reflecting a deep-seated suspicion of any suggestion that his Islamic Republic could be bound by rules that had been devised mainly by Western powers.

Four distinct perceptions of international society had emerged by the 1960s. These may be characterized as 'traditional', 'progressive', 'reformist', and 'revolutionary'. The traditional outlook, two of whose leading exponents were Britain and France, proceeded from the central Westphalian assumptions: states were sovereign in their internal (including their colonial) affairs; the principal norms of international society were those that defined the prerogatives of states and the bases of orderly relations among them; standards of international legitimacy should concern themselves primarily with such long-standing criteria for entitlement to membership of international society as effective control over a given territorial base. The progressive approach, represented primarily, if unevenly, by the United States, attempted to promote certain additional values as international norms, such as democratic government and observance of human rights. The other two groups drew their membership mainly from the Third World, with some support from the Soviet Union. For the reformers, such as India, international society was defined not just in politico-legal but in socio-economic terms. The UN Charter was seen as the basis of a radically revised international society, encompassing a new economic and cultural order, with opposition to racism and imperialism enshrined as basic norms. The revolutionaries also conceived of international relations as taking place within a complex system embracing economic and social as well as political and legal structures. However, they saw them essentially as instruments of Western oppression rather than as the basis of any genuine future community. They also tended to reject the reformers' belief in the possibility of achieving peaceful change within an existing international system whose fundamental feature in their view was a struggle between two opposing sides, one of which was doomed by history to inevitable defeat. Hence, although all four groups upheld the idea of sovereign equality, there was far less agreement amongst them in relation to other norms of

---

[12] My thanks to Professor Adam Roberts of Balliol College, Oxford, for bringing this remark to my attention.

international society. Indeed, sovereignty was perceived in different ways, with the revolutionaries going beyond a narrow legal definition by claiming that 'true' sovereignty required full control of a national economy, something that was denied to the poorer states by the imperialistic practices of the richer.

The international outlook of these four groups was shaped by their different historical experiences and domestic political situations. A leading student of revolutionary states suggests that domestic factors are more critical in the formation of the foreign policies of revolutionary regimes than of other states for four principal reasons.[13] The process of internal revolutionary change has 'inevitable international repercussions'; revolutionary regimes 'are prone to extremes of factional conflict' which affect foreign policy; victors in such conflicts are liable to seek to accuse their defeated opponents of having had treasonable relations with foreign partners; and the regime's domestic legitimacy depends in part upon its adoption of the appropriate external posture.[14] There are also slight variants upon these four themes, as when national unity under a particular revolutionary regime is so precarious that foreign policy issues are used deliberately to unite contending factions behind the leadership, or when a radical faction uses such issues to shift a revolutionary coalition towards its own preferred objectives.

The linkage between domestic politics and foreign policy is likely to be particularly strong in the case of revolutionary states in the Third World for four additional reasons. First, revolutions there will invariably have had an important external target either directly, as with colonial liberation struggles, or indirectly, where the revolution overthrows an *ancien régime* that is perceived as an 'imperialist puppet'. Second, two major goals of Third World countries, whether revolutionary or not, are nation building and modernization. The latter process will tend to create tensions between the old and the new modes of production, with foreign—usually Western—countries frequently associated with the unpopular new technology. Given the link already perceived by many in the Third World between their economic underdevelopment and 'Western imperialism', it is easy to see how the process of

[13] F. Halliday, *Revolution and Foreign Policy: The Case of South Yemen, 1967–1987* (Cambridge, 1990), 53–4.
[14] Ibid.

modernization can provoke anti-foreign reactions. So far as national unity is concerned, many of the new states have boundaries that reflect the convenience of their former colonial masters rather than any principle of nationality or geographical appropriateness. This has led to many irredentist issues in the Third World, which leaders have sometimes exploited for their own domestic ends. In other cases revolutionary regimes have sought to promote a broader unity with other states or peoples, on racial, religious, or ideological grounds, partly to deflect opposition from their own national minorities. A third distinctive feature of Third World revolutions has been the role of the charismatic leader, who has sometimes appealed to a far wider audience than his own countrymen, or has sought such an appeal to bolster his image at home. A fourth important factor has been the impact of the Cold War. The great majority of Third World revolutionaries have at some point adopted a stance hostile to the United States, widely seen as the principal element in the global system of imperialist exploitation and oppression which various revolutionary ideologies see as the ultimate cause of poverty and backwardness in the Third World. Such hostility has frequently evoked a counter-revolutionary response from the United States and support from the Soviet Union, which has inevitably increased American antagonism. The process has often been exacerbated by confiscation of foreign-owned assets by the revolutionary state, in pursuit of its own economic objectives. The loss of access to Western technology and investment that this may occasion, combined with a perceived threat from the United States, has sometimes drawn the revolutionary state into a close relationship with the Soviet Union.[15] Hence the revolution has become an important issue in the Cold War, since it has affected both the competition for influence between the superpowers and the contest between the politico-economic systems that each represents. In this respect the Cold War may be said to have intensified the familiar pattern whereby revolutionary states provoke counter-revolutionary responses from other states, with a general increase in international tension the inevitable consequence.

---

[15] F. Halliday, 'States and Revolution in the South', in C. Thomas and P. Saravanamuttu (eds.), *The State and Instability in the South* (New York, 1989), 99–111.

INDONESIA, 1960–1965

Sukarno's Indonesia is almost a paradigm of the domestic–international linkages discussed above. Without a strong power
base other than his own prestige as leader of the anti-colonial
struggle against the Dutch, Sukarno had to keep in check two
contending forces, the army and a large communist party (the PKI).
Their mutual hostility ensured an approximate internal balance of
power, but one that was always threatened by the prospect of civil
war between the two—an eventuality that threatened Sukarno's
position whichever side won. Hence, his dominating preoccupation
was to prevent the conflict between the two from erupting into
violence. His chosen means to this end were internally to promote a
social and political revolution and externally to lead Indonesia into
increasingly confrontational postures both in its general international stance and in its relations with its neighbours. In this way he
sought to associate the army and the PKI with a revolutionary cause
at home, of which he had made himself the guiding inspiration,
while at the same time keeping the army preoccupied with external
threats.[16]

This domestic context forms part of the explanation for
Indonesian foreign policy during the 1960–5 period. However,
Indonesia's international behaviour may also be seen as deriving
from Sukarno's revolutionary nationalism, which was evident well
before Indonesian independence. Sukarno saw Indonesia as having
been denied its true place in the world by Western imperialism.
After independence, the international system was still seen as
structured in ways that prevented Indonesia from realizing its full
potential. The ultimate solution was for the international system to
be restructured; in the meantime Indonesia should not feel
constrained by arguments to the effect that it was a member of an
international society with certain rules and standards of conduct
which it was bound to observe. Sukarno had an essentially
dialectical view of international relations, which he saw as a
constant struggle between declining and rising forces, defined by
him as 'old established forces' (OLDEFOS) and 'new emerging
forces' (NEFOS), with the future belonging to the latter. This led
him not only to line up with international groupings which he

[16] H. Feith and P. Castles, *Indonesian Political Thinking* (Ithaca, NY, 1970),
37–8.

perceived as part of the NEFOS, such as Afro-Asian organizations, but to seek to shift them towards more confrontational postures *vis-à-vis* the OLDEFOS. By 1965 he was aligning Indonesia more emphatically with the most radical elements within the Afro-Asian world, such as China and North Korea.[17]

In common with other revolutionary leaders, Sukarno discerned a close link between his international and his domestic struggles:

Since we are in a revolution, we should launch a confrontation to destroy the old order and create a new order. In launching a confrontation we will have enemies at home and abroad who want to preserve the old order. In the broader sense of the word, there will be a collision between the old and new forces or between the new emerging forces and the old established forces.[18]

As with other revolutionary states, radicalism in foreign policy was employed in part as a legitimizing device for the regime's domestic policies, since it enabled the Indonesian revolution to be portrayed as part of a world-wide movement:

The Indonesian Revolution and the Revolution of Asia and Africa are to uproot imperialism, to uproot colonialism, to uproot capitalism in order to build socialism, to consolidate a new world.[19]

In such a global revolution Indonesia could not regard itself as bound by international law or by any international agreement which ran counter to the revolutionary objective of greater justice:

if [an international agreement] contains elements which are in conflict with human justice—whether in the political field, the economic field or the military field—then it is an obligation to revise that agreement at the time when the balance of power alters ... We may not leave alone eternally and forever a certain law which is based upon the power of the strong over the weak.[20]

The culmination of this opposition to the existing structures of international society came at the beginning of 1965, when Sukarno

---

[17] See J. D. Armstrong, *Revolutionary Diplomacy: Chinese Foreign Policy and the United Front Doctrine* (Berkeley and Los Angeles, 1977), 114–49, for a fuller discussion of Indonesian foreign policy under Sukarno.

[18] D. E. Weatherbee, *Ideology in Indonesia: Sukarno's Indonesian Revolution* (Yale University, Southeast Asian Studies, Monograph Series, 8: (New Haven, Conn., 1966), 2.

[19] Ibid. 25.   [20] Ibid. 80.

announced Indonesia's withdrawal from the United Nations, a body that he had described earlier as 'a product of the Western state system'.[21]

Sukarno was unusual amongst Third World revolutionaries in that his foreign policy did not acquire an explicitly anti-American orientation until 1964. His specific foreign enemies were, first, the Dutch, and later the British; he saw the latter as the creators and controllers of Malaysia, against which he embarked upon a policy of 'Confrontation' from 1963. As Confrontation left Indonesia increasingly isolated diplomatically, she drew closer to the Soviet Union, and more so to China, whose military assistance was essential for Confrontation.[22] Another factor impelling Indonesia upon the same diplomatic course was that the radicalization of Indonesian foreign policy acquired its own dynamic and momentum, so that each move leftwards further narrowed the country's options internationally. Sukarno's speech of 17 August 1964, 'A Year of Living Dangerously', marked the first occasion when he was openly anti-American; further steps in this direction, including Indonesia's recognition of the Democratic Republic of Vietnam, occurred during 1965.[23]

The failed communist coup against the army in September 1965, which was followed by a massive purge of the PKI by the army, severely reduced Sukarno's real power and led to a reorientation of Indonesian foreign policy in more moderate directions. This may perhaps be seen as an example of 'socialization', albeit of a rather unusual kind. Indonesia had commenced its international life with a predictably anti-colonial outlook but not with a particularly radical foreign policy orientation, identifying itself primarily as part of the non-aligned movement. Its development of a more assertive foreign policy followed internal political changes at the end of the 1950s, and this assertiveness became more pronounced during the 1963–5 period, when Indonesia found itself drawing ever closer to the small camp of revolutionary states. However, both the domestic situation and Indonesia's external stance were becoming increasingly untenable and counter-productive. Whether Sukarno would have been prepared to recognize this or to reverse course without the army's effective assumption of power is uncertain. In many

[21] D. E. Weatherbee, *Ideology in Indonesia: Sukarno's Indonesian Revolution.*
[22] Armstrong, *Revolutionary Diplomacy.*
[23] Ibid.

respects he appeared to be trapped by the circumstances he had helped to create, partly in order to maintain an internal balance that proved in the end to be unsustainable.

CUBA

Like Indonesia, Castro's Cuba has displayed in its international relations some characteristics that are to be found in virtually all revolutionary states, some that are common amongst Third World revolutionary states, and some that are unique to it. Similarly, the interaction between Cuba and the international society, although in many respects following familiar lines, has certain distinctive features.

Central to Cuba's uniqueness has been a strong belief in the necessity for international revolution and a willingness at times to let this override more immediate and obvious interests. Although this is inseparable from its antagonism towards the United States, it is also essentially an ideological position, in the sense that it is only fully comprehensible if it is seen as part of a *Weltanschauung* that conceives of the world as in the throes of the final crisis of capitalism, with the end result assured, but capable of being hastened if Marxist-Leninists do their revolutionary internationalist duty. In many respects Cuba's position may be compared with that of the left-wing opponents of the Brest-Litovsk treaty, such as Bukharin, who took the view that unless international revolution followed closely upon the heels of the Bolshevik revolution, the revolution in Russia would be defeated.

Cuban resentment of perceived American mistreatment of their own country in the past may be what has given their antagonism toward the USA its emotional intensity, but the foundation of their belief in the necessity for world-wide revolution is their conviction that imperialism constitutes an interconnected global system, with the United States at its head. Support for international revolution, therefore, is not only required by the international nature of the system to be overthrown, but is also a means of hitting at Cuba's immediate enemy. In Castro's words:

The imperialists are everywhere in the world. And for Cuban revolutionaries the battleground against imperialism encompasses the whole world . . . And so our people understand . . . that the enemy is one and the same, the same one who attacks our shores and our territory, the same one who attacks everyone else. And so we say and proclaim that the revolutionary movement in every corner of the world can count on Cuban combat fighters.[24]

Moreover, although history's destination is clear and inevitable, it is 'improper revolutionary behaviour to sit at one's doorstep waiting for the corpse of imperialism to pass by'.[25]

Although the confrontation with imperialism takes many forms, its spearhead is direct armed struggle, as epitomized by the Vietnam War since this presents the confrontation in its sharpest terms, and helps to raise the consciousness of those engaged in the struggle as well as those observing it.[26] In this respect the Cubans found themselves diverging during the 1960s from the official Soviet line, which supported the thesis that states might be able to make a 'peaceful transition' to socialism. Another contentious issue was Cuba's insistence from 1966 that 'reformist' parties, even when they called themselves 'communist', should be shunned in favour of 'those who, without calling themselves communists, conduct themselves like real communists in action and in struggle'.[27]

Given such a comprehensive dismissal of even moderate Marxist-Leninist positions, more conventional standards of international conduct could clearly not be expected to constrain Cuba. As early as 1960, Castro was complaining that the 'dead letter' of international law had provided no protection for Cuba against America's act of 'economic aggression' in cutting its sugar quotas from Cuba, since 'reality imposes itself on the law set forth in international codes' and reality dictated that the powerful prevailed over the weaker.[28] In 1959 the Cuban journal *Revolución* had acclaimed Cuba's new foreign policy for not being 'encased in the old moulds of international law'.[29] By 1966 Castro was defiantly declaring that Cuba would not seek to re-establish diplomatic relations with those Latin American states that had broken off

[24] Cited in J. I. Dominguez, *To Make a World Safe for Revolution: Cuba's Foreign Policy* (Cambridge, Mass., 1989), 116.
[25] Ibid.
[26] M. Kenner and J. Petros (eds.), *Fidel Castro Speaks* (Harmondsworth, 1969), 218.
[27] Ibid. 201.
[28] Ibid. 48.
[29] Dominguez, *To Make a World Safe*, 117–18.

relations but would base its diplomatic position on new, revolutionary principles:

We will not re-establish diplomatic relations with any of those governments that obeyed imperialist orders; we have no interest in doing so; we have no desire to do so. We will only establish diplomatic relations with revolutionary governments in those countries; and, therefore, with governments that show they are independent.[30]

Cuba has supported its revolutionary internationalist position with action in three distinct ways. First, it has sent troops to Algeria, Angola, Ethiopia, and Grenada, to help ideologically compatible governments to deal with internal or external foes. Second, it has provided material and moral support for revolutionary forces in many South American countries, and several outside its own region. In one case, that of Bolivia, it attempted, through Che Guevara's expedition, virtually to create a revolution *ab initio*. Finally, it has used its membership of various international fora, such as the non-aligned movement, to promote 'anti-imperialist struggles'.

Although Cuba's international behaviour might be explained in part as the attempt of a weak state faced with an extremely powerful enemy to maximize the few weapons at its disposal, and hence as less ideological and revolutionary than it appears, such an interpretation would be inadequate and misleading. American hostility towards Cuba was not inevitable in 1959 and did not become implacable until 1960, mostly as a consequence of Cuba's own unremitting antagonism and newly proclaimed Marxist views.[31] Moreover, Cuba's policies in the 1960s damaged not only its relations with the United States and its South American 'lackeys' but also those with Morocco, during the Algeria–Morocco conflict, and China, during the 1979 Sino-Vietnamese border war, even though Cuba had stronger economic links with Morocco and China than with Algeria or Vietnam. In such cases Cuba appears clearly to have opted for ideological correctness, in the shape of a judgement as to the moral rights and wrongs of each conflict, over more concrete interests.

However, Cuba has not been able entirely to ignore more practical considerations, and these have been responsible for the

[30] Kenner and Petros, *Fidel Castro Speaks*, 202–3.
[31] Dominguez, *To Make a World Safe*, 16–26.

strongest pressures upon it to conform to the accepted canons of international conduct: to become 'socialized'. For example, Castro rebuked unofficial attempts by over-enthusiastic Cubans in 1959 to spread their revolution to Panama and elsewhere. This amounted to direct intervention in a country's internal affairs, he declared, adding that the principle of non-intervention provided some protection for Cuba's own sovereignty and should not be violated.[32] Cuba's later government-sponsored support for revolutions elsewhere made adherence to an unqualified principle of non-intervention less easy to maintain, although by 1975 Castro was offering a somewhat ambiguous declaration of Cuba's willingness to abide by generally accepted rules of international conduct:

We live in a world where respect for international norms is a must, and we have always been willing to respect them. But those who have tried to export counterrevolution will never have the right to demand that we respect international norms.[33]

More concretely, when revolution had failed to materialize throughout South America by the late 1960s, Cuba, confronted with the high political and economic costs of its isolation, felt obliged to resort to more conventional diplomatic means in order to achieve such equally conventional objectives as the restoration of official relations. It was relatively successful in this endeavour, even to the extent of reaching an agreement in 1973 with its arch-enemy the United States, about aerial hijacking, while achieving a general improvement in its relations with most countries in the region. However, its quest for international respectability did not prevent it from sending military assistance to the Marxist government of Ethiopia in 1977, or from supporting revolution in Colombia in 1980. By 1990, with socialism in headlong retreat elsewhere, Castro was still defiantly reiterating his socialist internationalism.

CHINA

In certain respects, Chinese foreign policy under Mao Zedong derived from influences similar to those that determined Cuba's revolutionary internationalist stance. In both cases an ideology that

---

[32] Dominguez, *To Make a World Safe*, 117–18.
[33] Ibid. 121.

postulated an ongoing global conflict with imperialism as the motive force of history appeared to be confirmed by confrontational experiences with the leading 'imperialist' power in Korea, the Bay of Pigs, and elsewhere. Both doctrine and national interest, therefore, appeared to dictate a policy of revolutionary internationalism aimed at weakening the USA world-wide and eventually bringing it to its inevitable defeat. Certainly, viewed through American eyes, the two were hardly to be distinguished: both represented a revolutionary Marxism that was not merely anti-American but fundamentally disruptive of any kind of stable international order.

There were, however, some important differences. Cuba was a small state whose capacity to play a world role was only made possible through Soviet protection and finance. China was a potential great power in its own right, but one whose legitimate entitlement to such symbols of great power status as a seat on the UN Security Council and even general diplomatic recognition was denied for many years by American support for the rival claimant to the right to govern all China: the Kuomintang regime on Taiwan. Hence the People's Republic of China had one entirely conventional international aim—to break free from its US imposed diplomatic isolation and receive general acknowledgement of its legitimacy—existing alongside its declared revolutionary objectives. Moreover, as a major power it had a substantial interest in the outcome of events in its own region, during a period of considerable tension and instability across its entire southern frontier. Some of its policies—for example in relation to the Indian subcontinent—were dictated by straightforward security and defence considerations, with little or no revolutionary purpose discernible. In other cases, the degree of support for revolution in a particular country varied directly with the level of attachment between that country and the United States.[34] Far fewer were the instances, such as China's Indonesian policy in the mid-1960s, where a very high priority was given to revolutionary prospects.[35]

This general pattern should not, however, be taken as evidence that China merely manipulated revolutionary rhetoric in a cynical fashion to explain and justify policies that were in fact determined

[34] For a detailed exposition of this thesis, see P. Van Ness, *Revolution and China's Foreign Policy* (Berkeley, Calif., 1970).

[35] Armstrong, *Revolutionary Diplomacy*.

by other considerations. As with the Soviet Union, the legitimacy and *raison d'être* of the ruling regime derived both from its ideology and from its capacity to organize society according to socialist principles. Unlike Lenin, Mao Zedong, China's revolutionary leader and chief ideologue, lived on for twenty-six years after the revolution and retained an essentially revolutionary outlook throughout that period. China's standing in the world was to some extent bound up with its claim that its revolution was a model for Third World states. Its credibility as a revolutionary state was important in its developing confrontation with the Soviet Union during the 1960s, since Beijing accused Moscow of 'revisionism', or a less than wholehearted devotion to the sacred scriptures of Marxism-Leninism. A consistent attempt was therefore made until the 1980s to relate China's foreign policy to a conceptual and terminological framework derived from Marxism-Leninism as filtered through the prism of 'Mao Zedong Thought'.

Claims that Mao had developed a variant—or a 'concrete application'—of Marxism-Leninism that was of significance for all developing nations appeared as early as 1936, and throughout the 1950s there were frequent assertions to the effect that Mao had 'solved the problems of revolution in colonial and semi-colonial countries'.[36] However, it was only after the sharp deterioration in Sino-Soviet relations from the late 1950s that the Chinese attempted to formulate a comprehensive statement of their distinctive views on international affairs in the course of pursuing their polemics with the Soviets and other 'revisionists'.

The Chinese singled out for their fiercest criticism the new Soviet line on peaceful coexistence that had appeared from 1956. This argued that the emergence of nuclear weapons had created a fundamentally new situation, in which the highest priority was to prevent a new world war, with the implication that circumstances that might lead to a US–Soviet conflict should be avoided, if necessary through Soviet–US collaboration. Hence the orthodox Leninist views, that war was inevitable while class divisions remained and that certain kinds of wars might actually assist the world revolutionary process, needed to be amended. Other 'revisionists', such as the Italian communist leader, Togliatti, went even further and suggested the existence of a potential community

[36] Lu Ting-yi, 'The World Significance of the Chinese Revolution', *People's China*, 1 July, 1951.

of interests between all states in which it was possible to 'renovate the structure of the whole world' and to establish 'a new world order' by building 'an economic and social order capable of satisfying all the aspirations of men and peoples for freedom, well-being, independence and the full development of and respect for the human personality, and for peaceful co-operation of all states'.[37]

In the Chinese view, such arguments were not merely 'revisionist', they were tantamount to capitulation to the class enemy. The Chinese contended that struggle against US-led imperialism was the dominant feature of the current era. The 'main battlefields' of this struggle were located in Africa, Asia, and Latin America and national liberation wars constituted its cutting edge. The threat of nuclear war had diminished since the launch of the first earth satellite by the Soviets in 1957. This, in Beijing's view, had shifted the balance of forces decisively in favour of the socialist camp, making it possible for the Soviets to support national liberation wars against American allies in the Third World without fear of an American nuclear response. In fact, armed struggle against 'US imperialism' and its 'lackeys' was necessary 'to smash the nuclear blackmail practised by US imperialism and defeat its plan for launching a new world war', as well as to push the world revolution forward.[38] Not only was Togliatti's advocacy of a community of interests between states unacceptable idealism but it stemmed from a false perception of an international society structured in terms of states rather than classes. The Chinese analysis of international affairs did not 'deny the class struggle' in this way but depicted US power as being confronted by a broad transnational coalition that embraced 'the world socialist camp, the international working class, the national liberation movement, all countries which oppose war, and all peace loving forces'.[39]

Another aspect of 'Soviet revisionism' with which the Chinese profoundly disagreed was the argument that it was possible for countries to make a peaceful transition from capitalism to socialism. During the 1950s Moscow had moved a considerable distance from its original categorization of India and other former

[37] 'The Differences Between Comrade Togliatti and Us', *Peking Review*, 4 Jan. 1963.
[38] *Two Different Lines on the Question of War and Peace* (Peking, 1963), 36.
[39] 'A Great Anti-Imperialist Call', *Red Flag*, 16 Dec. 1960, *Survey of Chinese Mainland Magazines*, 28 Dec. 1960.

colonies as not truly independent to a point where its relations with such states formed an important part of its global diplomacy. Clearly, for Moscow to appear to be advocating violent revolution against governments with which it was cultivating close relations would be potentially extremely harmful to Soviet interests, so a less embarrassing formulation was required. However, both ideology and the experience of their own revolutionary war led the Chinese communists to opposite conclusions. Armed struggle against the 'bourgeoisie' was not only virtually inevitable, it was desirable for its consciousness-raising side-effects upon the 'revolutionary masses'.[40] Peaceful transition to socialism was not a practical proposition and might even damage the revolutionary cause. Communist parties, in Beijing's view, needed to differentiate themselves clearly from social democratic and other parties and prepare for their historical role of seizing state power through armed force. 'Parliamentary struggle' had, at best, only a limited and secondary part to play in this process.[41]

In their denial of interests shared by socialist and 'imperialist' states, their class-based and transnational analysis of world affairs, their support for revolution and for armed confrontation with the United States, and their apparent attempt to base policies upon long-term assumptions about the future course of history, China's international relations were conceived and conducted outside the Westphalian framework. Their effect was particularly extreme during the Cultural Revolution of 1966–73, when China's internal convulsions spilled over into her foreign affairs to such an extent that she had relations that could be considered normal only with a handful of states.

The Chinese claimed throughout this period that, far from being a subversive force, they were the true defenders of sovereignty for Third World countries, since, in their view, true sovereignty required a government that was fully independent of 'imperialism'. However, opposition to 'reactionary' governments was also an imperative imposed by long-term revolutionary considerations:

The central problem of revolution is State Power. If the State power of the nationalist countries in Asia and Africa falls into the hands of the agents of

---

[40] 'Outline of Views on the Question of Peaceful Transition', in *The Origin and Development of the Differences between the Leadership of the CPSU and Ourselves* (Peking, 1963), 58–62.
[41] Ibid.

imperialism, it means the forfeiture of independence and the return to the status of a colony. Therefore, to the Asian and African countries, to combat imperialist subversion, first and foremost US subversion, has become an urgent task. It is necessary for Afro-Asian countries to be vigilant against imperialism's frontal attacks and particularly against its stab in the back, and against its bribery of reactionary militarymen to engineer counter-revolutionary *coups d'état.*[42]

Inevitably, things were not seen in this light by those 'reactionary' governments which suspected China of interfering in their internal affairs for its own revolutionary purposes. Such suspicions received some confirmation both from Chinese support for opposition groups in various Afro-Asian states and from Chinese analyses of Afro-Asian developments, such as that contained in secret Chinese army documents captured in 1961. These argued that Africa was 'now the centre of the anticolonialist struggle' but needed to be guided along 'the road of healthy development' so that its revolution could take a socialist course. If only one or two African countries were to 'complete a real national revolution', the effects might spread across the whole continent. China needed to 'take long range views' of the situation.[43]

Revelations of this kind, combined with the extreme militancy of the Cultural Revolution, led to rifts in China's relations with many Third World countries. A revolutionary posture had not only failed to achieve any gains on its own terms but had seriously damaged China's relations with many states at a time when China was threatened by the United States and, to an even greater extent, the Soviet Union. As other revolutionary states had done, China was discovering that its capacity to enjoy the benefits of normal inter-state relations were hindered by its apparent unwillingness to abide by the rules governing such relations. In the face of opposition from ultra-leftist factions, Beijing reached the inescapable conclusion that the pursuit of a revolutionary foreign policy would have to take second place to ensuring China's security. This required, first and foremost, *rapprochement* with the United States, a move which would simultaneously act as a balancing factor against the Soviet threat and enable China to break out of the diplomatic and

---

[42] *New China News Agency*, 2 June 1966, in *Survey of the China Mainland Press*, No. 3713.
[43] J. Chester Cheng, *The Politics of the Chinese Red Army* (Stanford, Calif., 1966), 484–5.

economic isolation that had been imposed upon it by the United States and by its own revolutionary extremism. From the end of 1968 Beijing began to signal its willingness to base its relations with the United States upon the principles of peaceful coexistence.[44] In 1971 Henry Kissinger's visit to China marked the conclusion of nearly three years of delicate diplomatic manœuvring between the two states, and initiated a rapid sequence of events during which China was formally recognized by many states and assumed the membership of the United Nations that had previously been held by Taiwan.

Tactical 'twists and turns' to deal with difficult circumstances or exploit new opportunities have been in the Marxist lexicon since Lenin's day. So long as the underlying strategy remains one of revolution, they involve, supposedly, no betrayal of fundamental principles. Developments as diverse as Brest-Litovsk, the Nazi–Soviet pact, and Khrushchev's policy of peaceful coexistence have been rationalized in this way. However, the Chinese went much further than depicting their *détente* with the United States as a 'twist and turn' (although they did that, too).[45] During the 1970s they developed a set of formulations that amounted to an entirely new conceptual framework for explaining their international relations. Moreover, the whole thrust of the new terminology was to shift the emphasis away from world revolution as a goal and from interpretations of world politics in terms of class and other transnational concepts, towards a more conventional analysis of international relations—one that could be more readily accommodated within a Westphalian perspective.

I have discussed these developments in detail elsewhere,[46] but their most important features may be briefly summarized here. Beijing had previously characterized world politics as an ongoing struggle between a dominant but historically doomed force, defined as 'imperialism', which was in alliance with various reactionary elements. 'Soviet revisionism', relabelled 'social imperialism' after the Soviet invasion of Czechoslovakia, was a secondary enemy. Imperialism was opposed by a broad coalition headed by national liberation movements and embracing 'oppressed nations' and 'revolutionary peoples'. All of these categories of 'enemies and

---

[44] Armstrong, *Revolutionary Diplomacy*, 95–104.
[45] Ibid.   [46] Ibid.

friends' derived from Marxist-Leninist classifications, as did the long-term historical context that Beijing employed for its evaluation of events. From 1970 this terminology was significantly amended by China's premier Zhou Enlai and others. The word 'superpowers' was used to refer to the United States and the Soviet Union, the terms 'hegemony' and 'power politics' to describe the undesirable features of the superpowers, and 'medium and small states' to denote one of the main forces thought to be antagonistic to 'superpower hegemony'.[47] Although the old language was not abandoned immediately, the message conveyed by these changes was clear enough. The Soviet Union had never fitted very easily into a Marxist-Leninist conceptualization of 'class enemies', nor was it easy to rally non-communist states around a banner of opposition to 'revisionism' or even 'social imperialism'. Both problems were avoided if international relations were depicted more conventionally in terms of a dichotomy between powerful and less powerful states. Such designations were also less harmful to China's relations with states which might feel threatened by the long-term revolutionary implications of the earlier formulations.

The change in language was accompanied by changes in China's external behaviour. Support for revolutionary groups was cut back during the 1970s and 1980s, as China began to make increasing use of the conventional diplomatic means for pursuing its objectives that became available in 1971. With the rise to power of moderate forces, headed by Deng Xiaoping, much of what remained of the old language of international revolution was effectively dropped. China proclaimed its primary goal to be modernization, and declared an economic 'open door' policy toward the rest of the world, encouraging external investment and, to some degree, internal capitalism. Demands for political liberalization to match what was taking place in the economic sphere tended to be met with repression and calls for China's 'socialist' goals to be safeguarded from foreign interference. However, this was never accompanied by a shift to a more radical international posture. In 1989, following the killing of student demonstrators in Tiananmen Square, China briefly reoccupied its former role of international pariah, but Beijing's response was quietly to seek to regain its status as a 'respectable' member of the international community by such

---

[47] Ibid. 100–1.

means as acquiescing in UN action against Iraq and giving comparatively short prison sentences to some of the Tiananmen demonstrators. In both cases China was attempting to show that the process of 'socialization' which it had undergone during the 1970s was firmly based. In the case of the Gulf Crisis Beijing was signalling its readiness to abide by those rules of international society that sought to sustain the rights of sovereign states. By its lenient treatment of its own dissidents it was implicitly acknowledging the existence of the new principle of international legitimacy embodied in the UN Charter, which called upon states to observe certain minimum standards of human rights within their own domain. Whether its motives in either case were entirely free from expediency or opportunism is immaterial to the central point for this study, which is that China's internal and external behaviour had been influenced and constrained by the very un-Marxist conception of an international society. However, cynicism about Chinese motivation may be unnecessary. After China's disastrous Cultural Revolution, many Chinese concluded, in the words of a senior Chinese official in 1988,

that we must reform; we must open up, we must invigorate our society, we must welcome anything, any measure, any set of values that would promote the welfare of the Chinese people, and not some high-sounding theory about the world revolution.[48]

Socialization is a process in which a potential entrant to a society internalizes the norms and values of that society. In its search for 'any set of values that would promote the welfare of the Chinese people', China was clearly embarking upon a multifaceted attempt to become integrated with several distinct systems—the Western international economic order, for example. But well before its adoption of the market economy, the first stage in China's retreat from its previous, ideologically defined social identity occurred in its initial steps to conform to the norms of the society of states. This was a deliberate act, taken in the face of great opposition that included an attempted *coup d'état* in 1971. Chinese policy decisions in 1990–1 were a continuation of a process that had commenced many years earlier.

---

[48] China's Vice-Minister of Culture quoted on *International Assignment*, BBC Radio 4, 15 Apr. 1988.

LIBYA

In September 1969, following the successful *coup d'état* of a group of Libyan army officers, the revolutionary leaders gave this assurance to foreign governments: 'our enterprise is in no sense directed against any state whatever, nor against international agreement or recognized international law. This is purely an internal affair.'[49] Less than a year later, after the seizure of the assets of several foreigners in Libya, in apparent violation of Libya's treaty obligations, the revolution's leader, Muammar Gaddafi, declared: 'No provisions or treaties will stand in our way because treaties and agreements which do not recognize our rights will be treated as such.'[50] Gaddafi had, in effect, announced Libya's commitment to a revolutionary international posture that was to dominate Libya's foreign relations during the next two decades. The specific policies which derived from this revolutionary outlook represented an attempt to make concrete Gaddafi's personal ideological creed, which was itself an idiosyncratic and often confused collection of ideas, none of which, taken separately, was in any sense original but which, taken as a whole, did constitute a distinctive perspective on international affairs and a multifaceted challenge to the Westphalian conception of international society.

The main tenets of Gaddafi's creed were Arab unity, anti-imperialism, Islam, a form of popular socialism, and a vaguely conceived universalism.[51] He was greatly influenced in his early years by the example of Nasser, who had written of Egypt's location within 'a group of circles which should be the theatre of our activity',[52] namely the Arab world, Africa, and Islam, and of imperialism as 'the great force that throws around the whole region a fatal siege'.[53] Nasser had in turn been influenced in his youth by his membership of the Young Egypt Society, which aimed to restore Egyptian greatness by making Egypt the leader of the Arab and Muslim worlds.[54] While such an aspiration was at least credible for

---

[49] J. Bearman, *Qadhafi's Libya* (London and New Jersey, 1986), 55.

[50] Ibid. 72–3.

[51] R. B. St John, *Qaddafi's World Design: Libyan Foreign Policy, 1969–1987* (London, 1987), 28–32, and B. S. Amoretti, 'Libyan Loneliness in Facing the World: The Challenge of Islam', in A. Dawisha (ed.), *Islam in Foreign Policy* (Cambridge, 1983), 54–67.

[52] Gamal Abd El-Nasser, *The Philosophy of the Revolution* (Cairo, 1954), 54.

[53] Ibid. 65.

[54] P. J. Vatikiotis, *Nasser and his Generation* (London, 1978), 73–5.

a country of Egypt's size and population, it was hardly realistic for
Libya, and many of Gaddafi's energies in the first years after the
revolution went into the pursuit of unity with Libya's neighbours,
in order to provide a larger platform from which to launch the
campaign for a single Arab nation. When these initial endeavours
failed, Gaddafi adopted a more aggressive attitude towards unity,
shifting his focus to African states like Tunisia, Sudan, and Chad, in
all of which Libya intervened in some way. By 1985 he had
concluded that his efforts had failed because of the close links
between corrupt and reactionary Arab regimes and 'imperialism',
which meant in his view that no notice should be taken of doctrines
of territorial sovereignty in the Arab world since these existed
primarily for the benefit of the imperialists:

We do not recognize the borders which have been drawn up by the colonial
powers to partition the single Arab people. We support, as of now, the
realization of Arab unity by force—we support it, accept it and place our
resources at its disposal . . . This is what should be done now to save the
Arab nation from becoming several nations and from replacing the nation
by states. The Libyan state, the Kuwaiti state, the Mauritanian state and
the Lebanese state will replace the Arab nation, and this is dangerous,
especially as we are now in the stage of the international social revolution.
The stage of the national revolution has passed.[55]

Gaddafi's disregard for the legitimacy of states and their
boundaries is reinforced by his interpretation of Islam. One of the
consequences of colonialism, in his view, is that Arabs lose sight of
their culture, central to which is their religion. In common with
many other advocates of Islamic revivalism, he perceives the
continuing plight of Arabs and other Muslims as stemming from
their deviation from the true path of Islam, a return to which will
restore their fortunes and lead eventually to Islam's victory
world-wide. But this is a process that cannot take place in isolation
in a single Muslim country, and this implies that all Muslims have a
legitimate interest in the revolutionary regeneration of every
Muslim society.[56] Moreover, since the chief enemy of Islam is
imperialism, the global struggle for Islam—or jihad—is also a
struggle against imperialism. It is therefore the case that 'any
contribution to liberate the world from imperialism should be
considered an integral part of *jihad*'.[57] Since imperialism is the chief

[55] Cited in M. Sicker, *The Making of a Pariah State* (New York, 1987), 128–9.
[56] Amoretti, 'Libyan Loneliness'.
[57] St John, *Qaddafi's World Design*, 36.

enemy of Libya's own regeneration in line with Gaddafi's theories, her support for revolutionary movements in Latin America and Central America was a form of self-defence[58]—an example, of course, of a type of proposition that has been advanced by many other revolutionary states. If any further explanation is required of Libya's tendency to determine its international relations within a framework provided by its own version of the 'great community', it may be found in Gaddafi's interest in natural law doctrines and the ideas of Rousseau.[59] Finally, the existence of the state of Israel, seen by Gaddafi as a colonial imposition on the Arab nation, has been used to justify any action anywhere in the world against Israel or in support of the Palestinian people.

Libya has employed the full gamut of potential instruments in pursuit of its goals. These include, for example, payments to African states to encourage them to break off diplomatic relations with Israel, and the propagation of Islamic culture through the establishment of schools, institutes, and mosques in any country prepared to accept them.[60] But it is Libya's sponsorship of terrorism and foreign revolutionary movements that has aroused the greatest controversy, and most hostility from other governments. The true extent of this sponsorship is impossible to establish with any precision. In some cases, such as that of a Muslim separatist movement in the Philippines, Libya has provided finance, weapons, and status in the shape of a diplomatic mission in Tripoli.[61] Revolutionary movements as far apart as Thailand, Burma, Northern Ireland, sub-Saharan Africa, the United States, and Latin America have all received varying degrees of Libyan support. Another form of violent intervention in other countries has involved the dispatching of assassination teams to murder Libyan opponents of the regime living abroad.

In the context of this discussion, Libya is perhaps best seen as an outlaw state rather than as the leading force behind an alternative vision of international society. This is because it has violated numerous international norms but, unlike several of the other revolutionary states that have been considered in this study, won little support for its universalist ideology, which is, in any case,

[58] Sicker, *The Making of a Pariah State*, 121.
[59] Amoretti, 'Libyan Loneliness', 61.
[60] Ibid. 65.
[61] Bearman, *Qadhafi's Libya*, 106.

often confused, contradictory, and unclear. Libya's oil wealth has given it an influence that it would not merit if judged by any other criterion of international importance, as Cuba has been enabled to take on a world role by the Soviet Union's money. Precisely how great this influence has been is difficult to calculate since such information is seldom freely offered either by Tripoli or by the recipients of Libyan cash. Although Libya may have made a marginal contribution to the growth of Islam in Africa and elsewhere, its financial and other support has been given to wide variety of groups, each of which has its own agenda and cannot really be considered as part of a single movement with Libya at the centre.

IRAN

Iran's Islamic revolution was of much greater global significance than the Libyan revolution, notwithstanding the best efforts of Colonel Gaddafi, since it not only had universal aspirations, but undoubtedly struck a chord with Muslims in many other countries, whether Shiite or not. Whether the Iranian revolution turns out to have had an enduring significance may be another matter. The Ayatollah Khomeini was never the universally acknowledged spokesman of Islam, nor even the undisputed interpreter of Shiism but rather an individual of enormous personal charisma, whose widespread appeal to others may have perished with him. Tehran may be contrasted with Moscow, which was for a period of nearly forty years the only centre and source of doctrinal truth for a world-wide revolutionary movement.

At one level the Iranian revolution may be interpreted as part of the pattern of 'revolt against the West' that we have been considering in this chapter. Iran, a country with a rich culture and memories of past glories, has undergone a more recent history of humiliation at the hands of the West. Attempts by its rulers after the First World War to impose modernization upon Iran through the adoption of Western mores did not meet with the success they had enjoyed in Turkey, but rather tended to associate the government of the Shahs with the hated imperialists. Similarly, the oil wealth of the 1970s served mainly to confirm the view of the Shah's opponents that he was an American puppet, bent upon destroying traditional values in Iran, since it brought economic disruption, conspicuous over-consumption by a few, rising but unfulfilled expectations in the many, and a large increase in the American role in Iran, symbolized by the presence of 35,000 Americans in the country by 1978.[62] However, what differentiated the Iranian from other Third World revolutions, and what made it a 'revolutionary state' as the term has been employed here, was its self-definition as the world's first Islamic Republic and the universalism flowing from Iran's identification of itself with a world-wide Islamic revolution. Since the Ayatollah Khomeini was the chief ideologue of Iran's version of revolutionary internationalism, it is to his ideas that we now turn.

The central pillar of Khomeini's world-view is his belief that history consists of the unfolding of God's purpose for man. Various biblical prophets had revealed parts of this purpose but the final, and most authoritative, revelation was that of Muhammad in the Koran. From these basic tenets, shared by all Muslims, Khomeini drew some more controversial conclusions. The first is that the dependent status of Muslim countries and their underdevelopment and other problems stems from their deviation from Islam:

If the Muslim governments and countries had relied on Islam and its inherent capabilities and powers instead of depending on the East (the Soviet Union) and the West, and if they had placed the enlightened and liberating precepts of the Quran before their eyes and put them into practice, then they would not today be captive slaves of the Zionist aggressors, terrified victims of the American Phantoms, and toys in the hands of the accommodating policies of the satanic Soviet Union. It is the disregard of the noble Quran by the Islamic countries that has brought the Islamic community to this difficult situation full of misfortunes and reversals and placed its fate in the hands of the imperialism of the left and of the right.[63]

Second, Khomeini gave a particular slant to the standard Islamic representation of the world in terms of an ongoing confrontation between believers and unbelievers.[64] Khomeini's preferred dichotomy is that between 'oppressors' and 'oppressed', clearly a much more overtly political distinction than the traditional Islamic

---

[62] H. Munson, Jr., *Islam and Revolution in the Middle East* (New Haven, Conn., and London, 1988), 124.

[63] Ibid. 12–13.

[64] P. J. Vatikiotis, *Islam and the State* (London and New York, 1987), 23.

one, particularly as Khomeini identified the oppressors with imperialism—headed by the United States, and supported by their 'political agents', the rulers of most Muslim countries.[65] The Constitution of the Islamic Republic of Iran explicitly calls upon Iran to support 'the just struggle of the oppressed and deprived in every corner of the globe'.[66]

The most controversial part of Khomeini's creed, and that with the most profoundly revolutionary implications, was his view of the legitimacy of contemporary nation states. His starting-point was the basic Shii belief that the only completely legitimate earthly authority belongs to the imams—the line of male descendants of Muhammad's cousin Ali—the twelfth of whom became supernaturally concealed in the ninth century AD. Until the reappearance of the twelfth imam, all earthly government is equally temporary and illegitimate.[67] This belief may be used to justify either an acquiescent or a militant attitude towards existing governments. Khomeini derived two essential principles from it. The first was that:

It is the duty of all of us to overthrow the *taghut*; i.e., the illegitimate political powers that now rule the entire Islamic world. The governmental apparatus of tyrannical and anti-popular régimes must be replaced by institutions serving the public good and administered according to Islamic law. In this way, an Islamic government will gradually come into existence.[68]

The second principle was that in the absence of the twelfth imam, government could approximate to legitimacy only if it was guided by 'trustees of Islam', or *fuqaha*: men learned in Islamic law. Khomeini, who depicted himself as the 'representative of the Imam',[69] clearly saw his own position in the Islamic Republic as the model for others to emulate.

Khomeini's genius as a revolutionary leader lay in his ability to represent essentially religious and mystical beliefs, such as the above, in ways that made them accessible to the Muslim masses and

[65] *Islam and Revolution: Writings and Declarations of Imam Khomeini*, trans. and annotated Hamid Algar (Berkeley, Calif., 1981), 49–50.

[66] D. Hiro, *Iran under the Ayatollahs* (London, 1985), 289.

[67] N. R. Keddie, *Roots of Revolution* (New Haven, Conn., and London, 1981), 5–9.

[68] *Islam and Revolution*, 147.

[69] M. Zonis and D. Brumberg, *Khomeini, the Islamic Revolution of Iran and the Arab World* (Harvard Middle East Papers, 5, Cambridge, Mass., 1987), 13.

relevant to their lives. He achieved this principally by linking each religious tenet to his other great theme: the struggle between the oppressed and the oppressors. Government in the Muslim world was not merely illegitimate; it was unjust, and the struggle to replace it with Islamic rule was also a struggle for justice. In Khomeini's view the injustice of temporal government stems from its concern with social order rather than with the perfecting of man:

There is a great difference between all the various manmade forms of government in this world, on the one hand—whatever their precise nature—and a divine government, on the other hand, which follows divine law. Governments that do not base themselves on divine law conceive of justice only in the natural realm; you will find them concerned only with the prevention of disorder and not with the moral refinement of the people. Whatever a person does in his own home is of no importance, so long as he causes no disorder in the street . . . Divine governments, however, set themselves the task of making man into what he should be . . . In the prophets' view, the world is merely a means, a path by which to achieve a noble aim that man is himself unaware of but that is known to the prophets. They know what the final destiny of man will be if he continues in his unfettered state, and they also know how different it will be if man is tamed and follows the path leading to the noble rank of true humanity.[70]

For Khomeini, in an extremely radical departure from Westphalian propositions, not only were earthly governments illegitimate but the state itself and the concept of nationality were equally invalid. In opposition to the Westphalian division of the world into sovereign states, each defined by territorial boundaries ('the product of a deficient human mind'), Khomeini offered his own version of the 'great community', asserting that the 'world is the homeland of humanity. All people should reach the salvation of both worlds here.'[71] The only important social identity for Muslims was their membership of the community of believers, or *umma*, which was defined by the leading Iranian ideologue Ali Shariati, as follows:

The ideal society of Islam is called the *umma*. Taking the place of all the similar concepts which in different languages and cultures designated a human agglomeration or a society, such as 'society', 'nation', 'race', 'people', 'tribe', 'clan', etc., is the single word *umma*, a word imbued with

---

[70] *Islam and Revolution*, 330–1.
[71] Cited in F. Rajaee, *Islamic Values and World View* (Lanham, Md., and New York, 1983), 77.

progressive spirit and implying a dynamic, committed and ideological social vision . . . Islam by choosing the word *umma* has made intellectual responsibility and shared movements toward a common goal the basis of its social philosophy.[72]

The centrality of the *umma* is written into the Islamic Republic's constitution:

According to the Koran all Muslims are of the same and one single religious community, and the Islamic Republic of Iran is bound to base its general policies on the coalition and unity of Islamic nations, and it should exert continuous efforts to realize the political, economic and cultural unity of the Islamic World.[73]

For Khomeini, Islamic unity was not just a religious requirement but a political necessity, in order to confront the 'imperialist conspiracy' to subjugate the Islamic world.[74]

If Khomeini had little time for the state itself, he had even less for the notion of a society of states with rules, norms of behaviour, and institutions to which Iran was supposed to adhere. For Khomeini the correct approach to international relations, as to everything else, was determined by Islam: 'the relations between nations should be based on spiritual grounds'.[75] These placed the trans-national bonds of the *umma* above unnatural territorial boundaries that merely served to divide Muslims from each other. Relations with non-Muslim societies were also to be conducted according to traditional Islamic principles, and in accordance with Khomeini's simpler distinction between the oppressed and oppressors of the world.[76] The condition of the former provided major opportunities for the further extension of the 'abode of Islam':

Today, we see the prospects for exporting the Islamic Revolution to the world of the oppressed and the meek more than ever before. The movement, which has been initiated by the oppressed and the meek . . . against the oppressor and the powerful . . . gives us hope for a bright future.[77]

[72] Amoretti, 'Libyan Loneliness', 58.

[73] Cited in C. Bernard and Z. Khalilzad, *'The Government of God'—Iran's Islamic Republic* (New York, 1984), 222 n. 3.

[74] Ayatollah Khomeini, *A Clarification of Questions*, trans. J. Borujerdi (Boulder, Colo., and London, 1984), 379–80.

[75] Cited in Rajaee, *Islamic Values*, 80.

[76] Ibid. 78–9.

[77] M. Zonis and D. Brumberg, 'Shi'ism as Interpreted by Khomeini: An Ideology of Revolutionary Violence', in M. Kramer (ed.), *Shi'ism: Resistance and Revolution* (Boulder, Colo., 1987), 57.

Institutions of international society such as the United Nations were merely part of the superpowers' structure of oppression[78] while, so far as international law was concerned, 'whatever is in accordance with Islam and its laws we will obey with humility. However, whatever contradicts Islam and the Qur'án, be it constitutional law or international treaties, we will oppose it.'[79]

In keeping with his beliefs in a global struggle against oppression and in his duty to extend the boundaries of the 'abode of Islam', Khomeini consistently called for the export of Iran's revolution. As in the utterances of other revolutionary leaders on this subject, there was sometimes a studied ambiguity on the precise means to be employed to this end, but as to the end itself there was no ambiguity:

We will export our Revolution throughout the world because it is an Islamic revolution. The struggle will continue until the calls 'there is no God but God' and 'Muhammad is the messenger of God' are echoed all over the world. The struggle will continue as long as the oppressors subjugate people in every corner of the world.[80]

Iran's internationalist duty followed inescapably from the Islamic nature of its revolution:

The Iranian Revolution is not exclusively that of Iran, because Islam does not belong to any particular people. Islam is revealed for mankind and the Muslims, not for Iran . . . An Islamic movement, therefore, cannot limit itself to any particular country, not even to the Islamic countries; it is the continuation of the revolution by the prophets.[81]

On other occasions Khomeini offered a third rationale for exporting the revolution, together with promoting Islam and fighting for the oppressed:

We must strive to export our Revolution throughout the world, and must abandon all idea of not doing so, for not only does Islam refuse to recognize any difference between Muslim countries, it is the champion of all oppressed people. Moreover, all the powers are intent on destroying us, and if we remain surrounded in a closed circle, we shall certainly be defeated.[82]

---

[78] Ibid. 53.   [79] Cited in Rajaee, *Islamic Values*, 81.
[80] Ibid. 83.   [81] Ibid. 82.
[82] *Islam and Revolution*, 286.

In arguing that exporting the revolution was a means of defending Iran itself, Khomeini was in part merely repeating similar assertions made by revolutionary leaders since 1789, but he was also concerned with a practical issue: breakaway nationalism by minority groups inside Iran. His emphasis on the unity of all Muslims and the irrelevance of nationality held a clear message for separatist movements in Iran itself.

Khomeini was less clear, if not actually evasive, on the subject of what exporting the revolution meant in practice. Sometimes he went to considerable lengths to remove any threatening implications for Iran's neighbours: 'When we say we want to export our Revolution we mean we would like to export our spirituality which dominates Iran . . . We have no intention to attack anyone with swords or other arms.'[83] On other occasions he appeared to argue that the revolution should be spread primarily through propaganda and also by the example set by Iranians both inside and outside Iran. Iranian diplomats were instructed by Khomeini:

It does not take swords to export this ideology. The export of ideas by force is no export. We shall have exported Islam only when we have helped Islam and Islamic ethics to grow in those countries. This is your responsibility and it is a task you must fulfil. You should promote this idea by adopting a conduct conducive to the propagation of Islam and by publishing the necessary publications in your countries of assignment. This is a must. You must have publications. You must publish journals. Such journals should be promotive and their contents and pictures should be consistent with the Islamic Republic, so that by proper publicity campaigns you may pave the way for the spread of islam in those areas.[84]

Similarly, Khomeini told Iranian athletic students going abroad:

our way of exporting Islam is through the youth who go to other countries where a large number of people come to see you and your achievements. You must behave in such a way that these large gatherings are attracted to Islam by your action. Your deeds, your action, and your behaviour should be an example; and through you the Islamic Republic will go to other places, God willing.[85]

The practice of Iran's revolutionary internationalism was rather more complex than these general principles might indicate. As in

[83] Rajaee, *Islamic Values*, 83.

[84] R. K. Ramazani, 'Khumayni's Islam in Iran's Foreign Policy', in A. Dawisha (ed.), *Islam in Foreign Policy* (Cambridge, 1983), 19.

[85] R. K. Ramazani, *Revolutionary Iran: Challenge and Response in the Middle East* (Baltimore and London, 1986), 26.

the case of Libya, hard facts about Iran's support for terrorist activities, its use of assassination squads against enemies overseas, its responsibility for unrest in other Muslim countries, and the other murkier aspects of its export of revolution are not easy to verify amidst a quagmire of rumour and sensationalism. Moreover, the confusion attendant upon any revolutionary situation, with many discordant voices claiming to speak for the revolution and no clear location of authority, sometimes made it hard to tell, in the early years of the Iranian revolution, whether every statement emanating from Tehran or every act of pro-Iranian groups abroad represented a definite policy decision by the Iranian government.

The revolution had a profound and multifaceted impact upon Iran's foreign relations. Previous policies towards the United States, Israel, and Egypt were reversed. Iranian support for Iraqi Shiite revolutionaries was one of the factors that led to the outbreak of the Iran–Iraq war in 1980, while Khomeini's determination to overthrow the Iraqi regime and replace it was largely responsible for Iran's refusal to end the war on relatively favourable terms when these were on offer from Iraq during the mid-1980s. Iran has also been at the centre of, or significantly involved in, various international revolutionary networks, most notably the Hizbollah (Party of Allah), which has been linked with numerous terrorist acts, especially in Lebanon.[86] Iran has also been implicated in violent acts of insurrection in Bahrain (over which Tehran has long claimed sovereignty), in Kuwait, and elsewhere, and it has used the Muslim pilgrimage to Mecca, the Hajj, as an opportunity for propaganda, both against Saudi Arabia and of a more general sort, in line with Khomeini's 1981 edict:

the aim of Islam in making the pilgrimage a duty for Muslims was the awakening of Muslims and their service of the interests of peoples and the world's oppressed.[87]

More orthodox means employed by Iran to spread its revolutionary message include broadcasts, conferences, pamphlets, and training camps.

Despite the considerable effort it has put into the export of revolution, Tehran has enjoyed very little success. There are some

[86] A. Taheri, *Holy Terror* (London, 1987), 77–89.
[87] Cited in F. Halliday, 'Iranian Foreign Policy since 1979: Internationalism and Nationalism in the Islamic Revolution'. Paper presented to the 1984 British International Studies Association Conference, p. 26.

obvious reasons for this. While many Muslims would endorse Khomeini's attacks on the West as the cause of the relative poverty of their states, and his call for a more authentic Islamic culture—'neither East nor West'—to be created, there is no consensus among them as to what concrete form a true Islamic society should assume. The peculiarly Shiite aspects of Khomeini's ideology are not accepted by the vast majority of Sunni Muslims, nor indeed by all Shii.[88] Moreover, nationalism remains a strong countervailing force to Islamic universalism. One leader threatened by Iranian internationalism, the Iraqi dictator Saddam Hussein, was able to deflect Iranian propaganda directed at Iraqi Shii, partly through a mixture of persecution and conciliation of his Shii population, but also by his ability to appeal to Iraqi nationalism against the ancient Persian enemy. Similarly, Kuwait employed pan-Arabist rhetoric in its attempt to counter Iranian inspired terrorism.[89] In the one country where Iranian-style fundamentalism did make some headway, Lebanon, it did so primarily because of the near anarchy prevailing inside Lebanon, and also because of the propaganda opportunities created by Israeli intervention.

The outbreak of war with Iraq had damaging consequences for Iran. Although the war helped Khomeini in his efforts to unify the country, it led in the end to compromises, in order to obtain arms, even with such hated enemies as Israel and the United States, and to highly pragmatic alliances with other enemies of Iraq, notably Syria. When the war eventually began to turn against Iran and Khomeini was forced to swallow the bitter pill of ending the war without having brought about the downfall of Saddam Hussein, more moderate forces in Iran were given the opportunity to bolster their position and ensure their succession to Khomeini. The Ayatollah was to show himself still capable of shrewd manœuvring to promote his own revolutionary faction, notably in the incident of his 'death sentence' against the British author Salman Rushdie. However, while this gave him back the initiative in Iran and sparked rioting elsewhere, it was essentially a temporary phenomenon, incapable of acting as a serious catalyst to international Islamic revolution. After Khomeini's death, although Iran remained publicly committed to his revolutionary cause, no fundamentalist

---

[88] J. L. Esposito, *Islam and Politics* (New York, 1987), 152–301, provides a detailed analysis of this question.
[89] Zonis and Brumberg, *Khomeini*, 45–6.

leader possessed anything approaching his charisma, and the new leadership under President Rafsanjani concentrated on gradually mending fences with Iran's neighbours and other countries which had become alienated from Iran during the Khomeini years. Rafsanjani has a delicate path to tread, since he needs to deflect accusations that he is abandoning the principles upon which the Islamic Republic was founded, and a restoration of Iran's relations with the United States (to say nothing of Israel) is some years in the future. None the less, the current government of Iran has clearly signalled its intention to restore Iran to a position of leadership in the region and, more generally, to re-establish the country within the world economy and the international community.

CONCLUSION

The revolutionary states that have been considered here share certain common characteristics. All were led by regimes whose hold on power was precarious, at least in the early years. This made it extremely important for them to strengthen their claim to legitimacy, which derived mainly from their identity as revolutionary standard-bearers. Second, all had suffered from various forms of imperialism, which gave their revolutions an international dimension from the outset. This was further emphasized when the regime's chief opponents had either fled to Western states or were supported by the United States or other Western powers. Third, the ideologies of all five depicted world politics in terms of an ongoing confrontation between good and evil, rich and poor, oppressed and oppressors, old and new, which helped to make them advocates of international revolution in some form. Fourth, all were hostile to any notion of an integrated international society, and in particular to any idea that they were bound by established rules of law. Finally, all departed in certain respects from currently accepted norms of international conduct, in their use of terrorism, support for revolutionary movements elsewhere, and other forms of interference in the domestic politics of foreign countries.

Considered purely in terms of their economic and military power, their impact on international affairs should not have been great, since all were relatively poor societies, even those which possessed oil. However, all five became involved in serious international conflicts. In several of these conflicts one factor that contributed greatly to their intensity was the American perception that the revolutionary state had openly disregarded the canons of acceptable international conduct. It was this element which turned what, from another perspective, might have been seen as civil wars of unification in Korea and Vietnam into major international wars and which gave impetus to American policy towards Iran in the 1980s. In these cases, as with the French and Russian revolutions, the increase in international disorder that followed the revolutions was a consequence of the reaction of established powers as well as of the deliberate policy of the revolutionary states.

What was true of the broader interaction between the revolutionary state and world politics was also the case of the impact of these states upon the post-1945 international society. Their direct impact was very limited. A world in which the majority of states were recently created was inevitably likely to find it difficult to reach a consensus over common norms and rules and these five states exacerbated this problem, as well as adding to the overall level of international insecurity. Their indirect impact was somewhat greater, since they contributed to the determination of the United States to assume a hegemonic role in the post-war world. All except Indonesia (which was a more localized problem and one being met by a British-led rather than an American response) found themselves confronted at various times by a range of American inspired economic, diplomatic, and cultural sanctions. This in turn helped to increase the use of such sanctions as a means of expressing the collective disapproval of international society and bringing pressure to bear upon offending states. Such sanctions formed part of the pressure towards socialization that these states encountered and the use of economic and other sanctions became an increasingly familiar socializing device in other cases of international rule-breaking.

6

Norms, Rules, and Laws

THE NATURE AND SOURCES OF INTERNATIONAL LAW

Order in social life generally is upheld by a wide range of different kinds of rules which in turn are supported by various distinct networks of social relationships. The 'law of the land', the most important of these systems of rules, is upheld by a structure of relationships involving legislature, judiciary, police, and populace. At a more informal level, a particular society's notions of what constitutes correct personal conduct are upheld by various smaller groups of family, friends, tribes, neighbours, colleagues, etc. Complex systems of rewards, ranging from national recognition to peer group approval, and punishments, ranging from death to the incurring of personal shame or dishonour, help to socialize individuals into behaviour that is in accordance with these different sets of rules.

In international society the nature, significance, and content of rules of state behaviour are more controversial matters. Even their existence may be disputed. In the absence of an authoritative law-making body, violation of whose edicts incurs sanctions which are enforced by courts and police forces, it has been argued that international law is not really 'law proper' but merely a set of moral injunctions.[1] Similarly, former American Secretary of State, Dean Acheson, asserted in 1963 that discussion of the legality of American actions during the Cuban Missile Crisis of the previous year was not well founded because 'much of what is known as international law is a body of ethical distillation' rather than true law.[2] Moreover, while one of the functions of law inside a state

[1] The most famous exponent of this view is John Austin (1790–1859), who defined law as the commands of a sovereign authority, backed by force. For a discussion of Austin's views, and their limited applicability to international law, see G. L. Williams, 'International Law and the Controversy Concerning the Word Law', *British Year Book of International Law* (1945), 146–63.

[2] Cited in P. E. Corbett, *The Growth of World Law* (Princeton, NJ, 1971), 18.

may be to enforce the community's moral code, morality has in general played a much less significant role in the relations among states. In a world of Christian, Buddhist, Hindu, Muslim, Marxist, and other states it is doubtful whether there is such a thing as a universal morality. In addition, states, it has been argued, occupy a different moral universe from individual human beings: the primary obligation of the agents of a state is to the citizens of that state and such an obligation may permit actions to be taken in the interests of the state which are deemed morally impermissible by the normal canons of personal behaviour. Finally, the intimate social relationships which help to ensure an individual's adherence to all of the written and unwritten rules of his own society have no exact parallel in the case of states; they have no friends, families, colleagues, or compatriots.

Writers on international law have offered many kinds of counter-arguments to claims such as the above.[3] Ultimately, however, the question 'is international law really law' is best answered by the fact that states clearly act as if their international conduct is constrained by rules which confer rights and impose obligations upon them. Moreover, the areas of international life that are affected by these rules have grown enormously over the last two hundred years. International law is an important part of the reality that confronts revolutionary states; it is also the part that most unequivocally affirms that states are members of an international society and that they share a collective responsibility for the maintenance of international order. Neither proposition is, prima facie, likely to win immediate or uncritical acceptance from a revolutionary state.

A useful, if unconventional, way of distinguishing the different kinds of obligations that states incur in international society classifies them under four broad headings; *norms*, *laws*, *rules*, and *standards*. This ordering of these four categories also represents the hierarchical ordering of their significance for states, although this is very approximate since the precise class to which a specific obligation belongs is in many cases a matter of debate, if only because the law of nations, like any system of law, does not stand still but develops in line with changing circumstances.

A *norm*, is a general principle that expresses some obligation that is fundamental and inescapable for all states. One such norm is

---

[3] Williams, 'International Law'.

pacta sunt servanda (treaties must be observed), which is partially qualified by another principle, *jus cogens*, according to which states may not enter into treaty commitments that contradict a peremptory norm of international law. *Jus cogens*, therefore, places legal norms in first place in the hierarchy of types of international obligations.[4] A *law* may be defined as a norm which has been given a concrete and specific definition, sometimes in an international convention, but failing that in the customary practice of states where states clearly perceive that practice to constitute a binding obligation for them. For example, the norm that diplomats are inviolate has been given clear expression as law in the 1961 Vienna Convention on Diplomatic Relations. A *rule* is one of the many thousands of lesser regulations that govern the day to day relations of states. In some cases these rules relate to some specific aspect of a law, such as the Article in the Vienna Convention which exempts diplomats from taxation in their receiving state. In other cases the rule may form part of an international regime that regulates some technical area of inter-state relations, such as telecommunications. A *standard* may be seen as an embryo norm, in the sense that it expresses some principle that certain states, but not all of them, would like to see become part of international law. Since 1945 these standards have frequently concerned matters that had previously been regarded as falling exclusively within a state's domestic jurisdiction. That is, they attempt to lay down criteria for a state's conduct of its internal as well as its external affairs. The endeavours of the UN General Assembly and other international organs over many years to make racial discrimination or colonialism internationally unacceptable relate to this category, and some would argue that these particular principles have evolved from standards into norms. The status of other standards, including the requirement for states to respect various human rights, is more controversial, while General Assembly calls for a new international economic order favouring the Third World remain aspirations. However, international law does not stand still; indeed, it is the formal expectation of the international community, embodied in the UN Charter, that it will 'progressively develop'. Texts on

---

[4] The *jus cogens*, principle has not been free of controversy amongst jurists, although it achieved a degree of formal legitimation by being written into the 1969 Vienna Convention on the Law of Treaties. See C. L. Rozakis, *The Concept of the Jus Cogens in the Law of Treaties* (Amsterdam, 1976), 4–6.

international law in the sixteenth century dealt mainly with the 'high politics' of inter-state relations: war, diplomacy, and the criteria for statehood and for determining the precise territorial boundaries of states. Today, although such concerns remain central, works on international law are equally likely to discuss the rights of sub-state groups and of individuals, and obligations which states owe to the international community as a whole, such as pursuing environmentally sound policies or protecting the 'common heritage of mankind'. Changes of this kind form part of the process whereby international standards acquire the status of norms and laws of international society.

The domestic law of a state derives from two principal sources: statutes passed by the state's legislature and, in countries with a common law tradition, legal precedents set by courts deciding particular cases. As there is no international legislature, and since cases decided by international courts are regarded as binding only upon the parties to the case, the question of the sources of international law has always been one of the more complex aspects of the theory of international law.

For Grotius the obligations of states stemmed not only from natural law but also from the nature of the society that existed among states. Just as individuals needed to live in society in order to achieve personal security ('tranquillity') and self-fulfilment, so too did states.[5] The basis of any society was 'that every one may have what is his own in safety, by the common help and agreement'.[6] In the international context this meant, essentially, acceptance of the various connotations of state sovereignty. In the case of international law, these included the fact that 'this Law of Nations is not like Natural Law, which flows in a sure way from certain reasons; but this takes its measure from the will of nations'.[7]

As this last phrase implies, the notion that the consent of states was required in some form for an international obligation to have the force of law was present from an early stage in the development of international law. By the nineteenth century natural law was less frequently alluded to, while the 'positivist' approach gained ground. This saw international law as a deliberate creation by

---

[5] Hugo Grotius, *De Jure Belli et Pacis*, ed. W. Whewell (Cambridge, 1853), Preface, p. iii.
[6] Ibid. i. 34.   [7] Ibid. ii. 206.

states and tended to stress the liberty of states, their rights and the need for them to consent to obligations more strongly than the constraints upon states, their duties and the categorical nature of certain kinds of obligation. However, if the 'will of nations' constituted the essential source of international law, that still left open the central question of how that will was to be made manifest: what kinds of actions by states counted as evidence that states believed themselves to be legally bound in particular cases?

Three means of determining states' consent to rules—or three 'sources' of international law—are encapsulated in the first three clauses of Article 38 of the Statutes of the International Court of Justice:

The Court, whose function is to decide in accordance with international law such disputes as are submitted to it, shall apply:

(*a*) international conventions, whether general or particular, establishing rules expressly recognized by the contesting States;

(*b*) international custom, as evidence of a general practice accepted as law;

(*c*) the general principles of law recognized by civilized nations.

In its use of the words 'recognized' in (*a*) and (*c*) and 'accepted' in (*b*), this Article draws attention to the need for some evidence that states have consented to be bound by rules, whether these be drawn from treaties, custom, or 'general principles'. The Article is also seen by some as implying a hierarchy of sources, with formal treaty obligations in first place, giving added emphasis to the doctrine of consent. Some would dispute this on various grounds, and would also dispute the relegation, in Article 38 (*d*), of judicial decisions to a 'subsidiary means for the determination of international law'.[8] However, there can be little doubt that the Article is a faithful reflection of the attitude of most governments to the order of importance of the various sources of international law. Obligations that states have freely entered into by signing treaties present fewer problems for governments than those that derive from some less tangible source, such as custom or general principles of law. It is possible to argue that, logically, custom is prior to treaties as a source of basic international law and that treaties are essentially 'evidence' of the existence of a customary norm but for all practical purposes treaties, as instruments controlled by governments, retain

[8] I. Brownlie, *Principles of Public International Law* (Oxford, 1973), 19–23.

their pre-eminence. Yet treaties are, for the most part, bilateral and so do not create universal legal norms, and although there has been an increasing trend since 1945 towards multilateral conventions in areas like diplomacy or the law of the sea, custom, in the sense of a general practice that states recognize as involving binding obligations, remains an indispensable source of general international law.

The third source of law referred to in Article 38 is capable of sustaining at least two meanings. The first is drawn from the old natural law tradition and the idea that there are universal moral imperatives to which all are subject. As with any theory of law, this presupposes the existence of a community, in this case the 'great community of mankind', that upholds certain universal values transcending the narrower values and interests of its members. The second interpretation of 'general principles of law' is that it refers to principles of jurisprudence that are widely accepted in the domestic legal systems of most states. This interpretation also implies a conception of an international society, in this case one in which the rudimentary notion of a society of states linked only by their common attribute of sovereignty is taken a stage further by having added to it the idea that states constitute a broader legal community in the sense that they share a common legal language, methods of legal reasoning, and basic legal concepts.

THE FRENCH REVOLUTION AND THE EMERGENCE OF MODERN INTERNATIONAL LAW

Even this brief discussion of the nature of international law suggests several obvious reasons why revolutionary states might have difficulties with the concept. These may be summarized as follows:

1. International law implies that its subjects, states, are identical in certain respects as members of an international society and that they share the same interest in upholding the common values of that society. Many revolutionary states, certainly including America, France, Russia, Libya, and Iran, have, by contrast, seen themselves as unique and most, with the partial exception of America, have commenced their international life by rejecting any notion of inter-state solidarity in the service of common interests or values.

2. International law is primarily concerned with the maintenance of order in international relations, whereas revolutionary states invariably perceive themselves as promoting their particular conception of justice. The requirements of order may not always be compatible with the claims of justice.[9] This is in part because, like any system of law, international law does not simply uphold order in general, it may also serve to underpin a particular international social order or hierarchy of states. Conversely, demands for greater justice invariably involve the necessity of transforming the existing social order. For example, in international society claims made, in the name of justice, in support of national self-determination have required the destruction of existing dynastic or colonial orders. The *ancien régime* of which revolutions see themselves as the foe may dictate the rules upholding the existing international structure of power as well as the domestic one.

3. Revolutions tend to embrace a cosmopolitanism that perceives the world in terms of transnational or 'great community' analytical categories, whose social universe is composed of classes, religious communities, or peoples rather than states. International law has traditionally concerned itself only with the members of the society of states, which, with only a few very limited exceptions, have been deemed to be the sole entities endowed with international legal personality.

4. The implication of customary international law is that new states may be bound by rules to which they have not given their express consent. Moreover, treaty obligations are regarded as binding upon the states that are party to them, not merely upon the governments that signed them: a change of government is not in itself deemed to be sufficient grounds for a treaty obligation to cease. Both of these assumptions are likely to appear objectionable to revolutionary states. As will be seen, the French and Russian revolutionary theories of the state added to the problems experienced by those states in accepting the traditional sources of international law.

5. Revolutionary states invariably see themselves as serving a higher and more permanent law—whether they define it in terms of god, nature, or history—than any transient, man-made substitute.

---

[9] See H. Bull, *The Anarchical Society* (London, 1977), 77–98 for a discussion of this problem.

Furthermore, their teleological perspective ill accords with the limited and static objective of any legal system, namely to regulate in an orderly fashion the affairs of the society to which it belongs.

A degree of cynicism concerning international law has never been entirely absent from public discourse about it, even, or perhaps especially, when states invoke it most loudly. This was certainly the case during the French revolutionary wars, when the law of nations was both broken and appealed to on numerous occasions by both sides. None the less, it would be wrong to see international law as simply an irrelevance during this period. The coalition against France acted from the outset upon the assumption that the French had threatened not merely some specific part of the law of nations but the entire body of formal and informal rules, principles, and practices that made up what was termed 'the political system of Europe'. It was their belief that this system had been fundamentally endangered by France that led them to make their comprehensive attempt to re-establish it after the defeat of Napoleon. For their part, the French revolutionaries were equally conscious that their most cherished principles challenged some of the time-honoured norms of international law. Contemporary international law was born out of the clash between the old system of European public law and the new ideas of the French.

Although all of France's enemies made frequent reference to their determination to restore the 'public law of Europe', they did not spell out in any great detail what they understood by this concept. For the absolute monarchies one pressing requirement was undoubtedly to reassert the legitimate rights of princes. The threat posed by revolutionary France to specific treaties, such as Munster, Osnabruck, and Utrecht, which had long underpinned the balance of power in Europe, was cited by all. A more general concern with France's somewhat cavalier attitude towards the very principle of treaty observance, *pacta sunt servanda*, was also much in evidence, as expressed powerfully by Edmund Burke in December 1792:

If a treaty opposed their ambition, they immediately affirmed that it was contrary to the laws of nature; and reduced every moral obligation to the same levelling principle . . . Thus the [revolutionists'] laws of nature superseded the laws of nations.[10]

[10] Cited in P. J. Stanlis, 'Edmund Burke and the Law of Nations', *American Journal of International Law*, 47/3 (1953), 404–5.

By the simple device of terming existing monarchies illegitimate under natural law, the revolutionaries had 'got rid of the law of nations and the obligation of treaties'. Indeed, their theory of the state amounted to the invention of a new law of nations.[11]

Burke shared with the leading statesmen of the anti-French coalition a view of international law that saw it as part of an overall system, encompassing the balance of power, alliances, good faith, etiquette, diplomacy, limitations on states' territorial ambitions, and 'compensations' to prevent unequal gains, through which the 'tranquillity' of Europe was ensured. This was the 'political system of Europe' which brought some degree of predictability to international life and some constraint to bear upon the worst excesses of which states were capable. He was well aware of the precarious nature of such an informal structure and of the need for self-restraint in maintaining it. He had also, accurately, perceived at the time that the first partition of Poland in 1772 was a major assault upon the principles on which European order rested:

The breach that has been now made, in those compacts that unite states for their mutual benefit, establishes a most dangerous precedent; it deprives, in a great measure, every separate power in Europe, of that security which was founded in treaties, alliances, common interest, and public faith. It seems to throw nations collectively into that state of nature, in which it has been supposed that mankind separately at one time subsisted.[12]

The first breach in the 'public law of Europe' may thus have been made by the established powers, and Sorel's cynical judgement that France after 1789 simply imitated their amoral ways is not unjustified.[13] Yet the determination with which the victorious powers went about their task of restoring international order, and their willingness from 1814 to accept a far more extensive management role in international affairs than anything Europe had previously witnessed, suggests that the Revolution had delivered a shock to the European system that was far greater than that caused by the rapaciousness of the Polish partition. The Revolution, in effect, forced the powers to look more closely at, and define more precisely, the underlying premises and basic norms of what they

[11] Ibid. 405.   [12] Ibid. 406.
[13] A. Sorel, *Europe and the French Revolution*, vol. i, trans. and ed. A. Cobban and J. W. Hunt (London, 1969), 66.

had—somewhat casually and uncritically up to that point—been accustomed to term the 'public law of Europe'.

The French revolutionary challenge to international law was at first implicit, in the sense that its doctrines contained an inherent contradiction of existing orthodoxies about the state. Some, such as Camille Desmoulins, were aware from an early stage of the potential confrontation between the new French ideas and the established principles of international law, and insisted that: 'The public law of Europe ought to be treated as Luther treated the canon law: all the books about it should be thrown into the fire.'[14] Others were more cautious about advocating such an open rift with international law, and in the early years there were frequent attempts to show how French conduct could be reconciled with it. Nevertheless, the challenge was there from the outset, since it stemmed from some of the most basic ideas of the French Revolution.

This was most obvious in the case of the new French doctrines about the nature of the state and the location of sovereignty. As early as 27 August 1789 the Declaration of the Rights of Man and Citizen, which laid down the basis of the new revolutionary theories, maintained in its second, third, sixth, and sixteenth articles that

2. The aim of every political association is the preservation of the natural and inalienable rights of man; these rights are liberty, property, security and resistance to oppression.

3. The source of all sovereignty resides essentially in the nation; no group, no individual may exercise authority not emanating expressly therefrom.

6. Law is the expression of the general will.

16. Every society in which the guarantee of rights is not assured or the separation of powers not determined has no constitution at all.[15]

The Declaration clearly implied, *as universal norms*, that the only fully legitimate states were those in which basic rights were guaranteed, that state sovereignty belonged to the people, and that popular consent was required to validate any laws. To these central ideas about the nature of legitimacy both in the state as such and in

[14] Cited in P. Gaxotte, *The French Revolution* (London and New York, 1932), 188.

[15] Full text of Declaration in J. H. Stewart, *A Documentary Survey of the French Revolution* (New York, 1951), 113–15.

obligations undertaken by the state was added the later principle that a state had the right to exist within its 'natural boundaries'.

One clear implication of the new doctrines was that pre-revolutionary treaties could no longer be regarded as binding upon France. This was on two grounds: they had been agreed between what were now deemed to be illegitimate rulers and they had not received the express consent of the French nation. Both arguments were advanced on numerous occasions in the first four years of the Revolution whenever an existing treaty appeared to obstruct French interests.

One such occasion concerned the Nootka Sound incident of October 1790, when Spain appealed for French help in pressing its claim to Vancouver Island against England, basing its appeal on the Family Compact of 1761 between the two states. Not only was the Family Compact a treaty of the old regime, it was a dynastic arrangement between two Bourbon monarchs. Although the Revolution had not yet entered its regicide phase, appeals to such an obviously antiquated principle were certain to arouse strong opposition, as indicated by this report from the British diplomat Earl Gower of the proceedings of one of the revolutionary clubs:

They say that they cannot adhere to engagements which never were just, which are incompatible with the rights of man and the principles of a free constitution and which render the nation dependent upon the will of one man and that man a stranger. They declare such treaties between Kings to be conspiracies against the people of their respective countries.[16]

As well as producing a negative response to Spain's request for assistance, the National Assembly debate on this question led to the comprehensive scrutiny, by a Diplomatic Committee especially appointed for the purpose, of all existing treaties, as well as of the whole process of foreign policy formulation. This will be considered in greater detail in the next chapter.

The issues that brought into the open the latent conflict between the new revolutionary ideas and the old principles of European public law were the French annexations of Corsica in 1789, the papal enclaves of Avignon and the Venaissin in 1791 and of Nice, Savoy, and the Rhineland during the first years of the revolutionary wars, and the abolition in 1789 of the remaining feudal rights held

[16] O. Browning (ed.), *The Despatches of Earl Gower* (Cambridge, 1885), 11–12.

by German princes in Alsace under the Peace of Westphalia. The cases of Corsica and Alsace were the least controversial of these, since formal sovereignty was vested in France, with Genoa and the German princes respectively retaining only certain limited rights. Such cases of ambiguous sovereignty had become rarer since 1648 than they were before it, but while the Holy Roman Empire continued to exist, disputes of this kind were inevitable. In both cases the National Assembly was able to conduct much of its debate in terms of existing public law and French rights under various treaties. But even as early as 1789, in the debate over the Corsican request for full union with France, there were voices urging that international law should be disregarded even if it *supported* French claims, since the only rightful basis for such decisions was the will of the peoples involved.[17] Over Alsace, a far longer debate about the rights and wrongs of the French case under existing international law took place, and the 'legalists' in the Assembly were able to carry their argument that, if the old feudal rights were abolished, the German princes were entitled to compensation in accordance with the Peace of Westphalia. None the less, Merlin of Douai, reporting for the committee that had considered this matter, went to some lengths to present the revolutionary as well as the public law bases of the French claim, and urged the Assembly to take primary account of the 'sacred and inalienable rights of nations'.[18] Kings were now only the delegates and mandatories of nations, where until recently they had been proprietors.[19] The will of the people, not the Treaty of Munster, was what counted.

A more dangerous argument advanced by Merlin was that only one of the competing claimants in Alsace—France—was a true, united state, possessing full legitimacy under the new revolutionary criteria.[20] Merlin's purpose in advancing this proposition was the strictly practical one of attempting to forestall any possibility that the argument that the self-determination principle gave a people the right to secede from one political association in order to join another might be used against France herself. One central problem with the idea of self-determination (it has persisted since the French

[17] *L'Ancien Moniteur*, xii. 194.
[18] *Archives parlementaires*, 28 Oct. 1790 (Paris, 1885), xxii. 75.
[19] *L'Ancien Moniteur*, vi. 241.
[20] J. P. McLaughlin, 'The Annexation Policy of the French Revolution', Ph.D. thesis (University of London, 1951), 47–9. The argument that follows is in part based upon Dr McLaughlin's analysis.

Revolution to the present day) was that, without a strict definition of the 'self' which had the right to form a sovereign state, there was no reason why any dissatisfied group of people should not attempt to assert this right. Plebiscites, which the French used on numerous occasions to determine the 'will of the people' were no solution.[21] Even assuming the fairness of a plebiscite conducted under the benevolent gaze of French soldiery, on what basis should the right to participate in a plebiscite be determined? Did all those living in a region have the right, or just those born there? How, in any case, were the territorial boundaries of a region to be determined? Did the minority in a plebiscite have the same right to a subsequent exercise in self-determination as the majority? Merlin's answer to the chaos that would result from an unlimited right of separatism was that when a people has solemnly expressed its desire to form a union, such a union was indissoluble except by the consent of the whole people. Although intended essentially to provide a basis for resisting separatist tendencies in France, this thesis carried the implication that the vast majority of existing states could be dissolved since they lacked France's legitimacy.

What had been mainly a potential conflict between revolutionary principles and existing international law became an open confrontation when the Assembly decided to annex Avignon and the Venaissin in 1791, following revolts there against papal authority. These territories had been under papal sovereignty for centuries, although there were grounds under European public law on which the papal title could be questioned, and these were duly brought before the Assembly.[22] However, even those who used public law to support annexation showed an increasing impatience with the notion that the future of the people of Avignon should be determined by such means. Pétion de Villeneuve, for example, after outlining the legal basis for the French claim, declared:

Who will deny that force, through the centuries, has been the sole public law of kings? To examine the way in which they traffic in peoples, in which they exchange them, in which they conquer them, in which they dictate their laws to them, is it not clear that they treat them as worthless cattle of which they are the owners? Yet it is this public law that is being appealed

[21] R. Redslob, *Histoire des grands principes du droit des gens* (Paris, 1923), 320–1.

[22] E. Nys, 'La Révolution française et le droit international', in *Études de droit international et de droit politique* (Brussels and Paris, 1896), 363–9.

to, it is these maxims that one cannot touch, so it is said, without disturbing social order, without destroying harmony. Great God! What order is it that reverses all morality and justice?[23]

The eventual decree incorporating the territories did cite the basis in international law of the French claim, and negotiations with the Vatican were commenced with a view to determining appropriate compensation, in accordance with established principles of law. But the greatest emphasis was given to the fact that the peoples of Avignon and the Venaissin had given their consent to incorporation.

The wider implications of the self-determination principle, including the danger of its being turned against France itself, were raised again during the debates on the papal enclaves. Once again the argument was advanced that French unity was based upon a genuine social contract which could not be dissolved without the consent of the whole people. As the *rapporteur* for the Diplomatic Committee put it, giving an ingenious twist to social contract theories:

The contract that a people makes with its administrators is of an entirely different nature from that which two peoples are able to make between themselves. The people, who instituted it without loss of their sovereignty, does not need the consent of the government to have the right to change it. I think that these truths are incontestable principles, which could shock only the enemies of liberty and the rights of nations. But, I will be told, the result of these principles would be for each part of the French empire to declare itself independent. I reply that no part of the French empire is actually independent because it is part of a society with which it has contracted. Without doubt, before the revolution, each part would have had the right of separation from the whole because no social pact united them with each other . . . But today, by a solemn confederation, the twenty four million French are bound amongst themselves, with the exception of some enemies of the public good, perhaps, by a social pact which creates obligations for each one towards all and all towards each one; no part of the empire has the right to break this contract.[24]

Of course, if this argument were taken to its logical conclusion, only France and the United States could count as truly legitimate states. All others could be dismantled if sections of their peoples so wished. They could also, if some real or contrived 'consent' could

[23] *L'Ancien Moniteur*, vi. 401.

[24] Cited in McLaughlin, 'The Annexation Policy', 102 (my translation).

be demonstrated, be amalgamated with France. Indeed, it was difficult to discover a norm in existing international law that could justify the annexations carried out by France during the revolutionary wars as conveniently as the new revolutionary principles, and public law was less frequently cited as the wars proceeded.[25] Not only could the self-determination argument be used to support French expansionism, but other revolutionary principles, such as 'reason' or 'natural law' could also be utilized. If all else failed, there was always the argument that, since France was the only legitimate state in Europe and since it was the standard-bearer of the revolution, its national interests should prevail over those of other, less advanced states.

All of these arguments were deployed in one of the definitive statements of French annexationist policy by Carnot, in presenting the Diplomatic Committee's decree on the incorporation of Monaco with France on 14 February 1793. It would be easy, he maintained, to argue the case for taking over Monaco in terms of the public law of the old diplomacy but he intended to confine himself to the new revolutionary basis for annexation.[26] However, the Diplomatic Committee had felt it necessary to devise 'a theory on territorial reunions', given that this issue 'involved the law of nations in its entirety'.[27] One possible theoretical basis for future French policy, which had been urged in some recent debates, he dismissed at once. This was the assertion that France was the centre of a future universal republic which any people that wished to do so could join by right. The problem with this idea was that purely French interests might be neglected in such an association:

To say that sovereignty resides in the universality of mankind is to say that France is only a portion of the sovereign, that it does not have the right, in consequence, to introduce the laws that suit it in its own home.[28]

French policy, declared Carnot, would be determined by natural law, national interest, and justice. From the first of these could be derived the principle that France should expand only to its 'natural frontiers'. From national interest, 'which will always be the first of our principles', and justice could be derived two central maxims:

[25] Ibid. 198.
[26] *Archives parlementaires*, 14 Feb. 1793 (Paris, 1900), viii. 549.
[27] Ibid. 546.   [28] Ibid. 547.

1. Every political measure is legitimate whenever it is required by the security of the state.
2. Every act which harms the interests of others without being indispensably necessary is unjust.

For Carnot, these maxims 'comprise the whole of the law of nations and are the foundation of private morality as they are of that of the nations'.[29] Significantly, however, although he claimed to derive these principles from natural law and universal morality, he also saw them as following logically from a conception of international society which perceived states as legal persons, much as the Westphalian conception did:

In effect the nations have a political order amongst themselves, just as individuals have a social order. They have, like them [individuals] their respective rights: these rights are independence, external security, internal unity, national honour, all those major interests, in a word, that a people could only lose if seized by force and which it can always take back when the occasion offers itself.[30]

The most serious French departure from existing public law was the declaration in 1792 that the Schelde was an open river. This directly contradicted the Peace of Westphalia and the Treaty of Utrecht, and brought Britain into the revolutionary wars. Lebrun, the French Foreign Minister, in his report on the Schelde decision, managed to employ every conceivable rationale for it, declaring to the National Convention that his reply to British objections had drawn upon 'arguments founded on the law of nature, on the law of nations, on all the principles of justice and liberty that the French people has made sacred and whose full and complete enjoyment it could not deny to the Belgians'.[31] However, in the subsequent debates on this issue, Brissot, reporting for the Committee of General Defence, could see little point in denying that opening the Schelde broke several existing treaties. The important point was that if France did otherwise it would violate the 'principles that will always guide its armies, the principles of eternal justice'.[32] A few minutes later on in his speech, he saw no contradiction in using equally strong words to attack Britain's violations of various

[29] *Archives parlementaires.*
[30] Ibid.
[31] Ibid. 19 Dec. 1792, p. 165.
[32] Ibid. 12 Jan. 1793, pp. 18–19.

treaties with France by its refusal to receive the French ambassador, its commercial policies, and the protection it gave to French *émigrés*.[33] However, the main thrust of his speech and of the debate over the Schelde issue was to make a clear break with the treaties that had defined the European order in the eighteenth century.

By this point the French had effectively declared their refusal to be bound by the public law of Europe where it conflicted with fundamental revolutionary principles or vital state interests. They had not, as certain Soviet jurists were to do in their turn, denied the validity of international law as such but had concentrated their fire essentially upon three specific complaints: existing public law had more to do with the rights of monarchs and with legitimizing vestigial feudalism than with the rights of peoples; treaties were deemed to bind a state even after it had undergone an internal revolution; the territorial distribution enshrined in the Westphalian and other treaties took no account of the new principles of popular consent and self-determination. They had also put forward a succession of general principles upon which a new law of nations might be built: the rights of peoples, natural law, reason, justice, and the rights and interests of states. By 1793 the last of these was becoming dominant, with frequent assertions of the right of all states to defend their interests.

A relatively pragmatic approach to international law was apparent from 1793, with France willing to appeal to it if it served some state interest but to ignore it where necessary on the grounds that it contradicted revolutionary principles. This pragmatism was a major reason why the National Convention did not adopt a 'Declaration of the Law of Nations' proposed by Abbé Grégoire. This contained the following twenty-one articles, which comprise a mixture of new revolutionary principles, ideas culled from Montesquieu and Vattel, and some traditional maxims of international law:[34]

1. Peoples are in a state of nature amongst themselves; they have universal morality for a bond.
2. Peoples are respectively independent and sovereign whatever the number of individuals who constitute them and the extent of the territory that they occupy. This sovereignty is inalienable.

---

[33] Ibid. 21.
[34] See Redslob, *Histoire*, and Nys, 'La Révolution française', 318–44, for discussion of the intellectual origins of the French ideas about international law.

3. A people must act towards others as it desires others to act towards it; what a man owes to a man, a people owes to others.

4. Peoples must do each other the most good in peace and the least possible harm in war.

5. The particular interest of a people is subordinated to the general interest of the human family.

6. Each people has the right to organize and to change its forms of government.

7. A people does not have the right to interfere in the government of others.

8. Only governments based on equality and liberty conform to the rights of peoples.

9. That which has an inexhaustible or innocent use, like the sea, belongs to all and cannot be the property of any people.

10. Each people is master of its territory.

11. Immemorial possession establishes the right of prescription between peoples.

12. A people has the right to refuse entry to its territory and to expel foreigners when its security requires.

13. Foreigners are subject to the laws of the country and punishable by them.

14. Banishment for crime is an indirect violation of a foreign territory.

15. Any actions taken against the liberty of one people are an assault upon all the others.

16. Leagues formed with the object of waging offensive war, or treaties which can harm the interest of a people, are an assault upon the human family.

17. A people can undertake a war to defend its sovereignty, its liberty, its property.

18. Peoples who are at war must not impede negotiations likely to bring about peace.

19. The emissaries of peoples are immune from the laws of the country to which they are sent in everything that concerns the object of their mission.

20. There is no order of precedence amongst the emissaries of nations.

21. Treaties between peoples are sacred and inviolable.[35]

The decree failed to secure final adoption, as it did when Grégoire presented it again two years later. On both occasions opponents of the decree cited as major obstacles the problems that it would cause for France in her relations with other powers.[36]

The Revolution had, in effect, shifted in its attitude towards international law from the radical reformism of its early period

---

[35] Nys, 'La Révolution française', 395–6.
[36] Ibid. 403–6.

through a contemptuous dismissal of international law whenever it conflicted with French aims to a prudent acknowledgement that international law—even in its current form—might be of some value after all. This was in part a product of the pragmatism of a nation at war, in part the outcome of what amounted to a four-year debate in which the French had attempted to work out a new basis for international law that took account of revolutionary principles. The idealistic cosmopolitanism that was associated with the 'great community' conception never won widespread acceptance. The more substantial debate revolved around the French conception of the state as the expression of the general will of its people rather than of the particular will of its sovereign. From this flowed the notions that international law concerned the relations between peoples and that states possessed legitimacy to the degree to which they met the essential criterion of popular consent. Moreover, a state that truly embodied the liberty of a people was an even more sacrosanct object than the product of Westphalia had been, and the dominant tendency in pronouncements from about 1792 onwards was to emphasize the inviolable rights of states, particularly of that state which most fully met the revolutionary criteria, France.

The contrasting approaches to international law of the early and later periods are best illustrated by the decree on non-aggression adopted in 1790, and the resolution on non-intervention of 1793. The French renunciation of wars of aggression was seen by delegates to the National Assembly as following naturally from the new basis upon which international relations were to be conducted: the solidarity and inherent peacefulness of peoples, all of whom were members of the same great community. As Volney put it in a proposed resolution, the Assembly should solemnly declare:

1. That it regards the universality of mankind as forming one and the same society, whose object is peace and the happiness of each and every one of its members.
2. That in this overall great society, the peoples and the States considered as individuals enjoy the same natural rights and are subject to the same rules of justice as are the individual members of particular and secondary societies.
3. That in consequence no people has the right to invade the property of another people nor to deprive it of its liberty and natural advantages.
4. That any war initiated by another motive and for another object than the defence of a just right is an act of oppression which it is important for

the whole of the great society to suppress since the invasion of one State by another State tends to threaten the liberty and security of all.[37]

By contrast, the principle of non-intervention derived unmistakably from a conception of states as sovereign entities with rights and duties that related to their membership of a society of states, not to any more broadly based moral imperative. The decree was one of a number of measures taken during the spring and early summer of 1793 that were intended to signal a retreat from both the revolutionary internationalism of the previous November and the idealistic cosmopolitanism of 1789–90. The aim now was to declare France's right to have whatever constitution it wished, while at the same time endeavouring to secure foreign recognition of the Republic through various steps designed to indicate what one author terms France's 'desire to return to the world of positive legal norms'.[38]

All of the new concepts and principles, whether these derived from cosmopolitanism, internationalism, or statism, that the French attempted to bring to bear upon the public law of Europe were honoured more in the breach than the observance. The same is true of their proclamations that the revolutionary wars would be conducted in accordance with the humanitarian ideas of the Enlightenment on the laws of war.[39] Yet this is not to say that the French Revolution was without significance for the evolution of international law. The ferocious struggle in which Europe was to be engaged for more than twenty years was not the best environment for a considered reform of the law of nations to take place in. But all of the French ideas entered the public discourse on international law and stayed there. The Revolution also had an indirect impact. The reaction to it by the victorious allies in 1814–15 did not simply put the clock back to 1789, even if that was what some may have believed had happened. The Concert of Europe represented a new international system, not a reconstitution of the old one, not least in its attempts to conduct the affairs of Europe in accordance with generally acknowledged rules of behaviour. Its more conservative objectives were unrealized. The nationalism which the French Revolution helped to unleash has dominated international relations to the present day and self-determination, arguably, now forms

[37] Nys, 'La Révolution française', 361.
[38] Kyung-Won Kim, *Revolution and International System* (New York, 1970), 89.
[39] G. Best, *Humanity in Warfare* (London, 1983), 75–127.

part of public international law, along with other principles such as non-aggression and non-intervention.

THE UNITED STATES: INCORPORATION AND REFORM OF THE LAW OF NATIONS

Unlike the French, Soviet, Iranian, and other revolutionary leaders, the American revolutionaries did not draw their inspiration from ideas that contained an inherent challenge to the state. Rather, their most urgent wish was to have their state accepted as a full and equal member of the society of states: to 'assume among the Powers of the earth the separate and equal station to which the Laws of Nature and of Nature's God entitle them', in the words of the Declaration of Independence. Hence, their initial response to that body of norms which defined the rights and duties of sovereign states—the law of nations—was, in the main, to embrace it enthusiastically as an important means of consolidating America's sovereign status. After the end of the War of Independence the move to a federal constitution also tended to enhance the standing of international law while in the 1790s internal political developments had the same effect. However, although most leading Americans emphasized the necessity of accepting the law of nations throughout this period, there were some significant differences of opinion as to what the content of that law was, or should be. This laid the foundations for a distinctive American approach to certain parts of international law.

Justice James Wilson, in a much cited comment during a case in 1796, declared: 'When the United States declared their independence, they were bound to receive the law of nations in its modern state of purity and refinement.'[40] A similar statement had been made four years earlier by Edmund Randolf, the first Attorney-General:

The law of nations, although not specially adopted by the constitution or any municipal act is essentially part of the law of the land. Its obligation commences and runs with the existence of a nation subject to modifications on some points of indifference.[41]

[40] Cited in E. Dumbauld, 'Independence under International Law', *American Journal of International Law*, 70/3 (July, 1976), 426.
[41] Cited in P. E. Corbett, *Law in Diplomacy* (Princeton, NJ, 1959), 39.

All were agreed that the body of rules and norms thus incorporated was the 'European law of nations'. In 1815 a judge in a prize court case went further and suggested that, as the United States was the successor to the state rights previously exercised by Britain, it had also inherited British obligations under the law of nations:

The law of nations is the great source from which we derive those rules respecting belligerent and neutral rights which are recognised by all civilized and commercial states throughout Europe and America . . . The United States, having, at one time, formed a component part of the British Empire, their prize law was our prize law. When we separated, it continued to be our prize law, so far as it was adapted to our circumstances, and was not varied by the power which was capable of changing it.[42]

These pronouncements by lawyers found their echo in the practice of American statesmen. As early as November 1775 George Washington was setting in motion measures to ensure that American naval activities were carried out in accordance with the existing law of the sea.[43] In their endeavours to determine the rules governing specific situations, American leaders turned to such authorities as Grotius, Pufendorf, and especially Vattel. For example, Franklin, thanking a friend for sending him copies of Vattel's work, said 'It came to us in good season, when the circumstances of a rising state make it necessary frequently to consult the Law of Nations.'[44] Jefferson had a similarly high opinion of Vattel, asserting that American policy was:

dictated by the law of nature and the usage of nations; and this has been very materially inquired into before it was adopted as a principle of conduct. But we will not assume the exclusive right of saying what that law and usage is. Let us appeal to enlightened and disinterested judges. None is more so than Vattel.[45]

Hamilton also frequently used citations from Vattel to support his case on various issues. The revolutionaries went to some lengths to ensure th⸍ ⸌riendly or neutral states were not alienated by actions

[42] Cited in H. H. Sprout, 'Theories as to the Applicability of International Law in the Federal Courts of the United States', *American Journal of International Law*, 26/2 (Apr. 1932), 285.
[43] H. J. Bourguignon, 'Incorporation of the Law of Nations during the American Revolution', *American Journal of International Law* 71 (1977), 271.
[44] Daniel Lang, 'Alexander Hamilton and the Law of Nations', in N. A. Graebner (ed.), *Traditions and Values: American Diplomacy 1790–1865* (Lanham, Md., New York, and London, 1985), 2.
[45] Ibid.

contrary to international law, and in 1777 the Committee of Secret Correspondence informed one of its agents that the Congress had 'an utter abhorrence of all irregular and culpable violation of the law of nations'.[46]

During the War of Independence, Americans placed great emphasis upon international law because they saw it as a means of enhancing their legitimacy, and also because they wished to be seen as acting 'responsibly' by potential allies against Britain. After the war the need for the thirteen states of the Confederation to accept a common interpretation of the law of nations and apply it in a consistent manner was an important part of the Federalists' case for stronger central control of foreign policy.[47] Jay, Madison, and Hamilton, the authors of the Federalist Papers, all paid particular attention to the need for a unified approach to such central issues of international law as making treaties, sending and receiving ambassadors, punishing piracy, and regulating commerce.

Hamilton was no starry-eyed idealist on the subject of international law. For example, in 1790, discussing the question of whether British troops had a legal right to pass through American territory in the event of a war with Spain, he wrote, after consulting all the relevant legal authorities:

Perhaps the only inference to be drawn from all this is, that there exists in the practice of nations and dogmas of political writers a certain vague pretension to a right of passage in particular cases and according to circumstances which is sufficient to afford to the strong a pretext for claiming and exercising it when it suits their interests, and to render it always dangerous to the weak to refuse.[48]

None the less, the need to promote respect for international law amongst the American people was central to his view of the United States as a weak but potentially very strong state which needed to pursue a prudent external policy in a world of contending sovereign powers. International law was also a valuable weapon in his

[46] F. Wharton, *The Revolutionary Diplomatic Correspondence of the United States* (Washington, 1889), ii. 256.

[47] See G. S. Rowe and A. W. Knott, 'The Longchamps Affairs (1784–86), the Law of Nations and the Shaping of Early American Foreign Policy', *Diplomatic History*, 10/3 (Summer, 1986), 199–220, for an account of some of the political debates over the law of nations in the period leading up to the adoption of the Federal Constitution.

[48] Cited in S. P. Rosen, 'Alexander Hamilton and the Domestic Usages of International Law', *Diplomatic History*, 5/3 (Summer, 1981), 193.

endeavours during the 1790s to strengthen the executive branch of government. As Bemis puts it, 'the law of nations, all too vaguely defined, was by executive proclamation made to supply the deficiency of domestic law'.[49]

Hamilton saw the law of nations as comprising a set of norms and rules that had evolved from long practice amongst the European states, not as some embryo moral order. Part of the attraction of international law to some Americans was that certain of its principles were derived by reasoning from natural law ideas, particularly the principles that formed the so-called 'necessary law of nations', rules that all states were obliged to follow. However, Hamilton was more concerned with the 'voluntary law of nations': the norms that states had worked out amongst themselves to regulate the unique institution of a society of sovereign entities. The following passage illustrates all of his underlying notions about the moral neutrality of international law, its pragmatic purposes, and its relation to the Westphalian conception of international society:

as to the external effects of war, the voluntary law of nations knows of no distinction between the justice or injustice of the quarrel; but in the treaty of peace puts the contrasting parties upon an equal footing; which is a necessary consequence of the independence of nations; for as they acknowledge no common judge, if in concluding peace both parties were not to stand upon the same ground of right, there never could be an adjustment of differences or an end of war. This is a settled principle.[50]

It was entirely consistent with such thinking, and also with his view of the United States as a weak and vulnerable state that he should be prominent among those who argued that the United States had, in effect, incorporated the 'established maxims' of international law, and that it should not seek unilaterally to amend them so that they were more in line with its ideals. In 1795 he issued the fullest statement to that date of the doctrine of incorporation:

A question may be raised. Does this customary law of nations as established in Europe bind the United States? An affirmative answer to this is warranted by conclusive reasons.

[49] S. F. Bemis, *The Jay Treaty* (New Haven, Conn., 1962), 193; cited in Rosen, 'Alexander Hamilton', 197. See also G. L. Lycan, *Alexander Hamilton and American Foreign Policy: A Design for Greatness* (Norman, Okla., 1970), 61, and *passim.*

[50] First public letter from 'Phocion' to the citizens of New York, Jan. 1784, in *The Papers of Alexander Hamilton*, iii. 490.

I. The United States when a member of the British Empire were in this capacity of a party to that law, and not having dissented from it when they became independent they are to be considered as having continued a party to it.

II. The Common law of England which was and is in force in each of these states adopts the Law of Nations, the positive equally with the natural, as a part of itself.

III. Ever since we have been an Independent nation we have appealed to and acted upon the modern Law of Nations as understood in Europe. Various resolutions of Congress during our revolution—the correspondence of Executive officers—the decisions of our Courts of Admiralty, all recognise this standard.

IV. Executive and legislative Acts and the proceedings of our Courts under the present government speak a similar language. The President's Proclamation of Neutrality refers expressly to the *modern* Law of Nations, which must necessarily be understood of that prevailing in Europe and acceded to by this Country. And the general voice of our Nation, together with the very arguments used against the Treaty [the Jay Treaty] accord in the same point. 'Tis indubitable that the customary law of European Nations is as a part of the common law and by adoption that of the United States.[51]

Hamilton's views were not shared by all. Some objected to them because they believed that international law could not be reconciled with republican ideals, others because the law of nations appeared to be being used to rationalize the consolidation of power in the hands of the federal executive. A more significant body of opinion, however, accepted the law of nations in principle but sought for opportunities to reform it. This group included John Adams, Franklin, and Madison, but its most significant figure was Jefferson.

Jefferson was as capable as Hamilton of using international law to justify American policy decisions that actually derived from concrete interests. He did so, for instance, in his various pronouncements on American territorial claims, which, he had maintained on one occasion, were based on the '*jus gentium* of America' rather than on a universally applicable law of nations.[52] In general, however, he was anxious to see international law serve the interests of justice and morality as well as order. He was particularly

[51] 'The Defence', No. XX, Oct. 1795, xviii. 341–2.
[52] C. M. Wiltse, 'Thomas Jefferson on the Law of Nations', *American Journal of International Law*, 29/1 (Jan. 1935), 69.

concerned to establish the principle that 'War between two nations cannot diminish the rights of the rest of the world remaining at peace.'[53] To this end he supported the liberal commercial principles for neutral ships that Americans had been advancing in various treaties since 1776.[54] These obviously served America's interest, first by ensuring supplies during the War of Independence, then by giving America the maximum freedom to trade during the French revolutionary wars; but Jefferson also believed that

Reason and usage have established that when two nations go to war, those who chose to live in peace retain their natural right to pursue their agriculture, manufactures, and other ordinary vocations, to carry the produce of their industry for exchange to all nations, belligerent or neutral, as usual, to go and come freely without injury or molestation, and in short, that the war among others shall be for them as if it did not exist.[55]

As well as espousing the rights of neutrals, Jefferson urged greater humanity during wars.[56] He was, in addition, instrumental in promoting a liberal approach to naturalization of foreigners, which limited the rights of their country of origin to extradite them.[57] Finally, he saw the system for judicial settlement of disputes amongst the thirteen American states as a model for the rest of the world, although in fact it was the Hamiltonian Jay Treaty with England that included the first reference to arbitration in an international treaty.[58]

It is a reasonably safe supposition that no European statesman cited Grotius, Vattel, and the other publicists as frequently as did either Hamilton or Jefferson. There were, it has been suggested, compelling practical reasons during the first twenty years of American history for its leaders to take international law so seriously. Even in considering Jefferson's more idealistic proposals, a concrete American interest can be discerned in each case. None the less, the net effect of the attention being paid to international law during this period was to create a foreign policy style in

[53] C. M. Wiltse, 'Thomas Jefferson on the Law of Nations', *American Journal of International Law*, 78.

[54] For an account of American endeavours in this respect, see G. L. Lint, 'The American Revolution and the Law of Nations 1776–1789', *Diplomatic History*, I/I (Winter, 1977), 20–34.

[55] Wiltse, 'Thomas Jefferson', 76–7.

[56] Ibid. 79.

[57] *The Papers of Thomas Jefferson*, ed. C. T. Cullen, viii (Princeton, NJ, 1954), 317–19.

[58] Ibid. vi. 505–6.

which legal arguments had a more significant place than they had in those of many European powers. The culmination of this tendency was the creation of the League of Nations, although a deeply seated isolationist impulse that also dated back to the post-revolutionary period prevented the United States from joining that organization. America's ascent to superpower status was marked by numerous violations of such current norms of international law as non-intervention. However, Jefferson's reformism was apparent even during this period, surfacing in areas like the United States' human rights policy. In its approach to international law, as in other aspects of its international behaviour, the United States remained both Jeffersonian and Hamiltonian.

THE SOVIET UNION AND THE QUEST FOR A THEORY OF RECONCILIATION

International law embodies one central and obvious proposition: that states belong to a society with its own norms and rules to which new entrants automatically subscribe upon attaining statehood. The Bolsheviks proceeded from an entirely different set of assumptions. For them, law was part of the 'superstructure' that had its basis in a particular set of economic relations. Capitalist economic relations would give rise to one type of law, socialist economic relations to another. The idea of a law common to the two systems was a logical paradox. Law was also a means of maintaining the dominance of a particular class, whose interests it reflected. It was a bourgeois fallacy to regard law as a genuine means of promoting or maintaining social order. Finally, the fundamental characteristic of the relationship between socialism and capitalism was struggle, given that one was historically destined to supplant the other. Rules whose aim was to promote their long-term coexistence, still more their co-operation, were meaningless.

In the context of international law, six central problems could be distinguished for Marxist theory and revolutions inspired by it:

1. Was the Soviet Union a state with the same legal attributes and obligations as bourgeois states or was it the vanguard of a social class, and therefore an international or transnational entity?

2. How could there be a system of law common to two distinct economic and social systems? Or, in the similar formulation of this

question by a leading Soviet international lawyer, Korovin, 'How is it possible in the light of Marxist-Leninist teachings concerning the basis and the superstructure, and those concerning state and law, that there exist norms of international law which are equally binding for socialist and bourgeois states?'[59]

3. On what grounds could the Soviet state co-operate with other states in the working of a system of rules and institutions that supposedly derived from a set of common interests and values which it denied?

4. How could the concept of sovereignty, which is basic to international law, be reconciled with a transnational perception of the world?

5. Could the Soviet state accept custom as a source of law in view of the fact that it had had no part in the development of existing customary norms?

6. On what legal basis were relations amongst socialist states to be conducted and how could two separate systems of international law (one for socialist states and one for all) be reconciled with each other?

The task of formulating theoretical answers to these questions fell to the lot of certain Soviet legal experts whose efforts will be considered shortly. However, the philosophical and logical issues involved did not greatly trouble the men who controlled the Soviet state. Their initial response to international law was to ignore or reject it when it suited their purposes and to utilize it when it supported their case. From the start, this selective approach was resisted by the other members of the international community, whose pressure led Moscow into an increasing acceptance of existing international law. In the 1930s, the threat from Germany caused the Soviets to pose as the leading champions of international law and order. The role of Soviet legal theorists became more and more that of providing a legal justification for every twist and turn of Soviet foreign policy. In the process, their initial quest for a means of reconciling ideology and practice tended to be forgotten.

Several of the earliest acts of the Soviet state involved a clear denial of international law. Treaties accepted by both the Tsarist and Kerensky regimes were abandoned, with Trotsky declaring in

[59] Cited in R. J. Erickson, *International Law and the Revolutionary State* (Dobbs Ferry, NY, 1972), 10.

1917: 'There exists for us only one unwritten but sacred treaty, the treaty of the international solidarity of the proletariat.'[60] All existing foreign loans were annulled, which also involved breaking treaties signed by previous Russian governments. The initial justification for repudiating treaties was revolutionary and Marxist: they had no validity in the relations between two entirely distinct social orders. However, as the anticipated world revolution failed to materialize and as the Soviets came increasingly to seek a firm basis in treaties for their commercial and diplomatic relations with the outside world, they resorted increasingly to an intriguing and somewhat novel justification for their earlier repudiation of treaties. This was the argument that the fundamental doctrine *pacta sunt servanda* had always been qualified by the subclause *rebus sic stantibus*, which expresses the principle that treaty obligations may be invalidated by a fundamental change of circumstances. The first use of this argument, by the Soviet delegation to the Genoa Conference, attempted to give it a revolutionary flavour by asserting the existence of a new legal norm that had come into being in consequence of previous revolutions:

the Russian delegation feels obliged to recall that principle of law according to which revolutions which are a violent rupture with the past carry with them new juridical relations in the foreign and domestic affairs of States. Governments and systems that spring from revolution are not bound to respect the obligations of fallen Governments. The French Convention, of which France declares herself to be the legitimate successor, proclaimed on 22 December 1792, that 'the sovereignty of peoples is not bound by the treaties of tyrants'. In accordance with this declaration revolutionary France not only tore up the political treaties of the former régime with foreign countries but also repudiated her national debt. She consented to pay only one-third of that debt, and that from motives of political expedience .... This practice, which has been elevated to the rank of doctrine by eminent legal authorities, has been followed almost universally by governments born of revolution or a war of liberation.

The United States repudiated the treaties of its predecessors, England and Spain.[61]

This argument managed simultaneously to assert that Soviet practice was grounded in existing law, that revolutionary states had

[60] Cited in E. H. Carr, *The Bolshevik Revolution 1917–1923* (Harmondsworth, 1971), iii. 26.

[61] J. Degras, *Soviet Documents on Foreign Policy*, i (London, 1951), 308–18.

succeeded in forcing the acceptance of a new doctrine in international law, and that the Soviet state was part of a continuous tradition created by revolutionary states. The claim that revolutionary states had amended international law in a progressive direction, which implicitly made that law more acceptable to the Soviet Union, continued to appear in Soviet discussions. A 1953 textbook, for instance, praised the French Revolution for advancing the principle of non-intervention, the right of asylum, the use of plebiscites to establish the will of the people, the rights of riparian countries to use of their rivers, the humane treatment of prisoners of war, and the principle of freedom of the seas. It also claimed that the October Revolution had advanced the 'democratization of international law' and introduced new principles such as the 'peoples' right to peace' and the notion that aggressive war was a 'crime against humanity'.[62]

The implied argument that 'bourgeois' and socialist states could accept a common body of norms because these had been reformed by revolutionary states did not solve the central ideological dilemma, that such norms were a priori impossible. Nor was it likely to win the acceptance of 'bourgeois' lawyers and statesmen, and Korovin, in a 1928 article aimed at Western international lawyers, confined himself to asserting that revolutions involved one example of the *rebus sic stantibus* principle:

Every international agreement is the expression of an established social order, with a certain balance of collective interests. So long as this social order endures, such treaties as remain in force, following the principle *pacta sunt servanda* must be scrupulously observed. But if in the storm of a social cataclysm one class replaces the other at the helm of the State for the purpose of reorganizing not only economic ties but the governing principles of internal and external politics, the old agreements, in so far as they reflect the pre-existing order of things, destroyed by the revolution, become null and void. . . . Thus in this sense the Soviet doctrine appears to be an extension of the principle *rebus sic stantibus*, while at the same time limiting its field of application by a single circumstance—the social revolution.[63]

One problem with such assertions was that they ignored the fact that there were several instances in which the Soviets found it

---

[62] *International Law* (Institute of State and Law, Moscow, 1953), 9, 46.
[63] E. Korovin, 'Soviet Treaties and International Law', *American Journal of International Law*, 22 (1928), 763, cited in A. Cassese, *International Law in a Divided World* (Oxford, 1986), 59–60.

convenient to base their diplomacy upon existing treaties. Despite some early suggestions that the Bolsheviks should treat prisoners of war differently according to their class origins—that officers should be treated as class enemies, and so forth—Trotsky insisted that they should adhere to existing conventions.[64] In August 1918 the Bolsheviks formally recognized that their national Red Cross society had not ceased to exist following the Revolution and that the Geneva Conventions on the laws of war bound the Soviet government as they had the Tsars.[65] Far more dubious, not to say hypocritical, were the several assertions by the Soviets of rights deriving from previous treaties. In 1920 Chicherin, protesting against an international conference that had granted the island of Spitzbergen to Norway, on the grounds that this matter was the subject of previous treaties signed by Tsarist Russia, sought an additional ideological rationale by arguing that Moscow stood for the interests of the working masses, who included fishermen and whalers with traditional rights in the area.[66] A later protest, against a meeting in 1923 of British, French, and Spanish representatives to arrive at a new statute on the international position of Tangier, referred solely to the Soviet right to participate under previous treaties.[67]

The Soviets did not only invoke their rights under old treaties, they increasingly found treaties to be a valuable means of defining their relations with other states, signing more than 250 treaties and other agreements between 1917 and 1922.[68] In some of these, they formally accepted an obligation not to foment revolution in their co-signatory's state. Treaties came increasingly to be cited by Soviet legal authorities as the most important source of international law. However, the Soviets found it impossible to ignore the fact that a great many international norms were based on custom, and as early as 1924 custom was implicitly acknowledged as a source of law in a treaty with Afghanistan, Article 3 of which stated that the embassies and consulates of the two states 'shall enjoy all

---

[64] Degras, *Soviet Documents*, i. 70–1, I. Lapenna, 'The Soviet Concept of "Socialist" International Law', *Yearbook of World Affairs* (London, 1975), 251.

[65] *Rapport général du CICR 1912–1920*, Bibl. CICR, 363, 191/7, p. 188.

[66] Degras, *Soviet Documents*, i. 181–2.

[67] T. J. Uldricks, *Diplomacy and Ideology: The Origins of Soviet Foreign Relations, 1917–30* (London, 1979), 151.

[68] J. F. Triska and R. M. Slusser, *The Theory, Law and Policy of Soviet Treaties* (Stanford, Calif., 1962), 27.

diplomatic privileges in conformity with the customs of international law'.[69] Even the far more difficult concept of 'general principles of law', which implied some commonality of values between socialist and 'bourgeois' states, found a place in early Soviet practice.[70]

In their first ten years, the Soviets thus accommodated in their international practice many of the basic elements of international law, albeit in a somewhat selective fashion. Their jurists were less successful in resolving the fundamental question of how such an acceptance of 'bourgeois' principles could be reconciled with Marxist ideology. The first to make a serious attempt to resolve this paradox was Korovin, whose ambitious aim was to 'create for the internationalist theoretician and practitioner a new outlook for a new reality'.[71] He began by attacking virtually the entire body of existing international law together with the basic concepts on which it was founded. For example, he opposed the concept of state sovereignty and the associated notion that the state was the sole subject of international law by arguing that both were based on the false claim of the state to be able to conciliate opposing interests within its borders.[72] However, he also rejected the anarchism of some Bolsheviks who claimed that international law was unnecessary and in any case impossible to conceive of in the relations between a proletarian state and bourgeois states. In his opinion, international law of some kind was inescapable because the Soviet Union had proved unable to isolate itself completely from the outside world and therefore some means of defining and regulating its relations with the bourgeois countries had to be found.

Korovin's solution was to suggest that, since the Soviet Union found itself in an interim situation in which world-wide socialist revolutions had not yet ushered in a new world, a new framework of international law was required for the period of transition between socialism and capitalism. His theory of international law for the transition period raised almost as many questions as it answered. For instance, was the law itself to be transitory, doomed abruptly to pass away with the end of capitalism? Korovin replied

---

[69] Cited in T. A. Taracouzio, *The Soviet Union and International Law* (New York, 1935). See also Erickson, *International Law*, 6.

[70] Triska and Slusser, *The Theory, Law and Policy of Soviet Treaties*, 14.

[71] Cited in J. Y. Calvez, *Droit international et souveraineté en URSS* (Paris, 1953), 43.

[72] Ibid. 44–6.

that the international law which he envisaged would, under the influence of the Soviet Union, be able to evolve in a progressive direction in line with the actual evolution of the world towards socialism.[73] Did the possibility of even a new system of international law imply the existence of a community of values and interests between the bourgeois and socialist worlds? Korovin could not fully accept this clearly un-Marxist proposition, but was too honest to be able to deny that his conception of international law did in fact carry this implication. However, he declared that only a partial community of interests was possible, in the limited area of trade and other economic matters, and with regard to a very restricted set of norms and values which he held to be eternal and classless, such as the eradication of disease and the preservation of artistic works. How could there be international law when he had denied the validity of the concept of state sovereignty? Here Korovin in effect resorted to two semantic devices. First he stated that while *state* sovereignty was inadmissible international law could be based on the concept of *national* sovereignty.[74] He claimed that the actual practice of the Soviet Union was a shining example of the observance of this principle, both in the rights which had been accorded to the nationalities which had comprised the former Tsarist empire, and in its treaties with Turkey, Iran, Afghanistan, and Mongolia, all of which had referred to national self-determination. Second, he maintained that the new international law would regulate the relations between the two *systems* of socialism and capitalism, rather than between states. The new legal order would construct a 'bridge between the bourgeois and socialist halves of humanity'.[75] In saying this Korovin was well ahead of his time: he had in effect given to the concept of 'peaceful coexistence' a meaning which went beyond even that given it by Khruschev more than thirty years later.

It did not take long for Korovin's writings to come under attack; his principal assailant was Pashukanis, whose work provided the theoretical basis of the Soviet attitude to international law until 1935. Pashukanis opposed as un-Marxist Korovin's contentions that a community of values and interests could exist between the two social systems and that international law could evolve in a

[73] Ibid. 82–5.   [74] Ibid. 58.   [75] Ibid. 79.

progressive fashion. He also asserted that Korovin had been guilty of abstract thinking in not taking sufficient account of the actual practice of the Soviet state. Pashukanis accepted Korovin's theory of international law for the transition period, but argued that all that was implied by this was that the Soviet Union regarded its acceptance of international law as a temporary compromise.[76] There should be no question of creating a new body of international law: the Soviet Union should simply accept in its entirety, for the moment, the existing structure of bourgeois international law. Unlike Korovin, who had stressed treaties as the principal source of law, Pashukanis felt that both treaties and customs were acceptable because the whole idea of international law was a bourgeois fallacy, but none the less one which could be used as a weapon for the defence of the Soviet state. In other words, Pashukanis proposed that the correct Soviet attitude towards international law, as towards any involvement with bourgeois society and its rules and values, should be one of dualism. He maintained that the Soviet dual policy towards international law should distinguish between its form and procedures on the one hand and its content on the other. The Soviet Union could accept the first, while in practice making international law serve its own ends.[77] The struggle between the two systems would thus take place within the formal structures and processes of bourgeois society: 'The significance of this period of transition is found in its changeover from an open struggle of annihilation . . . into a struggle within the framework of "normal" diplomatic relations and treaty agreements. International law becomes interclass law.'[78] However, Pashukanis was not able to avoid some of the complex philosophical questions which had troubled Korovin—for example, those concerning the personality accorded to the state by international law. On this point he argued that although the state was an instrument of oppression with regard to its *internal* functions, it did present a kind of unity in its *external* relations which permitted it to be personified and regarded as a legal subject.

By 1937 Pashukanis was himself the object of harsh criticism from Vyshinsky and others. The background to this new debate was very clearly the changes which the international situation had

---

[76] Cited in Calvez, *Droit international et souveraineté en URSS* (Paris, 1953), 100.

[77] Erickson, *International Law*, 8.

[78] Calvez, *Droit international*, 101.

been undergoing in the previous five years. For example, amongst other charges levelled against Pashukanis was that of 'nihilism', because of his refusal to see any intrinsic value in international law. The political reason for this charge is to be found in the new posture of the Soviet Union as champion of international law, in the face of assaults on that law by the fascist states. However, after Pashukanis's there were no major attempts at a new formulation of the Soviet attitude to international law. The subject was clearly dangerous, and the problems were intractable. Vyshinsky's thesis that international law was a means of regulating the 'struggle *and* cooperation among states'[79] was a half-hearted attempt at a 'reconciliation' theory, but one which did not confront any of the fundamental ideological questions which had concerned Korovin and Pashukanis. From 1951 the Soviet jurist Kozhevnikov began to stress coexistence and co-operation in what amounted to an 'adaptation' of theory: 'At the foundation of contemporary international law there are not two bases existing in separation from each other but the objective factor of the coexistence of these two bases.'[80]

Later on, the tendency was not so much to seek for ways of adapting theory as to ignore ideological questions altogether. For example, G. I. Tunkin, the most important Soviet international lawyer in the post-war period, felt able to urge his colleagues to set aside the ideological issues: these were not 'an insufferable obstacle to creating norms of international law'.[81] However, he was emphatic that the 'concept that the basis of law is community, particularly a common ideology, is completely unfounded'. Law resulted from the *division* of society into classes.[82] Given his pragmatic approach, Tunkin had no problem with accepting the conventional sources of international law. Treaties were still the most important source, but custom was also a valid source since customary norms emerged in practice by consensus, although this could be tacit in form.[83] Even 'general principles of law' were acceptable as a source, but these should not be seen as normative principles that bourgeois and socialist societies had in common.

[79] Triska and Slusser, *The Theory, Law and Policy of Soviet Treaties*, 15.
[80] Cited in Erickson, *International Law*, 11–12.
[81] G. I. Tunkin, *Theory of International Law*, trans. W. E. Butler (Cambridge, Mass., 1974), 48.
[82] Ibid. 27.   [83] Ibid. 133.

This was still 'very definitely' unacceptable. However there were 'legal concepts, logical rules, modes of legal technique, which are used in interpreting and applying law in general, both international and national, irrespective of the social essence of the law'.[84]

Tunkin also supported the concept of *jus cogens*—indeed, he claimed that the Soviet Union had been largely responsible for its adoption, against Western objections, at the Vienna Convention on Treaties.[85] However, he rejected both the idea that *jus cogens* derived from natural law and the notion that it represented the common principles of different legal systems. Like all international law, in Tunkin's view, *jus cogens* resulted from agreement.[86] The concept was evidently valuable as a means of supporting any principle that the Soviets might wish to advance as an international norm, but the danger that it could be turned against the Soviet Union needed to be guarded against. This caution had the effect of considerably diluting the concept, which, if it means anything, implies a norm (such as the prohibition of genocide) which exists as a moral imperative which states have no choice but to accept as an obligation. Such was, at any rate, the interpretation of Soviet jurists of the Gorbachev era, who disputed Tunkin's definition of the concept.[87]

By the mid-1950s fundamental ideological issues had all but disappeared from Soviet discussions of international law and there was a clear consensus identifiable around three basic propositions:

1. Existing international law was acceptable as a basis for Soviet relations with non-socialist states, but it was preferable for there to be clear evidence of implied or explicit Soviet consent to any specific rule or norm.

2. The principles of peaceful coexistence formed 'the criteria of the legality of all other norms formulated by states in international relations'.[88]

3. International Law had developed in a progressive and democratic direction under Soviet influence. Of the following list of basic principles of international law suggested by a Soviet jurist in

---

[84] G. I. Tunkin, *Theory of International Law*, 200.

[85] Ibid. 154.

[86] Ibid. 158–9.

[87] R. A. Mullerson, 'Sources of International Law: New Tendencies in Soviet Thinking', *American Journal of International Law*, 83 (1989), 494–518.

[88] Speech by a Soviet representative to the UN General Assembly in 1962, cited in Erickson, *International Law*, 47.

1959, numbers 1, 2, 4, 5, 6, and 7 were regarded by the Soviets as largely to their credit: 1. Peaceful coexistence. 2. Sovereignty and territorial integrity. 3. Non-interference in the internal affairs of other states. 4. The right of nations to self-determination. 5. Non-aggression. 6. Prohibition of aggressive wars. 7. The principle of just and democratic peace. 8. Equality of states. 9. Inviolability of diplomatic representation. 10. *Pacta sunt servanda*. 11. Freedom on the high seas. 12. Peaceful settlement of disputes.[89]

Rules and norms for relations of peaceful coexistence during a transitional period of 'struggle and cooperation' were clearly not appropriate to the 'new type of international relations' that was declared to exist amongst members of the socialist camp after 1945. Intra-bloc relations were said to be so substantially different from those amongst capitalists or between capitalists and socialists that even as early as 1947 a new form of international law was discerned by Soviet scholars. The countries of the socialist camp were, of course, declared to be sovereign: indeed, they were more fully so than 'bourgeois' states, since they alone embodied the popular will. But their relations were also said to be marked by the highest possible levels of co-operation, fraternal feelings, and solidarity with the socialist camp as a whole. A model for the legal basis of relations amongst such entities already existed, in the Soviet view, in the Soviet Union itself, which

is a prototype for the future association of the working masses of all states. The new socialist state evolved a new socialist legality and new legal forms and principles of governmental relations.

At the same time the socialist state did not reject all earlier legal forms of international relations which had evolved in the course of past history but, on the contrary, used individual old forms, filling them with a qualitatively new democratic content, in accordance with the principles of the socialist law.[90]

The purpose of this new socialist law was not merely to regulate intra-bloc relations in an orderly fashion; it was also teleological. Trade agreements, for example, were 'an important instrument for planned coordination of the development of national economies within the framework of the world socialist system'.[91]

[89] Ibid. 63 n. 2.
[90] Soviet jurist Kozhevnikov, cited in K. Grzybowski, *The Socialist Commonwealth of Nations* (New Haven, Conn., and London, 1964), 256–8.
[91] Ibid. 261.

The notion that there were, in effect, two distinct systems of international law, one for all states and one just for socialists, was at the heart of the attempts by Soviet jurists and others to justify the 1968 invasion of Czechoslovakia. Objections to the invasion on the grounds that it conflicted with 'the Marxist-Leninist principle of sovereignty and the rights of nations to self determination' were fundamentally flawed because they were 'based on an abstract, non-class approach'.[92] Norms of law could not be interpreted 'narrowly, formally, and in isolation from the general context of class struggle in the modern world'.[93]

Tunkin provided the fullest, if most contorted, attempt to explain the invasion in terms of the new legal norms that derived from 'socialist internationalism'. Class struggle, he declared, 'comprises the basic content of contemporary international relations' and given that, unity within the socialist camp against attempts by 'the forces of the old world to destroy or subvert any socialist state of this system' was an absolute imperative. Moreover, the sovereignty of socialist states meant something more than a narrow legal independence. It was in form and substance popular sovereignty and in these circumstances 'respect for the sovereignty of states is becoming, in content, respect for the rights of the peoples of the respective states'.[94] Brezhnev offered a similar argument in 1981, when he declared that in the 'world of socialism' relations among states had become relations among peoples.[95] By implication, therefore, an intervention against the government of a socialist state could in fact be an action in support of the socialist principle of sovereignty since it was in defence of the people of that state. While it is not unreasonable to dismiss such assertions as *ex post facto* rationalizations, they may also be seen as part of the alternative framework of ideas and assumptions to which many revolutionary states subscribe. In the Soviet case, they added a new layer of complexity, if not confusion, to the Soviet attitude towards international law. The existing norms of international law, which derived from the Westphalian conception of international society, could apparently be accepted even if such acceptance created an irreconcilable contradiction with Soviet ideology. But a wholly

[92] *Pravda*, 25 Sept. 1968, cited in J. N. Moore and R. F. Turner, *International Law and the Brezhnev Doctrine* (Lanham, Md., and London, 1987), 9.
[93] Ibid. 10.
[94] Tunkin, *Theory of International Law*, 434–40.
[95] Moore and Turner, *International Law and the Brezhnev Doctrine*, 86.

different system of legal norms was supposed to operate amongst socialist states, thus creating a further conflict between the two legal systems to which the Soviets supposedly adhered.

The Gorbachev revolution brought about a profound change in the Soviet perspective on international law. Shevardnadze's remark

We should not pretend, Comrades, that norms and notions of what is proper, of what is called civilized conduct in the world community do not concern us. If you want to be accepted in it you must observe them[96]

was a considerable understatement of what amounted to a revolution in the Soviet approach to international law. Central to this revolution were an acceptance of the idea that there were common values amongst states with different social systems, and an insistence that international law should have primacy in the relations between states. According to one recent Soviet attempt to redefine international law:

Contemporary international law is neither bourgeois nor socialist; it is a common human, general democratic normative system based on a common humanity. Its rules and standards based on the principles of the UN Charter express the balance of interests between individual states and the international community as a whole. It legalizes many common human values.[97]

Numerous actions designed to demonstrate the Soviet Union's genuine adherence to international law accompanied such statements.

Gorbachev did not set out merely to have the Soviet Union become a fully accepted member of the international community, but to reform it; his view of international law was also coloured by his 'new thinking'. The tone was set in his December 1988 General Assembly address, in which he said:

Our ideal is a world community of States which are based on the rule of law and which subordinate their foreign policy activities to law.[98]

The reference here to 'States which are based on the rule of law' is significant, since it implies a modern version of the nineteenth-century conception of a 'standard of civilization'. States are, in

---

[96] *International Affairs* (Moscow), Oct. 1988, p. 23.

[97] V. Vereschetin and R. Mullerson, 'The Primacy of International Law in World Politics', in A. Carty and G. Danilenko (eds.), *Perestroika and International Law* (Edinburgh, 1990), 7.

[98] M. Gorbachev, 7 Dec. 1988, UN Document A/43/PV.72, 22.

other words, to conform to certain domestic standards of good governance and legitimacy, laid down by all that is embodied in the term 'rule of law', in order fully to qualify as members of the international community. The notion of a 'rule-of-law state' was reiterated by numerous Soviet international lawyers, as in the following example:

International legality can be reliably ensured only in relations of rule-of-law States. Domestic and international legality are closely interconnected. Just as a rule-of-law State can not function without an adequately high level of legal consciousness and legal culture, so too does international law require an appropriate international legal consciousness and culture from leaders and populace.[99]

Even Tunkin wholeheartedly accepted this aspect of 'new thinking' and in fact went further than others in pointing to the hierarchical implications of the concept:

Beyond doubt a State in which democracy and legality predominate and respect for human rights is ensured can be expected to respect international law in the international arena more than a State in which arbitrariness predominates. Therefore, the existence of the greatest possible number of rule-of-law States which can set the tone of international life is an important prerequisite for the primacy of international law in politics.[100]

REVOLUTION AND INTERNATIONAL LAW SINCE 1945

In its communications to the International Court of Justice in December 1979 and March 1980, in reply to the United States' submission to the ICJ concerning the American diplomats who had been taken hostage in Iran, the Iranian government rejected the Court's right to concern itself with this case. One of its reasons was that the hostage issue 'only represents a marginal and secondary aspect of an overall problem'.[101] The issue had to be seen in the context of more than twenty-five years' interference in the internal affairs of Iran by the United States and of 'numerous crimes

---

[99] I. I. Lukashuk 'People's Diplomacy and International Lawyers', in W. E. Butler (ed.), *Perestroika and International Law* (Boston and London, 1990), 98.

[100] G. I. Tunkin, 'On the Primacy of International Law and Politics', *Theory of International Law*, 9.

[101] 'Official Documents, Case Concerning United States Diplomatic and Consular Staff in Tehran', *American Journal of International Law*, 74 (1980), 751.

perpetrated against the Iranian people, contrary to and in conflict with all international and humanitarian norms'. Hence, the 'problem involved in the conflict between Iran and the United States is . . . not one of the interpretation and application of the treaties upon which the American Application is based, but results from an overall situation containing much more fundamental and more complex elements'.[102] A further consideration was:

the deep-rootedness and the essential character of the Islamic Revolution of Iran, a revolution of a whole oppressed nation against its oppressors and their masters, the examination of whose numerous repercussions is essentially and directly a matter within the national sovereignty of Iran.[103]

As these extracts demonstrate, there had been little change by the 1980s in the ability of revolutionary states to adopt a dichotomous position towards international law. On the one hand, the idea that there existed such things as 'international norms'—an expression used three times in the Iranian communication—was potentially too valuable to be discarded. The same was even more true of the concept of national sovereignty. However, Iran preferred to focus upon those norms which supported its ideas of justice rather than those that sustained the notion of lawful state behaviour in international society, and to rely upon the classic revolutionary justification of demanding that issues should be assessed in the context of the 'overall situation' rather than by the more specific criterion of one of the most basic international legal norms. Ultimately, Iran was prepared to fall back upon the quintessential revolutionary argument: the revolution itself conferred legitimacy upon its 'numerous repercussions'.[104]

The Iranian perspective on international law was complicated by the Shiite position regarding the precedence of Islamic law over all other legal systems and the right of the leading Islamic jurists to interpret and lay down the law. Treaties and other international agreements with well-disposed non-Muslim states were deemed to

[102] Ibid.
[103] Ibid. 269, 750. The principal difference between Tehran's communications of Dec. 1979 and Mar. 1980 is that, in the former, this argument is placed last, while in the latter it appears first.
[104] For a detailed consideration of some of the legal issues involved in this case, see O. Schachter, 'International Law in the Hostage Crisis: Implications for Future Cases', in W. Christopher *et al.*, *American Hostages in Iran: The Conduct of a Crisis* (New Haven, Conn., and London, 1985), 325–73.

be possible, but Muslims retained the right to proselytize their 'absolute truth' while denying the same right to non-Muslims. Attempts by the latter to 'intrigue against' Muslims would invalidate international agreements. This was essentially the same dualism of outlook that characterized the early Bolsheviks.[105]

The approach to international law of most other post-1945 revolutionary states was not very different from that of the majority of Third World states. International law in general was somewhat suspect, since it had been developed by their former colonial masters, and was believed to reflect the interests of the powerful over those of the weak, the preservation of the status quo rather than the pursuit of radical change. On the other hand, it provided some protection for the sovereignty of recently established states and, through its norm of sovereign equality, for their dignity.

Two areas of international law that illustrated the divergent perspectives of Western and Third World states, particularly in the 1960s and 1970s, were the laws of war and international economic law. In the former case, international law has traditionally restricted the legitimate right to use force to sovereign states. More recently, it has attempted to set strict limits even to the right of states to use force. Both norms have been challenged by Third World and revolutionary states, on the grounds that national liberation movements have the right to use force, since they are acting in the name of another norm, self-determination.[106] China exceeded the more limited demands of most other states when it withdrew from the Geneva Conference on humanitarian law after its request for the concept of 'just wars' to be included in the laws of war was rejected by other participants.[107] The main target of the Third World opponents of international economic law has been the requirement that compensation for the foreign owners of any property taken over by the state should be 'prompt, adequate and effective'. The chief precedent here was set by the Bolsheviks in 1917, although similar issues were raised during the American and French revolutions. More recently, this question has been central to

[105] M. H. Behishti and J. Bahonar, *Philosophy of Islam* (Salt Lake City, 1982), 501–73.
[106] For a detailed discussion of this question, see H. A. Wilson, *International Law and the Use of Force by National Liberation Movements* (Oxford, 1988).
[107] M. Mushkat, 'The Development of International Humanitarian Law and the Law of Human Rights', *German Yearbook of International Law*, 21 (1978), 150–68.

the Third World demands for a restructuring of the international economy along lines that it would see as more just.[108]

Simple economic necessity, together with the fact that living within the accepted framework of international legal norms conferred more benefits than being an 'outlaw' state, meant that even the most radical of states encountered strong pressures to become 'socialized'. Chinese discussions of international law in the 1960s stated flatly that 'bourgeois international law' was 'the superstructure of an economic base' and as such was a 'tool of oppression used by big capitalist powers against weak and small countries', and that a universal 'world law' was impossible because there was no unified economic system in the modern world.[109] Such assertions did not prevent Chinese diplomats from appealing to rights deriving from earlier treaties, and to established legal norms, in cases such as those of its boundary dispute with India and its claim to Taiwan. China's reluctance to accept the notion that it shared a common body of rules and norms with 'imperialists', however, remained unaltered, and in fact increased during China's Cultural Revolution. However, by the 1980s China's attitude had undergone a complete transformation. The uncompromising dogmatism and radicalism of earlier years evaporated in the quest for foreign trade, investment, and international respectability. By 1981 a Chinese textbook on international law was able not only to offer an essentially 'bourgeois' definition of international law as 'the sum total of principles, rules, regulations and systems which are binding and which mainly regulate interstate relations', but even to declare that 'in international society there is no ruling class nor is it possible to have such a class'.[110]

The reason for such a wholesale retreat from what the Chinese themselves described as 'nihilist and liquidationist' approaches to international law was openly acknowledged by a leading Chinese scholar:

China's economic and cultural exchanges with foreign countries involved increasingly complicated legal relations, as could be seen in the assimilation

---

[108] See Cassese, *International Law in a Divided World*, 317–75, for a discussion of some of the legal issues involved in the Third World demand for a new international economic order.

[109] J. A. Cohen and H. Chiu, *People's China and International Law: A Documentary Study* (Princeton, NJ, 1974), 41–3.

[110] Cited in S. S. Kim, 'The Development of International Law in Post-Mao China: Change and Continuity', *Journal of Chinese Law*, 1/2 (1987), 125.

of foreign investment, the importation of advanced technology, the joint development of resources with foreign countries, the establishment of joint ventures and other forms of economic cooperation, the contracting of loans, foreign trade, maritime affairs, insurance and tourism, all of which had to be governed and regulated through various forms of law. It was [therefore] necessary to step up the study of these questions and relevant international conventions, regulations and customs.[111]

There is an intriguing parallel here with China's experience in the nineteenth century. Then China was placed under intense pressure by Western powers, who conducted their international relations in accordance with what were, for the Chinese, alien principles of sovereign equality and diplomacy. Eventually the Chinese government felt that it had no choice, if it was to defend China's integrity, but to learn about the rules that governed this strange society of states by which the Western powers justified their behaviour, in order to use them on China's behalf. Accordingly it sent out for the works of Vattel and other leading authorities on the law of nations. Without stretching the analogy too far, it seems that neither traditional Confucian China nor its revolutionary Maoist successor has proved able to conduct its foreign relations according to non-Westphalian principles and thereby avoid the inevitable consequences of socialization.

CONCLUSION

International law is a loose and decentralized system that lacks an effective means of enforcing compliance. For this reason, it has often been thought of as irrelevant to the 'real' world of power politics or, at least as having only a marginal significance. Most states have disregarded some aspect of international law at some time so two questions immediately arise: whether the hostility of revolutionary states towards the law of nations is really any different from the attitude of most states and whether, given the apparent inconsequentiality of international law, their response to it matters?

The first of these questions is relatively easy to answer. Most states break rules of international conduct occasionally; revolu-

---

[111] Huan Xiang, Vice-President of the Chinese Academy of Social Sciences, cited in Cassese, *International Law in a Divided World*, 72.

tionary states have systematically and comprehensively denied their validity or applicability to their own conduct. They have objected to international law on ideological grounds, and also because it implies that they themselves are part of a larger society of states. Hence, the response of revolutionary states to international law has not simply been different in degree but different in kind as well.

But if international law is unimportant, does this matter? Paradoxically, international law seems to grow in significance whenever it is placed under the greatest pressure by a cataclysmic event, such as war, or by the deliberate challenge of a revolutionary state. Major revolutions appear to force established states to rediscover and redefine both their social identity as members of a society of states and the normative and juridical principles upon which that society is based. If the alternatives to the Westphalian international society seem to be an anarchic free-for-all, or a world order refashioned in accordance with new revolutionary doctrines, the value of sustaining what states already have is likely to seem more persuasive.

The sharper focus into which international law has been placed by revolutionary challenges to it has contributed markedly to the two processes with which this study is concerned: international socialization and change within international society itself. International law gave intellectual coherence as well as authority to the established powers' response to revolutionary states. In so doing, it served to inform the revolutionary states that they were challenging not merely the existing global power structure but a clear and determinate set of rules of international conduct. International law also defined the common language of the discourse among states. Hence, a revolutionary state's acceptance of international law entailed a concrete and unambiguous form of socialization since it required adherence to specific rules of conduct. It also clearly illustrated the nature of the process of socialization as one involving the avoidance of 'punishment' in the form of international censure and sanctions including the possible use of force, and the receipt of 'rewards' including international legitimacy and access to participation in the international discourse. But revolutionary states also obliged established states to re-examine their own attitude to international law, as well as introducing new ideas into the international discourse. In this way they acted as important catalysts for change by strengthening the commitment of the great powers to international law, by encouraging them to lead in its defence, and by contributing to its further development.

7

Diplomacy

Revolutionary leaders display a remarkable unanimity on the subject of diplomacy. For Jefferson it was 'the pest of the peace of the world'.[1] Robespierre believed all of France's diplomats to be traitors to the revolution.[2] Engels thought that the 'diplomats of all countries constitute a secret league as against the exoteric public and will never compromise one another openly'.[3] Stalin, who numbered many Soviet diplomats among his victims in the purges, was even more contemptuous:

For a diplomat, words *must* have no relation to actions—otherwise what sort of a diplomat would he be? Words are one thing, actions absolutely another. Good words are a mask for the concealment of unprincipled acts. To speak of a sincere diplomat is the same as talking about dry water or wooden iron.[4]

Libya, China during the Cultural Revolution, and Iran all attempted to restructure their diplomatic services along revolutionary lines, while also engaging in repeated abuse of their own diplomatic privileges and violations of the rules relating to diplomats stationed in their countries.

What is the nature of this institution which has incurred so much revolutionary displeasure and what is its role in international society? Why was it singled out for attack, and what impact did revolutionary states have upon their own diplomatic practice? And how has diplomacy evolved as a central institution of international society in the face of so much revolutionary distrust and hostility?

[1] F. Gilbert, *To the Farewell Address: Ideas of Early American Foreign Policy* (Princeton, NJ, 1961), 72.
[2] D. A. Silverman, 'Informal Diplomacy: The Foreign Policy of the Robespierrist Committee of Public Safety', Ph.D. thesis (University of Washington, 1973), 246.
[3] Cited in F. Petrenko and V. Popov, *Soviet Foreign Policy: Objectives and Principles* (Moscow, 1981), 25.
[4] Cited in E. R. Goodman, *The Soviet Design for a World State* (New York, 1960), 81.

DIPLOMACY AND INTERNATIONAL SOCIETY

Definitions of diplomacy tend to see it as a particular form of dialogue between two or more parties in which they seek peaceful means to adjust their differences or advance their common interests.[5] Although the term may be used to refer to a great many different kinds of dialogue, in its most specific context—international relations—a more complete definition needs to take account of two additional characteristics: diplomacy involves dialogue that takes place between sovereign states who are members of an international society.

There are both formal and practical reasons why a complete definition of diplomacy needs to incorporate these two requirements. The formal reason derives from the framework of legal concepts that defines the sovereign state and, by extension, the nature of the relations of sovereign states with each other. Sovereign statehood (as distinct from nationhood, or political or economic independence, or some other property which states may possess) means, essentially, that the sole source of legitimate authority over a given group of individuals resides in their state and not in some external source. As Alan James puts it, sovereignty denotes 'constitutional independence', which means, most simply, that 'a state's constitution is not part of a larger constitutional arrangement'.[6] At one time, absolute monarchs were the living embodiments of most states and the relations between states were formally defined as the relations between individual monarchs. Even as late as the French Revolution, George III could declare, in reply to a French threat to appeal directly to the British people; 'This nation . . . will never have with foreign powers connexion or correspondence, except through the organ of its King.'[7] This was not some princely conceit, but a simple statement of the sovereignty principle as applied to the British constitution. A sovereign was, by definition, unable to come under the jurisdiction of one of his peers, and this principle applied, by extension, to his personal repre-

---

[5] Cf. A. Watson, *Diplomacy: The Dialogue Between States*, (London, 1982), esp. 9, 14, 16–17, and 33.

[6] A. James, *Sovereign Statehood* (London, 1986), 25.

[7] Cited in H. Temperley and L. M. Penson, (eds.), *Foundations of British Foreign Policy* (London, 1966), 7–8.

sentatives. It was not merely that ambassadors represented in their persons the dignity, honour, and prestige of their sovereign lords; they embodied sovereignty itself. Hence, juridical logic entailed the necessity for diplomatic immunity, since without it the sovereign's representative would be subject to an external jurisdiction.[8]

But sovereignty itself had little meaning except in the context of a society of states which acknowledged it as the central principle from which their other norms and rules derived. And, since it is almost impossible to conceive of a society whose members do not communicate regularly with each other about their common business, and in which such communication does not take place in accordance with generally understood conventions of discourse, the existence of a society of sovereign states also presupposes a system of diplomatic relations based upon certain universally accepted rules and practices.[9] Indeed, diplomats in their relations with each other may be seen as the personification of international society and as the symbolic evidence for its existence.[10]

Vattel derived similar conclusions from natural law, which, he said,

imposes on all sovereigns the obligations of consenting to those things, without which it would be impossible for nations to cultivate the society that nature has established among them, to keep up mutual correspond-ence, to treat of their affairs, or to adjust their differences. Now, ambassadors, and other public ministers, are necessary instruments for the maintenance of that general society, of that mutual correspondence between nations. But their ministry cannot effect the intended purpose, unless it be invested with all the prerogatives which are capable of insuring its legitimate success, and of enabling the minister freely and faithfully to discharge his duty in perfect security.[11]

---

[8] See the discussion of the theoretical bases of the principle of diplomatic immunity in C. E. Wilson, *Diplomatic Principles and Immunities* (Tucson, Ariz., 1967), 1–25.

[9] Here I reach a different conclusion from H. Bull, *The Anarchical Society* (London, 1977), 167, who says that international society does *not* presuppose 'the diplomatic institutions of today'. However the difference is less than it might appear since Bull is essentially arguing that the particular set of contemporary diplomatic institutions took some time to evolve. I am merely stating that diplomacy as such—dialogue within a context of agreed rules and procedures—is a necessary part of international society.

[10] Ibid. 182–3.

[11] Emerich de Vattel, *The Law of Nations*, ed. J. Chitty (London, 1834), 470.

Violence against an ambassador constituted, for Vattel, an attack against 'the common safety and well-being of nations',[12] an observation echoed in 1784 by the American Chief Justice:

> The person of a public minister is sacred and inviolable. Whoever offers any violence to him, not only affronts the sovereign he represents, but also hurts the common safety and well-being of nations; he is guilty of a crime against the whole world.[13]

Diplomacy between independent political communities, and its concomitant principle of diplomatic immunity, however, long pre-dated the Westphalian state system. This was essentially because they met practical as well as theoretical needs. Regular communication between states brought numerous reciprocal benefits: commerce, the reduction of friction, and assistance in dealing with common dangers. No state would be willing to send representatives abroad if the lives or property of its envoys were endangered, or if they came under other forms of pressure from the governments which received them.

As already stated, diplomacy functions as an important symbol of the existence of an international society. Diplomats stand not merely for the dignity of their states and for the sovereignty principle, but for these as agreed and upheld by states *in association*. Their existence forms the most basic evidence that states observe rules in their relations with each other. It was suggested in an earlier chapter that, while the minimum basis for the Westphalian international society was agreement among states to observe such rules as were necessary to uphold sovereignty as the central principle of international life, international society could develop beyond this rudimentary stage and that it had in fact done so during the nineteenth century. It was possible after 1815 to talk in terms of an elementary *community* and not just a *society* of states: that is, one which shared certain values as well as common interests. The dominant powers were all European, with similar levels of economic, social, and political development, a common culture, and numerous personal links amongst their leading families. They also collaborated to a much greater extent than previously in the management of the international system through such common institutions as the Concert of Europe. Their criteria

---

[12] Ibid. 464.
[13] Cited in Wilson, *Diplomatic Principles*, 3 n. 13.

for international legitimacy, and hence membership of international society, became more complex and refined, with the introduction of the 'standard of civilization'. Diplomacy reflected these changes, with diplomats, in their personal relations with each other in the major capitals of Europe, coming to resemble an inner circle of like-minded individuals of similar quality and background who shared a 'diplomatic culture' of etiquette, manners, rituals, and values. A somewhat idealized description given in the 1850s by the former French premier, Guizot, makes a similar point:

The professional diplomats form, within the European community, a society of their own which lives by its own principles, customs, lights and aspirations, and which, amid differences and even conflicts between States, preserves a quiet and permanent unity of its own. Moved by the divergent interests of nations, but not by their prejudices or momentary passions, that small diplomatic world may well recognize the general interest of the great European community with sufficient clearness and fill it with sufficient strength, to make it triumph over differences, and cause men, who have long upheld very different policies without ever quarrelling among themselves, and who have almost always shared the same atmosphere and horizons, to work sincerely for the success of the same policy.[14]

Diplomacy, then, may be defined as dialogue between sovereign states which perceive themselves to be members of an international society. Its function, so far as the sovereign states are concerned, is to provide them with a non-violent means to pursue their individual objectives, to accommodate or resolve their differences and to advance their common aims. So far as the international society as a whole is concerned, its function is to assist in preserving international order and to symbolize the existence of an international society. Two further fundamental attributes of diplomacy are the immunity of diplomatic agents and the acceptance of what have been termed here 'conventions of discourse'. These last may vary over time in their specific content—French has supplanted Latin and English French as the universal language employed by diplomats—but they must always comprise the following elements:

1. A common diplomatic language. This does not simply denote language in the literal sense but what Raymond Cohen refers to as a

---

[14] Cited in H. Morgenthau, *Politics Among Nations*, 3rd edn. (New York, 1965), 247.

'language of diplomacy making use of specialized terms and conventions so that messages can be conveyed, both orally and in writing, with a minimum of unnecessary misunderstanding'.[15]

2. Accepted rules relating to protocol and ceremonial procedures and rituals. This aspect of traditional diplomacy has aroused particular contempt from various quarters, including several revolutionary states. However, it is possible to see ceremonial and protocol as not peripheral to diplomacy but central to it. As Jules Cambon explains in a noted essay:

These solemn frivolities, when all is said and done are not altogether meaningless. Foreign envoys stand for something more important than themselves. The honours rendered them are paid to the super-personal entity of which they are merely the symbol. Besides, people are inclined to overlook the fact that the protocol makes no difference between victors and vanquished, and compels even hostile peoples to treat one another with consideration, regardless of any question of might. It is only a matter of form, of course, which does not affect the real issue, but for once Bridoison was right in stressing the importance of formality. The latter implies respect for the dignity and independence of weaker nations, and that is saying a great deal. It is the whole law of nations in a nutshell.[16]

As this quotation suggests, it is not too far-fetched to see diplomatic ceremonial as involving a formal celebration of the Westphalian international society and its central principle of sovereign equality.

3. An acceptance of the principle that, while each individual diplomat represents the special interests of his own state, the primary functions of diplomatic *dialogue* are to facilitate peaceful solutions to disputes and to accommodate differences. When François de Callières wrote in 1716 that 'the secret of negotiation is to harmonize the real interests of the parties concerned',[17] it was not because he was naïvely unaware that diplomatic dialogue could be put to other purposes, such as deception or the issuing of threats. Rather, he was arguing that what distinguished diplomacy from other, more competitive modes of interaction among sovereign states was its intrinsic relationship to international society as a whole:

To understand the permanent use of diplomacy and the necessity for continual negotiations, we must think of the states of which Europe is

---

[15] R. Cohen, *Theatre of Power* (London and New York, 1987), 1.

[16] J. Cambon, *The Diplomatist* (London, 1931), 99.

[17] Cited in H. Nicolson, *The Evolution of Diplomatic Method* (London, 1954), 63.

composed as being joined together by all kinds of necessary commerce, in such a way that they may be regarded as members of one Republic and that no considerable change can take place in any one of them without affecting the condition or disturbing the peace of all the others.[18]

Hence, the orderly functioning of international society—indeed the continued existence of an international society—required clearly recognized processes for the adjustment and accommodation of separate national interests in a peaceable fashion. This was the distinctive role of diplomatic dialogue.

4. A high degree of mutual respect among diplomats for each other's rights and prestige. As with other aspects of diplomacy, this has both formal and practical facets. The diplomatic corps in a foreign capital has the high purpose of standing for the society of states as well as the sovereignty of each individual state. But it is also the case that the common duty of all diplomats to engage in dialogue is greatly facilitated if there exists some sense of solidarity or collegiality among them.

5. Some degree of self-restraint by diplomats in exercising the privileges that derive from their status. This expresses the essential principle that the rights conferred by any society upon its members can continue to be exercised by all only if they are not abused by some. In the case of international society, the line between what a diplomat needs to do in legitimate pursuit of his country's interest and what he may do given the constraints of his state's membership of a rule-governed society can sometimes be hard to determine. When, for example, does intelligence gathering become espionage? When does a reasonable degree of communication with opposition groups become subversion? Hard and fast rules in such cases do not exist, which increases the onus upon the self-imposed limitations of the individual diplomat. Self-restraint of this order tends to be associated with a high level of social consciousness, or awareness and acceptance of one's responsibilities as a member of society.

As it developed from the late seventeenth century to the nineteenth century, diplomacy came to acquire other characteristic features. When criticisms were made of the 'old diplomacy', it was often these elements that were singled out for particular hostility, especially by revolutionary states. To its opponents, diplomacy

---

[18] A. F. Whyte, *The Practice of Diplomacy*, trans. of F. de Callière's *De la manière de négocier avec les souverains* (London, 1919), 11.

appeared an amoral activity, carried out in secret by cynical members of Europe's aristocratic élite whose main concern was to manipulate the equally amoral balance of power in their favour, with little regard for the interests of weaker states or the welfare of the masses.

REVOLUTIONARY DIPLOMACY

It is the function of diplomacy as symbol and sustainer of international society—what Adam Watson refers to as 'the diplomacy of *raison de système*'[19]—that gives rise to the most fundamental revolutionary objection to it. If the underlying premiss of the Westphalian international society is unacceptable to revolutionaries, one of the principal institutions of that society is unlikely to be less so. The initial response of revolutionary states to diplomacy tends to reflect the relative intensity of their opposition to the idea of international society. The Americans accepted it without enthusiasm as an unavoidable necessity that should be treated with extreme circumspection. The French, following the urgings of *philosophes*, who provided much of the ideological underpinning for the Revolution, sought to reform it.[20] The Soviets rejected 'bourgeois' interpretations of it but saw it as something that could be exploited. The Chinese during the Cultural Revolution viewed it as a form of struggle against 'imperialism, revisionism and reaction'.[21] Iran commenced its revolution with one of the most striking violations of diplomatic immunity in recent decades.

In practice, even those revolutions whose ideologies, in principle, could not accommodate the idea of a society of sovereign states engaged in a process of continual dialogue with each other found themselves unable to dispense altogether with some system of formal or informal relations with foreign powers. But diplomacy was never liked or trusted. To Barère, speaking in 1794, it was a

[19] Watson, *Diplomacy*, 201.
[20] F. Gilbert, 'The "New Diplomacy" of the Eighteenth Century', *World Politics*, 4/1 (Oct. 1951), 1–38. See also J. Der Derian, *On Diplomacy* (Oxford, 1987), 163–7.
[21] Philippe Ardant, 'Chinese Diplomatic Practice During the Cultural Revolution', in J. A. Cohen (ed.), *China's Practice of International Law: Some Case Studies* (Cambridge, Mass., 1972), 86–128.

'lying and crafty science' that the onward march of liberty would put an end to.[22] No less emphatically, Trotsky declared in 1917:

Secret diplomacy is a necessary tool for a propertied minority which is compelled to deceive the majority in order to subject it to its interests. Imperialism, with its dark plans of conquest and its robber alliances and deals, developed the system of secret diplomacy to the highest level. The struggle against the imperialism which is exhausting and destroying the peoples of Europe is at the same time a struggle against capitalist diplomacy, which has cause enough to fear the light of day. The Russian people, and the peoples of Europe and the whole world, should learn the documentary truth about the plans forged in secret by the financiers and industrialists together with their parliamentary and diplomatic agents . . .

The abolition of secret diplomacy is the primary condition for an honest, popular, truly democratic foreign policy.[23]

Essentially, the problem with diplomacy, at least the one that united all revolutionary states in their suspicion of it, was that it involved unavoidable contact with foreigners and hence the risk that pure revolutionary virtues could become contaminated. This risk appeared particularly strong because the foreigners concerned were perceived to be uniquely devious and cunning. In 1803 Jefferson solemnly advised Madison that diplomacy with the English would be futile because 'an American contending by stratagem against those exercised in it from their cradle would undoubtedly be outwitted by them'.[24] In this respect Jefferson found himself in agreement with his political opponent John Adams, who said in 1783, 'I confess I have sometimes thought that after a few years it will be the best thing we could do to recall every minister from Europe and send embassies only on special occasions.'[25] Even as late as 1885 an American senator could still lament:

This diplomatic service is working our ruin by creating a desire for foreign customs and foreign follies. The disease is imported by our returning diplomats and by the foreign ambassadors sent here by monarchs and despots to corrupt and destroy our American ideals.[26]

[22] *Archives Parlementaires*, 15 Apr. 1794 (Paris, 1912), lxxxviii. 609.
[23] J. Degras, *Soviet Documents on Foreign Policy*, i (London, 1951), 8.
[24] Cited in B. Spivak, 'Thomas Jefferson, Republican Values and Foreign Commerce', in N. A. Graebner (ed.), *Traditions and Values: American Diplomacy, 1790–1865* (London, 1985), 38.
[25] Cited in W. F. Illchman, *Professional Diplomacy in the United States 1779–1939* (Chicago, 1961), 18.
[26] Ibid. 27.

It was not just American virtue that stood in such peril from contact with the outside world. French revolutionary diplomats such as Talleyrand may have been less troubled than Jefferson about their ability to match other Europeans in low cunning, but their political masters remained apprehensive about the capacity of republican virtues to survive unsullied amidst the 'obscure intrigues' of the old diplomacy.[27] Early in 1791 Mirabeau insisted that diplomatic personnel must not include individuals who were 'strangers to the new language of which they must be the mouthpieces'.[28] Later in that year Brissot went much further in demanding the recall of several diplomats and attacking the Foreign Minister, whom he found to be too deeply 'imbued with the prejudices of the old diplomacy'.[29] The Bolsheviks, Chinese, Iranians, and other revolutionary states were similarly to recall large numbers of diplomats at various times due to a basic mistrust of their commitment to revolutionary principles. Numerous instructions from the French Foreign Ministry to its ambassadors made it clear that they were expected to behave with the virtue appropriate to the representatives of a new republic and that they were to avoid 'the ridiculous disputes with which the old diplomacy was so occupied'.[30] In case such instructions failed to bring about the correct attitude on the part of existing diplomats, the French Revolution became the first of many revolutionary states to decide to send out trustworthy political agents to ensure that the diplomats did not deviate from the accepted line. Barthélemy, one of France's senior diplomats, received the following explanation of this move from his Minister:

An inconvenience, Citizen, attached to the position of diplomatic agents employed abroad is to perceive in the Revolution only the results which mark its different periods . . . it is important that those who are involved in the general administration of the Republic do not serve merely with probity; it is necessary that the agents of the Republic are its most zealous and ardent partisans.

[27] Minister of Foreign Affairs, Deforgues, 24 June 1793, *Archives parlementaires* (Paris, 1902), lxvii. 111.
[28] F. Masson, *Le Département des affaires étrangères pendant la révolution, 1787–1804* (Paris, 1877), 88.
[29] Ibid. 128.
[30] Le Brun to Barthélemy, 8 Oct. 1792, in J. Kaulek (ed.), *Papiers de Barthélemy*, i. (Paris, 1886), 327–8; see also 'Instructions générales pour les agents politiques de la république en pays étranger', ibid. ii. 290–4.

But if, absent from their country, they are not in a position to grasp the mood and to follow the march of events, if they cannot be witnesses of the energy which their compatriots display, if, on the contrary, they see all around them only those who are indifferent to or even enemies of the French Revolution, it is to be feared that they will not raise themselves to the high level of the occasion and that their patriotism is only a vague and indeterminate attachment to their country when it should be an enthusiasm supported by republican virtues.

These considerations, citizen, have determined me to send to be close to some of the agents of the Republic in foreign countries some enlightened patriots who, having followed the whole progress of the Revolution and contributed to the acceleration of its forward movement, will bring to them [the French envoys] knowledge of facts of which they cannot remain unaware and a gauge of the public spirit in France.[31]

Apart from recalling diplomats or stationing political watchdogs and 'thought police' in embassies, various other strategies were open to revolutionary states that wished to limit the risks attendant upon contact with foreigners. Early suggestions that the United States should limit its relations with the outside world to commercial matters have already been noted. While that extreme was never reached, various measures were taken to reduce contact by other means. Even during the War of Independence, the Continental Congress proposed that diplomats should spend no more than three years abroad. Thomas Jefferson cut back the size of the diplomatic service when he became President, and the United States retained a determinedly amateurish approach to diplomacy until the twentieth century.[32] An early action of the French Revolutionary Assembly was similarly to decree a substantial cut in the budget for foreign affairs, although the exigencies of war soon reversed this decision.[33] A series of articles written during 1793 ('New Diplomacy', 'The Rout of the Old Diplomacy', and 'Commercial Diplomacy') also put the case for France to enter only into commercial relations with the rest of Europe.[34] The even more suspicious Communist and other revolutionary regimes of the twentieth century concentrated their efforts on another aspect of the problem of foreign contact: the presence of foreign diplomats in their own countries. Extensive restrictions were placed on the

---

[31] Kaulek (ed.), *Papiers de Barthélemy*, iii. 263–4.

[32] Illchman, *Professional Diplomacy*, 1–2, 23, 26.

[33] Masson, *Le Département des affaires étrangères*, 69.

[34] These articles appeared in *Le Moniteur Universel* on 9 June, 30 Oct. and 5 Dec., respectively.

freedom of movement of diplomats in capitals like Moscow and Beijing.[35] Local nationals employed by Western embassies for minor duties found themselves subjected to various forms of harassment by their own governments.[36]

Another revolutionary objection to diplomacy concerned its secrecy. Even the Soviet Union, which was to become one of the world's most secretive states, was to commence its international life with sweeping criticisms of secret diplomacy and the publication of numerous Tsarist Russian treaties and other diplomatic documents. While not going so far, Woodrow Wilson called for 'open covenants, openly arrived at'. The mood of both states recalled sentiments that had been expressed during the eighteenth-century revolutions.

However, the common experience of many revolutionary states has been the discovery that secrecy and confidentiality in international discourse have their uses after all. When Thomas Paine, a frequent critic of the old diplomacy, revealed certain facts about the secret negotiations that were going on between France and the United States to secure French support against Britain, French displeasure caused him to be dismissed from his position of secretary to the Committee of Foreign Affairs.[37] The issue of secret diplomacy recurred in 1796 when a Republican Congressman, Edward Livingston, debating the Jay treaty, demanded that the President should make public details of the instructions that had been given to Jay. This provoked a full defence of secret diplomacy from Alexander Hamilton. Confidentiality in international discussions was necessary, he wrote to Washington, first because breaking a confidence would destroy others' faith in the US government's 'prudence and delicacy'. Secondly, the other side in a negotiation might feel that it had to adopt a harder stance if it thought that its own domestic audience might discover that concessions were being offered. Thirdly, instructions to diplomats often contained observations on the views and motives of the other side, which it would be offensive to make public. They might also reveal too much about American plans in future contingencies, which could either help or give grounds for suspicion to other powers. Finally, if one side did not reveal its hand at the start of a

---

[35] Ardant, 'Chinese Diplomatic Practice'.
[36] Wilson, *Diplomatic Principles*, 203–15.
[37] W. C. Stinchcombe, *The American Revolution and the French Alliance* (New York, 1969), 40.

negotiation, it might be able to gain more in the subsequent treaty than had been required of it by its official instructions.[38] In the event, Livingston amended his motion by requiring instructions to be tabled 'excepting such papers as any existing negotiation may render improper to be disclosed'.[39] However, Madison was unable to secure Congressional agreement to a further amendment excepting such papers as, in the President's judgement, 'it may not be consistent with the interest of the United States, at this time, to disclose'.[40]

The French revolutionaries had similar experiences and, as in the American case, the issues of secret diplomacy and democratic control of foreign policy became intertwined. This was perhaps clearest during the period between the Declaration of Pillnitz on 27 August 1791 and the French declaration of war on Austria on 20 April 1792. In 1790 the Assembly had assumed various powers with regard to the making of foreign policy that had previously been the exclusive preserve of the executive. This process was taken a stage further with the constitution of 1791.[41] The Legislature appointed a Diplomatic Committee to manage its foreign affairs role, while at the same time subjecting it to strict democratic controls, including a vote every three months on the Committee's membership.[42] In practice, the Committee became for a period the instrument of Brissot and the Girondins and functioned, in effect, as an alternative Foreign Ministry. Brissot and his pro-war allies were able, by helping to whip up and then cleverly playing upon the anti-Austrian sentiments and general paranoia of the Assembly, to lead the nation step by step towards the war they desired. During this process, not only were more moderate voices unable to make themselves heard above the general hysteria, but the room for subtle diplomatic manœuvring, which might have been able to limit the war in various ways, was severely circumscribed.

When Montmorin, as Foreign Minister, presented his report on the current international situation on 31 October 1791, he asked the Assembly to respect 'the limits within which I have thought it necessary to confine myself'. In his view a large Assembly, in the

---

[38] *The Papers of Alexander Hamilton*, xx. 88.
[39] Ibid. 65.
[40] Ibid.
[41] J. E. Howard, *Parliament and Foreign Policy in France* (London, 1948), 13–23.
[42] Masson, *Le Département des affaires étrangères*, 113.

interest of the nation as well as its own dignity, should not expect its Foreign Minister to reveal certain details, such as correspondence with foreign powers.[43] Given the prevailing mood, a plea for secret diplomacy was unacceptable to the Assembly and Montmorin was obliged to resign. A semi-official report on foreign policy some months later attacked Montmorin's 'mysterious dogma' that there were details that a large Assembly should not ask of the Foreign Minister. The report went on to urge the Diplomatic Committee to exercise constant surveillance over the Minister, to unveil his 'perfidies' and comment on or refute his assertions. It demanded that the Minister should also communicate to the Committee all correspondence, while lower ranks in the Foreign Ministry should also have access to the Committee. The effect would be that 'state secrets will no longer exist. Our diplomacy will be sincere.'[44] Montmorin's replacement, De Lessart, soon found himself coming under criticism for his strategy of negotiating with Austria to prevent a concert of foreign powers from being formed against France—a classic exercise in traditional diplomacy on his part. Brissot called for blunter language to be used in dealing with Austria—'language worthy of free men'—but questioned whether one could look for such language in 'the old diplomacy, this diplomacy so respectful towards tyrants, so insolent towards peoples'.[45] He added that little could be expected of the French Foreign Ministry, which preserved 'the same forms, the same mystery, the same falseness of language. It sees everywhere only the kings; the nations seem not yet to exist for diplomacy.'[46]

France's relative diplomatic isolation in late 1792 and 1793 led to a reconsideration of various aspects of revolutionary diplomacy, including the negative effects of public diplomacy, which tended on the one hand to inflame passions at home and on the other to irritate and alarm foreign governments. By the time of the Directory (November 1795–November 1799) traditional diplomacy had clearly been completely rehabilitated, as the following instruction from the Directory to its ambassadors abroad suggests:

The Executive Directory of the French Republic, anxious to prove to the governments with which it is at peace that it recognizes no other policy

---

[43] Ibid. 114–17.
[44] Ibid. 154.
[45] *Archives Parlementaires*, 29 Dec. 1791 (Paris, 1891), xxxvi. 610.
[46] Ibid.

than that which tends to render men happy, believes that it should trace for its agents . . . the [rules] of conduct they should observe to cause the great character of the French nation that they have the honour to represent to be esteemed, loved, and respected in them.

A French agent should be dignified; should give an example of purity of character; should respect the political, civil, and religious laws of the country, and make other Frenchmen respect them, should acknowledge and defend only the tranquil French patriot.

If he is forced to complain of abuses, he does so with decency and moderation . . . He should mix with no faction. He should increase the number of his friends without injuring the foreign government. He should regard himself as the link joining . . . two nations which are seeking happiness each in its own way, and which, more or less advanced toward perfection in the social scale, ought to guide each other in their quest only by reciprocal consideration.[47]

A further focal point for revolutionary criticisms of diplomacy has been behaviour seen as excessively formal and subservient to tradition in areas like etiquette, protocol, and forms of language. Even the clothing worn by diplomats has been a target, with both American and French diplomats going to some lengths to demonstrate republican simplicity through their attire.[48] When a would-be helpful French diplomat tried to advise the first American diplomats sent to Paris to pay more heed to observing the existing diplomatic formalities, John Adams brusquely informed him that:

the dignity of North America does not consist in diplomatic ceremonials or any of the subtleties of etiquette; it consists solely in reason, justice, truth, the rights of mankind, and the interests of the nations of Europe.[49]

Litvinov, who was sent to London by the Bolsheviks to try to obtain British recognition, was not accorded the status that would have been due to a properly accredited diplomat, but claimed, 'like Mr. Trotsky, I do not attach much importance to matters of etiquette and unnecessary formalities'.[50] The matters of precedence amongst diplomats and diplomatic titles also exercised the minds of

[47] Cited in S. S. Biro, *The German Policy of Revolutionary France* (Cambridge, Mass., 1957), ii. 507.

[48] L. S. Kaplan, *Colonies into Nation: American Diplomacy, 1763–1801* (New York, 1972), 93–4; J. H. Clapham, *The Abbé Sieyès* (London, 1912), 207.

[49] F. Wharton, *The Revolutionary Diplomatic Correspondence of the United States* (Washington, 1889), iv. 590.

[50] A. E. Senn, *Diplomacy and Revolution* (Notre Dame, Ind., and London, 1974), 44.

the revolutionary leaders. For many years after winning independence, the United States retained a studied amateurism in its approach to foreign relations, in part out of a continuing distaste for what it regarded as the aristocratic pretensions of Europe's professional diplomats. It believed consular representation to be appropriate to most of America's needs, and paid little attention to arguments in favour of a professional, well-rewarded foreign service until well into the twentieth century.[51] Proposals were put forward during the early years of the French Revolution to replace the then current range of diplomatic titles with the single title 'nonce de France' (French nuncio), while other questions of etiquette were carefully scrutinized with a view to arriving at politically correct alternatives.[52]

Diplomatic ranks in the Soviet Union were abolished in 1918, being replaced with the single title of Polpred (plenipotentiary). At the same time the Bolsheviks made known their intention to treat equally all foreign diplomats, regardless of their ranks.[53] The full flavour of Soviet revolutionary diplomacy in the early days was experienced at the Brest-Litovsk negotiations with Germany. The Russian delegation included representative soldiers, sailors, workers, and peasants, the member of the last category having been virtually press-ganged at the last minute as the Bolshevik delegation was making its way to the Petrograd railway station.[54] Once in Brest-Litovsk, the Bolsheviks insisted that their delegation be treated according to the rules of 'revolutionary etiquette' on social occasions, with the proletarian representatives seated in the more favoured positions.[55] As early as 1922, Andrei Sabanin, a member of the People's Commissariat for Foreign Affairs (NKID), had noted the disadvantages of the Soviet policy with regard to diplomatic ranks:

It should be noted that in determining actually the place of the Russian representative among the representatives of other states, the decree of 1918

[51] Illchman, *Professional Diplomacy*, 36–48; and A. L. Steigman, *The Foreign Service of the United States* (Boulder, Colorado, 1985), 11–30.
[52] Masson, *Le Département des affaires étrangères*, 155, and Der Derian, *On Diplomacy*, 179–80.
[53] T. J. Uldricks, *Diplomacy and Ideology: The Origins of Soviet Foreign Relations, 1917–30* (London, 1979), 33, and K. Von Beyme, *The Soviet Union in World Politics* (Aldershot, 1987), 18.
[54] J. W. Wheeler-Bennett, *Brest-Litovsk, The Forgotten Peace* (London and New York, 1966), 85–7.
[55] Ibid. 113–15.

raises certain difficulties for the NKID; we have been required to wage a complicated struggle to assure for our plenipotentiary representatives a status [actually] befitting them. This has proved necessary perhaps to a certain extent in contradiction with the idea that was at the foundation of the decree of 1918 since the 1918 decree can acquire real force only when all states are equally pervaded with the sense of the justice of the principles that were made its foundation.[56]

This plea (from one of the few Russian diplomats practising before October 1917 to have been allowed to continue) for an attempt to live in the world as it was rather than as one would like it to be was followed in 1924 by a partial bow to the inevitable: the distinction 'with the title of Ambassador' was bestowed upon certain Polpreds.[57] This illustration of the process of socialization might be compared with the following observations by Felix Gilbert of the experiences of American envoys to Paris during the War of Independence:

Closer acquaintance with the European diplomatic scene had modified the views of those who had come to France with proud feelings of superiority over a world corrupted by a love for rank, distinctions and formalities. The American agents began to notice that these arrangements instead of being meaningless reflected the influence and the position which a country had in the society of states. Soon after Deane's first interview with Vergennes, in which the American had vaunted his ignorance of diplomatic customs, Deane admitted that 'something is due to the dignity of old and powerful States or, if you please, to their prejudice, in favour of long established form and etiquette'.[58]

While many aspects of the etiquette and other formalities that the French and American revolutionaries took exception to were essentially eighteenth-century phenomena, it may be noted that the dignified titles used in the diplomatic world can still cause problems for revolutionary states, as evidenced by Libya's decision to call its embassies 'People's Bureaux'. The subtleties and controlled politeness of diplomatic language have also tended to be early casualties of more recent revolutionary diplomacy. This can potentially be a more dangerous matter than changes in nomenclature, since it may directly affect the conventions of

---

[56] Cited in J. F. Triska and R. M. Slusser, *The Theory, Law and Policy of Soviet Treaties* (Stanford, Calif., 1962), 210.

[57] Von Beyme, *The Soviet Union*, 18.

[58] Gilbert, 'The "New Diplomacy" ', 77.

diplomatic discourse. For example, if, during some disagreement between two states, one refuses to communicate in the measured and careful tones of traditional diplomacy but insists upon adopting a confrontational posture from the outset, the prospects of a peaceful resolution may be severely circumscribed. Soviet negotiating behaviour has resulted in just such difficulties from the outset, and similar problems have been experienced with many other Communist states, as well as with Iran and Libya.[59]

Soviet negotiating practices reflected in part the influence of Marxist dialectics, which assume that every encounter between the 'proletariat' and 'bourgeoisie' is of necessity a form of struggle. A Soviet handbook on diplomacy, written in 1964, argued:

The theoretical foundation of Soviet diplomatic activity is a Marxist-Leninist understanding of the international situation, of the laws of social development, of the laws of class struggle . . . a Marxist-Leninist evaluation of international events and the formulation of a line of diplomatic struggle on this basis is a powerful element in Soviet diplomacy.[60]

If diplomacy is a form of struggle, its ideological purpose is to pursue a policy of revolutionary internationalism, and this perception is at the root of the suspicion with which the diplomatic missions of revolutionary states have frequently been regarded, even when they have outwardly conformed to the conventional norms of diplomatic behaviour. This problem of the possible dual identity of revolutionary diplomats is far older even than the French Revolution. An emissary sent to Spain by England shortly after Oliver Cromwell's parliament had executed King Charles I made the following speech on his arrival:

With the example afforded by London all kingdoms will annihilate tyranny and become republics. England has done so already; France is following in her wake; and as the natural gravity of the Spaniards renders them somewhat slower in their operations, it will take Spain ten years to make the revolution.[61]

[59] R. F. Smith, *Negotiating with the Soviets* (Bloomington and Indianapolis, 1989), 3–50.

[60] V. A. Zorin, *Rôle of the Ministry of Foreign Affairs of the USSR: The Bases of Diplomatic Service* (Moscow, 1964), reproduced in US Congress Senate Committee on Government Operations, *The Soviet Approach to Negotiations* (Washington, 1969), 85.

[61] Cited in J. W. Thompson and S. K. Padover, *Secret Diplomacy: Espionage and Cryptography, 1500–1815* (New York, 1970), 82–3.

This, of course, was hardly diplomatic in any sense of the word but Cromwell himself had made no secret of his desire to see monarchy overthrown elsewhere.[62]

Furthering the revolutionary cause was also suspected to be amongst the responsibilities of French diplomats during the early years of the Revolution. The most notorious case involved Edward Genêt, who was sent to the United States in 1793 and engaged in a range of activities while there that went far beyond the normal duties of an ambassador. He was perhaps misled by the enthusiastic popular reception he received on arrival into believing that he could safely ignore American governmental attempts to restrain him by appealing over the heads of the government directly to the people. This attitude, however, merely served to lose him any last vestiges of support from such enthusiasts for the French Revolution as Jefferson.[63] Genêt's instructions were to attempt to foster anti-monarchical sentiments in those parts of North America that were still controlled by Spain and England.[64] He made himself head of a political club on his arrival in the United States and (this was more serious in its possible implications for American neutrality) attempted to fit out two ships for use against the English navy. On this occasion the views of Hamilton and Jefferson were identical. Hamilton argued that although ambassadors enjoyed, under the law of nations, 'privileges and immunities of a high and peculiar character', these imposed a moral obligation upon an ambassador to act with circumspection and propriety: 'his only justifiable weapons are negociation, remonstrance, representation'.[65] Of Genêt's threat to appeal directly to the American people, Hamilton argued:

The general security of nations has established it as a sacred and inviolable maxim, forming an essential bulwark of their internal tranquillity, that no agent of a foreign sovereign shall, on any pretext, attempt to create a schism between the citizens and the rulers of a state.[66]

Jefferson cited the law of nations against Genêt's naval activities, and was angered by Genêt's dismissive response, remarking:

[62] Cited in J. W. Thompson and S. K. Padover, *Secret Diplomacy: Espionage and Cryptography, 1500–1815* (New York, 1970), 82–5.

[63] Kaplan, *Colonies into Nation*, 228.

[64] F. L. Kidner, 'The Girondists and the "Propaganda War" of 1792', Ph.D. thesis (Princeton University, 1971), 263–81.

[65] 'No Jacobin', No. VI, 16 Aug. 1793, in *The Papers of Alexander Hamilton*, xv. 249.

[66] Ibid.

To these principles of the law of nations Mr. Genêt answers, by calling them 'diplomatic subtleties' and 'aphorisms of Vattel and others'. But something more than this is necessary to disprove them.[67]

The use of diplomacy as a means of promoting international revolution has been most commonly associated with the Soviet Union and subsequent communist regimes. Initially, the Soviets took the view that all encounters with the West would take the form of an overt or disguised struggle between socialism and capitalism. The revolutionary purpose of participating in such negotiations, for the Soviets, was to exploit them for propaganda purposes, with the aim of putting their enemies on trial before world public opinion, as Trotsky candidly explained in discussing his tactics at the forthcoming Brest-Litovsk conference:

Sitting at one table with them we shall ask them explicit questions which do not allow any evasion, and the entire course of the negotiations, every word they or we utter, will be taken down and reported by radiotelegraphists to all peoples, who will be the judges of our discussions. Under the influence of the masses, the German and Austrian Governments have already agreed to put themselves on the dock. You may be sure, comrades, that the prosecutor, in the person of the Russian revolutionary delegation, will be in its place and will in due time make a thundering speech for the prosecution about the diplomacy of all imperialists.[68]

The manœuvres of the Bolsheviks during November 1917 perfectly illustrated their belief that diplomacy was revolutionary struggle by other means. They had published the secret treaties, and now issued a call for an armistice on terms that no belligerent power could possibly accept. When their appeal met with its inevitable lack of response, they used this lack as propaganda against the allied governments, as, presumably, had been their intention all along. In a radio broadcast on 28 November to the peoples of the belligerent countries, they made traditional diplomacy an explicit target of their attacks:

The Government of the victorious revolution does not require recognition from the professional representatives of capitalist diplomacy, but we do ask the people: Does reactionary diplomacy express their ideas and aspirations? Are they willing to allow the diplomats to let the great

[67] F. Dumbauld, 'Independence under International Law', *American Journal of International Law*, 70, 3 (July 1976), 429.
[68] Cited in Uldricks, *Diplomacy and Ideology*, 152.

opportunity for peace offered by the Russian revolution slip through their fingers?[69]

When world revolution failed to appear, the Soviets adjusted their approach, opting for a general observance of the conventional norms of diplomacy in their formal relations with other states, while continuing to support the cause of world revolution through Comintern. They insisted that they bore no responsibility for the propaganda and other subversive activities of Comintern, a pretence with which other governments were prepared to go along most of the time for the sake of ensuring some continuity and stability in their relations with the Soviets. However, they sometimes tried to secure Soviet agreement to a clause in trade and other treaties in which each side undertook to refrain from propaganda activities against the other. The first such clause appeared in the 1921 Trade Agreement between Great Britain and the Soviet Union.[70]

If formal Soviet diplomacy showed itself to be prepared to adhere to the established conventions, this did not yet make it 'normal'. Soviet diplomats retained an almost systematic suspiciousness towards their Western counterparts that derived from their ideologically conditioned view of them as implacable enemies. As one reporter noted of Molotov's attitude during the 1947 London Foreign Ministers' meeting, 'He is innately suspicious. He seeks for hidden meanings and tricks where there are none. He takes it for granted that his opponents are trying to trick him and put over something nefarious.'[71] The generally negative attitude of the Soviets towards diplomacy probably also resulted in their frequently noted tendency in negotiations to treat any offered concession as a sign of weakness and immediately raise the stakes.[72] Diplomatic relations with foreign powers, in the words of an American ambassador to the Soviet Union, have tended to be seen by the Soviets as 'armistice relations' pending a renewal of open battle.[73]

[69] Degras, *Soviet Documents*, i. 11.

[70] L. Preuss, 'International Responsibility for Hostile Propaganda Against Foreign States', *American Journal of International Law*, 28, 4 (Oct. 1934) 649–68.

[71] *New York Times*, 7 Dec. 1947, cited in G.A. Craig, *War, Politics and Diplomacy* (New York), 1966, 242 n. 86.

[72] Ibid. 242–4.

[73] United States, Department of State, *Foreign Relations of the United States: The Soviet Union, 1933–39* (Washington, 1952), 224.

The negotiating style of communist China in its first fifteen years closely paralleled that of the Soviet Union, suggesting that this was essentially a product of ideological preconditioning rather than of Russian national culture.[74] During the Chinese Cultural Revolution, however, the Chinese went far beyond even Soviet conceptions of diplomacy as a form of struggle. A *People's Daily* editorial at the height of the Cultural Revolution, entitled 'Salute the Red Fighters for Chairman Mao's Revolutionary Diplomatic Line', asserted:

The diplomatic personnel of great socialist China are proletarian diplomatic fighters. At any time and in any place, they conscientiously study Mao Tse-tung's thought, resolutely put it into practice, earnestly propagate it and valiantly defend it. With Mao Tse-tung's thought, that matchless weapon, in their hands they show a dauntless revolutionary spirit, a firm and correct political orientation, an unconquerable fighting will. They are capable of accomplishing all the missions of proletarian revolutionary diplomacy however complicated or perilous the situation.[75]

Such statements were accompanied by various kinds of deliberately confrontational behaviour by Chinese diplomats abroad, and by government-encouraged demonstrations against, and attacks upon, foreign embassies in China. It should be noted, however, that when Chinese behaviour provoked equal or worse outrages against Chinese diplomats, China was quick to accuse the relevant foreign state of violating the established international principles relating to diplomacy. On such occasions China claimed that its own conduct was in line with 'the guiding principles of international relations' or with 'international usage'.[76]

A different use of diplomacy for revolutionary purposes was witnessed in the cases of Iran and Libya. Although Iran's revolution certainly perceived itself as the precursor of similar developments elsewhere in the Muslim world, it failed to win more than a relatively small number of adherents outside Iran. Libya was even less successful in its internationalist pretensions. However, both revolutionary states saw certain of their citizens living abroad as significant dangers to their survival, and their embassies—suitably

---

[74] K. T. Young, *Negotiating with the Chinese Communists* (New York, 1968), *passim*.
[75] Cited in Ardant, 'Chinese Diplomatic Practice', 92.
[76] Ibid. 88–9.

purged of individuals of dubious loyalty—were used to carry out surveillance of the Iranian and Libyan communities in other countries, as well as to conduct propaganda campaigns amongst those communities.

The essential principles of Iranian diplomacy were laid down by the Ayatollah Khomeini:

In the case of political relations between Muslim states and foreign states, if it is feared that the foreigners will gain control of the Islamic countries, even if that control is purely political and economic, it is the duty of the Muslims to oppose such relations and to force the Islamic states to sever them. . . .

If the establishment of relations, whether political or commercial, between one of the Muslim states and foreigners is contrary to the interest of Islam and the Muslims, such relations are not permissible and if a Muslim government moves to establish such relations, it is the duty of the other Muslim governments to compel it, by any means possible, to sever relations.

If certain heads of state of Muslim countries, or certain members of either house of the Majlis, permit foreigners to expand their influence, whether that influence is political, economic, or military, [in a manner] contrary to the interests of Islam and the Muslims, they automatically forfeit their posts—whatever their posts may be—by virtue of this reason, even if it is supposed that the post [in question] was legitimately obtained. Furthermore, it is the duty of the Muslims to punish them by any means possible.

[The establishment of] commercial and political relations with states like Israel that are the tools of the tyrannical superpowers is not permissible and it is the duty of the Muslims to oppose such relations in any way possible. Merchants who establish commercial relations with Israel and its agents are traitors to Islam and the Muslims, and they are aiding in the destruction of the ordinances of Islam. It is the duty of the Muslims to discontinue all dealings with those traitors, whether they are governments or merchants, and to compel them to repent and renounce their relations with such states.[77]

Islamic law formally acknowledges the principle of diplomatic inviolability.[78] However, in Khomeini's interpretation at least, this principle takes a poor second place to the need to guard against

[77] Khomeini, *Islam and Revolution: Writings and Declarations of Imam Khomeini* (Berkeley, Calif., 1981), 440.

[78] N. R. Keddie, *Roots of Revolution* (New Haven, Conn., and London, 1981), 266.

'Control' by foreigners and to the even more all-embracing 'interests of Islam'. Governments disregarding these principles did so at their peril. Khomeini established what amounted to a separate diplomatic system to ensure that his ideas were implemented.[79]

Revolutionary states are not the only ones to have abused diplomatic privileges or violated norms of diplomatic conduct, but they have been involved in some of the most serious cases in recent times. Here, a distinction needs to be made between actions committed in the heat of the revolutionary moment and those involving some clear degree of governmental approval or sponsorship. For example, it is quite possible that the Iranian government did not order the attack upon the American Embassy by militant students in 1979, but there can be no question that this incident was exploited by the Khomeini faction to push the revolution further to the left.[80] Interestingly, when the possibility of holding foreign diplomats hostage was debated by the French revolutionaries, it was done so in the context of fears that other governments might not respect the rights of French envoys.[81]. In other words, when the French Assembly considered hostage-taking, it did so as a possible means of enforcing compliance by other states with the established principles of international law. Indeed some of the worst violations of diplomatic immunity during the French Revolution were perpetrated by its opponents, as when Austria captured and imprisoned two fully accredited French diplomats in 1793.[82] Perhaps the central point here is that revolutions help to create an atmosphere in which respect for the conventions of international society tends to diminish on all sides.

Other violations of diplomatic norms or abuses of privileges by revolutionary states have included the use of diplomatic bags for importing arms, which in the most notorious case were used by someone in the Libyan People's Bureau in London to kill a British policewoman. Cuban and Vietnamese diplomats were expelled by Britain in 1988 for incidents involving guns.[83] The use of embassies

[79] D. Hiro, *Iran under the Ayatollahs* (London, 1985), 133.
[80] F. Halliday, 'Iranian Foreign Policy since 1979: Internationalism and Nationalism in the Islamic Revolution'. Paper presented to the British International Studies Association Conference, 1984.
[81] A. Mathiez, *The French Revolution* (London, 1951), 215.
[82] A. Sorel, *Europe and the French Revolution*, vol. i, trans. and ed. A. Cobban and J. W. Hunt (London, 1969), 106.
[83] G. V. McClanahan, *Diplomatic Immunity* (London, 1989), 157.

for espionage purposes has also been associated with revolutionary states ever since the French Revolution, although they are hardly the only states to have engaged in this practice.

In general, revolutionary states have eventually come to see some value in conventional diplomacy, even if they have not necessarily accepted that they are bound by prevailing diplomatic norms and rules. In diplomacy, as in other aspects of foreign affairs, it is impossible to escape from some of the consequences of being a state in a society of states, a point partially conceded by Litvinov in 1929:

Unlike other Commissariats, the Commissariat for Foreign Affairs cannot, unfortunately, put forward a five-year plan of work, a plan for the development of foreign policy. It is not difficult to see why. In putting forward control figures and drawing up a plan of economic development we start from our own aspirations and wishes, from a calculation of our own potentialities, and from the firm principles of our entire policy, but in examining the development of foreign policy we have to deal with a number of factors that are scarcely subject to calculation, with a number of elements outside our control and the scope of our action. International affairs are composed not only of our own aspirations and actions, but of those of a large number of countries, built on different lines from our Union, pursuing other aims than ours and using other means to achieve those aims than we allow.[84].

As with other aspects of the international impact of revolutionary states, not all of the adverse consequences for diplomacy of the appearance of a revolutionary state flow directly from that state's ideology or antisocial behaviour. Revolutions can create uncertainty and unpredictability whatever the intentions of their leaders. The reaction of other powers may also play a part in disrupting the international climate.

One obvious example concerns the diplomatic recognition of a new revolutionary regime.[85] Sometimes it may not be perfectly clear that what purports to be the new government of a state does indeed exercise *de facto* control, which is the normal criterion necessary for other states to recognize it. On other occasions, as with France in 1792–3, other governments may wish to withhold recognition as an expression of disapproval of the domestic policies

[84] Degras, *Soviet Documents*, i. 408.
[85] See the discussion on this subject in P. Calvert, *Revolution and International Politics* (London, 1984), 151–2.

of the revolutionary state. Finally, they may use refusal of recognition as a weapon against a state which, for various reasons, they do not wish to achieve international acceptability, as happened in the case of American policy towards China for two decades after 1949. Recognition does not create a state; statehood derives from the objective fact of sovereignty. However, recognition is part of the process whereby a state enters into all of the rights and obligations that are attendant upon being a member of the society of states. Without recognition from at least the major powers a state may find itself in an ambiguous situation with regard to international society. As a state it is expected to adhere to all of the obligations that go with statehood, yet its non-recognition by important states may deny it some of the entitlements that it has a right to expect. The communist government of China was unable to take up its seat at the United Nations, along with the great power rights that went with membership of the Security Council, until 1971 because of the American policy of non-recognition.[86] Some legal authorities take the view that the fact that recognition is an act with consequences for international society as a whole and not just for individual states implies that states have an international duty to recognize governments which exercise effective control over a clearly defined territory: in other words, which are objectively sovereign.[87] The American government dismissed this theory in relation to its China policy, arguing that recognition was a matter 'solely to be determined as the national interest dictates' and that American interests were against recognition of the People's Republic of China.[88] Without entering into what Michael Akehurst terms a 'bitter theoretical quarrel' about the precise legal effects of recognition,[89] it is reasonable to suppose that a state that was already disinclined to see its statehood as imposing obligations upon it as a member of international society would be even less ready to do so if other states persisted in treating it as an outlaw.

These are not new issues in the relationship between revolutionary states and international society. The Protocol of Troppau of

[86] Ibid.

[87] e.g. H. Lauterpacht, *Recognition in International Law* (London, 1947), 6.

[88] US Government Statement, 20 November 1958, cited in D. J. Harris, *Cases and Materials on International Law*, 2nd edn. (London, 1979), 148.

[89] M. Akehurst, *A Modern Introduction to International Law* (London 1987), 59.

November 1820 asserted the following general principle on behalf of all the members of the Concert of Europe except Britain:

States which have undergone a change of government, due to revolution, the results of which threaten other states, *ipso facto* cease to be members of the European Alliance, and remain excluded from it until their situation gives guarantees for legal order and stability. If, owing to such alterations, immediate danger threatens other states, the powers bind themselves, by peaceful means, or if need be by arms, to bring back the guilty state into the bosom of the Great Alliance.[90]

This of course went considerably further than calling for recognition to be denied, since it countenanced armed intervention to force delinquent states to observe all of the prevailing norms of international society, including what Metternich was trying to establish as a specific principle of international legitimacy that protected all established governments. A similar issue emerged during Woodrow Wilson's presidency, when he shifted away from America's traditional policy of recognizing governments that were in effective control of their countries towards using the denial of recognition as a weapon against Mexico following the seizure of power there by General Huerta. The same period saw American interventions in Haiti, the Dominican Republic, and Cuba when revolutionary violence threatened stability in the region.

CONCLUSION

It is easy to see why diplomacy has become a particular target of revolutionary states. Especially in its eighteenth- and nineteenth-century forms, diplomacy represented everything that revolutionaries tend to stand against. It was an activity carried out by aristocrats who saw themselves as the physical incarnation of international society and the upholders of international order, and whose role was to endeavour to achieve agreement and compromise solutions through secret negotiations that were to be conducted in accordance with well-established rules of courtesy and etiquette. Furthermore, traditional diplomacy belongs to a world dominated by such post-Westphalian assumptions as reason of state, the primacy of foreign policy, the rights of great powers, and the importance of the

[90] Cited in F. B. Artz, *Reaction and Revolution, 1814–1832* (New York, 1934), 164–5.

balance of power. In its fundamental principles, in its form, and in its content, therefore, diplomacy could be seen as the antithesis of revolutionary values.

Yet it has been virtually impossible for revolutionary states to avoid becoming involved in conventional diplomacy. However transnational or universal their conception of themselves, they could not escape the only kind of identity that could legitimize their existence in the eyes of others: sovereign statehood, a status that, they soon discovered, conferred benefits as well as obligations. But statehood entailed membership of a society of states whose chief medium of communication was through diplomacy. As in other areas of international society, it was the pressures of socialization that brought revolutionary states to engage in diplomatic relations with the rest of the world. Many had their own separate agendas in so doing. Diplomacy could still be used for subversion, espionage, propaganda, or other revolutionary purposes. Moreover, not all of its traditions and customs were wholeheartedly embraced by revolutionary states. Until the end of the Cold War there were few instances of diplomacy between Western and communist states functioning in quite the same way as it did between Western states, at least over major political issues. Yet whatever private reservations revolutionary states may have had about the operational norms and conventions of diplomacy, in most cases they found it difficult to conduct their formal relations by other means.

This is not to say that diplomacy was any more immune to the challenge of new revolutionary ideas than were other institutions of international society. Several developments in diplomatic practice in the twentieth century, not all of them necessarily beneficial to the orderly conduct of international affairs, may be partially attributed to the impact of revolutionary states. The propaganda element in some areas of contemporary diplomacy, for example, stems from the spread of democracy, with its creation of attentive domestic audiences for foreign policy ventures, and also from the ideological confrontations of the post-1945 era. Both developments owe something to the major revolutions of the last two hundred years. The relative decline in the importance of the activities of professional diplomats compared with that of high-level meetings among political leaders similarly reflects the higher public profile that diplomacy has acquired in this century. The emergence of 'parliamentary diplomacy' in the League of Nations and UN assemblies and elsewhere owes something to the demands for 'openness' and 'democracy' in international relations with which successive revolutionary states have been associated. Diplomacy, like other institutions of the Westphalian international society, has retained its essential character and purposes since 1648, but it has not survived unchanged.

8

Statecraft and
the Balance of Power

THE BALANCE OF POWER AND INTERNATIONAL SOCIETY

In *The Anarchical Society*, Hedley Bull devotes a chapter to each of the following institutions, which he sees as upholding order in an anarchical international society: the balance of power, international law, diplomacy, war, and the preponderant role of the great powers. In this chapter I propose to consider the balance of power, war, and the great powers as parts of a single 'institution', in Bull's sense of 'a set of habits and practices shaped towards the realization of common goals'.[1] Since I depart from Bull's schema in this respect, it is appropriate to begin with an explanation of why.

As numerous writers on the balance of power have pointed out, the concept is one that is capable of sustaining a great many different meanings.[2] However, the task of definition is simplified by narrowing the focus to its role as an institution of international society. In this context the balance of power may be seen as a shorthand expression for 'a set of habits and practices' that, alongside international law and diplomacy, serve the purpose of providing some degree of order in a society of sovereign states which share one central common interest: protection and preservation of their sovereign rights. Although the 'habits and practices' that have some bearing upon the balance of power are many (alliances, spheres of influence agreements, guarantees, compensations, and arms control arrangements, to name but a few), the central institution that they serve—the balance of power—has only two closely related meanings that concern its role in international society. The first defines it as a *tendency* in a world of competing

---

[1] H. Bull, *The Anarchical Society* (London, 1977), 74.
[2] See, for example, the essay by Martin Wight, 'The Balance of Power', in H. Butterfield and M. Wight, *Diplomatic Investigations* (London, 1966), 149–75.

sovereign states for an attempt by one state to achieve preponderance over the rest to be met by sufficient resistance from other states for the attempt to fail. In this sense, the balance of power operates either to deter such endeavours or to ensure that they do not succeed. In the second definition, this natural tendency is consciously manipulated and encouraged so that it becomes a deliberate *contrivance* of states. In this sense the balance of power is part of a structure of international 'governance', a term denoting such regulatory or managerial devices as may be found in conditions of anarchy like those that prevail in international society.[3] Governance through the balance of power may be achieved either by all states exercising 'that national jealousy, and anxious attention to the affairs of other states, which is the master principle of the modern system',[4] or by a single state undertaking the role of 'balancer' for the system as a whole, or by the major powers acting in concert.

Four specific functions of the balance of power as an institution of international society were identified during the hundred years from the Treaty of Utrecht to the commencement of the Concert of Europe. The first three of these recur in most discussions of the concept, while the fourth represented an attempt to make the balance of power underpin the conservative principle of legitimacy which was at the heart of Metternich's approach to the concert system. There was universal agreement upon the first function, elaborated here by Fenelon in 1720:

This care to maintain a kind of equality and balance among neighbouring nations, is that which secures the common repose; and in this respect such nations, being joined together by commerce, compose, as it were one great body and a kind of community. Christendom, for example, makes a sort of general republic which has its interests, its dangers, and its policy. All the members of this great body are to one another for the common good, and to themselves for their particular security, that they oppose the progress of any one member which may destroy the balance, and tend to the inevitable ruin of the other members. Whatever alters the general system of Europe is dangerous and draws after it many fatal consequences.[5]

[3] L. S. Finkelstein, 'What is International Governance?' Paper presented to the Annual Meeting of the International Studies Association, Vancouver, 1991.

[4] Henry Brougham, 'Balance of Power', in M. Forsyth *et al.*, *The Theory of International Relations* (London, 1970), 265.

[5] From 'Two Essays on the Balance of Europe', in M. Wright, *Theory and Practice of the Balance of Power, 1486–1914* (London, 1975), 41.

The emphasis here is upon the security of individual states and the potential danger for international order (or the 'common repose') of insecurity arising from a perceived threat to the balance of power.

Although Fenelon also mentioned 'liberty' as a goal of the balance of power system, he did not, as Vattel does in the following passage, make 'liberty' an objective equal to 'order' in international society:

Europe forms a political system, an integral body, closely connected by the relations and different interests of the nations inhabiting this part of the world. It is not, as formerly, a confused heap of detached pieces, each of which thought herself very little concerned in the fate of the others, and seldom regarded things which did not immediately concern her. The continual attention of sovereigns to every occurrence, the constant residence of ministers, and the perpetual negotiations, make a modern Europe a kind of republic, of which the members—each independent, but all linked together by the ties of common interest—unite for the maintenance of order and liberty. Hence arose that famous scheme of the political balance, or the equilibrium of power; by which is understood such a disposition of things, as that no one potentate be able absolutely to predominate, and prescribe laws to the others.[6]

'Liberty' in this context meant the freedom of states, although it was also possible to link the notion of an international balance with the liberal constitutionalist idea of a separation of powers, and to see both as promoting individual freedom.[7]

A third purpose of the balance of power which may be identified in these writings is to sustain the idea of an international society as an influence upon the behaviour of states. Heeren suggests that this was achieved through the promotion, by the 'principle' of a balance of power, of 'a general feeling of respect for independence, and a system of politics of a higher order than that arising from individual gratification'.[8] In other words, not only was the central value of the Westphalian international society—sovereign equality—protected by the balance of power, but respect for it was enhanced, which created the possibility of international relations being conducted on a less anarchical basis than would otherwise have been the case.

[6] Emerich de Vattel, *The Law of Nations*, ed. J. Chitty (London, 1834), 311–12.

[7] M. S. Anderson, 'Eighteenth-Century Theories of the Balance of Power', in R. Hatton and M. S. Anderson, *Studies in Diplomatic History* (London, 1970), 183–98.

[8] A. H. L. Heeren, *A Manual of the History of the Political System of Europe and its Colonies* (New York, 1971 edn.), 9.

In the nineteenth century numerous attempts were made by writers and statesmen to make the balance concept serve other interests than those of order, freedom, and the preservation of international society. For Metternich, the balance of power was a fundamental principle of an international society that displayed a high degree of solidarity in defence of the legitimate rights of the established states:

What characterizes the modern world and distinguishes it from the ancient is the tendency of states to draw near each other and to form a kind of social body based on the same principle as human society . . . In the ancient world isolation and the practice of the most absolute selfishness without other restraint than that of prudence was the sum of politics . . . Modern society on the other hand exhibits the application of the principle of solidarity and of the balance of power between states . . . The establishing of international relations, on the basis of reciprocity under the guarantee of respect for acquired rights . . . constitutes in our time the essence of politics.[9]

The restoration of the 'legitimate' order in Europe was also stressed by Talleyrand, who argued that the Congress of Vienna:

wished that every legitimate dynasty should be either preserved or reestablished, and that every legitimate right should be respected, and that vacant territories, meaning those without a sovereign, should be distributed conformably with the principles of political equilibrium, or, in other words, with those principles which tend to preserve the rights of each and the tranquillity of all.[10]

Although the Congress of Vienna had gone to some lengths to try to establish a durable balance of power, defined literally in terms of territorial adjustments and state creation with the aim of devising an overall balance of forces, Talleyrand's broader use of the concept foreshadowed an evolution in the way in which the idea was interpreted in the nineteenth century. Paul Schroeder's definitive study suggests that these changes are implicit in the employment by Talleyrand and others of the term 'political equilibrium' rather than 'balance of power':

Subjectively political equilibrium meant the enjoyment of stability, peace and guaranteed rights; freedom from threats and isolation; the recognition

---

[9] E. V. Gulick, *Europe's Classical Balance of Power* (New York, 1967), 32.
[10] Letter from Talleyrand to Metternich, cited in Wright, *Theory and Practice*, 100.

of one's legitimate interests, sphere of influence, and the right to a voice in general affairs; and especially for the great powers, assurance of equality in rank, status and dignity, even if not in power . . . In objective terms, political equilibrium required that (1) the rights, influence and vital interests claimed by individual states in the international system be somehow balanced against the rights, influence and vital interests claimed by other states and the general community and (2) that a balance or harmony exist between the goals pursued by individual states, the requirements of the system, and the means to promote one's interests. Oversimplified, political equilibrium meant a balance of satisfactions, a balance of rights and obligations and a balance of performance and payoffs, rather than a balance of power.[11]

The notion that the balance of power was part of a system of international governance was clearly present in the eighteenth century, although it was honoured more in the breach than in the observance. After the Treaties of Utrecht, which attempted to reach a general settlement of European affairs by confirming the legitimacy of the Westphalian arrangements and constructing an overall balance, larger European considerations played little part in the struggle for advantage that underlay the numerous wars and partitions up to the French Revolution.[12] This is not to say that the frequent allusions to the 'balance of power', the 'European political system', the 'public law of Europe', and the 'common repose' during this period were entirely hypocritical and meaningless. At the most basic level they were significant because statesmen evidently believed that they needed to justify their conduct by reference to the norms and rules of the Westphalian system. If the competition amongst the powers was frequently fierce, it was always carried on in accordance with certain tacitly agreed 'rules of the game', which brought some constraints to bear upon the actual conduct of warfare and helped to regulate its conclusion in a relatively orderly fashion. Moreover, Europe as a whole was still seen as able to confer legitimacy upon certain kinds of political arrangement within states. For example, the emperor Charles VI sought guarantees from several European powers of the Pragmatic Sanction, which ensured that the Habsburg possessions in Austria would pass intact to his heirs, whether male or female. The system

[11] P. Schroeder, 'The Nineteenth-Century System: Balance of Power or Political Equilibrium', *Review of International Studies*, 15/2 (Apr. 1989), 135–53.
[12] K. J. Holsti, *Peace and War: Armed Conflicts and International Order, 1648–1989* (Cambridge, 1991), 73–102.

of diplomatic representation that had developed in the previous century became ever more sophisticated and comprehensive, with French accepted by most states as the language of diplomatic exchange. Linked by the many blood ties between their monarchs, and by a high level of artistic interchange, the European powers shared in many respects a common culture. Finally, if preserving or restoring an overall balance was seldom a deliberate objective of the many wars during this period, nonetheless the balancing *tendency* in European diplomacy remained, a natural consequence of what Brougham called 'the perpetual attention to foreign affairs which it [the balance of power] inculcates; the constant watchfulness which it prescribes over every movement in all parts of the system'.[13]

A true system of international governance did not emerge, however, until the creation of the Concert of Europe following the Napoleonic Wars, when the victorious great powers agreed in 1814 to devise the 'relations from whence a system of real and permanent balance of power in Europe' was to be achieved. The Concert system regulated much more than the European balance, with great power congresses regarded as authoritative means of resolving numerous issues of general interest and conferring legitimacy upon various territorial settlements and political arrangements. It also, as suggested earlier, presided over a more complex and sophisticated conception of equilibrium than is implied by the term 'balance of power'. All the same, the 'political equilibrium' was underpinned by a distribution of power which, if not a perfect mathematical balance, contained sufficient checks, constraints, and counterpoises to inhibit excessive ambition on the part of any single power. Even when this distribution of power came under threat with German unification and the increasing fragility of the Habsburg and Ottoman empires, Bismarck sought to consolidate his position by constructing a new balance of power rather than by making a bid for European hegemony. He also, with rather less success, tried to revive the essential Concert principle that matters of general European interest should be settled by great power consensus.[14]

As this brief discussion suggests, the conception of the balance of power as an institution of international society is inseparable from

[13] M. Forsyth, *et al.*, *The Theory of International Relations* (London, 1970), 269.
[14] G. A. Craig and A. L. George, *Force and Statecraft* (New York and Oxford, 1983), 35–40.

the role of great power management. It is that which turns the balance of power from a 'natural' phenomenon into a deliberate contrivance. The outbreak of war may be evidence of the collapse of a particular balance of power or of a more general breakdown of international society. However, war may also play a positive role in upholding international society, and it is in this sense that it may be seen as part of a single 'institution', in conjunction with the balance of power and great power management. Bull distinguishes two principal functions of war: enforcing international law and preserving the balance of power.[15] Since the First World War it has been frequently asserted that the destructiveness of modern warfare has made war dysfunctional in the latter respect. The assertion has had even greater force since the advent of nuclear weapons. Against that it might be argued that, while the damage caused by global nuclear war (or perhaps any nuclear war) would far outweigh any possible gains for international society, states continue to act on the assumption that war remains an instrument of last resort in defending both the global and regional balances, while the United Nations Charter makes it a legitimate instrument for upholding international law in certain circumstances. War was used for both purposes by the UN coalition against Iraq in 1991, while, arguably, the United States believed itself to be upholding the principles of the Westphalian international society, as well as the regional balances of power, in the Korean and Vietnam wars.

One further point needs to be made about the balance of power. It may be seen at one level as the only logical means of preserving order in a system of sovereign states without creating international structures of authority and mechanisms of control that would diminish sovereignty more than they protected it. However, at another level balance of power thinking stems from an essentially pessimistic view of human nature and a conservative assessment of the realistic possibilities for fundamental change. It assumes that men and states will seek power unless constrained by some external force and that a struggle for power is therefore at the heart of the relations among states. These assumptions also form the basic premises of the so-called 'Realist' theory of international relations.[16]

---

[15] Bull, *The Anarchical Society*, 186–9.
[16] For the fullest exposition of a 'realist' perspective on international relations, see H. Morgenthau, *Politics Among Nations*, 3rd edn. (New York, 1965).

In a world characterized by power politics more than by agreement on what constitutes morality, 'statecraft'—a term which first appeared in Europe shortly before the Peace of Westphalia and which meant the art of conducting state affairs, particularly in its foreign relations—assumed a particular importance. By the eighteenth century, certain key assumptions about statecraft were generally accepted throughout Europe:

1. The conduct of foreign policy was the highest responsibility of government since it was intimately connected with the security and possibly even the survival of the state.

2. The primary function of statecraft was the pursuit and the protection of the vital interests of the state.

3. Given the existence of numerous equally powerful states, all contending for their own advantage, the highest skill of statecraft was the successful manipulation of the balance of power.

4. However, all states shared an interest in the survival of the society of states. Statecraft that was prudent and far-sighted needed to take account of this larger interest, and this meant not simply manipulating the balance of power in one's favour but preserving the balance of power system as a principal ordering mechanism of international society. There was an inherent tension between these two objectives, which helps to explain the constant fluctuations in the eighteenth-century balance.

REVOLUTION AND THE BALANCE OF POWER

Revolutionary states viewed the balance of power with considerable ambivalence. On the one hand, it appeared to epitomize many of the 'old order' qualities against which they believed themselves to be in revolt, in its pessimism, its cynicism, its essential conservatism, and its implicit rejection of solutions to the dilemma of states which appealed to internationalism or solidarity among peoples. On the other hand, all revolutionary states in the early period of their revolutions tended to perceive their survival as seriously threatened by established powers. Any means that might be available to ensure their survival had to be utilized, and balancing the power of one adversary by cultivating the friendship of another state that was also opposed to that adversary was an obvious and unavoidable stratagem. This, of course, did not mean willing acceptance of the balance of power as an *institution* of an international society that was itself rejected by many revolutionary states, but it did mean that revolutionary states had to understand and exploit one of the basic tools of 'old order' statecraft.

The balance of power was one of the targets of the writings of the French *philosophes*, who provided much of the intellectual background for the French, and to a much lesser extent the American, revolution. Hence it is not surprising to find, for example, a French Foreign Ministry official attacking 'the system of the political balance' as 'harmful and degrading to the human spirit' and urging its replacement by a confederation in which 'the common interest' would reign supreme.[17] Similarly, Brissot spoke scornfully of politicians 'who still believe in the old European balance',[18] and called for French diplomacy to be 'raised to its true height' by breaking with the old power politics, with their reliance on 'treaties devised by ignorance and corruption', which, he suggested, should be replaced by a treaty of friendship with the human race.[19] In this instance he was specifically attacking France's alliance with Austria, which stemmed from the diplomatic revolution of 1756.

The American revolution also produced opponents of the balance of power, although these were far fewer than in the French case, for reasons that will be given shortly. Silas Deane, for example, showed that he was aware of the conventional rationale for the balance of power principle, but dismissed it, albeit on 'realist' rather than 'idealist' grounds:

Universal monarchy has at many periods been feared from the House of Bourbon, and England has been exhausted to prevent it; she has engaged allies pretendedly to keep the balance of power in Europe, as it is ridiculously and unintelligibly termed by European politicians; but you will permit an American to give his sentiments; . . . From the period when the feudal system prevailed over all Europe, when every lord was sovereign, to this hour, the number of kingdoms or distinct powers in Europe has been decreasing [so that] the whole must, at some very distant period, be brought into one; for not an age passes, and scarce a single war, without annihilating or swallowing up several of them. But from what quarter is

---

[17] Cited in J. Der Derian, *On Diplomacy* (Oxford, 1987), 180.
[18] *Archives parlementaires*, 12 Jan. 1793 (Paris, 1900), lvii. 20.
[19] Ibid. 17 Jan. 1792.

this universal empire in Europe to originate? . . . not from the house of Bourbon but . . . [from] Great Britain.[20]

Deane added that, despite the prospect of the United States exercising a joint hegemony with England and Russia in the future, he wished America to remain 'unconnected with the politics or interests of Europe' except by commercial links.[21] Benjamin Franklin was another of America's first diplomats who spoke disparagingly of 'whims about the Ballance of Power'.[22]

Criticisms of the balance of power concept were also heard during the American debate over federalism, although, like Deane's comments, they reflected an essential realism about international relations rather than an idealistic optimism about the prospects for changing the world. For example, Alexander Hamilton's chief objection to the balance concept was not that anything better could be expected but that if the American states retained their independence in foreign affairs, North America would reproduce the worst features of the balance of power system in Europe, since these were virtually a law of life for separate sovereign states. Americans should not expect any more from mere treaty arrangements among the thirteen American states than Europe had experienced:

In the early part of this century there was an epidemical rage in Europe for this species of compacts; from which the politicians of the time fondly hoped for benefits, which were never realised. With a view to establishing the equilibrium of power and the peace of that part of the world, all the resources of negotiation were exhausted, and triple and quadruple alliances were formed; but they were scarcely formed before they were broken, giving an instructive but afflicting lesson to mankind, how little dependence is to be placed on treaties which have no other sanction than the obligations of good faith; and which oppose general considerations of peace and justice to the impulse of any immediate interest or passion.[23]

A similar argument was advanced by President Polk in 1845, although by that time the issue was the rising power of the United States itself, power which some European states had suggested

---

[20] F. Wharton, *The Revolutionary Diplomatic Correspondence of the United States* (Washington, 1889), ii. 332–3.
[21] Ibid.
[22] G. Stourzh, *Benjamin Franklin and American Foreign Policy* (Chicago, 1969), 254–5.
[23] C. Rossiter (ed.), *The Federalist Papers* (New York, 1901), 109.

should be contained by a balance of power system on the American continent. The balance of power, Polk asserted, 'can not be permitted to have any application on the North American continent, and especially to the United States'.[24] Although Jefferson clearly regarded the balance of power with distaste, he was convinced of its value in keeping the great European powers at each others' throats, rather than America's.[25] It was not until the advent of Woodrow Wilson that a leading American emerged whose critique of the balance of power derived from American revolutionary ideas and who attempted to replace it with a conception of a 'community of power'.

Of the other revolutionary states that have been considered here, those which espoused Marxism-Leninism had their own unique variant of the balance of power concept, which will be assessed shortly. However, Marxist ideas about the 'balance of forces' had little or nothing in common with the concept of the balance of power system as an institution of international society. The latter was normally criticized by Soviet theorists as designed in reality to favour the leading 'imperialist' powers. In a similar vein, Stalin (who was no stranger to the manipulation of power) responded contemptuously to Stafford Cripps's suggestion in 1940 that Britain and the Soviet Union should seek to re-establish the European balance:

The so-called European balance of power had hitherto oppressed not only Germany but also the Soviet Union. Therefore the Soviet Union would take all measures to prevent the re-establishment of the old balance of power in Europe.[26]

The Ayatollah Khomeini had a very similar view of the balance of power system, which he believed had been used as a weapon against Islam, first through the division of the Islamic Ottoman Empire into numerous smaller countries and secondly through the creation of the state of Israel.[27] At a more fundamental level, Khomeini's rejection of the territorial state was also a denial of a basic premise of the balance of power principle.

[24] N. A. Graebner, *Ideas and Diplomacy* (New York, 1964), 224–5.
[25] L. S. Kaplan, *Entangling Alliances with None: American Foreign Policy in the Age of Jefferson* (Kent, Ohio, and London, 1987), 111–26.
[26] Wight, 'The Balance of Power' in Butterfield and Wight, 155.
[27] F. Rajaee, *Islamic Values and World View* (Lanham, Md., and New York, 1983), 86–7.

If revolutionaries were uneasy about the balance of power as an institution of international society, especially where their own freedom of action was concerned, they were less troubled about exploiting the natural dynamics of a balance of power system to their own advantage. The American revolutionaries in particular saw the value of the European system for their own purposes, first in their quest for allies against England and later in safeguarding their independence. So long as the system remained in its European home, it might be unsavoury but it could be useful. Some Americans went so far as to believe that the balance system, along with religious freedom, was a sign 'of progress . . . in the order and perfection of human society'.[28] More common were the views of John Adams, who proceeded from a coldly realistic appraisal of the nature of international relations in the Old World, but who made it clear that understanding and exploiting something did not mean approving it. He noted the deficiencies in human nature which had given rise to the balance of power system:

Men are so sensible of a constant tendency in others to excesses, that a signal superiority of power never appears without exciting jealousies and efforts to reduce it.[29]

This principle had led to coalitions being formed against Charles V of Spain and Louis XIV of France; now it was the turn of the English. This law of nature applied whether the effort to achieve hegemony involved the traditional domination of land or, as in the case of the English, of the sea:

It is an observation made some years ago by a great writer of this nation [France], de Mably, that the project of being sole master of the sea and of commanding all the commerce is not less chimerical nor less ruinous than that of universal monarchy on land . . . France has already repeated several times that it was necessary to establish an equilibrium, a balance of power at sea.[30]

To those who argued that differences of language, religion, or culture would prevent America from aligning herself with France or other enemies of England, Adams replied with a realism reminiscent of Hamilton's that 'the circumstances of modes,

---

[28] John Witherspoon, 30 July 1776, cited in J. H. Hutson, *John Adams and the Diplomacy of the American Revolution* (Lexington, Ky., 1980), 10.
[29] Wharton, *The Revolutionary Diplomatic Correspondence*, iii. 278–9.
[30] Ibid. 542.

language and religion have much less influence in determining the friendship and enmity of nations than other more essential interests'.[31]

Towards the end of the War of Independence Adams, in his most extensive statement on the balance of power, argued that skilful exploitation of the balance in Europe had been, and should remain, the governing principle of the foreign policy of the Continental Congress:

Gentlemen can never too often [be] requested to recollect the Debates in Congress in the Years 1775 and 1776 when the Treaty with France was first in Contemplation. The Nature of those connections, which ought to be formed between America and Europe will never be better understood than they were at that time. It was then said, there is a Ballance of Power in Europe. Nature has formed it. Practice and Habit have confirmed it, and it must forever exist. It may be disturbed for a time, by the accidental Removal of a Weight from one Scale to the other; but there will be a continual Effort to restore the Equilibrium. The Powers of Europe now think Great Britain too powerful. They will see her Power diminished with pleasure. But they cannot see Us throw ourselves headlong into the Scale of Bourbon [power] without Jealousy and Terror. We must therefore give no exclusive priviledges in Trade to the House of Bourbon. If we give exclusive priviledges in Trade, or form perpetual Alliances offensive and defensive with the Powers in one Scale, We infallibly make Enemies of those in the other, and some of these at least will declare War in favor of Great Britain. Congress adopted these principles and this System in its purity, and by their Wisdom have succeeded most perfectly in preventing every Power in the World from taking Part against them.[32]

In general, Adams's views on the practical utility of the European balance of power system were shared by most other leading Americans of the period, although there were some differences of nuance. Even when Britain was virtually the sole balancing factor against Napoleon, Jefferson's Anglophobia made it difficult for him to adjust America's foreign policy in the pro-British direction that Adams's advocacy of maximum flexibility demanded. In essence, Jefferson had very little time for the amoral manœuvrings that balance of power policies required and preferred America to have as little involvement in European affairs as possible. Only Hamilton really addressed the contradiction that was implicit in a policy of,

[31] Ibid. 687.
[32] Graebner, *Ideas and Diplomacy*, p. xiii, and Hutson, *John Adams*, 28–9.

on the one hand, exploiting the European balance to America's advantage and, on the other, avoiding entangling commitments in Europe. In his view Americans should not expect too many political benefits to accrue from their country's potential commercial importance. A more direct engagement in the balance system might eventually be required. In particular, the nation needed to build a sizeable navy which 'if it could not vie with those of the great maritime powers, would at least be of respectable weight, if thrown into the scale of either of two contending parties'.[33] Adams expressed the more commonly held opinion when he urged Americans to exploit the balance, but to guard against the machinations of the European powers, who 'will be continually manoeuvring with us, to work us into their real or imaginary balances of power'.[34] Whether it was possible to work to maintain the European balance, which all agreed was in America's interest, while remaining outside the European system as a whole, as most hoped, would remain a critical issue in American foreign policy until the middle of the twentieth century.

Although the French revolutionary wars began, in part, as an act of defiance against the balance of power system that the Westphalian settlement and other treaties had devised, and although they became, under Napoleon, a quest for French hegemony in Europe, the intervening years saw numerous attempts by the French leaders to return to traditional balance of power policies. Robespierre, for example, sought to divide the anti-French coalition and to bring Turkey, Sweden, and other powers into the equation as counterweights to France's enemies.[35] The treaties concluded by the Directory in 1795 with Prussia, Spain, and some of the smaller German states were indistinguishable from earlier eighteenth-century treaties in the priority given to balance of power considerations over the newer revolutionary principles, such as nationality.[36] In the same year Merlin of Douai argued that, while it was right and proper that Belgium should receive its liberty, this

[33] Cited in Stourzh, *Benjamin Franklin*, 197.

[34] A. Deconde, 'The French Alliance in Historical Speculation', in R. Hoffman and P. J. Albert (eds.), *Diplomacy and Revolution: The Franco-American Alliance of 1778* (Charlottesville, Va., 1981), 22.

[35] S. T. Ross, *European Diplomatic History, 1789–1815: France Against Europe* (New York, 1969), 86.

[36] Kyung-Won Kim, *Revolution and International System* (New York, 1970), 102.

should not take a form that would harm France. A completely independent Belgium would work to England's advantage, so Belgium's 'freedom' should take the shape of union with France.[37]

The overall design of France's foreign policy at this time was the responsibility of the Abbé Sieyès, who presented his plan to the Committee of Public Safety in April 1795. His grand design essentially represented a return to orthodox balance of power principles, with some concessions to the new forces that had been unleashed by the Revolution.[38] Its ultimate objective was 'durable, if not perpetual peace', an aim that would be achieved by redrawing the map of Europe with a view to creating a stable balance. However, he noted that France's new political status had given rise to a new source of insecurity: 'A republic is always subject to dissensions; nothing is more dangerous for it than a powerful neighbour.'[39] Hence, the new 'natural' frontiers that France had attained by force of arms needed to be secured by a lasting balance of power. This could only be achieved through a perfect balance between Prussian and Austrian power, with the frontiers of the two German states redrawn some distance away from their 1789 borders with France. Fortunately, 'compensations' were available for them in the form of the ecclesiastical principalities, whose existence, in any case, rested upon clearly outmoded ideas.[40]

The same awareness of underlying balance of power considerations was evident in the early foreign policies of other revolutionary states, even where they rejected the balance of power as a necessary principle of the international system. Nowhere was this more the case than in the Soviet Union. For example, Chicherin's statement on the Straits at the 1923 Lausanne Conference, while flavoured with a pinch of Bolshevik rhetoric, was indistinguishable from the Black Sea policies of his Tsarist predecessors:

Any solution based on the presence in the Straits of forces belonging to certain Powers, and tending to create a preponderant situation for one Power or group of Powers, will encounter determined opposition not only from Russia and her allies, but also from public opinion in all countries,

---

[37] S. S. Biro, *The German Policy of Revolutionary France* (Cambridge, Mass., 1957), i. 439.

[38] J. H. Clapham, *The Abbé Sieyès* (London, 1912), 180–3.

[39] A. Sorel, *L'Europe et la révolution française*, 21st edn. (Paris, 1892), iv. 299.

[40] Ibid.

which desires to eliminate those causes of conflict in the Near East which constitute a permanent menace to the cause of peace.[41]

Stalin's speech on the international situation in January 1925 was even more open in its advocacy of a Soviet policy of exploiting the balance of power:

Our banner remains as before the banner of peace. But if war begins, we shall not be able to sit by with folded hands. We shall have to make a move, but we shall be the last to come out, and we shall make a move in order to throw the decisive weight into the balance, the weight that might tip the scales.[42]

One of the reasons why this kind of thinking came naturally to Stalin and other Marxist-Leninist leaders was that it was relatively easy to depict it as ideologically sound as well as self-interested. The dialectical view of history saw events as proceeding along certain predetermined paths in accordance with 'objective' laws of motion, which took the form of the working out of the 'contradiction' or tension between opposing class forces. The contribution of Lenin, and later Mao, to Marxist theory was to take Marx and Engels' historicism and make it the basis of the strategy and tactics of a political party whose supposed historical role was to employ its 'advanced' awareness of these laws to help history progress towards its inevitable ends. This required a careful assessment of the particular 'correlation of forces' at any point in time with a view to planning the 'correct' tactics. The same principles could be applied to international relations as well as to the politics of revolution inside a country. In Lenin's words:

The fundamental task of proletarian tactics was defined by Marx in strict conformity with the general principles of his materialist-dialectical outlook. Nothing but an objective account of the totality of all the mutual relationships of all the classes of a given society without exception, and consequently an account of the mutual relationship between it and other societies, can serve as the basis for the correct tactics of the advanced class.[43]

It is possible to deduce certain basic principles of a 'dialectical' foreign policy, which may be contrasted with the principles of eighteenth-century statecraft that were outlined earlier:

[41] J. Degras, *Soviet Documents on Foreign Policy*, i. (London, 1951), 346–51.
[42] Ibid. ii. 2.
[43] Cited in R. L. Garthoff, 'The Concept of the Balance of Power in Soviet Policy-Making', *World Politics*, 4/1 (Oct. 1951), 90.

1. The world is in a state of constant flux and any apparent equilibrium will be temporary and unstable.

2. Change and development in the social universe are governed by the nature of the contradictions between social forces. At any point in time these will be arranged in a particular correlation which can be accurately perceived by those possessing the correct 'consciousness'.

3. Correct policy-making will involve an understanding of process as well as situation. That is, it will take account of the fact that underlying any political situation is a changing relationship among forces, and it must accurately perceive the direction of the change as well as the point in a situation's dialectical evolution that has been reached at a particular time. This implies that policy may be made with reference to long-term assessments of probable future outcomes as well as to short-term considerations.

4. The principal contradiction in which socialist states are involved is the hostility towards them of 'imperialist' states, since the latter are at the head of the system which it is socialism's historical destiny to destroy. However, there are numerous other important contradictions of which a Marxist-Leninist foreign policy must take full account, and which it must exploit, especially contradictions amongst the imperialist powers and between them and other, non-socialist forces such as national liberation movements.

5. International, transnational, and intranational structures and processes all contain their own contradictions, all of which need to be taken full account of in a correct Marxist-Leninist foreign policy.

It is impossible to gauge with any precision the extent to which such ideological formulations were reflected in actual Soviet policy. While numerous Soviet or Chinese decisions may be interpreted as following logically from a dialectical mode of analysis of world politics, they can also be given more conventional explanations.[44] However, what is indisputable is that communist leaders from Lenin to Brezhnev consistently explained their own actions in these terms. At the very least, it appeared that policy had to be rationalized by reference to these ideological criteria, while those

---

[44] I have attempted a fuller investigation of this problem in *Revolutionary Diplomacy: Chinese Foreign Policy and the United Front Doctrine* (Berkeley and Los Angeles, 1977).

Western states which were the putative ultimate losers by whatever assistance Moscow might give to historical forces had little choice but to take them seriously.

In the early years of the Soviet state the exploitation of 'contradictions amongst the imperialists' was portrayed as an inescapable consequence of Soviet weakness. As Lenin explained in 1920, the fundamental rule of Soviet foreign policy:

the rule which we have not only adopted theoretically, but applied in practice, and which will be our rule until the final victory of socialism throughout the world [is] to exploit the contradictions and antagonisms between the two imperialisms, between the two systems of capitalist states, inciting them one against the other. So long as we have not won the entire world, so long as, from the economic and military point of view, we remain weaker than the rest of the capitalist world, so long shall we keep to that rule.[45]

But a correct assessment of the 'correlation' of forces was deemed no less important in 1960, when it was claimed that the balance had shifted in favour of the Soviet Union:

the distribution of power between the two systems is steadily changing. For several years now these changes have obtained for socialism a preponderance of power over capitalism in the scales of the planet.[46]

This, according to Khrushchev had created the preconditions necessary for the socialist camp to be able 'to determine, in growing measure, the character, methods and trends of international relations'.[47] A Soviet spokesman felt able to claim in 1974:

One of the characteristic features of the international situation is the constantly changing correlation of class and political forces on the world arena in favour of socialism, the steady strengthening of the forces of peace and social progress on the one hand, and the faster rate of disintegration and breakdown of the old world on the other.[48]

Chinese foreign policy statements during the Maoist era were also generously flavoured with dialectical rhetoric. Mao saw world history as involving a constant struggle between a dominant

---

[45] Cited in Degras, *Soviet Documents*, i. 221.

[46] Cited in W. Zimmerman, *Soviet Perspectives on International Relations, 1956–67* (Princeton, NJ, 1969), 181.

[47] Ibid.

[48] R. J. Mitchell, *Ideology of a Superpower: Contemporary Soviet Doctrines on International Relations* (Stanford, Calif., 1982), 59.

oppressive force, which, although dominant, represented the interests of only a tiny minority, and a variety of other forces which, though oppressed, represented those of the overwhelming majority.[49] Revolutionary strategy consisted essentially of translating the 'true' preponderance of the progressive forces, which was concealed by the apparent strength of the oppressors, into real power:

in the struggle against the class enemy, the proletariat and other revolutionary people must, first of all, make a correct estimate of the overall balance of class forces, must show dauntless revolutionary spirit and revolutionary aspirations, and must have a firm faith that the revolutionary forces, which are outwardly weak, are certain to defeat the counter-revolutionary forces, which are outwardly strong.[50]

This 'firm faith' in the inevitable tendency of the balance of forces to favour the course of revolution led Mao in the 1950s to coin several slogans—'the east wind is prevailing over the west wind', 'imperialism and all reactionaries are paper tigers', and so forth—which reflected his belief that the socialist camp was in a position to assert itself more forcefully against 'imperialism', particularly through greater support for revolution in the Third World. This was one of the issues that provoked an eventual rift between China and the Soviet Union. Although the Soviets accepted the essential thesis of the preponderance of socialism, they tended to argue that this should be used to compel imperialism to accept *détente* and peaceful coexistence rather than to raise the level of struggle. In the 1960s their opposition to China's more 'adventuristic' line tended to derive from their apprehensions about the impact of nuclear weapons on the great power equation. However, it may be noted that Stalin drew similar conclusions in 1925 about the effects of what was perceived as a 'temporary equilibrium' between capitalism and socialism:

What is fundamental and new, deciding and permeating all events for this period in the sphere of foreign relations, is that a certain temporary equilibrium of forces has been established between our country, which is building socialism, and the countries of the capitalist world, an equilibrium which has determined the present phase of 'peaceful coexistence' between

---

[49] Mao Zedong, 'On Contradiction', *Selected Works* (Peking, 1969), i. 313–42.
[50] Shao Tieh-chen, 'Revolutionary Dialectics and how to Appraise Imperialism', *Peking Review* (11 Jan. 1963), 10–15.

the land of the Soviets and the capitalist lands. That which we at one time thought of as a brief breathing space after the war has changed into an entire period of respite.[51]

It is possible that the different Chinese and Soviet views of the correct policy implications of favourable balances of forces reflected not so much alternative interpretations of Marxism as the different perspectives of a would-be superpower and a far weaker Third World state. A favourable balance could be used to shape world events in accordance with Soviet global interests, while a world-wide revolutionary upsurge that would tie down hostile American forces was a better guarantee of security for China.

The Ayatollah Khomeini did not formulate Iran's foreign policy in terms of correctly appraising and exploiting the existing balance of forces. However, he was closer to Mao in his depiction of the world as divided between the oppressors, led by the two super-powers, and the oppressed. Like Mao, he called for a united front of the oppressed, and saw the future course of history as entailing their inevitable victory:

Beware that the world today will be that of the oppressed; sooner or later they will be victorious. God has promised that they will inherit and rule the earth. Once again I declare my full support for all movements, groups and parties who struggle against the superpowers of left or right.[52]

The spearhead of this struggle he envisaged as unity amongst Muslims:

all Muslims in the world are about to join together and achieve mutual understanding between the different schools of thought in Islam, in order to deliver their nations from the foul grasp of the superpowers.[53]

If a conception of the balance of power is discernible in the ideologies of many revolutionary states, this, of course, is very far from meaning that they were participants in a balance of power system, in which the balance of power was regarded as a major regulatory mechanism of international society. The French and Americans sought to exploit the competition for power amongst other states for their own ends, with little or no acceptance of the notion of the balance of power as an institution. Marxist and

[51] Cited in Degras, *Soviet Documents*, ii. 69–76.
[52] Cited in Rajaee, *Islamic Values*, 79.
[53] Khomeini, *Islam and Revolution* (Berkeley, Calif., 1981), 300.

Islamic revolutionaries proceeded from a long-term vision, in which history was seen as working towards an overwhelming *imbalance* in their favour.

There are several other respects in which the advent of revolutionary states had potentially disruptive consequences for the orderly functioning of the balance of power as an institution of international society.

1. Their conception of the global revolutionary struggle envisaged alignments on the basis of doctrinal considerations and also depicted the overall balance of forces in terms of intranational and transnational as well as international factors. Hence the Ayatollah hoped that the Islamic revolution would cause the downfall of the more traditional Middle Eastern regimes; Gaddafi used international terrorism to 'balance' the conventional power of his enemies; Comintern, the communist-controlled parts of the labour and peace movements in the West, and links with Third World revolutionary forces, have all, at times, been seen (both by Moscow and by its Western opponents) as elements in the balance of power between the Soviet Union and the capitalist world; the French revolutionaries believed that they could appeal over the heads of foreign governments to their peoples; while China and Cuba supported revolutionary struggles in Asia and Latin America partly because they perceived these as a countervailing force against American power. Factors such as these complicate conventional calculations of the relative power of adversaries, and this in turn introduces new elements of instability and distortion into the balance of power. It was suggested earlier that order in international relations is partly a matter of perceptions, and nowhere is this more true than in the case of the role of the balance of power in international society. For instance, the balance of power in the Middle East during the 1980s was seen as more precarious than ever on account of the fundamentalist threat to conservative regimes in the Gulf and elsewhere arising out of the Iranian revolution. The United States saw its sphere of influence in South and Central America as jeopardized by Cuban activities in the region. The massive American commitment to South Vietnam derived in part from a belief that Vietnamese communism represented an arm of Chinese power. Burke wrote of the French revolutionaries that:

Exploding, therefore, all sorts of balances, they avow their design to erect themselves into a new description of empire, which is not grounded on any balance, but forms a sort of impious hierarchy, of which France is to be the head and the guardian.[54]

Exactly the same argument was to be used many times after 1917 of the Soviet Union.

2. Revolutions frequently lead to abrupt and fundamental shifts in the existing structure of interstate alignments. This was first illustrated by the French Revolution, which overturned the alliance pattern that had been created by the so-called Diplomatic Revolution of 1756. The latter had ranged France, Austria, Spain, and Russia, together against a triple alliance of England, Prussia, and Holland, a somewhat uneasy balance of power. The Austrian connection had always been unpopular in France, and so was an easy target of the Girondins. The Bolshevik revolution took Russia out of the First World War and later brought it into a temporary alignment with another outsider state, Germany. China, Iran, and Cuba had all been closely tied to the United States prior to their revolutions, an association that was promptly reversed by their revolutionary leaders. In all of these cases an existing alignment which owed something to broader balance of power considerations was ended when a new, essentially ideological element was introduced into the equation.

3. A phenomenon that is harder to pin down with any accuracy than alliance reversals, but which is none the less real and important, concerns the impact of a revolution upon the actual power that can be mobilized by the state. The most famous and dramatic case here was that of France. In 1789 France was in a state of deep financial crisis, its ability to play its former leading role in European affairs apparently exhausted. However, the potential ability of the so-called 'absolute' monarchs elsewhere in Europe to deploy all of the resources of their states for war-making purposes was severely circumscribed, with major limitations upon their capacity to raise revenue and conscript citizens for armed service.[55] The French revolutionaries were able not only to extend state control into economic and financial areas hitherto undreamt of, but

[54] Cited in M. Wight, *Power Politics*, ed. H. Bull and C. Holbroad (Harmondsworth, 1986), 182.

[55] Kim, *Revolution and International System*, 6–7, and Ross, *European Diplomatic History*, 15–16.

also to recruit a huge conscript army and enthuse it to a high pitch of martial fervour.[56] This was achieved most notably through the *levée en masse* of August 1793 which commanded the French people to be 'in permanent requisition for army service'. Under its auspices the French army grew in size from under 400,000 to more than one million by the following August.[57] Although the *levée en masse* was introduced by Robespierre in response to military defeats, the consequences of the Revolution for warfare had been fully anticipated by the Girondin-dominated Convention in its proclamation of 23 January 1793:

We have no allies in the courts of Europe; but it is up to free nations to save themselves. A war waged slowly and parsimoniously would be uncertain and ruinous. Liberty wages only short and terrible wars and liberty counts only victories. Stand before an astonished Europe. To sustain your armies and your fleets you have a security, still tremendous, in the national territory; your enemies have only loans and precarious riches. The resources of a great and free nation are inexhaustible; the means of absolute governments are soon exhausted. Let the entire nation arise again, and these colossi used by despotism will soon collapse.[58]

No other revolutionary state illustrates this point quite so dramatically as did that created by the French Revolution, but suggestive comparisons may be drawn with China's success in fighting American forces to a stalemate in Korea shortly after its revolution, and with the ferocity of the Islamic Republic of Iran's defence of its territory after the Iraqi attack upon it in 1980. Khomeini explained Iranian successes in 1982 in terms reminiscent of the French proclamation:

Our Revolutionary Guards Corps and Mobilization Force had just been formed from the people and had just been armed with rifles, not having had proper military education and not having proper warfare machinery at their disposal, and with all the signs of weakness apparent in them. Only their faith in God, love of martyrdom for Islam and a spirit of self-sacrifice assisted them in this unequal war.[59]

4. The prospects of a stable balance of power in whose maintenance and operation all states co-operate are diminished by

[56] Holsti, *Peace and War*, 104–5.
[57] Ross, *European Diplomatic History*, 80.
[58] J. H. Stewart, *A Documentary Survey of the French Revolution* (New York, 1951), 392–6.
[59] A. Dawisha (ed.), *Islam in Foreign Policy* (Cambridge, 1983), 24,

two characteristic features of many revolutionary states. The first is their teleological view of events. Clearly if history is working towards some ultimate goal, whether it be the realization of God's purpose on earth or the attainment of communism world-wide, any equilibrium that falls short of these objectives can only be temporary and will be regarded as such by adherents of the revolutionary ideology. Secondly, the classical balance of power system requires some degree of mutual self-restraint and moderation on the part of its members. Hence, in the eighteenth century, war aims tended to be limited to the achievement of relatively small gains, and there was a general acceptance of the principle that other powers were entitled to reciprocal 'compensations' in the event of one of their number threatening to acquire disproportionate territorial gains that might jeopardize the overall balance.[60] This principle was sometimes even applied to the losers of military contests, so long as they were great powers; lesser states were not so fortunate, at times being obliged to supply the 'compensatory' territory even if they had not been involved in the war. The consequence was that states tended to seek only relatively marginal adjustments in their territorial holdings except where all could agree upon the equal apportionment of some larger cake, such as Poland. The aims of war were limited in other respects. Monarchs did not challenge each other's legitimate right to rule, only the precise extent of their domains; nor did they attempt to overthrow such essential parts of the Westphalian settlement as the status of the Schelde. A revolutionary foreign policy is not constrained in this way. France fought for the destruction of tyrants and later for a universal empire. Soviet ideology committed Moscow to the overthrow of capitalism world-wide. The Iran–Iraq war might have ended earlier and on more favourable terms for Iran if the Ayatollah had not made the fall of Saddam Hussein's regime one of his war aims. Even where revolutionary states might be prepared to accept less than their ideology would seem to require, their uncompromising image may cause others to distrust them. When they do appear to engage in conventional horse-trading along balance of power lines, they may have radically different understandings of what an agreed compromise should entail. For example, Churchill had in mind a much looser form of Soviet

---

[60] Gulick, *Europe's Classical Balance of Power*, 70–2.

influence than had Stalin when the two leaders reached their famous 'percentages' agreement over their respective spheres of influence in the Balkans.

CONCLUSION

The balance of power, like all of the institutions of a loosely associated society of states, has never functioned perfectly, as an ever-reliable mechanism for attaining international order. It has succeeded to the extent to which the great powers have co-operated in its working, and have been deterred from actions that might overturn the prevailing equilibrium by their perception that an approximate balance does indeed exist. Like any social institution, it requires the members of the society that it serves to have similar assumptions about their goals, and to have a common understanding about the principles of conduct necessary in order to uphold it. In particular, it requires some measure of self-restraint and moderation from states in defining both their national objectives and the means that they are prepared to employ to achieve them.

As we have seen, although revolutionary states tend to reject the balance of power as a system, institution, or principle, their ideologies have found it relatively easy to accommodate certain aspects of the concept in their formulations of foreign policy. However, they have normally seen the balance of power as something to exploit or overturn, rather than as the basis of an overall political equilibrium in whose management and maintenance the great powers might be able to collaborate. This, together with the other aspects of revolutionary states' behaviour that have been discussed here, may introduce a destabilizing or distorting element into the operation of a balance of power system.

The actual impact of revolutionary states upon the prevailing balance over time is harder to assess. It was suggested earlier in this chapter that the balance of power may be defined, basically, as a natural tendency within an anarchical state system; the additional element of great power management enables this inherent tendency to function as an institution. To the extent that there is a tendency towards equilibrium in international relations, the net effect of revolutionary states may be only marginal. The French Revolution, which ended in a bid for universal hegemony, may be the exception rather than the rule. Successive revolutions in the Middle East have frequently disrupted the pattern of international relations there for short periods, but the forces working towards a rough equilibrium have always reasserted themselves. Faced with a threat from India along their common border, China's instinctive response was to seek a closer relationship with the conservative, Islamic, anti-communist state of Pakistan. The Soviet Union could see advantages for itself in the stability provided by a long-term equilibrium both in the inter-war years and during the Cold War.

In all such cases, a balance of power, if one emerged, was the product of an accidental conjuncture of forces, much as it was in the eighteenth century, despite great power rhetoric to the contrary. The political equilibrium of the nineteenth century was a facet of a much more fully developed structure of international governance. Revolutionary states are not alone in their rejection of a system of international order that depends upon a broad consensus about goals and values and an acceptance of self-restraint in the pursuit of national objectives. Any state that is dissatisfied with the existing international distribution of goods such as land, natural resources, or military power is unlikely to accept a managed political equilibrium that underwrites the prevailing division of such things. However, it may only take relatively marginal changes to appease most dissatisfied states; the 'dissatisfaction' of revolutionary states is not so easily accommodated.

Conclusion

This study has ranged over a fairly wide terrain but it has sought to maintain a focus throughout upon the interaction between revolutionary states and the sovereignty-based notion of international society that has been termed here the 'Westphalian conception of international society'. In the broadest sense, this interaction has involved a dialectic between the Westphalian conception and the two alternative formulations of international society that have been described here as the 'universal society' and the 'great community'. Both of these offer fundamental challenges to the Westphalian conception since they call into question its doctrinal corner-stone: the idea of sovereignty. A further dialectic has taken place within the revolutionary state itself, between its revolutionary identity and its statehood.

The term 'dialectic' implies an ongoing tension between ideas, and it is the existence of both types of dialectic that has meant that revolutionary states frequently bring in their wake a major disturbance to international order. Order was defined in the Introduction to this study as denoting:

stability and regularity in the pattern of assumptions, rules, and practices that are accepted as legitimate among the members of a given society and that concern the mechanisms of and limits to the process of change within that society.

Every aspect of this conception of order as applied to international relations has been contested by revolutionary states. Almost by definition, such states have been disturbers of 'stability and regularity' in many existing patterns of things, but they have posed a particular challenge to the underlying set of 'assumptions, rules, and practices' by which the society of states has conducted its affairs. An orderly society is not one that permits no change but one possessing recognized procedures for change that are seen to be effective by its members. But demands for change that go far beyond the established consensus as to the acceptable boundaries of change can have profoundly disorderly consequences. Where, as in the case of international society, a society has relatively conservative and restrictive notions concerning the 'mechanisms of and limits to' change, the threshold of tolerance is reached relatively quickly. This is partly because order—the 'tranquillity' or 'repose' of the European society of states—depends upon the subjective perceptions of the established powers as well as upon objective conditions. Insecurity is inherent in statehood in an anarchical society and states are easily roused to fear by real or imaginary threats, both of which have arisen in abundance from the existence of revolutionary states. Conversely, some measure of paranoia often appears to be part of the mind-set of revolutionaries, and the readiness of each side to perceive and believe the worst of the other has contributed extensively to the international disorder that has accompanied the appearance of revolutionary states.

All historical experiences are unique, but it is possible to discern elements of a pattern in the interaction between international society and revolutionary states. This is essentially for two reasons. First, the main features of the Westphalian society of states have changed only slowly and marginally over three centuries. Hence, the social context, and the ways in which this has conditioned behaviour, have remained fairly constant both for new arrivals to statehood and for existing international actors. Second, as many studies have sought to demonstrate, revolutions themselves tend to exhibit numerous similarities in, for example, their leaderships and the typical stages through which they proceed.

Some facets of this pattern have been indicated in the course of this book. Others include the phenomenon of 'revolutionary optimism'—the sense that the revolution, since it represents an improved order of things, will inevitably bring victory for the revolutionary state in its external struggles. This, combined with the fact that revolutions may have authentically regenerative effects that assist their mobilization for war, may sweep the revolutionary state along in a mood of mass enthusiasm and willingness to endure sacrifices that deny a hearing to counsels of prudence.

Another common pattern in the international relations of revolutions is for them to move from an early, idealistic cosmopolitan phase, when foreign radicals are made welcome, to a later suspiciousness of foreigners, including those who were initially fêted. The earlier phase is liable to feed the fears of other states that the revolutionary state intends to export its revolution, while the latter may contribute to the overall mood of paranoia which frequently takes hold in a revolutionary state.

Another generalization that may be made about most revolutionary states concerns the relationship between their domestic politics and foreign policies. The foreign policies of all states are to some degree an extension of their internal situations but this is even more true of revolutionary states for two reasons. First, they are likely to see spreading the word of their revolutionary cause, if not the actual export of their revolution, as an important part of their foreign policy. Second, a revolution is invariably followed by a period when the revolutionary leaders' hold on power is, to say the least, precarious. This may lead revolutionary élites to see overseas adventures as a means of consolidating their power base. In addition, many face an *émigré* problem: their enemies may have taken up residence abroad and be conducting a campaign of opposition from there. Such power struggles have spilled over into the domiciles of the *émigrés* in numerous ways, including the dispatching of assassination squads, whose array of arms has included ice-picks, poisoned umbrellas, guns, and bombs. This is one aspect of the more general tendency of revolutionary states to disregard the principle of non-intervention in the domestic affairs of other states.

Many revolutionary states have a teleological view of world politics—they see them as proceeding inevitably in accordance with some iron law of history which they are uniquely privileged to perceive. This can colour their approach to international relations in all sorts of ways, contributing to such erroneous judgements as the Soviet miscalculation in the early 1930s of the respective prospects of social democratic and Nazi forces in Germany.

Recurring patterns are in evidence not only in the behaviour of revolutionary states, but in the reaction to them of established states. The multiplicity of discordant voices, the frightening rhetoric, the implicit or explicit threat of subversion, the appeal to disaffected elements outside the revolutionary state's borders: all are likely to disturb the repose of existing states even without the accompaniment of declarations of universalist intent, sudden reversals of alliances, and other such normal manifestations of revolutionary foreign policy. Any over-reaction, or even reaction, by the established powers is likely to be seen as confirming the predictions of the more radical revolutionaries, and so to impel the revolution towards more extreme postures and acts.

All such phenomena add to the negative implications of revolutionary states for international order. The root cause of the problem that revolutionary states pose for order is that international order requires some measure of consensus as to the assumptions, rules, and practices by which international society conducts its affairs. Revolutionary states are by nature consensus breakers. This study has considered their particular objections to three of the main foundations of international order: international law, diplomacy, and the balance of power. It has suggested that a common sequence, although one that has manifested itself in different ways, is for an initial hostility towards these institutions of international society to give way to a grudging acceptance of their value, albeit sometimes coupled with a desire to reform them. This process, along with other adjustments in the behaviour of revolutionary states to accord more with the normal patterns of international conduct, has been defined as a process of 'socialization'.

The experience of socialization has not been uniform for all revolutionary states. The United States was, by and large, anxious to gain rapid acceptance as a 'respectable' state, although it retained a sense of its particularity and an intermittent reformism that continued to set it apart to some degree from other established states. The French moved to disown some of the internationally objectionable aspects of their revolution as early as 1793, but by then events had acquired an unstoppable momentum. The Soviets adapted some of their international behaviour quite quickly to the requirements of membership of the society of states, although their ideologues encountered enormous difficulties in their search for doctrinally acceptable explanations of this. However, the Soviet Union maintained a dual identity until the Gorbachev era, when its decision to opt for respectability as a state helped to untie the bonds that had held both the Soviet Union and the socialist camp together.

Many factors have combined to impel states towards socialization. The need to gain access to the international trading and financial system, the need for allies and more generally for greater security, and even an appreciation of the possibility of exploiting the conventional structures and processes of international society for revolutionary purposes have all played a part. But the deeper forces at work in the socialization process all revolve around one central fact. Whatever the larger and longer-term aspirations of victorious revolutionary leaders, after the revolution they were no longer merely directing a revolutionary movement, but had assumed control over a determinate territorial unit which had been a state and which, short of global revolution, they had no option but to continue to manage as a state. Indeed, the internal policies of the revolutionaries were normally directed towards transforming it into a stronger, more efficient state and to harnessing all of its latent power. Yet statehood had external as well as internal aspects, and here the will of the revolutionary élite was not the only variable that counted. The external dimension of statehood involved rules, practices, norms, and institutions whose legitimacy derived from the will of the society of states as a whole. Full statehood meant not only the effective exercise of power internally but international conduct that conformed to these externally determined prerogatives and responsibilities. Achieving the highly desirable goal of statehood, therefore, entailed a high degree of socialization.

The fact that so many revolutionary states were obliged to adapt their behaviour to the Westphalian conception of international society is some testimony to the durability of that conception. But although the essential elements of the Westphalian structure remained in place, the system was far from changeless. Developing ideas about the state itself, direct attempts to reform the institutions of international order, and the great increase in the number of states after 1945 have all contributed to the evolution of international society since 1648. Since revolutionary states played a part in all three of these forces for change it is clear that the interaction between revolutionary states and international society was far from being a one-way process.

Taking each of these three forces in turn, changes in conceptions of the state have, at one level, involved a continual expansion in the functions performed by the state, and correspondingly in the expectations of citizens about what their state can and should do on their behalf. From another perspective, these changes have involved an evolution in the collective judgement of international society about what constitutes a legitimate state. The Westphalian judgement was simple enough—any entity exercising sovereignty that happened to be in existence at the time could qualify, whether it was a dynastic state, a constitutional monarchy, or even, in one or two cases, a republic. The American Revolution indirectly, and the French Revolution directly challenged this *laissez-faire* position with their new ideas of national self-determination and constitutional (ideally republican) government reflecting the popular will. Although many states that failed to meet these criteria remained in being, it became increasingly difficult after 1919 and even more so after 1945 for states to refuse at least to pay lip service to the new values. As the Cold War ended and a new world order has begun to emerge in the 1990s, a liberal polity and national self-determination have appeared to be becoming even more entrenched as yardsticks of legitimacy in late twentieth-century international society. The general understanding of what the idea of a liberal state encompassed has become ever broader through the nineteenth and twentieth centuries. To the original requirement of a democratic constitution has been added the need to meet increasingly demanding norms of internal governance, including the 'standard of civilization', the protection of human rights, and the rule of law. International society itself has developed a range of devices through which its collective judgements on such matters could be made known. International organizations like the League of Nations and the United Nations have played an important part in this process. By the early 1990s the leading Western powers, which had achieved a preponderance in international society with the collapse of the Soviet Union, appeared to be moving towards a loose great power concert based on numerous formal and informal mechanisms like the Group of Seven meetings and the UN Security Council. They also seemed to be engaging in a form of piecemeal international social engineering by linking aid to Third World and Eastern European states to firm commitments by those states to social, political, and economic reform. Statecraft was no longer simply a matter of manipulating the balance of power through a foreign policy whose imperatives were paramount, as in the original post-Westphalian international society. Now domestic policy had primacy and international society had adjusted to reflect this change.

The instruments of international order had also experienced change. The unmanaged power politics of the eighteenth century gave way to a more controlled balance of power system in the nineteenth. The great power concert of the nineteenth century was given institutionalized form (the League Council and the UN Security Council) in the twentieth century, while attempts were made to replace the discredited balance of power system with a 'community of power' in the shape of the collective security provisions of the Covenant and Charter. By the 1990s new concepts of 'co-operative security' were being mooted as international society sought to reflect the extraordinary changes that had taken place since 1989. The idea of an equilibrium of forces had not vanished from international discourse, and indeed it remained a crucial element in the international politics of certain regions. But the pessimistic assumptions about human nature that had seemed to make a balance of power system, however disguised, an inevitable part of the institutions of order in the Westphalian international society, appeared to be yielding at least some ground to the idea that international relations could develop in more harmonious directions than the balance of power allowed.

Equally striking developments had occurred in the other institutions of international society. 'Parliamentary' and other forms of public diplomacy, together with a great increase in 'summit' diplomacy, had not entirely replaced traditional diplomacy by the 1990s. But their growth, like the changes in the balance of power system, could be seen as evidence both of an increasing sense of dissatisfaction with traditional diplomacy within international society, and of the way in which the greater openness and democratization inside many states was being reflected in the conduct of international relations.

Similarly, the prodigious growth of international law after the eighteenth century brought with it some subtle amendments to the implicit Westphalian premiss that the sole purpose of international law was to protect and preserve sovereignty. Sovereign equality was still the central legal norm, but the rules that states were prepared to accept had come gradually to reflect a concern with other objectives than the preservation of the society of states and the sovereign rights of its members. This change may, very broadly, be characterized as a shift from rules that promoted *order* towards rules and practices that served the purpose of, first, a system of international *governance*, and later the direct *regulation* of certain aspects of international life. Promoting international order, it will be recalled, involved devising means of ensuring regularity and stability in the pattern of rules, assumptions, and practices that prevailed in international society. Diplomacy, a balance of power, and rules of coexistence were the principal devices employed by states towards these ends. All three could function with only a minimal degree of conscious manipulation by states. When the great powers undertook the role of management of international order in the nineteenth century, they were not challenging the essential principle of sovereignty, except to the limited extent that the conservative powers were able to obtain international support for their interventions against revolution. But they were implicitly acknowledging that membership of international society entailed responsibilities and duties as well as rights, and also that some measure of direct and deliberate involvement in the processes of rule formation in international society and of supervision of Europe's political equilibrium was needed if the goal of order were to be achieved. Later, in the nineteenth century, and even more in the twentieth, special institutions were set up separately from the great power concert to provide for the direct regulation of numerous functional areas of international intercourse. At first these were concerned with matters that aroused little controversy among states, such as postal services, telecommunication, and the control of epidemic diseases. After 1945 more sensitive issues, such as monetary relations, refugees, and, to a very limited degree, human rights, came to be the subjects of international regimes.

The third major factor contributing to the evolution of international society was the great expansion in its membership after 1945. Since the vast majority of new states were relatively poor, non-white former colonies, their concerns diverged sharply from those of the European great powers who had dominated international society until the Second World War. Issues such as colonialism, racism, and Third World poverty were placed on the international agenda, and new international norms emerged which made imperialistic or racialistic practices internationally reprehensible. Limited international sanctions were brought to bear against the racist regime of South Africa, and the use of violence in the cause of national liberation received at least some degree of international legitimation through resolutions in the United Nations and other fora.

It is impossible to measure with any accuracy the precise contribution of revolutionary states to this evolution of international society. In some cases they were the principal catalysts of change, as in the emergence of new principles of international legitimacy. They also played a critical part in promoting the demands for new international norms after 1945. In other cases change occurred as a consequence of the reaction of established powers to revolutionary states, as in 1814–15. On balance, the Westphalian conception of international society has proved more durable than revolutionary internationalism, so the impact of international society on revolutionary states through the socialization process may be judged to have been stronger than the reverse interaction. But there can be no doubt that both entities have influenced each other.

The international society perspective does not belong wholly within a single school of International Relations theory. It is most commonly associated with Realist theories because of its emphasis on the state, its scepticism about the possibility of fundamental change in the conduct of international affairs, and its pessimistic assumptions about human (and state) motivation. However, other aspects of the international society approach do not square with Realist hypotheses. The very idea of an international society presupposes that states have a social identity as well as a self-seeking one and that the behavioural implications of these two identities are quite different. It also suggests that states are constrained by rules. This, too, is very different from the Realist proposition that a tendency towards a balance of power may serve to limit the ability of states to achieve their ambitions, or the Neorealist refinement of this, which depicts the distribution of capabilities among states as a 'structure' that determines, in some measure, the behaviour of states.[1] Bull's important distinction between an international system and an international society is crucial in this context.[2] Most theoretical work in International Relations that postulates a macro-political framework which orders international behaviour in some sense derives more from a systemic than from a societal perspective. That is, it suggests the existence of regular patterns which assume their characteristic forms because of some system-wide features, such as anarchy, bipolarity, or multipolarity, that condition the behaviour of the units that belong to the system. Without disputing the importance of systemic features in determining certain recurring patterns and

[1] K. N. Waltz, *Theory of International Politics* (Reading, Mass., 1979).
[2] H. Bull, *The Anarchical Society* (London, 1977), 9–16.

regularities, the international society approach concludes that a more complete explanation of the behaviour of states must include the fact that they consider themselves to be members of a society of states organized around the sovereignty principle, and that they accept certain rules and sustain certain institutions which derive from their membership of such a society.

The international society concept should also be distinguished from a theoretical perspective with which it has much in common: regime theories. Regimes, according to the most widely accepted definition of the term, are 'implicit or explicit principles, norms, rules and decision-making procedures around which actors' expectations converge in a given area of international relations'.[3] Analysis of regimes has often been linked to two other theoretical insights—that international relations are characterized by growing interdependence and that the relative strength or weakness of particular regimes is closely related to the role of a hegemonic power.[4] Both regime theories and the international society approach, therefore, focus attention upon co-operative aspects of the relations among states and the importance of rules of international conduct. The international society approach also allows for a limited joint hegemony or even for leadership by a single hegemon, so long as neither threatens to lead towards what this study has termed a 'universal society'. However, there are several important differences between the two approaches. First, regime analysis tends to view the world as a system rather than a society, although the distinction between these two may sometimes become blurred. Regimes emerge in relation to particular issues as a consequence of a coincidence of interests among states and other international actors. They are outcomes of what may be conceived of as a bargaining process, which then help to structure behaviour within a given area of international transactions. They are, therefore, the products of spontaneous interactions among international actors. The international society approach suggests that, while the central Westphalian contrast endures, states will choose to co-operate, in limited but vitally important respects, to uphold the rules and

[3] S. D. Krasner, 'Structural Causes and Régime Consequences: Régimes and International Variables', in S. D. Krasner (ed.), *International Régimes* (Ithaca, NY, 1983), 2.

[4] S. Haggard and B. A. Simmons, 'Theories of International Régimes', *International Organization* 41/3 (1987), 491–517.

institutions of international society against fundamental challenges to them. Second, regimes are concerned with collaboration over limited subjects at an international subsystem level; international society is concerned with the fundamental rules of international association at the global level. Third, many regimes are essentially temporary phenomena; the Westphalian international society has lasted for more than three hundred years. Fourth, regimes are secondary aspects of international relations, which regulate specific international activities; international society establishes the primary norms and rules of international conduct. The prior existence of an international society makes regimes possible by laying down an elementary but crucial basis for orderly international relations, and it also, through its emphasis on sovereignty, conditions and limits the form regimes may take; regimes do not, in themselves, create an international society.

A very different perspective from that of the international society, but one which also analyses international relations from the level of the global structure, is the world system approach of Wallerstein and others.[5] This asserts that there is indeed an international society, or, more accurately, a world social system, but, far from reflecting a consensus about underlying values, it comprises an exploitative hierarchical system that developed alongside the emergence of capitalism in Europe. In this world system, economic processes are the main determinants of events, with the state (conceived as a pluralist conglomerate, not a unitary actor) defined by its economic role rather than, as in this study, in juridical terms. The principal feature of the world system is a global division of labour which produces a structure of dominance by a small, capitalist 'core' over a large, underdeveloped 'periphery'. The periphery remains economically dependent on the core because this suits the interests of world capitalism. Institutions such as international law and diplomacy serve, in effect, as tools of the dominant international capitalist class.

This analysis, which, of course, has much in common with several revolutionary ideologies, implies that the confrontation that

[5] I. Wallerstein, *The Modern World System* (New York, 1974), 1–13, 132–63, 346–57; B. Andrews, 'The Political Economy of World Capitalism: Theory and Practice', *International Organization*, 36/1 (1982), 135–63; J. Caporaso, 'Dependence, Dependency, and Power in the Global System: A Structural and Behavioural Analysis', *International Organization*, 32/1 (1978), 13–44.

has been portrayed in this study as one between the Westphalian conception of international society and the revolutionary state is, in truth, part of a global class struggle. It declares, in effect, that the revolutionary critique of international society is essentially correct. Here is not the place for a detailed rebuttal of the world system thesis. Its focus on economic processes involves a very different level of analysis from the legal–political framework that has been employed in this study. Whether it is more fruitful to depict economic processes as taking place within a legal–political structure that is an important determinant of their outcome, or vice versa, will doubtless continue to be a subject of heated speculation. To those who remain sceptical about the prospects for an all-encompassing general theory of international relations, it seems reasonable to suppose that significant phenomena may be discerned that belong primarily to one level of analysis rather than the other, and that both perspectives may afford valuable insights. It is also safe to assume that whichever of these two frameworks dominates at any time will depend upon the kinds of issues involved. In the case of international response to revolutionary states, it would be difficult to sustain an argument that economic considerations have been more than secondary factors. In the domestic politics of long-established states, fundamental constitutional issues, on the rare occasions when they arise, tend to dominate political debate, leaving questions of economic costs and benefits on the sidelines. A similar phenomenon appears to occur when there is a fundamental challenge to the international 'constitution'—the Westphalian social contract. International concern about the conduct of revolutionary France, Cuba, China, Libya, or even Iran or the Soviet Union bore little relation to the position of those states in the world economic system. Moreover, the response of established states was essentially the same, regardless of whether the revolutionary state concerned was a great power or a small, Third World nation.

Social order over any lengthy period of time does not depend simply upon the capacity of a society's institutions to maintain stability and regularity, but upon their ability to change in response to new circumstances. International society has shown itself to be adaptable, but all too often change (usually of a very limited nature) has taken place only after the extreme violence of war and revolution. This has been accepted by states because the foundation of their association has been the common defence of sovereignty. Their social contract has been a pact of association—an agreement to consider themselves members of a society—rather than a contract of government, or an agreement to surrender their independence in return for the benefits deriving from the acceptance of a central authority. There are no signs that states are any readier today than in the past to move towards some kind of world government, nor indeed would such a development necessarily be desirable. But such negative consequences of the division of the world into competing sovereign states as an extreme inequality in the apportionment of the world's material and non-material goods are still much in evidence, even if the incidence of major wars has decreased. Historical experience of the interaction between revolutionary states and international society has shown that, while fundamental change in the Westphalian international society is unlikely, none the less the basis of association among states may broaden and some change may be accommodated. Disaffected and alienated states still exist in large numbers and there is a long way to go before a true 'end of history' is reached with the universal triumph of the liberal state. It is safe to assume, therefore, that the dialectic between revolutionary states and international society has not yet concluded. There can be no doubt that the collapse of the Soviet Union has brought the world to a remarkable juncture at which the West has achieved a moment of ascendancy, to be used wisely or foolishly. While the lessons of the past cannot dictate the construction of the future, they may at least help to identify mistakes that do not need to be repeated.

BIBLIOGRAPHY

AKEHURST, M., *A Modern Introduction to International Law* (London, 1987).

AMANN, P., 'Revolution: A Redefinition', *Political Science Quarterly*, 86 (Mar. 1962), 36–53.

American Journal of International Law, 'Official Documents, Case Concerning United States Diplomatic and Consular Staff in Tehran', 74 (1980), 258–77 and 746–81.

AMORETTI, B. S., 'Libyan Loneliness in Facing the World: The Challenge of Islam', in A. Dawisha (ed.), *Islam in Foreign Policy* (Cambridge, 1983), 54–67.

Ancien Moniteur, L', Réimpression de l'Ancien Moniteur, Mai 1789–Novembre 1799.

ANDERSON, M. S., 'Eighteenth-Century Theories of the Balance of Power', in R. Hatton and M. S. Anderson, *Studies in Diplomatic History* (London, 1970), 183–98.

ANDREWS, B., 'The Political Economy of World Capitalism: Theory and Practice', *International Organization*, 36/1 (1982), 135–63.

Archives parlementaires de 1787 à 1860: Recueil complet des débats legislatifs et politiques des chambres français (127 vols., Paris, 1879–1913).

ARDANT, P., 'Chinese Diplomatic Practice During the Cultural Revolution', in J. A. Cohen (ed.), *China's Practice of International Law: Some Case Studies* (Cambridge, Mass., 1972), 86–128.

ARMSTRONG, J. D., *Revolutionary Diplomacy: Chinese Foreign Policy and the United Front Doctrine* (Berkeley and Los Angeles, 1977).

——*The Rise of the International Organization* (London, 1982).

ARTZ, F. B., *Reaction and Revolution, 1814–1832* (New York, 1934).

BAILEY, T. A., *A Diplomatic History of the American People*, 2nd edn. (New York, 1942).

BAILYN, B., *The Ideological Origins of the American Revolution* (Cambridge, Mass., 1967).

——*The Origins of American Politics* (New York, 1967).

BAKER, R. S., and DODD, W. E. (eds.), *The Public Papers of Woodrow Wilson* (6 vols.; New York, 1925–7).

BARRACLOUGH, G., *The Origins of Modern Germany* (Oxford, 1979).

BEARD, C. A., The Idea of National Interest (Chicago, 1966).

BEARMAN, J., *Qadhafi's Libya* (London and New Jersey, 1986).

BEHISHTI, M. H., and BAHONAR, J., *Philosophy of Islam* (Salt Lake City, 1982).

BEMIS, S. F., *The Diplomacy of the American Revolution* (New York and London, 1935).

——*The Jay Treaty* (New Haven, Conn., 1962).

BERLIN, I., *Karl Marx*, 2nd edn. (London, 1948).

BERNARD, C., and KHALILZAD, Z., *'The Government of God'—Iran's Islamic Republic* (New York, 1984).

BEST, G., *Humanity in Warfare* (London, 1983).

BIRO, S. S., *The German Policy of Revolutionary France* (2 vols.; Cambridge, Mass., 1957).

BLANNING, T. C. W., *The French Revolution in Germany: Occupation and Resistance in the Rhineland, 1792–1802* (Oxford, 1983).

——*The Origins of the French Revolutionary Wars* (London and New York, 1986).

BOURGUIGNON, H. J., 'Incorporation of the Law of Nations during the American Revolution', *American Journal of International Law*, 71 (1977), 270–95.

BRADLEY, E. D., *The Life of Barnave* (2 vols.; Oxford, 1915).

BRIDGE, F. R., and BULLEN, R., *The Great Powers and the European States System, 1815–1914* (London, 1980).

BRINTON, C., *A Decade of Revolution, 1789–1799* (New York, 1934).

BROUGHAM, HENRY, 'Balance of Power', in M. Forsyth *et al.*, *The Theory of International Relations* (London, 1970), 260–74.

BROWNING, O. (ed.), *The Despatches of Earl Gower* (Cambridge, 1885).

BROWNLIE, I., *Principles of Public International Law* (Oxford, 1973).

BRYCE, J., *The Holy Roman Empire* (London, 1907).

BULL, H., *The Anarchical Society* (London, 1977).

——and WATSON, A. (eds.), *The Expansion of International Society* (Oxford, 1984).

CALVERT, P., *Revolution and International Politics* (London, 1984).

CALVEZ, J. Y., *Droit international et souveraineté en URSS* (Paris, 1953).

CAMBON, J., *The Diplomatist* (London, 1931).

CAPORASO, J., 'Dependence, Dependency, and Power in the Global System: A Structural and Behavioural Analysis', *International Organization*, 32/1 (1978), 13–44.

CARLYLE, R. W., and A. J., *A History of Mediaeval Political Theory in the West* (6 vols.; Edinburgh and London, 1903–36).

CARR, E. H., *The Bolshevik Revolution, 1917–1923* (3 vols.; Harmondsworth, 1971).

CASSESE, A., *International Law in a Divided World* (Oxford, 1986).

CHENG, J. CHESTER, *The Politics of the Chinese Red Army* (Stanford, Calif., 1966).

CLAPHAM, J. H., *The Abbé Sieyès* (London, 1912).

CLARK, I., *Reform and Resistance in the International Order* (Cambridge, 1980).

COBBAN, A., *Aspects of the French Revolution* (London, 1971).
——*A History of Modern France* (3 vols.; London, 1957–65).
COHEN, G. A., *Karl Marx's Theory of History: A Defence* (Oxford, 1978).
COHEN, J. A., and CHIU, H., *People's China and International Law: A Documentary Study* (Princeton, NJ, 1974).
COHEN, P. S., *Modern Social Theory* (London, 1968).
COHEN, R., *Theatre of Power* (London and New York, 1987).
CORBETT, P. E., *The Growth of World Law* (Princeton, NJ, 1971).
——*Law in Diplomacy* (Princeton, NJ, 1959).
CRAIG, G. A., *War, Politics and Diplomacy* (New York, 1966).
——and GEORGE, A. L., *Force and Statecraft* (New York and Oxford, 1983).
DAVIES, J. C., 'Towards a Theory of Revolution', *American Sociological Review* (Feb. 1962), 5–18.
DAWISHA, A. (ed.), *Islam in Foreign Policy* (Cambridge, 1983).
DEBO, R. K., *Revolution and Survival: The Foreign Policy of Soviet Russia, 1917–18* (Liverpool, 1979).
DECONDE, A., 'The French Alliance in Historical Speculation', in R. Hoffman and P. J. Albert (eds.), *Diplomacy and Revolution: The Franco-American Alliance of 1778* (Charlottesville, Va., 1981), 1–26.
DEGRAS, J., *Soviet Documents on Foreign Policy* (3 vols.; London, 1951–3).
DER DERIAN, J., *On Diplomacy* (Oxford, 1987).
DEUTSCHER, I., *The Prophet Armed: Trotsky, 1879–1921* (London, 1954).
Documents on British Foreign Policy 1918–39, ed. E. L. Woodward and R. Butler (London, 1952–63).
Dokumenty vneshnei politiky (Moscow, 1957–).
DOMINGUEZ, J. I., *To Make a World Safe for Revolution: Cuba's Foreign Policy* (Cambridge, Mass., 1989).
DUKES, P., *A History of Europe, 1648–1948* (Basingstoke, 1985).
DULL, J. R., *A Diplomatic History of the American Revolution* (New Haven, Conn., and London, 1985).
——'France and the American Revolution Seen as Tragedy', in R. Hoffman and P. J. Albert (eds.), *Diplomacy and Revolution: The Franco-American Alliance of 1778* (Charlottesville, Va., 1981), 73–106.
DUMBAULD, E., 'Independence under International Law', *American Journal of International Law*, 70/3 (1976), 425–31.
EKIRCH, A. A., *Ideas, Ideals and American Diplomacy* (New York, 1966).
D'ENCAUSSE, H. C., and SCHRAM, S. R., *Marxism and Asia* (London, 1969).
ENGELS, F., *Anti-Dühring* (1st pub. 1878; Moscow, 1954).
——*Ludwig Feuerbach and the End of Classical German Philosophy*, 1888 edn. (Moscow, 1946) (including K. Marx, *Theses on Feuerbach*).
D'ENTREVES, A. P., *The Notion of the State* (Oxford, 1967).

ERICKSON, R. J., *International Law and the Revolutionary State* (Dobbs Ferry, NY, 1972).

ESPOSITO, J. L., *Islam and Politics* (New York, 1987).

EUDIN, X. J., and SLUSSER, R. M., *Soviet Foreign Policy, 1928–1934: Documents and Materials* (2 vols.; London, 1966).

EYCK, F. (ed.), *The Revolutions of 1848–49* (Edinburgh, 1972).

FALK, R. A., 'World Revolution and International Order', in C. J. Friedrich (ed.), *Revolution* (New York, 1969), 154–76.

FARRELL, J. C., and SMITH, A. P. (eds.), *Image and Reality in World Politics* (New York, 1967).

FEITH, H., and CASTLES, P., *Indonesian Political Thinking* (Ithaca, NY, 1970).

FINKELSTEIN, L. S., 'What is International Governance'. Paper presented to the Annual Meeting of the International Studies Association, Vancouver, 1991.

FLEMMING, D. F., *The United States and the League of Nations, 1918–1920* (New York, 1932).

FORSYTH, M., *et al.*, *The Theory of International Relations* (London, 1970).

GARTHOFF, R. L., 'The Concept of the Balance of Power in Soviet Policy-Making', *World Politics*, 4/1 (Oct. 1951), 85–111.

GAXOTTE, P., *The French Revolution* (London and New York, 1932).

GEYELIN, P. L., 'The Adams Doctrine and the Dream of Disengagement', in S. J. Ungar (ed.), *Estrangement: America and the World* (New York, 1985), 193–224.

GIERKE, O., *Political Theories of the Middle Ages* (Cambridge, 1900).

GILBERT, F., 'The "New Diplomacy" of the Eighteenth Century', *World Politics*, 4/1 (Oct. 1951), 1–38.

——*To the Farewell Address: Ideas of Early American Foreign Policy* (Princeton, NJ, 1961).

GOEBEL, J., *The Equality of States* (New York, 1923).

GONG, G. W., *The Standard of 'Civilization' in International Society* (Oxford, 1984).

GOODMAN, E. R., *The Soviet Design for a World State* (New York, 1960).

GRAEBNER, N. A., *Ideas and Diplomacy* (New York, 1964).

GROSS, L., 'The Peace of Westphalia, 1648–1948', *American Journal of International Law*, 42 (1948), 20–41.

GROTIUS, HUGO, *De Jure Belli et Pacis*, ed. William Whewell (3 vols.; Cambridge, 1853).

GRZYBOWSKI, K., *The Socialist Commonwealth of Nations* (New Haven, Conn., and London, 1964).

GULICK, E. V., *Europe's Classical Balance of Power* (New York, 1967).

HAGGARD, S., and SIMMONS, B. A., 'Theories of International Régimes', *International Organization*, 41/3 (1987), 491–517.

HALLIDAY, F., 'Iranian Foreign Policy since 1979: Internationalism and Nationalism in the Islamic Revolution'. Paper presented to the British International Studies Association Conference, 1984.

——*Revolution and Foreign Policy: The Case of South Yemen, 1967–1987* (Cambridge, 1990).

——'Revolutions and International Relations: Some Theoretical Issues'. Paper presented to the British International Studies Association Conference, 1989.

——'States and Revolution in the South', in C. Thomas and P. Saravanamuttu (eds.), *The State and Instability in the South* (New York, 1989), 99–111.

HAMILTON, ALEXANDER, *The Papers of Alexander Hamilton*, ed. H. C. Syrett and J. E. Cooke (26 vols.; New York and London, 1961).

HARRIS, D. J., *Cases and Materials on International Law*, 2nd edn. (London, 1979).

HATTO, A., 'Revolution: An Inquiry into the Usefulness of an Historical Term', *Mind* (Oct. 1949), 459–517.

HEEREN, A. H. L., *A Manual of the History of the Political System of Europe and its Colonies* (2 vols.; Oxford, 1833; repr. New York, 1971).

HINSLEY, F. H., *Power and the Pursuit of Peace* (Cambridge, 1963).

HIRO, D., *Iran under the Ayatollahs* (London, 1985).

HOFFMANN, S., *Primacy or World Order* (New York, 1978).

——'Report of the Conference on the Conditions of World Order', *Daedalus* (Spring, 1966), 455–78.

HOLSTI, K. J., *Peace and War: Armed Conflicts and International Order, 1648–1989* (Cambridge, 1991).

HOWARD, J. E., *Parliament and Foreign Policy in France* (London, 1948).

HSU, I. C. Y., *China's Entrance into the Family of Nations* (Cambridge, Mass., 1960).

HUTSON, J. H., 'The American Negotiations: The Diplomacy of Jealousy', in R. Hoffman and P. J. Albert (eds.), *Peace and the Peacemakers: The Treaty of 1783* (Charlottesville, Va., 1986), 47–65.

——'Early American Diplomacy: A Reappraisal', in L. S. Kaplan (ed.), *The American Revolution and 'A Candid World'* (Kent State, Ohio, 1977), 40–68.

——'Intellectual Origins of Early American Diplomacy', *Diplomatic History*, 1/1 (Winter, 1977), 1–19.

——*John Adams and the Diplomacy of the American Revolution* (Lexington, Ky., 1980).

ILLCHMAN, W. F., *Professional Diplomacy in the United States, 1779–1939* (Chicago, 1961).

INTERNATIONAL COMMITTEE OF THE RED CROSS, *Rapport général du CICR 1912–1920*, Bibl. CICR, 363, 191/7.

International Law (Institute of State and Law, Moscow, 1953).

IRIYE, A., *From Nationalism to Internationalism: US Foreign Policy to 1914* (London, 1977).

JAMES, A. (ed.), *The Bases of International Order* (New York, 1973).

——*Sovereign Statehood* (London, 1986).

JEFFERSON, THOMAS, *The Papers of Thomas Jefferson*, 1st ser., ed. C. T. Cullen (20 vols.; Princeton, NJ, 1950–83).

——*Thomas Jefferson, Writings*, ed. M. D. Peterson (New York, 1984).

JOHNSON, CHALMERS, *Revolution and the Social System* (Hoover institution, ser. 3; Stanford, Calif., 1964).

JONES, E. R. (ed.), *Selected Speeches on British Foreign Policy* (London, 1914).

JONES, R. A., *The Soviet Concept of 'Limited Sovereignty' from Lenin to Gorbachev* (London, 1990).

JORDAN, Z. A., *The Evolution of Dialectical Materialism* (Harmondsworth, 1967).

KAPLAN, L. S., *Colonies into Nation: American Diplomacy, 1763–1801* (New York, 1972).

——*Entangling Alliances with None: American Foreign Policy in the Age of Jefferson* (Kent, Ohio, and London, 1987).

——'Jefferson and the Franco-American Alliance of 1778: Reflections on Francophilia', in C. Fohlen and J. Godechot (eds.), *La Révolution américaine et l'Europe* (Paris, 1981), 403–27.

KAULEK, J. (ed.), *Papiers de Barthélemy* (6 vols.; Paris, 1886–1910).

KEDDIE, N. R., *Roots of Revolution* (New Haven, Conn., and London, 1981).

KENNER, M., and PETROS, J. (eds.), *Fidel Castro Speaks* (Harmondsworth, 1969).

KHOMEINI, AYATOLLAH, *A Clarification of Questions*, trans. J. Borujerdi (Boulder, Colo., and London, 1984).

——*Islam and Revolution: Writings and Declarations of Imam Khomeini*, trans. and annotated by Hamid Algar (Berkeley, Calif., 1981).

KIDNER, F. L., 'The Girondists and the "Propaganda War" of 1792: A Re-evaluation of French Revolutionary Foreign Policy from 1791 to 1793', Ph.D. thesis (Princeton University, 1971).

KIM, KYUNG-WON, *Revolution and International System* (New York, 1970).

KIM, S. S., 'The Development of International Law in Post-Mao China: Change and Continuity', *Journal of Chinese Law*, 1/2 (1987), 117–60.

KISSINGER, H., *A World Restored* (Boston, 1957).

KOHN, H., *Prelude to Nation State* (Princeton, NJ, 1967).

KOROVIN, E., 'Soviet Treaties and International Law', *American Journal of International Law*, 22 (1928), 753–63.

KRASNER, S. D., 'Structural Causes and Régime Consequences: Régimes and International Variables', in S. D. Krasner (ed.), *International Régimes* (Ithaca, NY, 1983), 1–23.

KRIEGER, L., *The Politics of Discretion and the Acceptance of Natural Law* (Chicago and London, 1965).

LANG, DANIEL, 'Alexander Hamilton and the Law of Nations', in N. A. Graebner (ed.), *Traditions and Values: American Diplomacy, 1790–1865* (Lanham, Md., New York, and London, 1985), 1–26.

——*Foreign Policy in the Early Republic* (London, 1985).

LAPENNA, I., 'The Soviet Concept of "Socialist" International Law', *Yearbook of World Affairs* (London, 1975), 242–64.

LAUTERPACHT, H., *Recognition in International Law* (London, 1947).

LEFEBVRE, G., *La Révolution française* (Paris, 1951).

LENIN, V. I., *Collected Works* (55 vols.; Moscow, 1961).

——*Karl Marx*, 1918 edn. (Peking, 1967).

——*The State and Revolution* (1st pub. 1917; repr. Peking, 1976).

LIGHT, M., *The Soviet Theory of International Relations* (Brighton, 1988).

LINKLATER, A., *Men and Citizens in the Theory of International Relations* (London, 1982).

LINT, G. L., 'The American Revolution and the Law of Nations, 1776–1789', *Diplomatic History*, 1/1 (Winter, 1977), 20–34.

LUKASHUK, I. I., 'People's Diplomacy and International Lawyers', in W. E. Butler (ed.), *Perestroika and International Law* (Boston and London, 1990), 97–105.

LYCAN, G. L., *Alexander Hamilton and American Foreign Policy: A Design for Greatness* (Norman, Okla., 1970).

LYNN, J. A., *The Bayonets of the Republic: Motivation and Tactics in the Army of Revolutionary France, 1791–4* (Chicago, 1984).

MCCLANAHAN, G. V., *Diplomatic Immunity* (London, 1989).

MCILWAIN, C. H., *The Growth of Political Thought in the West* (New York, 1932).

MCLAUGHLIN, J. P., 'The Annexation Policy of the French Revolution', Ph.D. thesis (University of London, 1951).

MAO ZEDONG, 'On Contradiction', *Selected Works* (Peking, 1969), i. 313–42.

MARANTZ, P., 'The Gorbachev Revolution: Emerging Trends in Soviet Foreign Policy'. Paper delivered to the International Society of Political Psychology, Tel Aviv, 20 June 1989.

MARX, K., *Capital*, 1887 edn. (3 vols.; London, 1954).

——and ENGELS, F., *The Communist Manifesto*, ed. H. J. Laski (London, 1948).

MASSON, F., *Le Département des affaires étrangères pendant la révolution, 1787–1804* (Paris, 1877).

MATHIEZ, A., *The French Revolution* (London, 1951).

MATTINGLY, G., *Renaissance Diplomacy* (London, 1955).

MEISNER, M., *Li Ta-chao and the Origins of Chinese Marxism* (Cambridge, Mass., 1967).

MELOGRANI, P., *Lenin and the Myth of World Revolution* (Atlantic Highlands, NJ, 1989).

MERK, F., *Manifest Destiny and Mission* (New York, 1966).

MIDGLEY, E. B. F., *The Natural Law Tradition and the Theory of International Relations* (London, 1975).

MILLER, D. H., *The Drafting of the Covenant* (2 vols.; New York, 1928).

MILLER, J. D. B., 'World Society and International Economic Interdependence'. Unpublished paper in the Seminar on World Society given by the Department of International Relations, Australian National University, 7 July 1975.

MITCHELL, H., *The Underground War against Revolutionary France: The Missions of William Wickham, 1794–1800* (Oxford, 1965).

MITCHELL, R. J., *Ideology of a Superpower: Contemporary Soviet Doctrines on International Relations* (Stanford, Calif., 1982).

MOORE, J. N., and TURNER, R. F., *International Law and the Brezhnev Doctrine* (Lanham, Md., and London, 1987).

MORGENTHAU, H., *Politics Among Nations*, 3rd edn. (New York, 1965).

MULLERSON, R. A., 'Sources of International Law: New Tendencies in Soviet Thinking', *American Journal of International Law*, 83 (1989), 494–518.

MUNSON, H., JR., *Islam and Revolution in the Middle East* (New Haven, Conn., and London, 1988).

MURLEY, J. T., 'The Origins and Outbreak of the Anglo-French War of 1793', D.Phil. thesis (Oxford University, 1959).

MUSHKAT, M., 'The Development of International Humanitarian Law and the Law of Human Rights', *German Yearbook of International Law*, 21 (1978), 150–68.

NARDIN, T., *Law, Morality and the Relations of States* (Princeton, NJ, 1983).

NASSER, GAMAL ABD EL-, *The Philosophy of the Revolution* (Cairo, 1954).

NICOLSON, H., *The Evolution of Diplomatic Method* (London, 1954).

NYS, E., 'La Révolution française et le droit international', in *Études de droit international et de droit politique* (Brussels and Paris, 1896), 318–406.

Origin and Development of the Differences between the Leadership of the CPSU and Ourselves, The (Peking, 1963).

PADOVER, S. K., *Thomas Jefferson on Democracy* (New York, 1939).

PARKER, G., *The Thirty Years War* (London, 1984).

PARRY, C. (ed.), *Consolidated Treaties Series*, i (Dobbs Ferry, NY, 1969).

Peking Review, 4 Jan. 1963.

People's China, 1 July 1951.

PETRENKO, F., and POPOV, V., *Soviet Foreign Policy: Objectives and Principles* (Moscow, 1981).

PLAMENATZ, J., *German Marxism and Russian Communism* (London, 1954).

POLISENSKY, J. V., *The Thirty Years War* (London, 1974).

PREUSS, L., 'International Responsibility for Hostile Propaganda Against Foreign States', *American Journal of International Law*, 28/4 (Oct. 1934), 649–68.

RAJAEE, F., *Islamic Values and World View* (Lanham, Md., and New York, 1983).

RAMAZANI, R. K., 'Khumayni's Islam in Iran's Foreign Policy', in A. Dawisha (ed.), *Islam in Foreign Policy* (Cambridge, 1983), 9–32.

——*Revolutionary Iran: Challenge and Response in the Middle East* (Baltimore and London, 1986).

REDSLOB, R., *Histoire des grands principes du droit des gens* (Paris, 1923).

RIDDELL, J. (ed.), *Lenin's Struggle for a Revolutionary International: Documents, 1907–1916* (New York, 1986).

ROIDER, K. A., JR., *Baron Thugut and Austria's Response to the French Revolution* (Princeton, NJ, 1987).

ROSEN, S. P., 'Alexander Hamilton and the Domestic Usages of International Law', *Diplomatic History*, 5/3 (Summer, 1981), 183–202.

ROSS, S. T., *European Diplomatic History, 1789–1815: France Against Europe* (New York, 1969).

ROSSITER, C. (ed.), *The Federalist Papers* (New York, 1901).

ROWE, G. S., and KNOTT, A. W., 'The Longchamps Affairs (1784–86), the Law of Nations and the Shaping of Early American Foreign Policy', *Diplomatic History*, 10/3 (Summer, 1986), 199–220.

ROZAKIS, C. L., *The Concept of the Jus Cogens in the Law of Treaties* (Amsterdam, 1976).

RUDDY, F. S., *International Law in the Enlightenment* (New York, 1975).

RUSH, M. (ed.), *The International Situation and Soviet Foreign Policy* (Columbus, Ohio, 1970).

RUSSELL, R. B., *A History of the United Nations Charter* (Washington, 1958).

RUYSSEN, T., *Les Sources doctrinales de l'internationalisme* (3 vols.; Paris, 1954).

SABINE, G. H., *A History of Political Theory* (London, 1963).

ST JOHN, R. B., *Qaddafi's World Design: Libyan Foreign Policy, 1969–1987* (London, 1987).

SAVELLE, MAX, *The Origins of American Diplomacy* (New York, 1967).

SCHACHTER, O., 'International Law in the Hostage Crisis: Implications for Future Cases', in W. Christopher *et al.*, *American Hostages in Iran: The Conduct of a Crisis* (New Haven, Conn., and London, 1985), 325–73.

SCHAMA, S., *Patriots and Liberators: Revolution in the Netherlands, 1780–1813* (London, 1977).

SCHROEDER, P. W., 'The Nineteenth-Century System: Balance of Power or Political Equilibrium', *Review of International Studies*, 15/2 (Apr. 1989), 135–53.

Second Congress of the Communist International, The (Washington, DC, 1920).

SELBY, F. G. (ed.), *Burke's Reflections on the Revolution in France* (London, 1906).

SENN, A. E., *Diplomacy and Revolution* (Notre Dame, Ind., and London, 1974).

SEYMOUR, C. (ed.), *The Intimate Papers of Colonel House* (4 vols.; London, 1928).

SHENNAN, J. H., *The Origins of the Modern European State* (London, 1974).

SICKER, M., *The Making of a Pariah State* (New York, 1987).

SILVERMAN, D. A., 'Informal Diplomacy: The Foreign Policy of the Robespierrist Committee of Public Safety', Ph.D. thesis (University of Washington, 1973).

SMITH, R. F., *Negotiating with the Soviets* (Bloomington and Indianapolis, 1989).

SOBOUL, A., 'Anacharsis Cloots, l'orateur du genre humain', *Annales historiques de la révolution française*, 239 (Jan.–Mar. 1980), 29–58.

——*The French Revolution, 1787–1799*, trans. A. Forrest (2 vols.; London, 1974).

SOREL, A., *L'Europe et la révolution française*, 21st edn. (8 vols.; Paris, 1885–1902).

——*Europe and the French Revolution*, vol. i, trans. and ed. A. Cobban and J. W. Hunt (London, 1969).

SPIVAK, B., 'Thomas Jefferson, Republican Values and Foreign Commerce', in N. A. Graebner (ed.), *Traditions and Values: American Diplomacy, 1790–1865* (London, 1985).

SPROUT, H. H., 'Theories as to the Applicability of International Law in the Federal Courts of the United States', *American Journal of International Law*, 26/2 (Apr. 1932), 280–95.

STANLIS, P. J., 'Edmund Burke and the Law of Nations', *American Journal of International Law*, 47/3 (1953), 397–413.

STEIGMAN, A. L., *The Foreign Service of the United States* (Boulder, Colo., 1985).

STEWART, J. H., *A Documentary Survey of the French Revolution* (New York, 1951).

STINCHCOMBE, W. C., *The American Revolution and the French Alliance* (New York, 1969).

STINCHCOMBE, W. C., 'John Adams and the Model Treaty', in L. S. Kaplan (ed.), *The American Revolution and 'A Candid World'* (Kent State, Ohio, 1977), 69–84.

STONE, L. S., 'Theories of Revolution', *World Politics*, 18 (1966), 159–76.

STOURZH, G., *Alexander Hamilton and the Idea of Republican Government* (Stanford, Calif., 1970).

——*Benjamin Franklin and American Foreign Policy* (Chicago, 1969).

SUAREZ, FRANCISCO, *Selections from Three Works*, ed. J. B. Scott (2 vols.; Classics of International Law; Oxford, 1944).

Survey of the China Mainland Press (US Consulate General, Hong Kong), No. 3713.

Survey of Chinese Mainland Magazines (US Consulate General, Hong Kong), 28 Dec. 1960.

SYDENHAM, M. J., *The French Revolution* (London, 1965).

——*The Girondins* (London, 1961).

TAHERI, A., *Holy Terror* (London, 1987).

TARACOUZIO, T. A., *The Soviet Union and International Law* (New York, 1935).

TEMPERLEY, H., and PENSON, L. M., *Foundations of British Foreign Policy* (London, 1966).

THOMPSON, J. W., and PADOVER, S. K., *Secret Diplomacy: Espionage and Cryptography, 1500–1815* (New York, 1970).

TIEH-CHEN, SHAO, 'Revolutionary Dialectics and how to Appraise Imperialism', *Peking Review* (11 Jan. 1963), 10–15.

TRISKA, J. F., and SLUSSER, R. M., *The Theory, Law and Policy of Soviet Treaties* (Stanford, Calif., 1962).

TROTSKY, LEON, *My Life* (New York, 1930).

TUNKIN, G. I., *Theory of International Law*, trans. W. E. Butler (Cambridge, Mass., 1974).

Two Different Lines on the Question of War and Peace (Peking, 1963).

ULDRICKS, T. J., *Diplomacy and Ideology: The Origins of Soviet Foreign Relations, 1917–30* (London, 1979).

ULLMAN, W., *The Church and Law in the Earlier Middle Ages* (London, 1975).

——*The Growth of Papal Government in the Middle Ages* (London, 1962).

——*Medieval Papalism* (London, 1949).

UNITED STATES CONGRESS SENATE COMMITTEE ON GOVERNMENT OPERATIONS, *The Soviet Approach to Negotiations* (Washington, 1969).

UNITED STATES, DEPARTMENT OF STATE, *Foreign Relations of the United States: The Soviet Union, 1933–39* (Washington, 1952).

——*Foreign Relations of the United States, 1950* (Washington, 1977).

VAGTS, A., and D. F., 'The Balance of Power in International Law: A History of an Idea', *American Journal of International Law*, 73 (1979), 555–80.

VAN NESS, P., *Revolution and China's Foreign Policy* (Berkeley, Calif., 1970).

VARG, P. A., *The Foreign Policy of the Founding Fathers* (Baltimore, 1963).

VATIKIOTIS, P. J., *Islam and the State* (London and New York, 1987).

——*Nasser and his Generation* (London, 1978).

VATTEL, EMERICH DE, *The Law of Nations*, ed. J. Chitty (London, 1834).

VERESCHETIN, V., and MULLERSON, R., 'The Primacy of International Law in World Politics', in A. Carty and G. Danilenko (eds.), *Perestroika and International Law* (Edinburgh, 1990), 6–14.

VON BEYME, K., *The Soviet Union in World Politics* (Aldershot, 1987).

WALLERSTEIN, I., *The Modern World System* (New York, 1974).

WALTZ, K. N., *Theory of International Politics* (Reading, Mass., 1979).

WATSON, A., *Diplomacy: The Dialogue Between States* (London, 1982).

WEATHERBEE, D. E., *Ideology in Indonesia: Sukarno's Indonesian Revolution* (Yale University Southeast Asian Studies, Monograph Series, 8; New Haven, Conn., 1966).

WEBSTER, C. K., *The Congress of Vienna* (London, 1934).

WENDT, A. E., 'The Agent–Structure Problem in International Relations Theory', *International Organization*, 41/3 (Summer, 1987), 335–70.

WHARTON, F., *The Revolutionary Diplomatic Correspondence of the United States* (Washington, 1889).

WHEELER-BENNETT, J. W., *Brest-Litovsk: The Forgotten Peace* (London and New York, 1966).

WHYTE, A. F., *The Practice of Diplomacy*, trans. of François de Callière's *De la manière de négocier avec les souverains* (London, 1919).

WIGHT, M., 'The Balance of Power', in H. Butterfield and M. Wight, *Diplomatic Investigations* (London, 1966), 149–75.

——*Systems of States* (Leicester, 1977).

——*Power Politics*, ed. H. Bull and C. Holbraad (Harmondsworth, 1986).

WILLIAMS, G. L., 'International Law and the Controversy Concerning the Word Law', *British Year Book of International Law* (1945), 146–63.

WILLIAMS, W. A., *The Roots of the Modern American Empire* (London, 1970).

——*The Tragedy of American Diplomacy* (New York, 1962).

WILSON, C. E., *Diplomatic Principles and Immunities* (Tucson, Ariz., 1967).

WILSON, H. A., *International Law and the Use of Force by National Liberation Movements* (Oxford, 1988).

WILTSE, C. M., 'Thomas Jefferson on the Law of Nations', *American Journal of International Law*, 29/1 (Jan. 1935), 66–81.

WOLFF, CHRISTIAN VON, *Jus Gentium Methodo Scientifica Pentractum*, trans. J. H. Drake (Oxford, 1934).

WOOD, G. S., *Creation of the American Republic, 1776–87* (Chapel Hill, NC, 1969).

WRIGHT, M., *Theory and Practice of the Balance of Power, 1486–1914* (London, 1975).

YOUNG, K. T., *Negotiating with the Chinese Communists* (New York, 1968).

ZIMMERMAN, W., *Soviet Perspectives on International Relations, 1956–67* (Princeton, NJ, 1969).

ZONIS, M., and BRUMBERG, D., *Khomeini, the Islamic Revolution of Iran and the Arab World* (Harvard Middle East Papers, 5; Cambridge, Mass., 1987).

————'Shi'ism as Interpreted by Khomeini: An Ideology of Revolutionary Violence', in M. Kramer (ed.), *Shi'ism: Resistance and Revolution* (Boulder, Colo., 1987), 47–66.

ZORIN, V. A., *Rôle of the Ministry of Foreign Affairs of the USSR: The Bases of Diplomatic Service* (Moscow, 1964); reproduced in US Congress Senate Committee on Government Operations, *The Soviet Approach to Negotiations* (Washington, 1969).

INDEX

Acheson, D. 199
Adams, J. 42, 44, 46, 48–9, 53, 58, 252, 284–5, 286
Adams, J. Q. 52, 71
Aix-la-Chapelle, Congress of 114
Alexander, Tsar 114
Alsace 35, 85, 87, 90
Articles of Confederation 55–6
Auckland, Lord 93, 99
Avignon 85

Bahrain 195
balance of power 29, 34–5, 40, 48, 76, 88, 109, 113, 273–98
  and American revolution 284–6
  and Chinese revolution 290–2
  and French revolution 284–6
  and Russian revolution 287–90
Barère de Vieuzac, B. 88, 107, 251
Barthélemy, F., marquis de 253
Bemis, S. F. 222
Beveridge, A. J. 72
Bismarck, Prince Otto von 278
Blanning, T. C. W. 81
Bodin, J. 33
Bolsheviks and international relations 120–6
Boulding, K. 126
Brest-Litovsk 135–7, 259
Brezhnev, L. 145, 151–4, 236
Brissot de Warville, J. P. 81, 85, 88, 91, 95, 98, 101, 214–15, 253, 256–7, 281
Britain 156
  and American revolution 43, 47, 48, 55
  and French revolution 87, 92, 99–100, 102–4, 214–15
  and Russian revolution 146
Brougham, Lord H. 278
Bukharin, N. I. 136, 173
Bull, H. vii, 4, 5, 7, 8, 15, 31, 36, 273, 279, 307
Burke, E. 100, 206–7, 293–4

Callières, F. de 249
Cambon, J. 106, 249
Carnot, L.-N. 213–14

Castlereagh, Viscount R. S. 114–15
Castro, F. 42, 173–6
Charlemagne 21
Charles VI 277
Chauvelin, marquis de 92
Chicherin, G. V. 140–1, 143–4, 229, 287
China 176–84
  and Africa 181
  imperial 17
  and the Soviet Union 148
  and the United States 179
  see also balance of power; diplomacy; international law
Christendom 20–2, 36
Churchill, W. S. 296–7
Cicero 18–19
Clark, I. 116
Clavière, E. 81, 95
Cloots, A. 81, 93
Cohen, P. 4
Cohen, R. 248–9
cold war 74–5
Communist International (Comintern) 140
Concert of Europe 113–14, 125, 218, 247, 278
Confucian world order 17
Continental Congress 47, 49
Cromwell, O. 261–2
Cuba 173–7
  and Africa 175
  missile crisis 199
  and the United States 175–6
Curzon, Lord 162
Custine, marquis de 95
Czechoslovakia 151, 236

Danton, G.-V. 106, 107
Deane, S. 281–2
Declaration of Rights of Man and Citizen 90, 208
Decree of French Foreign Policy 106
Deng Xiaoping 183
Desmoulins, C. 95, 208
diplomacy 16, 30, 38, 39, 166, 229–30
  American 251–62 passim
  Chinese 251, 265
  Cuban 267

diplomacy (*cont.*):
  French 88, 89, 251, 257–8, 267
  and international society 245-51
  Iranian 251, 265–7
  Libyan 260, 267
  new 160
  open 271
  secret 132, 133
  Soviet 154, 251, 258, 259–60, 261
  Vietnamese 263–4
Diplomatic Committee (of the French
  revolution) 209, 212, 256–7
Dumouriez, C.-F. 82, 88, 106

émigrés 100, 301
Engels, F. 121, 123, 124
  on diplomacy 244
Ethiopia, Italian invasion of 162

Falk, R. 3
federalism 53
Federalist Papers 221
Fénelon, F. 274
France 46, 47, 146
  see also French revolution
Franklin, B. 49, 52, 220, 282
Frederick William II 101
French revolution 36, 79–111, 206–19,
  253–4, 256–8, 262
  annexations policy of 209–14
  armies of 95–6
  Britain and 102–4, 110, 242
  Decree on Non-Aggression 217
  Spain and 90, 98
  United States and 59–63
  see also balance of power; diplomacy;
    international law; Westphalian
    conception of international society

Gaddafi, M. 42, 185–7, 293
Gagern, H. von 118
Galiev, Sultan 131
Genêt, E. 60, 262
Geneva Conventions 229
Genoa Conference 143, 227
Gentili, A. 26–7
Germany 35
  Nazi, international theory of 146
Gerry, E. 51
Gilbert, F. 46, 260
Girondins 81, 107
Gorbachev, M. 128, 152–5, 237
Gower, Earl 209
Greek revolt 71

Grenville, Lord 99
Grotius, H. 14, 27, 28, 202
Guevara, C. 175

Halliday, F. 10
Hamilton, A. 42, 50, 53, 54–62, 65,
  66–9, 76, 77, 220–3, 255–6, 262,
  282, 285–6
Heeren, A. H. L. 94, 275
Hitler, A. 163
Hizbollah (Party of Allah) 195
Hobbes, T. 7
Hoffmann, S. 5
Holy Alliance 114
Holy Roman Empire 21, 33, 85
House, Colonel E. 161

Indonesia 170–3
International Court of Justice 238
International Labour Organization 156
international law 16, 20, 22, 37, 64,
  87, 107, 115, 199–243
  China and 240–2
  France and 206–19
  nature and sources of 199–204
  Soviet Union and 225–38
  United States and 219–25
  see also natural law
international legitimacy 23, 36, 85,
  89–91, 119, 126, 165, 167
international society (and theory of
  international relations) 307–10
international system 9, 40–1, 307–9
Iran 186–97, 238–9
  see also balance of power; diplomacy
Iraq 196
  see also Saddam Hussein
Islam 189–92, 196
Israel 187, 196

Jacobin Club 105
James, A. 4, 5, 245
Japan 146, 163–4
Jay Treaty 73, 224
Jefferson, T. 42, 54–66, 69–70, 220,
  223–4, 244, 252, 254, 262–3, 283,
  285
Johnson, C. 3
jus cogens 201
jus gentium 19, 25, 27, 62–3, 68–9,
  115

Kaunitz, Prince von 100–1
Kennedy, J. F. 70

Khomeini, Ayatollah Ruh Allah 42,
167, 188–7, 266, 283, 292, 295
see also Iran
Khrushchev, N. 145, 148, 150, 290
Korovin, E. 226, 228, 230–2
Kozhevnikov, V. 233
Kuwait 196

Lafayette, marquis de 82
Laibach, Congress of 114
Lamartine, A. de 118
League of Nations 76, 141, 143, 146,
158–62, 225
Lebanon 195, 196
Lebrun, P.-H. 91, 92, 102–3, 214
Lee, R. H. 45
Leeds, Duke of 99
Lenin, V. I. 121, 122, 124, 127,
128–31, 135, 136–9, 288, 290
Leo III, Pope 21
Leopold, Emperor 91, 100
levée en masse 88–9, 108
Li Ta-chao 131
Libya 185–8
Litvinov, M. 140–2, 145, 258, 268
Livingston, E. 255–6
Louis XVI 89, 100, 101

Madison, J. 56, 60, 63, 65, 256
Mao Zedong 176, 187, 291
Marie Antoinette 100
Marx, K. 121, 122, 123, 124
Merlin of Douai 105, 210–11, 286
Merlin of Thionville 108
Metternich, Prince 71, 109, 114, 116,
117, 270, 274, 276
Miller, J. D. B. 4
Mirabeau, comte de 253
Molotov, V. M. 264
Monroe, J. 65, 70–1
Montmorin, comte de 256–7
Morris, R. 49
Munster, Treaty of 33

Napoleon 56, 108, 113
Narkomindel (People's Commissariat of
Foreign Affairs) 134, 140
Nasser, G. Abd El- 185
natural law 14, 18, 19, 24, 27, 30, 62,
67, 86, 87, 112
nonintervention 39, 218
Nootka Sound crisis 67, 209

obligation (political) 12–15
order 4–7, 41, 115–16, 125, 199, 205,
270, 273, 279, 297, 299–300,
304–5
Osnabruck, Treaty of 33
Oxenstierna, A. 34

Paine, T. 44, 93, 255
Paris Peace Conference 119–20
Pashukanis, V. 231–2
peaceful transition, theory of 148
philosophes 45
Pillnitz, declaration of 101, 256
Pinckney, C. 53
Pitt, W. 103–4, 110
Poland 159, 207
Polk, President J. 72, 282–3
Propaganda Decree 62, 85, 97, 99,
102, 106
Prussia 108
Pufendorf S. 28

Quadruple Alliance 114–15

Rafsanjani, President 147
Randolf, E. 219
Rapallo, Treaty of 144
Reagan, President R. 70
recognition, diplomatic 268–9
regimes, theory of 308–9
revolutions of 1848 117–18
Richelieu, Cardinal 39
Robert, P.-F. 107
Robespierre, M. 42, 93, 244, 286
Roman Catholicism 21, 22, 23
Roman Empire 18–20
Roosevelt, F. D. 157
Ross, S. T. 81
Rushdie, S. 196

Saddam Hussein 196, 296
Sardinia 85
Saudi Arabia 195
Savoy 85
Schelde (opening of) 62, 87, 102, 214
Schroeder, P. 116, 276
Shariati, A. 191
Shevardnadze, E. 237
Sieyès, Abbé 287
Smuts, J. 161
social contract 16, 19, 311
socialization 1–2, 7–8, 69, 75, 77,
104–8, 127, 139, 145, 155, 184,
198, 242–3, 271, 302–3

Sorel, A. 79–81, 82–4, 90, 96, 207
South Africa 166
sovereignty 4, 32–4, 245
Stalin, J. 139, 149, 244, 283, 288, 291–2
state, the (and international society) 15–16, 18–19, 32, 38–40
statecraft 280–1
Stoics 18, 24
Suarez, F. 26
Sukarno 170–3
Syria 196

Taft, President W. H. 72
Talleyrand, C.-M. 253, 276
Thirty Years War 32, 34
Tiananmen Square 183–4
Tito, President J. B. 149
Togliatti, P. 178–9
Troppau, Congress of 110, 114, 269–70
Trotsky, L. 42, 124, 131, 133–6, 142, 226–7, 252, 263
Truman, President H. S. 70
Tunkin, G. I. 233, 236, 238
Turkey 143

United States 42–78, 144–5, 156–7, 189, 195, 196, 198, 269
United Nations Organization 76, 164–6, 279
    see also balance of power; diplomacy; international law

Vattel, E. de 37, 112, 220, 242, 246–7, 275

Vergennes, C. V., comte de 50
Versailles, Treaty of 162
Vienna, Congress of 114
Vienna Convention on Treaties 234
Villeneuve, Pétion de 211–12
Vitoria, F. de 25
Volney, C. F. 217–18
Vyshinsky, A. 150, 232–3

Wallerstein, I. 309
Waltz, K. 9
Washington, G. 42, 59, 65, 220
Watson, A. 8, 251
Westphalia, Peace of 32–9, 57, 62
Westphalian conception of international society 4, 30–40, 113, 158–61, 165, 249, 277, 303–6
    American revolution and 69, 75, 76, 157, 222
    French revolution and 85–9, 103, 109–10, 214
    Iran and 191
    Libya and 185
    Russian revolution and 125, 132, 140, 152, 154, 155
Whipple, W. 51
Wight, M. 3, 22, 36
Wilson, J. 48, 219
Wilson, W. 70, 73, 126, 134, 155, 159–62, 255, 270, 283
Wolff, C. von 20, 28–9
world system 309–10

Zhdanov line 148
Zhou Enlai 183